ALSO BY ZEV BAR EITAN

ABRAVANEL'S WORLD OF TORAH
A Structured Interpretation

- Bereshit: Theory of Moral Evolution
- Shemot, Vol. I: Sinai Rules
- Shemot, Vol. II: Assembled at Sinai

ABRAVANEL'S
WORLD OF TORAH

A Structured Interpretation

Vayikra, Vol. I: The Meat of the Matter

ABRAVANEL'S
WORLD OF TORAH

A Structured Interpretation

Vayikra, Vol. I: The Meat of the Matter

ZEV BAR EITAN

Renaissance
Torah Press

Jacket Design: Dov Abramson
Typesetting: S. Kim Glassman

ISBN #978-965-91833-4-0
Library of Congress Control Number 2018934528

www.abravanelsworldoftorah.org
yabravanel@gmail.com

Printed in Canada

וְהִנֵּה הַסְּנֶה בֹּעֵר בָּאֵשׁ

To the Six Million of blessed memory הי"ד

וְהַסְּנֶה אֵינֶנּוּ אֻכָּל

and to the survivors of the Holocaust

ישיבה יוניברסיטי בישראל ע"ר
Yeshiva University in Israel
RIETS Kollel - Aaron Rakeffet
Caroline and Joseph S. Gruss Institute
40 Rechov Duvdevani,
Bayit Vegan, Jerusalem ISRAEL 9641423
Tel: 972-2-531-3000 Fax: 531-3021

בס"ד

Don Isaac Abravanel may be the most outstanding "statesman and philosopher" in the History of the Torah Nation. He was both a financier and count advisor in Portugal, Spain and Italy. In addition, Abravanel was a formidable Torah scholar and prolific writer. His most widely studied scholarship was his commentaries on the Pentateuch and the Prophets. His writings are generally verbose. At times it is challenging to grasp the essence of his insights.

Rabbi Zev Bar-Eitan has authored a structured interpretation and English translation of this classic commentary. He has achieved a rendition of the Abravanel which will enable all English readers to comprehend the depths and innovativeness of the original Hebrew text.

I gladly recommend Rabbi Bar-Eitan's works to you. To the author I declare:

יישר חילך לאורייתא, ויפוצו מעיינותיך חוצה!

Aaron Rakeffet

Aaron Rakeffet-Rothkoff

RABBI NAFTALI JAEGER
ROSH HAYESHIVA

בס"ד

ONE CEDARLAWN AVENUE • LAWRENCE, NY 11559 • (516) 239-9002 • FAX: (516) 239-9003

שאר ישוב
SH'OR YOSHUV
INSTITUTE

CONTENTS

THE PARSHIYOT

MORE PRAISE FOR "ABRAVANEL'S WORLD OF TORAH"

A masterful rendition…lucid, free-flowing and interesting.
Rabbi Zev Leff
Rabbi, Moshav Matityahu; Rosh Hayeshiva, Yeshiva Gedola Matityahu

Riveting and flowing elucidation of the text simplifies complex ideas leaving the reader readily able to grasp the Abravanel's inner meaning and purposeful explanation.
Rabbi Meyer H. May
Executive Director, Simon Wiesenthal Center and Museums of Tolerance

Open[s] our eyes and minds to the fascinating world of the Abravanel and his unique way of analyzing the Torah…in a user-friendly commentary.
Rabbi Steven Weil
Senior Managing Director, OU

It gives me great pleasure that the English-speaking world can now enjoy and appreciate the unique and original approach of this outstanding Torah giant to Sefer Shemos.
Rav Yitzchak Shurin
Darche Noam Institutions; Rosh Midrasha, Midreshet Rachel v'Chaya

The translation is as beautiful as the original Hebrew and the English reader loses nothing in this excellent rendition.
Rabbi Allen Schwartz
Congregation Ohab Zedek, Yeshiva University

Abravanel needs a redeemer…. Bar Eitan takes on this complex task.
Rabbi Gil Student
Jewish Action

At once a work of scholarship and a treat for the imagination…. Bar Eitan's Abravanel presents Exodus as great literature, as exciting and gripping as any great Russian novel.
Rabbi Daniel Landes
Rosh Hayeshivah, Machon Pardes

An uncommon treat.... Rabbi Bar Eitan is to be commended for providing an accessible entree to this timeless masterpiece.

Rabbi N. Daniel Korobkin
Beth Avraham Yoseph of Toronto Congregation

Relevant and accessible.... Ideal for teachers as well as Yeshiva High School, Ulpana, Yeshiva and Seminary students alike...a wonderful translation... enjoyable reading....

Rachel Weinstein
Tanach Department, Ramaz Upper School, NY

The clear, easy-to-read language and appended notes and illustrations bring the Abravanel to life, for scholars and laymen alike. A great addition to personal and shul libraries.

Rabbi Yehoshua Weber
Rabbi, Clanton Park Synagogue, Toronto

Of great value to those who have hesitated to tackle this dense, complex work.... Render[s] the Abravanel's commentary accessible to the modern reader.

Simi Peters
author, Learning to Read Midrash

A gift to the English-speaking audience.... An important "must have" addition to the English Torah library.

Chana Tannenbaum, EdD
lecturer, Bar-Ilan University

The thoughts of a Torah giant over 500 years ago in terminology understandable to the modern reader.

Deena Zimmerman, MD, MPH, IBCLC
author; lecturer

Allows the reader the opportunity to see firsthand the brilliance, creativity, and genius of this 15th-century Spanish biblical commentator.

Rabbi Elazar Muskin
Young Israel of Century City, Los Angeles

An excellent job bringing to life the profound ideas of one of the most original thinkers in Judaism and making them relevant and interesting 500 years later.

Rabbi Dr. Alan Kimche
Ner Yisrael Community, London

PREFACE

What a wonderful privilege and pleasure it is to present this most recent addition to the *Abravanel's World of Torah* series. Though I had not initially expected Sefer Vayikra to require two volumes, in fact that is what happened. It just kept growing.

Vayikra volume I covers the first five *parshiyot* (Vayikra–Metzora). Clearly, the bulk of this *sefer* centers on the vast subject of sacrifices, including Abravanel's methodical and lengthy introduction to it. But it isn't the sole matter. The book also features key discourses on *kashrut* (Parashat Shemini) and another pillar of Judaism: sensibly approaching sexual intimacy (Parashat Metzora).

Following is a thumbnail biography of Abravanel, followed by discussions of this book's format and suggestions concerning how readers might approach this work, insofar as it is a structured interpretation of the Hebrew original.

Biography. Don Yitzchak Abravanel[1] (1437–1508) was born into an illustrious and erudite family of court advisors in Portugal. A formidable scholar and prolific writer, he taught and regularly surrounded himself with a cadre of capable companions. Concurrently, he rose professionally through the ranks to become one of Portugal's—and later Spain's—trusted financial advisors to royalty. Really, his services were indispensable to them.

Abravanel's personal success, comfort, and security crashed abruptly when King Ferdinand and Queen Isabella ascended the throne. Unleashing wellsprings of Catholic fanaticism and violence, they cast a pall over Spain's non-Catholic population. As an eyewitness to ugly and turbulent times, Don Yitzchak harrowingly experienced the orchestrated and devastating disgorging of Spanish Jewry. This medieval holocaust concluded with the infamous expulsion of the Jews in 1492, though not before Don Yitzchak spurned the king's bilious dispensation employment package. Insidiously and cynically, Ferdinand extended Don Yitzchak an offer to remain in Spain. Unwilling to consider the plan, which called for him to hide cloistered and protected within the palace confines, Abravanel fled for his life and limb.

---

1. Some variations of the spelling for his last name include Avrabanel, Abarbanel, and Avravanel.

After much travel and travail, he settled in Italy, where he resumed his writings and professional life, serving in senior advisory capacities to the local Italian higher echelon. At the age of seventy-one, he passed away in Venice.

Format. This volume contains five chapters or *parshiyot*, each subdivided into seven *aliyot*. To further guide readers, each *aliyah* begins with its first or lead verse(s), marked in large, bold print.

For brevity's sake I omit translating Abravanel's introductory questions, which invariably precede each *aliyah* and/or particular section in his original work. Instead, I head directly to the *pshat*. Out of similar concerns for keeping up a steady pace, I have also generally left out translating many of his prefatory references and critiques of earlier commentators, especially when he later discards them. I do footnote such omissions, allowing interested readers to consult the original Abravanel.

Scattered scintillating essays (e.g., elucidating esoterica surrounding spiritual purity and defilement or providing a full-blown analysis of Nadav and Avihu's mysterious demise at the fiery inauguration of the Mishkan) are not bundled apart from the main body of the commentary. Instead, effort has been made to indicate topic shifts within *aliyot* by the insertion of subheadings.

Ample footnotes allow readers to delve further into sources and topics of particular interest. Tanach quotes are generally cited by Biblical chapter and verse except where references can be made to *Abravanel's World*. In those latter cases and to illustrate, a footnote may state, for example: "See *Abravanel's World: Bereshit*, Parashat Noach, second *aliyah*."

Structured interpretation. Abravanel's works do not easily lend themselves to literal translation. Besides often being repetitive, they tend to be very long—especially for today's readers, increasingly used to getting Torah in bite-size pieces. Until recent years and before present-day Israeli scholars put out new editions, just getting through a page or two of the older, antiquated versions took a fairly serious time investment plus copious effort. Add an overall element of non-reader-friendly two-columned pages, small letters, text without punctuation, bibliography, indices, or any other basic type of aid, and we arrive at a highly undesirable outcome: his classic works have sadly become predominantly overlooked and neglected.

From the outset, my aim has been to make Abravanel more accessible. Book titles, *parashah* titles, *aliyah*-by-*aliyah* format, graphs, tables, bullet points, maps, illustrations, and so on all contribute to a new design and model for this fifteenth-century treasure. This is Abravanel with a new look—but that is not only my stated goal and commitment with regard to the book's physical layout. More than infusing Abravanel with a contemporary look, I try to create a new standard. With that in mind, this guide and companion has a popular, if at times folksy, ring to it.

To be sure, though I have contemporized the tone and enlivened the text with added graphics, still and all I strive to purvey the master's words and intent faithfully. Please note that while this *sefer* reads smoothly on its own, readers may want to keep an open Sefer Vayikra (or Tanach) at hand, since uninterrupted Biblical text is not provided.

Translations are tricky business. To be perfectly up front, my translation does not purport to follow well-worn models in that genre. It is neither a linear nor a literal translation. Had I gone that route, I would have defeated my purpose. Contemporary language, catchy turn of phrase, and even a sprinkle of light-spiritedness are brought to bear in my effort to ease readers into this compelling fifteenth-century classic.

A footbridge, *Abravanel's World* gets readers over rough patches so they can better access and appreciate his breadth, genius, and relevance. Particular and unique challenges taunt any translator undertaking to translate a Torah commentary in general—and one penned in the fifteenth century in particular. In order to make the original Hebrew comprehensible and accessible to the modern English-speaking reader, I regularly translate before offering a transliteration. Then, at the first usage of the term or phrase, the Hebrew will be placed immediately afterwards in parentheses. Inserting Hebrew opens the gates for students to explore Hebrew text.

Our model of implementing transliteration and Hebrew is thus designed to optimize this book as an educational experience. This is particularly necessary when the subject matter—as translated to vernacular English—may become misleading due to the decidedly non-Jewish associations of some English terms. For example, "angels" conjures up winged cherubs instead of the Jewish concept of heavenly agents or facilitators, and the concepts of "Heaven" and "Hell" bring to mind Dante's vision.

Another technical qualifier is in order. Where I do translate from the Bible, I have not followed or adopted any one particular translation. Readers will encounter verses quoted that may be literal, figurative, or emotive depending on Abravanel's mood or inflection. As for transliterations, I have followed standard modern Israeli pronunciation.

Without a doubt, this blend of old and new proves to be a delicate if somewhat elusive mix. To the extent that readers open a chapter and peruse its *aliyot*, and not only get out of it the main gist but also experience Abravanel, this is testimony to my colleagues' skill and acumen. However, to the extent that readers get distracted by the author, I accept responsibility. *Mea culpa.*

ACKNOWLEDGMENTS

I turn to the shopworn analogy of giving birth—used for just about anything under the sun—for comparing that laborious act to the process of self-publishing a book. I better realize that, if I want to be generous, my original manuscript corresponds to the first trimester. Credit for the last two trimesters, that critical time when development and refinement occur in leaps and bounds, goes to my highly professional team of content editor, copy editor, proofreader, graphic designer, typesetter, and printer.

Accordingly, I extend sincere gratitude (and not a little awe) to Rabbi Yisrael Herczeg, Kezia Raffel Pride, Dov Abramson, S. Kim Glassman, and Friesens. Thank you for your top-notch work and perseverance. Writing a compendium, especially one of this nature, encompasses multiple challenges and can feel like a grueling trek. I am fortunate to have shared good company along this fourth leg of it.

Shuv, todah rabbah.

INTRODUCTION

From time immemorial, the Hebrew Bible (Tanach) has been universally revered and beloved. Jew and Gentile have pored over its pages, savoring its wisdom. Traditional and scholarly Jewish commentaries spanning centuries proclaim and share the fruits of their labor. Indelibly, their erudite marginalia line each page.

As in the past, the study of Tanach today still enjoys wide appeal. People of all backgrounds and faiths want to better understand the Bible. What better way to uncover the meaning of each word and passage than to enlist the sound counsel afforded by devoted sages of earlier generations? Ground rules and established principles handed down for posterity put us on the right track. These are the well-trodden pathways paved by the Talmudists, Geonim, and Rishonim.[1]

Don Yitzchak Abravanel (1437–1508), a tribune for Jewish tradition or *masoret*, joined that venerable cadre of trusted teachers who revolutionized Tanach scholarship when he penned his trailblazing commentary—a pursuit that occupied much of an extraordinarily productive lifetime.

With a seemingly boundless curiosity and a commanding intellect, Don Yitzchak illuminates Tanach, page by page. When people think of him, they see before their eyes an avalanche of questions which he uses to introduce a *parashah* or passage. Justifiably so. By my count, in the Five Books of Moses or Chumash as well as the major and minor prophets or Neviim these total 2,777.[2] His reach extended to Writings (Ketuvim), as well. When we include his commentary on Daniyel (*Maayenei Hayeshuah*), the astounding tally of his queries approaches three thousand (especially when we account for "unofficial" yet nuanced questions). Even though none of his questions run on as long as the first two in Parashat Bereshit (covering about fifteen pages, if they were to be translated word for word!), we're not talking about the more familiar "multiple choice," skeletal type, either.

In a nutshell, that captures but a scorecard stat of Abravanel's questions. There is, though, another aspect to them. Namely, what can be said about

---

1. Respectively, the eras of Mishnaic and Talmudic sages (400 BCE–600 CE), Geonim (600–1000 CE), and Rishonim (1000–1500 CE) flourished for nearly two millennia.
2. In this introduction, obviously, it is not feasible to cull more than a random sampling of his questions.

their no-nonsense, commonsense quality that cut to the core of the matter? By way of illustration, I paraphrase the third question in Parashat Shemot: The Torah teaches that Bnei Yisrael increased and grew more populous than the Egyptians. Abravanel wonders, if the Hebrews had already outnumbered and outmuscled the Egyptians, why did Egypt's top brass express concern lest they multiply further? They already had multiplied. Further, he muses that the real concern should not have been Jews representing a fifth column in the event of war, but rather something more rattling. That is, Hebrew hordes might just turn on their hosts, subdue them, and take over Egypt. And finally, the third prong of this question: Given the existential threat that the Jews posed, why should Paroh fear them packing up and leaving? Had that occurred, the Egyptians should have breathed a sigh of relief, counted their lucky stars, and said good riddance.

To be sure, questions and answers are a time-tested methodology. While Abravanel took it to new levels, there is a bigger part of the story to be shown. He really needs to be reintroduced to today's readership, who will upon reflection see in him an educator par excellence and more.

If we view Don Yitzchak's writings as his classroom, then before we sit down with the mentor, let us consider how he prepared his lessons, delved into the *parshiyot*. To do that, we allow ourselves to first tour his study, as it were.

What panoply of Hebrew *seforim*, secular books, and ancient tomes lay at his fingertips, piled upon his stately writing desk? Again, figuratively speaking, we begin with the disheveled Jewish stack, manifestly well thumbed. There we spy a Tanach, both Talmuds, and Midrash (*Rabbah, Tanchuma, Yalkut, Chazit*, and others). We also encounter the esoteric *Sefer Hayetzirah, Zohar*, and *Sefer Habahir*. Classic medieval-period commentators such as Yitzchak Israeli (d. 932), Hasdai Ibn Shafrut (d. 975), Shmuel Hanagid (d. 1056), Ibn Gavriol (d. 1058), Rashi (d. 1105), the Aruch (d. 1106), Yehudah Halevi (d. 1141), Ibn Ezra (d. 1167), Rambam (d. 1204), Radak (d. 1235), Ramban (d. 1270), Ralbag (d. 1344), Ibn Caspi (d. 1345), Ran (d. 1376), Albo (d. 1444), and Rabbi Yosef ben Shem Tov (d. 1480) served as his steadfast rabbis. Moreover, Abravanel regularly corresponded and conversed with contemporary scholars and students. Though far from an exhaustive list of references, these represent a fair number of the Jewish works and authors he was wont to acknowledge, berate, critique, debate, and esteem.

Now we move to the secular and ancient piles of books mercilessly weighing down a rapidly crowded, sprawling table. These include classic histories of all stripes—Hebrew (Josephus), Egyptian, Persian, Greek, Roman, and Christian. In addition to history, Abravanel delighted in sharing his familiarity with and often unabashed affection for Greek and Roman classics, featuring Pythagoras, Socrates, Plato, Aristotle, Claudius Ptolemy, Pliny the Elder, Seneca, and Claudius Galen, to name seven well-known figures.

Finally, we gaze agape at another sagging section of Abravanel's bureau. Our eyes focus on more tattered book spines. Squinting, we struggle to make out the titles of these Gentile sources, among them a Christian Old Testament (Septuagint). Some remain, at least for us, anonymous writers to whom he generically refers as "the mathematicians and cosmologists."[3] Others make the who's who list of Christian and Muslim thinkers. Four who come to mind are Jerome, translator of most of the Hebrew Bible into Latin; Nicholas of Lyra, a Franciscan Biblical exegete; as well as Al-Ghazali and Ibn Rushd. Even the noted Persian Ibn Sina (aka Avicenna) finds his works strewn over a perennially congested desk. Banished to the floor underneath Don Yitzchak's table could be found the works of sniggering and subversive scoundrels, disingenuous Biblical expositors. Some of these ignominious wretches Abravanel names; others he deems unworthy of mention. But in all of their faces, he rants, ridicules, and rails.

A bell sounds.

Abravanel enters. Class begins. Questions and answers churn with no less force and determination than a D9 bulldozer. What do we hear? If it is Parashat Bereshit, we learn more than cosmological theory. He introduces us to the world of angels or *malachim*, a theological subject he returns to throughout much of his Tanach commentary.[4] Parashat Shemot gives readers a taste of another subject Abravanel encourages us to better understand: prophecy.[5]

Abravanel, the consummate renaissance rebbi that he was, provides range. He serves his students a full repast of meaty dishes like the two just

---

3.　Abravanel references "the opinion of the mathematicians and cosmologists" or *daat hatechunin u'baalei hasivuv* (דעת התכונין ובעלי הסבוב).

4.　A study unto itself, the subject meanders in the Torah and Prophets. See his comments on Yeshayahu (chapter 6) and Yechezkel (Abravanel's introduction to it and first chapter), among others.

5.　Really, this topic is broached in Sefer Bereshit but gets elaborated in Parashat Shemot and Yitro in addition to the books of Yeshayahu, Yirmiyahu, Yechezkel, etc.

mentioned (savory and beefy Q and A sessions), but our plate quickly fills up, in a manner of speaking, with hearty side dishes, garnishes, and desserts.

To explain, Abravanel's writings cover overarching themes as well as titillating mini-essays.

- The literal versus figurative interpretations of the Garden of Eden narrative with Adam, Eve, and the talking snake
- Full-bodied portraits of the patriarchs
- Biblical dreams
- Moshe's real name, his prophetic legacy and achievement
- Exodus and Redemption: the Pesach story in all its hues and schemata
- Revelation at Sinai and the Ten Commandments
- The Tabernacle or Mishkan, its vessels, plus the priestly garments
- Sacrifices and Temple service
- Biblical poetry: Holy Writ or Hebrew Lit

Classroom discussion doesn't get bogged down with highfalutin notions. Verse-by-verse comments keep up a sprightly pace. To quote and translate Abravanel, we often come across a favorite line, which he uses to indicate the end of one prefatory discourse and the beginning of his running commentary: "And after Hashem has informed you of all this, we will explain verse by verse."[6] How he brims with delight over understanding (and sharing his understanding) of Torah!

A rich background in Tanach enabled him to unravel text via Hebrew etymology and grammar: linguistics reveal meaning. Here is one example of how Abravanel utilizes grammar to uncover simple meaning or *pshat*. Carefully contrast the first verse in Sefer Shemot with an earlier, similar-looking one from Sefer Bereshit. In Shemot we read, "And these are the names of Bnei Yisrael who came to Egypt. Each man with his family came, bringing Yaakov."[7] Compare that with this verse from Bereshit: "And these are the names of Bnei Yisrael—Yaakov and his sons—who came to Egypt. Yaakov's oldest son was Reuven…."[8] On the surface, the two verses seem to be a restatement of each other. Yet they convey different emphases or points of reference. The verse in

---

6. Bereshit 41:39.
7. Shemot 1:1.
8. Bereshit 46:8–27.

Bereshit gives a roster of people (seventy) who traveled down to Egypt. This list includes Yaakov, the family's patriarch. However, in Shemot we read of the sons who attended to and brought Yaakov to Egypt. The inclusion of the word *et* (את) holds the key. It clues readers in to the need to read Yaakov as an object (sons brought father) and not a subject (Yaakov came down). Not insignificantly, that also answers why Bereshit names all seventy sojourners, but in Shemot we only read of those men (eleven sons, since Yosef was already in Egypt) responsible for evacuating the venerable patriarch from famine's ravages.

In Parashat Beshalach's seventh *aliyah*, we read about Bnei Yisrael's first battle with Amalek: "And Amalek came and warred with Israel in Refidim."[9] Was Amalek's aggression preplanned or desultory? Though Bible students may be inclined to paint the Hebrews' wicked nemesis here as having purposely picked a fight, the text is less convincing. Abravanel quotes some who say that Amalek had not left their home territory in order to wage war with the Hebrews in the desert. Had that been the case, the verse should have been written, *And Amalek came to fight with Israel*. Abravanel is by no means whitewashing Amalek's despicable and cowardly militarism, which took aim at the camp's weak and infirm. Far from it. He does, though, allow readers to entertain the possibility that Amalek had, at the outset, other destinations in mind before coincidentally crossing paths (and swords) with Hebrew stragglers. The unscrupulous nation of miscreants known as Amalek beheld a pitiful human target too tempting to pass on. Instead of extending a helping hand, they pounced mercilessly.

To infuse another word about the classroom experience, if you will, it is integrative, restorative, and riveting. Abravanel synthesizes diverse goals. On the one hand he commits to providing running commentary, and yet on the other hand he interjects dozens and dozens of mini-essays on an array of bedrock issues. He sees the Tanach as complementary and supplementary, meaning that knowledge and understanding of a verse in, say, the Prophets sheds light on one in Sefer Bereshit.[10] Also, logic and reason and science cannot be seen as anathema to Torah. Rather, he adjures and insists that students reconcile cumulative human wisdom and divine, prophetic wisdom.

---

9. Shemot 17:8.
10. One illustration is Avraham's refusal to accept war spoils from the king of Sedom. This has reverberations in King David's time when he needs to divvy up spoils among his warriors.

Especially in the final *parshiyot* in Sefer Shemot, he waxes prolific on the Mishkan's symbolism. With authority, he confidently asserts that when man's knowledge ultimately masters what we call "the hard sciences," we will better secure the true essence of the Mishkan's mysteries, or at least some of them.

On many occasions, Don Yitzchak expresses dismay (and profound disappointment) that none of his illustrious predecessors were bothered by glaring gaps he perceived in Tanach. See his introduction to Sefer Devarim, in which he yearns to know why its style differs so greatly from the first four books of the Chumash: "I stand flabbergasted at the Torah's commentators. How could they not be bothered by this?" He strikes a similar incredulous stance in his introduction to Sefer Shmuel. He asks why there are such disparate accounts of Jewish history in Sefer Shmuel and Divrei Hayamim (Chronicles). "And I have not found anything of this subject discussed. Not among the early Talmudic sages nor latter exegetes and thinkers. Not a peep." More sadness prevails upon him when he ponders the dearth of commentary on Divrei Hayamim: "This greatly vexes and pains me." His writings set out to repair breaches and restore unacceptable lacunae.

Every inspiring teacher knows how to engage students. Indeed, a classroom must be a safe room to allow for questioning and exploration. Abravanel's lessons have been here described in terms of a rich multi-course repast. His questions may be seen as the bread and butter. Hard and liberal sciences—where appropriately integrated with Torah knowledge—are the meat and potatoes.

Don Yitzchak made room for dessert—those wonderfully quirky tidbits he sprinkles gingerly, sure to raise eyebrows. For example:

- How did Alexander the Great unwittingly substantiate the Torah's account of creation and prove the preeminence of Hebrew as the lingua sancta?
- Did Noach have four sons, and not three as is explicit in the Torah?
- A visit to Moshe's private study in Egypt
- A possible rationale behind Jewish dietary laws or *kashrut* from a custom prevalent in medieval England

In closing this introduction, let us advance a last word on Abravanel's complexities. We have described an ennobled personality who experienced personal uprooting and stood witness to national horror of historic proportions: the expulsion of 1492. Even as a court Jew, he was not spared the fate of his co-religionists. Exile to exile, he wandered. Calamity and penury doggedly shadowed him throughout Europe. Unbroken, he emerged with his ancestors' unshakable faith fully intact.

And his pen.

What motivated him to write? In a word, impassioned dedication to truth and love of Torah served as his cynosure. Here was a furious scribe who could neither compromise excellence nor abide attempts to undermine hallowed Jewish tradition.

Some try to portray Abravanel as a statesman, philosopher, or mystic. What a pity to reduce his stature to that of a mere political scientist, ivory tower academic, or messianic cultist. Such mischaracterization broadly misses the mark. After all, did he leave behind disquisitions, let alone dissertations in those fields?

Don Yitzchak Abravanel's legacy is, without a scintilla of doubt, his love of Torah or *ahavat Torah*. First and foremost, we hear the indefatigable voice of a defender and champion of Judaism. We sense a man who felt it his life's task to climb the highest intellectual and religious heights and give greater meaning and relevance to Holy Writ. His closeness with God is palpable throughout his writings; he is ever praising God or praying for strength to finish his life's task. Perhaps the most striking example—a modest sampling—of this may be found in his introduction to *Zevach Pesach*, his commentary on the Haggadah, in which he writes, "The Almighty caused my cup to run over when I arrived in Italy. He blessed me with unimaginable material riches. He blessed me with silver and gold, not to mention prestige among my co-religionists. Bounty and honor caused me to forget the tribulations of Spain and Portugal. To be sure, my good cheer came about as a result of immersing in Torah. How it stood me in good stead! O words of God, pure words of the Almighty…."

Indeed, his was quite the journey. Posterity is richer for his having liberally shared his momentous trek and breathtaking view of distant horizons and vistas. This is Abravanel's world of Torah.

Nof Ayalon, Israel
Tammuz 5778/June 2018

ABRAVANEL'S PROLEGOMENON TO SEFER VAYIKRA

The Torah's first book, Bereshit, revealed that the world was created ex nihilo. It also taught about the creation of man and succeeding generations of human history. Finally, Sefer Bereshit related detailed narratives pertaining to the three patriarchs, culminating in Yaakov's move to Egypt with his descendants.

In the Torah's second book, Shemot, we learned about the cruel bondage that Egypt inflicted upon the Hebrews. The story continued to chronicle their miraculous redemption led by Moshe and Aharon. Redemption abounded with first-rate wonders in Egypt and at the Red Sea leading up to the Sinai extravaganza. There, all of the people achieved prophecy in the course of receiving Torah and commandments from the Almighty. The Golden Calf debacle rapidly followed Sinai. Thereafter, atonement ensued.

For the express purpose of housing the mystical Shechinah, Jews built the Mishkan. Squarely, this undertaking intended to join the Holy Immanence as a permanent fixture among the people. It did. Divine providence lodged amidst the encampment. In the eyes of the Jews, proof positive of God's willingness to accompany them got a boost when Heaven showered fire upon the altar on the very day the Mishkan was inaugurated. God's cloud enwrapped the Tent of Meeting, and Hashem's glory—in ringing tones—filled the Mishkan. It was official. The Divine Spirit took up residence in the hallowed complex.

In that context it was crucial for this, the Torah's third book, to follow in sequence after the second one. The underlying theme of Sefer Vayikra traces the Mikdash service in all its splendid minutiae. How did the Kohanim officiate in their service to Heaven? What were the prescribed ways in which Bnei Yisrael received forgiveness from transgression? Which methods had been employed by the Kohanim to teach Jews right from wrong?

The Kohanim, Torah's pious teachers, became dedicated mentors. "For the lips of the Kohanim guarded wisdom."[1] People sought their goodly counsel, as it says, "And you shall come to the Kohanim—the Leviim—and they will instruct in matters of jurisprudence."[2]

---

1.   Malachi 2:7.
2.   Devarim 17:9.

Heaven acknowledged how Kohanim deserved the Jews' financial support. Through a system of tithes and gifts, their needs were taken care of. This not only freed them from having to make a living, but it also provided repose and sufficient peace of mind to allow them to do their jobs maximally. An equitable arrangement assured steady income for the Kohanim and their families.

Clearly the Torah foresaw how priests, a branch of the tribe of Levi, would accede to special status within the national fabric and rise to predominance. Their admirable erudition, refinement, and character were also marked by outward appearances. In this, particular vestments played a pivotal role.

Furthermore, Kohanim refrained from otherwise socially normative conduct. For example, they were cautioned against contact with death and against nicking their heads to draw blood, a custom prevalent among ancient mourners. Strict laws governed their daily grooming practices, such as the way they shaved and trimmed their hair.

Other restrictions placed upon them interfered with their choice of spouses. Only chaste women were deemed fit partners. While officiating in the Mikdash, they foreswore liquor and all intoxicating beverages.

Not every Kohen qualified to work in the Mishkan by dint of his patriarchal line. Certain physical blemishes rendered him unworthy to participate alongside his brethren. All told, priests answered to a higher calling. "Be holy" was a byword by which they lived. Holy men of God, the priests earned the nation's highest esteem.

Indeed, the bulk of Sefer Vayikra pertains to laws and customs particular to the priests. As we will see, many commandments are geared for that single purpose—preparing Kohanim for their life's mission. Apropos, the sages call this third book of Moses by the name Torat Kohanim.[3] Note its two distinct parts. One centers on the uniqueness of the priests and on their manner of officiating. It covers five and one half *parshiyot*. The second deals with certain constraints placed upon the nation as a whole, constraints that contribute to their refined character. "And you shall sanctify yourselves and be holy."[4] Those *parshiyot* make up the balance of the *sefer*'s ten chapters. Also sprinkled in this second section are woven various other commandments and warnings concerning Kohanim.

---

3. BT *Megillah* 30.
4. Vayikra 20:7.

Parashat Emor is a case in point, since there is a tight interface between directives aimed to produce a holy nation and a holy priesthood. From that perspective, the Mishnaic sages arranged the body of Jewish law traced to these *parshiyot* in Seder Kodashim (the Order of Holy Things). This reflects the following emphases: *kedushat haKohanim, kedushat ha'avodah, u'kedushat ha'am* (the sanctity of the priests, the sanctity of the worship service, and the sanctity of the people).

With the passage of time, a tragic anomaly has transpired. Despite an abundance of textual content surrounding the various sacrifices, little is known about them. This is due in large part, according to the Rambam, to the lamentable reality of Jews deprived of their Mikdash—that integral component of Hebrew religious life. Alas, the Temple has been destroyed, and Jewish glory with it. See his introduction to his commentary on the *mishnayot* on Seder Kodashim.

Another difficulty when it comes to understanding Sefer Vayikra is that the discussion of sacrifices is scattered throughout the Torah rather than grouped in one comprehensive block of text. Consider that some aspects are broached in Sefer Shemot (Parashat Tetzaveh) and others—such as those relating to the *sotah* and *nazir*—in Sefer Bamidbar (Parashat Naso). The sacrifices brought by the chiefs of the twelve tribes are dealt with there as well. Another place where the subject is recorded can be found in Parashat Behaalotcha. Specifically, we read there about *korban Leviim*. Parshiyot Shelach Lecha and Korach provide critical information concerning things that cause impurity to the Kohanim, and in Chukat the subject of the red heifer is broached. *Temidim* (daily sacrifices) and *musafim* (additional sacrifices) are to be found in Parashat Pinchas.

We will now address the challenge of putting the vast subject of sacrifices in cohesive order. Below is a thorough treatment of a subject that has not received its due on account of the lack of concentration of textual source material. Note, we do not intend to present novel observations on sacrifices. Indeed, texts abound—whether in the Torah or Oral Tradition—that adequately cover the subject of sacrifices. However, we will make an effort to expand on the words of the great Rambam. Has his discerning mind's eye not grasped profound meaning? We present his findings in a format and manner that will facilitate understanding.

Ultimately, it is anticipated that this presentation's structure will offer students a way to compartmentalize this multifaceted topic. Our contention is that when the material is presented in a logical structure, the matter of sacrifices will no longer confuse, put off, or intimidate readers. On the contrary, the subject will hopefully regain its former clarity as well as stimulate further interest and relevance.

1. The Three Types of *Korban*: Animal, Bird, and Plant

Strictly speaking, the terms *zevach* (זבח) and *korban* (קרבן) are not synonymous, though, on occasion, they are interchangeable. While it is true that every *zevach* is a *korban*, the inverse does not follow. That is, not every *korban* is a *zevach*. This is because *zevach* invariably refers to animal sacrifices requiring ritual slaughter. Animal parts are then brought to the altar. In Hebrew, ritual slaughter equals *zevichah* (זביחה) or *shechitah* (שחיטה). A verse bears this out: "And you shall slaughter [זבחת] from your herd and your flock as I have commanded."[5]

Therefore, every *zevach* by definition is a *korban* and is offered on Hashem's altar. However, certain *korbanot* (sacrifices) are not ritually slaughtered. An example of such a case is bird sacrifices. They require no ritual slaughter. Or take gift offerings as another illustration. They are sacrifices, though they are not animals and hence not called *zevach*. In sum, the term *korban* (sacrifice) is used far more loosely than the word *zevach*, since the latter always conveys a slaughtered animal offered on an altar. Now, concerning bird or gift offerings, despite the fact that they may be referred to as *korbanot*, they will never be called *zevachim*.

Let us further provide working definitions, beginning with the term *korban*. There are two types. One gets its name insofar as it is brought upon an altar. Type 2 relates to the act, or better the intent behind the act. Namely, a man who sacrifices attains closeness or *hakravah* with his Maker. "And who is the mighty nation whose God relates intimately [קרובים] with him?"[6]

The Torah lists the various kinds of sacrifices. From the animal category, all three are domesticated: bulls, sheep, and goats. Bird types include only

---

5.　Devarim 12:21.
6.　Devarim 4:7.

turtledoves and doves. Vegetable or grain sacrifices must comprise bread, oil, or wine. Frankincense or *levonah* (לבנה) is added to these.

An undisputed value hierarchy characterizes these different categories. Sacrifices ranking the highest or most desirable before the Almighty are bulls, sheep, or goats. Support for this assertion comes from the fact that no public sacrifices utilize birds, vegetables, or grains—but rather only animals.

It is appropriate to explain why sacrifices consist exclusively of those types delineated above. According to the Rambam, the three animals were offered for two reasons: (a) by nature and species they are all choice specimens of the animal kingdom, and (b) they are readily available. Had Heaven called for Jews to sacrifice wild animals,[7] procuring the means to bring a *korban* would have presented far greater exertion. God did not desire to trouble His children. A similar logic prevailed with regard to both bird types.

The Ralbag concurred with the Rambam's thinking. Both men are correct, though two more reasons are advanced.

First, the three large, domestic animals allude to the three saintly patriarchs. Bulls are reminiscent of Avraham. Just as bulls measure in as the largest domesticated animals, so too Avraham was the most prominent. A textual clue can be found: "And Avraham ran to the bulls and he took a tender and healthy bull."[8] Sheep correspond to Yitzchak, and they follow bulls with regard to choiceness. Also at the Akeidah, a ram burnt offering substituted for Yitzchak, as it says, "And he took a ram and offered it for a burnt offering instead of his son."[9] Goats line up with Yaakov. Their makeup places them after bulls and sheep so far as worthiness is concerned. Textual support comes from "And to Yaakov [Rivkah said]: Please go to the flocks and take for me two kid goats from among them."[10] Additionally, the Yaakov and goat dyad gets bolstered when he dresses up in goat skins and receives blessings from his father.[11]

Second, these choice animals and fowl relate back to the Jewish nation. Often, the prophets nicknamed the people "bulls," as this verse illustrates: "As a refractory cow is headstrong Israel."[12] Or "Cows of Bashan are Efraim,[13] a

---

7. Kosher non-domesticated animals such as gazelle, deer, and antelope, per Devarim 13:4.
8. Bereshit 18:7.
9. Bereshit 22:13.
10. Bereshit 27:9.
11. *Abravanel's World: Bereshit*, Parashat Lech Lecha, sixth *aliyah*.
12. Hoshea 4:16.
13. Amos 4:1.

calf [that acts by] rote."[14] Such examples are numerous. As stated above, all public sacrifices comprised bulls, sheep, or goats. To wit, when the congregation sinned unintentionally, atonement required bringing a cow from a herd.

Frequently, the prophets utilized other metaphors for the Jewish people. They were called lambs, sheep, or flock: "Israel is a stray sheep."[15] Yechezkel said, "And I judged between the sheep."[16] Accordingly, the two daily sacrifices in the Temple were sheep—one in the morning and another in the evening. More samples employing flock imagery follow: "And I give you My flock, the flock of My affection"[17] and "Lost flocks became of My people."[18]

Male and female goats were yet another regular designation for Hebrews. Yeshayahu writes, "Therefore strong people (עם עז) will honor You."[19] Yirmiyahu conjures, "Wherefore is the mighty rod (מטה עז) broken."[20] And Yechezkel adds this: "And I brought back the excellence (גאון עזים), the excellence of your might."[21] It can't escape notice that on Yom Kippur, part of the service featured a goat picked for Hashem's portion (גורל ה'), symbolizing the Jewish people. Note how these prophets literarily played on the two-letter cognate עז, invoking a shared meaning of either goat or *ez* (עז) or strength or *oz* (עוז). Following the prophets' lead, the sages list three kinds of goats or *izim*, Hebrews being among them.[22]

Clearly, literary device had been at work when the prophets likened the people to bulls, sheep, and goats. Another twist can be found when they borrowed animal imagery to drive home the pain and anguish of Jews in exile: "As sheep led to slaughter and like a ewe before her shearers—silently without a bleat."[23] Practically iconic, this depiction is ubiquitous. The Almighty expressly commanded Jews to sacrifice animal types so closely resembling themselves to better evoke emotion. They had been marched upon the altar, their flesh and blood spilled. "Man—when amongst you he offers sacrifice to

---

14. Hoshea 10:11.
15. Yirmiyahu 50:17.
16. Yechezkel 34:17.
17. Yechezkel 34:31.
18. Yirmiyahu 50:6.
19. Yeshayahu 25:3.
20. Yirmiyahu 48:17.
21. Yechezkel 7:24.
22. BT *Beitzah* 25.
23. Yeshayahu 53:7.

God."[24] Read literally: Yourselves and animals like yourselves (bulls, sheep, goats) get offered to Heaven.

Let us continue our broad discussion. Dispensation is provided for poor folk who cannot afford to pay for a domestic animal. Doves and turtledoves suffice, as Tanach verses freely associate the Hebrew nation with them, too. "My turtledove nestled in the rock's cleft."[25] Allegorically, this motif spilled over to Jewish liturgy and prayer on behalf of them: "Time for the songbird arrived. And the sound of the dove goes out in our land."[26]

The Ramban explains that those two birds were chosen because of their admirable traits. Doves only pair up with their mates. Fidelity is also an ingrained characteristic of turtledoves. Jews' loyalty to their Creator is permanent, Ramban observes. Fine words, and they are lent additional support from the following quote found in an ancient source: "And male turtledoves exclusively mate with their partners. Should the female die, it is extremely rare that the male will pair with another female. If the male dies, take it as axiomatic that the female will never be induced to mate with a second male."[27]

It is also possible to say that doves and turtledoves were used on account of their place in the zodiac.[28] Broadly, these subjects impinge upon celestial formations and phenomena.

In addition to domestic animal and bird usage for the Mikdash, we come to the third and final category. This is the gift offering taken from fine flour, oil, frankincense, and wine for libations. As this category's name implies, gifts are generally exchanged when a guest desires to please his host. For that reason, the gift must be worthy to be eaten on a table as part of a festive meal. Thus, we can reason that the food items listed above were all a most appreciated bill of fare. Moreover, bread, oil, and wine rate as delicacies fit for a royal dining table. King David acknowledged as much: "And wine gladdens man's heart to brighten his countenance more than oil. And bread brings a man's satiety."[29]

---

24. Vayikra 1:2.
25. Shir Hashirim 2:14.
26. Shir Hashirim 2:12.
27. Abravanel cites here the eighth chapter of a work entitled *Philosophical Theory* whose author he does not identify.
28. Abravanel quotes from *Reishit Chochmah*. He incorporates fifteenth-century theories of cosmology and physics that make little sense to modern readers. Some of his comments have therefore been omitted here.
29. Tehillim 104:15.

For these reasons, man brings gift offerings to his master. Specialties were, of course, seasonal; at harvest time a gift offering meant bringing produce of the land. If fresh fruit or grain was unavailable, then gifts consisted of flour, oil, and other spices to add flavor and aroma. Naturally, fine wine was a staple with the beau monde. This mode, then, was transferred to the Mishkan, where the Almighty commanded that similar opulence be brought before the Master of the Universe.

Minchat habikkurim (first fruits) were offered to Hashem in the Mishkan. At other junctures of the harvest times, Jews brought their gifts consisting of choice produce such as bread, oil, and wine seasoned with *levonah*, quality aromatics. Summing up, we count four gift offerings. That number alludes to the four main condiments and dishes served to nobility. Later in the second part of this *sefer*'s introduction, more will be discussed.

To recap, the choicest offering was taken from four-legged, domesticated animals. Beneath them was considered a gift from one of two types of birds: doves and turtledoves. For those who could not afford livestock or fowl gifts, other presents consisting of the three upscale grains were perfectly acceptable.

2. Categories of Sacrifices

This section deals with the various sacrifices' formats. When discussing *zevachim* or *menachot*, it is understood that they are brought and offered upon the altar.

Zevachim: Animal Sacrifices

We begin with *zevachim*'s four distinct subcategories.

(a) *Olah* (עולה)—burnt offering
(b) *Chatat* (חטאת)—sin offering
(c) *Asham* (אשם)—guilt offering
(d) *Shelamim* (שלמים)—peace offering

This is an exhaustive list of all of the types of *korbanot* mentioned in the Torah. Now let us present particulars.

Olah. The burnt offering is wholly offered on the altar, whether it is an individual or communal sacrifice. Accordingly, neither those who donated the animal nor the officiating priests partake of any of it. An exception is made for the animal's hide. It goes to the priest. Furthermore, its gender must be male regardless of whether it comes from bulls, sheep, or goats. Burnt offerings may be taken from turtledoves or doves, but when they are, gender does not matter. Either male or female birds are acceptable.

When bulls, sheep, or goats are brought, they must be without blemish. Old age is considered an imperfection and hence disqualifies. What is considered too old? Bulls may be up to three years old, sheep and goats up to two years. Animals older than those respective ages suffer attenuated strength and vigor.

The Torah dictates that animals brought to the altar must be choice, robust specimens. For bird sacrifices, that translates into plump turtledoves and slightly built doves. Beauty, in terms of those particular birds, is so judged.

The following terminology is used to describe animal sacrifices, as explained in *Masechet Parah*:

keves (כבש), *kesev* (כשב), *seh* (שה), or *ez* (עז)	young flocks, less than a year old
ayal (איל) or in plural *ayalim* (איילים)	male sheep or goats under the age of two
par (פר) or in plural *parim* (פרים)	bull within its first three years
egel (עגל)	a calf up to a year old
se'ir izim (שעיר עזים)	sheep or goats older than one year

Chatat. Discussion continues with sin offerings, of which there are two types. The first kind calls for innards to be burned on the altar, either of a bull taken from a herd or a goat from a flock. Specifically, internal fat (על הקרב מבפנים), kidneys together with surrounding fatty substance (שתי הכליות עם חלבהן), and a lobe over the liver (היותרת אשר על הכבד) make up the innards used for bulls. But when the sin offering is sheep, additional body parts are burned. This refers to a tail (האליה כלה עם הכליות אליה) and some connective kidney tissue. Comprehensively, these are the parts of an animal's anatomy that Hashem commanded to be burned on the altar. Kohanim may partake of whatever remains from the sin offering. In contrast to this first type, there is a second type of sin offering. It is wholly consumed by altar flames and therefore nothing remains to distribute to Kohanim. More details will emerge about this type below.

Asham.   The third category of *korban* is called the guilt offering. Individuals bring this kind of offering in one of two scenarios. First, when one is unsure whether he actually sinned in connection with a commandment for which, had he done it willfully, he would face *karet* (spiritual excision).[30] Perhaps he lacked adequate knowledge to assess his questionable behavior. Hedging, he brings a guilt offering. This remedial step essentially provides him with a safety net, pending clarification of his deed. If it can be ascertained that he indeed transgressed, then he is required to offer a sin offering.

Here is the governing principle and basic rule: each act necessitating a sin offering in the event of the perpetrator's perfect knowledge requires him to bring a guilt offering when he is unable to clearly ascertain his guilt. This situation only presents itself for individuals, but never with the community at large.

In terms of what animal parts get burned (or eaten by priests) on the altar, some guilt offerings mimic sin offerings. That is something both the sin and guilt offering share in common.

Shelamim.   Finally, the fourth and last type of sacrifice is the peace offering. Part of the animal is burned on the altar, similar to sin and guilt offerings. Priests take their due from the animal's breast and thigh. The remaining parts belong to the animal's owner. Sharing portions is what marks a goodwill or peace offering; it gets divvied up most amicably among the parties. For the most part, peace offerings are brought by individuals, but note one exception that is communal: Shavuot's two sheep or *shnei kevassei atzeret* (שני כבשי עצרת).

This concludes the delineation of the four different types of *zevachim* (animal sacrifices requiring ritual slaughter). They range from the *olah* (עולה), which gets totally burned on the altar, to sin and guilt offerings that

---

30. *Karet* may refer to an untimely death or it may mean becoming spiritually cut off in some way.

get partially burned and partially shared among Kohanim, to peace offerings, which are shared three ways—between the altar, the Kohanim, and the
animal's proprietors.

Menachot: Grain Sacrifices

Having wrapped up the subject of *zevachim*, we now proceed to *menachot*
(grain sacrifices). They get subdivided as follows. Some *minchah* offerings
(*menachot* is the plural of *minchah*) are burned together with corresponding
sacrifices. Underscoring their important role, if certain animal sacrifices are
missing *menachot*, the entire sacrifice is disqualified. This type of add-on
minchah is called *minchat nesachim* (מנחת נסכים). Other *menachot* are offered
independently.

Here are the criteria. Bird sacrifices never come with *menachot*, as is
laid down in the *Sifrei*.[31] The sages have also established that all sacrifices
stemming from vows (נדרים) or free volition (נדבות) need *menachot*. Since
sin and guilt offerings are obligatory, they don't require *menachot*. For that
same reason, other obligatory sacrifices such as the *bachur* (הבכור), *maaser
behemah* (מעשר בהמה), or *pesachim* (הפסח) do not get *menachot*. The pattern
is logical. When a sacrifice is optional, *menachot* are added, but when they
are compulsory, *menachot* are dropped. Thus to further illustrate, burnt and
peace offerings, due to their very nature of being optional, must have *menachot*
regardless of whether they are brought by individuals or are communal. Sin
and guilt sacrifices, theoretically, do not have *menachot*, though there are two
exceptions to the rule: *chatat hametzora* (חטאת המצורע) and *ashmat hametzora*
(אשמת המצורע).

The *minchah nechasim* consists of flour mingled with olive oil, and the
nechasim are wine libations. Burnt and peace offerings' *menachot* vary in terms
of the proportions of flour, oil, and wine. Quantities for the various *menachot*
break down as follows.

(a) When peace offerings are sheep or goats (relatively small in
body size and weight), their meat is accompanied by flour in the
amount of one-tenth or an *isaron* (עשרון) of an *eifah*, mingled

---

31. *Sifrei*, Bamidbar 15:3.

with one-fourth *hin* or *reviit hin* (רביעית הין) oil and one-fourth *hin* wine.[32]

(b) Male sheep or goats are bigger-framed and heavier, so that necessitates larger accompanying *menachot*. The *minchah* offering for a male sheep or goat is two *esronim* flour mingled with one-third *hin* oil and one-third *hin* wine.

(c) Bulls, irrespective of their particular size, get bigger measures than (a) and (b) above. Thus, they receive three *esronim* flour mingled with one-half *hin* oil per bull and that same one-half *hin* wine.

Note that these measures are per animal. But there are caveats to the established rule:

- The sheep offered on the second day of Pesach for the *korban hanafat ha'omer* (קרבן הנפת העומר) is a burnt offering, and the Torah records that its *minchah* is two *esronim* flour mingled in one-third *hin* oil. Its *nechasim* gets the standard one-fourth *hin* wine for sheep.

- The sin and guilt offerings for the *metzora* (Biblical "leper") each receive one *isaron* flour. To clarify, a *metzora* brings two male and one female sheep. They comprise one *chatat* (חטאת), one burnt offering or *olah* (עולה), and one guilt offering or *asham* (אשם). The Torah demands that the *minchah* that accompanies these offerings is three *esronim* (שלשה עשרונים).

This concludes that particular type of *minchat hanesachim* which is burned upon the altar together with its burnt offering or within the parameters of innards offered as peace offerings.

The second type of *menachot* is wholly independent of animal sacrifices and subdivides into individual versus communal offerings. Individual offerings are further distinguished among five kinds (a–e below), whereas communal offerings are of only three types (a–c below).

We begin with the communal or public type:

---

32. An *eifah* is a solid measure and a *hin* is a liquid measure. An *eifah* corresponds to the volume of 432 eggs; an *isaron* therefore is equal to 43.2 eggs. A *hin* is equivalent to 124 fluid ounces (just under a gallon) or 3.667 liters; one-fourth *hin* is therefore just under a quart or liter.

(a) *Omer hatenufah* (עומר התנופה) is brought on the second day of Pesach. A quantity called a *kometz* (קומץ) is brought to the altar with the leftover given to the Kohanim.

(b) *Shtei halechem* (שתי הלחם) is offered on Shavuot, as the verse teaches "from your dwelling places you shall bring *lechem hatenufah* [לחם התנופה]."[33] Another verse calls this offering a *minchah*, as it says, "In your offering a new *minchah* to Hashem on your Festival of Weeks."[34]

(c) *Lechem hapanim* (לחם הפנים) is eaten each Shabbat by Kohanim. It consists of twelve loaves of *challah*, with each loaf prepared from two *esronim* flour.

These three gift offerings supersede or take precedence over what is usually a halachic restraint, the presence of *tumah* (טומאה). In contradistinction, they may not be eaten if they themselves contract *tumah*, as decided in Talmud.[35] Another axiom is that "*minchat ha'omer*" (מנחת העומר) takes precedence over Shabbat.[36]

We continue with the five individual *menachot*.

(a) *Minchat choteh* (מנחת חוטא) or *chatat* (חטאת). This is brought by a man for a transgression committed inadvertently. For example, he entered the Mikdash in a state of *tumah* or handled items dedicated to the Mikdash while *tamei* (spiritually unclean). Alternatively, he erred with regard to solemn oaths (שבועת ביטוי או שבועת העדות), either wittingly or unintentionally. The law requires a man who transgresses any of the four sins mentioned above to bring a sacrifice. In the event that the transgressor is indigent and cannot afford to buy an animal, he may bring one-tenth part flour (עשירית האיפה סלת), though it is not mixed with oil or *levonah*. It is referred to as a *minchat choteh* (מנחת חוטא) or the shortened Torah term *chatat* (חטאת). According to *halachah*, a *kometz* is brought to the altar, and the Kohanim eat the remainder.

---

33. Vayikra 23:17.
34. Bamidbar 28:26.
35. BT *Pesachim* 76b.
36. BT *Menachot* 71a.

(b) *Minchat hasotah* (מנחת הסוטה). This is unique among other *menachot* insofar as it consists not of wheat flour but rather barley flour. Furthermore, no oil or *levonah* is added. Again, the measure used on the altar is a *kometz*, with the remainder going to the Kohanim. It is also referred to as *minchat kana'ut* (מנחת קנאות), or jealousy offering.

(c) *Minchah* (מנחה). By this general or catch-all term, we refer to *menachot* prescribed for various sacrifices, such as when a man undertakes to bring a thanksgiving offering (קרבן תודה) or volunteers to become a *nazir* (one who sanctifies himself through specific ascetic vows). Together with his animal sacrifice, he must bring a *minchah*. It takes the form of *challot* or wafers. Interestingly, though it accompanies the *nazir*'s ram offering, the Torah does not call it a *minchah*, nor is it listed anywhere among the *menachot*. Here is proof: If a Kohen personally brings a thanksgiving offering or ram for completing his nazirite term, he may eat the *challot* or wafers. This follows the standard practice if the donor is a non-Kohen. However, if this were a bona fide *minchah*, it would need to be burned on the altar in its entirety. The Torah demands this: "And every gift of the Kohen is fully burned and is not to be eaten."[37] The sages call this *minchah*. Note that this is a borrowed term, but not technically speaking a genuine *minchah*. Evidence of this is that a Kohen may eat it and is not required to burn it.

(d) *Minchat Kohen Mashuach* (מנחת כהן משוח). This refers to a *minchah* that the Kohen Gadol brings daily or subordinate Kohanim bring once during their lifetimes. It marks the first time that they officiate upon the altar. In the Kohen Gadol's case, it is called *chavitei Kohen Gadol* (חביתי כ"ג) and consists of one-tenth of an *eifah* (איפה). Half goes with the daily morning offering and the second half with the daily afternoon offering. It is entirely consumed, as it says, "An eternal statute to the Almighty—totally offered incense."[38] When other Kohanim bring it, it is called

---

37. Vayikra 6:16.
38. Vayikra 6:15.

minchat Kohen Mashuach, on account of its timing. That is, a Kohen performs this on the day when he is anointed (*mashuach*). As far as subordinate priests are concerned, they bring it only once. It is a gesture of the priest having reached majority (bar mitzvah). He brings two portions of flour. That gift is offered as a *minchah* and must be entirely burned on the altar. This is intimated by the verse "This is Aharon's and his sons' sacrifice which they offered before Hashem."[39] Woven into this verse's meaning is an allusion to the *minchat Kohen Gadol* brought daily in addition to that one-time *minchah* proffered by all subordinate Kohanim upon assuming official status in the Mikdash. From the time that a Kohen reaches majority, he is fit to serve there. As a matter of practice, though, his fellow Kohanim traditionally prevented him from serving until he reached the age of twenty.

(e) *Minchat nedavah* (מנחת נדבה). This *minchah* comes with an oath or volunteer sacrifice. It is prepared using five distinct methods.

> I) Flour mingled with oil:
>   *minchat solet* (מנחת סלת)
> II) Oven-baked *challot* or wafers:
>   *minchat maafeh tanur* (מנחת מאפה תנור)
> III) Stove-top offering:
>   *minchah al machavat* (מנחה על המחבת)
> IV) Pan offering:
>   *minchah al hamarcheshet* (מנחה על המרחשת)
> V) First fruit offering:
>   *minchat habikkurim* (מנחת הביכורים)

Let us consider the following case. When a man takes a solemn oath and thereby triggers an obligation to bring a *minchah*, how does he discharge his responsibility? What amount of *minchah* must he bring? Before discussing particulars, a minimum amount of flour to be offered is one portion.

Concerning the first four categories, here is what they share in common. They need to include oil and *levonah*. All must use finely sifted flour and all must take a *kometz* to offer on the altar with the remaining batter distributed

---

39. Vayikra 6:13.

to the Kohanim. The appropriate name for the leftover is *shiurei menachot* (שיורי מנוחות). These are exclusive gifts to the Kohanim, except in cases when Kohanim are the men presenting them. In that case, the entire quantity is brought to the altar.

In summing up, it is manifest that all of the *menachot* were made up of wheat flour aside from the *minchat hasotah* and *minchat ha'omer*, which were of barley flour. Also, the entire *minchah* was not offered on the altar, with three exceptions: *minchat hasotah*, *minchat Kohanim*, and the *menachot hanesachim* that accompanied burnt or peace offerings. Plausibly, the first four above carried deeper significance. Perhaps they correspond to the four main types of bodily fluids found in man.[40] The signal conveyed is that when one of these blood components is unregulated, man is weakened. But when Hashem supports an ailing man and gives him renewed strength so that he rises from his sick bed, gratitude pours. He is moved to bring a sacrifice and a *minchah* to the Almighty. Specifically, he will try to offer something akin to what had caused him severe ailment. That same principle of matching up *minchat maafeh tanur* or *machavat* applies. Namely, a recuperating patient will track an underlying spiritual reason for his illness and bring the appropriate *minchah* as a religious expression.

Rashi writes: "The *machavat* is a vessel that was used in the Mikdash. Since this vessel in the Mikdash was shallow, it caused the *minchah* inside it to harden, because the fire burned the oil."[41] The *minchat hamarcheshet* is likened to the white, and it is liquid. Rashi explains that the *marcheshet* was also a vessel used in the Mikdash, this one deep. "Oil inside it settled inside [to a depth] and the fire did not burn it, therefore the *maaseh minchah* inside was soft because of the liquid absorbed in it."[42] These, then, were the cardinal differences between the first four types of *menachot*. In contrast, the fifth kind was the *minchat bikkurim*.

This concludes the second section.

---

40. Abravanel refers to red, black, or white blood plus plasma. He based this on his knowledge of human physiology, something modern readers will find outdated. Accordingly, many of his comments on this subject have been omitted.
41. Rashi, Vayikra 2:5.
42. Rashi, Vayikra 2:7.

3. Who Brings Sacrifices?

This chapter identifies those whom the Torah commands to bring sacrifices. Though the officiating Kohanim assisted with sacrifices, that is not this chapter's subject. Here we address the layman who brings a sacrifice: the owner of the animal, bird, or grain. Some men acted voluntarily out of a higher, altruistic calling, whereas others were obliged to seek their atonement after having sinned. Four categories present themselves.

Communal or public sacrifices (11)	1. *Olot hatamid* (עולות התמיד) 2. *Musaf Shabbat* (מוסף שבת) 3. *Musaf Rosh Chodesh* (מוסף ראש חודש) 4. *Korban Chag Hamatzot* (קרבן חג המצות) 5. *Korban hanafat ha'omer* (קרבן הנפת העומר) 6. *Korban musaf yom atzeret Chag Hashavuot* (קרבן מוסף יום עצרת חג השבועות) 7. *Korban* specific to the Shavuot festival (קרבן שתי הלחם עם חג העצרת) 8. *Korban Rosh Hashanah* (קרבן ראש השנה) 9. *Korban Yom Hakippurim* (קרבן יום הכיפורים) 10. *Korban Succot*—first day (קרבן יום הראשון חג הסוכות) 11. *Korban musaf Shemini Atzeret* (קרבן מוסף שמיני עצרת)
Individual or personal sacrifices (5)	1. Brought on account of something a man did or said 2. A miscellany of matters concerning a man's body 3. Obligations due to matters concerning his property 4. Obligations incurred by calendric considerations 5. Incurred on account of oaths or goodwill
Communal sacrifices that mimic private ones (3)	1. *Chatat hakahal* (חטאת הקהל) 2. *Se'irei avodah zarah* (שעירי ע"ז) 3. *Par he'elem dvar shel tzibbur* (פר העלם דבר של ציבור) or *par haba al kol hamitzvot* (פר הבא על כל המצוות, "bull that comes for the commandments")
Private sacrifices that mimic communal ones	Not detailed by Abravanel.

Communal or Public Sacrifices

Let us begin with the first grouping of communal sacrifices. These include the twice-daily burnt offerings as well as offerings made each Shabbat and New Moon, besides those offered on the three annual festivals. Constant, all of them are fixed into Jewish law eternally. The eleven sacrifices comprise:

1. Daily offerings—morning and evening—were two sheep burnt offerings. They are called *olot hatamid* (עולות התמיד).

2. *Musaf Shabbat* (מוסף שבת). These were two additional sheep offered each Shabbat, between the morning and evening daily offerings. All tallied, on each Shabbat four sheep were slaughtered in the Mikdash.

3. *Musaf Rosh Chodesh* (מוסף ראש חודש). In addition to the two daily animals, these extras included two bulls, one ram, and seven one-year-old sheep. All of those were burnt offerings. Finally, the last extra one was a male goat sin offering. That brings the total New Moon count to twelve burnt offerings and one sin offering. When the New Moon fell on Shabbat, that day there were sixteen burnt offerings in addition to the one goat sin offering.

4. *Korban Chag Hamatzot* (קרבן חג המצות). Each of the holiday's seven days, the Kohanim would offer precisely as they did on Rosh Chodesh. That came to two bulls, one ram, seven sheep, plus one goat for a sin offering. When Shabbat coincided with the festival, two extra animals were slaughtered. When all are accounted for, we number fourteen burnt offerings and one sin offering.

5. *Korban hanafat ha'omer* (קרבן הנפת העומר). On the second day of Pesach, this was one sheep for a burnt offering.

6. *Korban musaf yom atzeret Chag Hashavuot* (קרבן מוסף יום עצרת חג השבועות). This was the same as the New Moon's offering, namely two bulls, one ram, and seven sheep—all of those were burnt offerings. One male goat served as a sin offering.

7. *Korban* specific to the Shavuot festival (קרבן שתי הלחם עם חג העצרת). This was one bull, two rams, and seven sheep—all were burnt offerings. One goat was a sin offering and two sheep were peace offerings. When the holiday fell on Shabbat, twenty-six sacrifices were burnt offerings and two goats were sin offerings.

8.   *Korban Rosh Hashanah* (קרבן ראש השנה). After the baseline offerings of daily plus New Moon sacrifices, there came others. That is, one bull and one ram plus seven sheep—all of them burnt offerings. One male goat was the sin offering. When Rosh Hashanah came together with Shabbat, there were twenty-three burnt offerings and two goats for sin offerings.

9.   *Korban Yom Hakippurim* (קרבן יום הכיפורים). This included one bull, one ram, and seven sheep—all of which were burnt offerings. One goat was a sin offering as per the sacrifices on Rosh Hashanah. But in addition there was another goat sin offering— a corresponding goat to one that was sent to the Judean Desert. The one that remained in the Mikdash was entirely consumed by flames, as the Torah makes plain.[43] Another ram was sacrificed as a burnt offering as per verses in Parashat Acharei Mot.[44] When Shabbat and Yom Hakippurim coincided, then all told there were sixteen burnt offerings and one goat for a sin offering.

10. *Korban Succot*—first day (קרבן יום הראשון חג הסוכות). Added to the Mikdash regulars came thirteen bulls, two rams, and fourteen sheep, plus one goat for a sin offering. On a coinciding Shabbat, adding the extras brings the count to thirty-three burnt offerings and a goat for a sin offering. This was the formula for all ensuing days of the festival so far as the rams, sheep, and goats were concerned. However, when it came to the bulls, note that their numbers diminished daily by one, so that by day seven of Succot, only seven bulls were offered. Overall on that last day of the festival there were seven bulls, seven rams, and two sheep, equaling sixteen burnt offerings and one goat sin offering.

11. *Korban musaf Shemini Atzeret* (קרבן מוסף שמיני עצרת). This consisted of one bull, one ram, and seven sheep—all burnt offerings plus one goat for a sin offering. On Shabbat the extras for Shabbat as well as the two daily offerings were added.

Now that all eleven add-ons have been identified, let us proceed to the order in which they were sacrificed. First to be offered was the morning daily

---

43. Vayikra 16:27.
44. Vayikra 16:3.

sacrifice. When Shabbat came, that *musaf* followed. If it was Rosh Chodesh or a festival or both together, Rosh Chodesh took precedence over festivals. And if Rosh Hashanah fell on Shabbat, then after the daily morning sacrifice came Shabbat, New Moon, and finally Rosh Hashanah offerings. The daily afternoon sacrifice always trailed last. This sequence is laid out clearly in the Talmud Bavli.[45]

These represent the regular communal sacrifices that transpired annually without exception or variation. Further note that each one took precedence over Shabbat and thus the seventh day did not hinder in the least bit the offerings mentioned above. Also noted was the fact that public sacrifices were not guilt offerings, nor were they goodwill or peace offerings. The exceptions were the two peace offerings of sheep during the Festival of Shavuot (see 7 above). Generally, public sacrifices utilized two types of sin offerings—those which were entirely burned or others from which Kohanim were allowed to eat. Of the former category was the goat brought on Yom Kippur.

Now our discourse continues with private or individual sacrifices.

Individual or Personal Sacrifices

This section has five subcategories in it.
1. Brought on account of something a man did or said
2. A miscellany of matters concerning a man's body
3. Obligations due to matters concerning his property
4. Obligations incurred by calendric considerations
5. Incurred on account of oaths or goodwill

1. Brought on account of something a man did or said. Type 1 takes into account Torah obligations for a man to bring sacrifices specifically because of something that he said or did. One who accidentally perpetrates severe prohibitions deserving of *karet* brings a sacrifice. If the perpetrator is unclear whether he did the deed, then he brings a guilt offering. Note that not all of the *karet* prohibitions are subsumed and uniform so far as sacrifices are concerned. Take for example a man who inadvertently did not bring his Pesach offering or a man who unintentionally was negligent and failed to have his son circumcised. While punishment for both offenses is *karet*, they do not have to bring sin offerings, since both are positive commandments. The Torah

---

45. BT *Zevachim* 91a.

is clear that only a man who accidentally performs a negative precept may bring a sin offering, as the verse states: "And he committed one of Hashem's [negative] commandments which ought not to have been done."[46]

Another illustration is the *megadef*, a man who expresses verbal heresy. Though considered a major offender (since his offense entails the ultimate hate speech), he does not bring a sacrifice because his crime is one of speech and not an act per se. Or another example is one who enters the Mikdash in a state of *tumah* (טומאה) or is *metamei* (מטמא) sanctified Mikdash food. Even though his sin carries *karet* and when done inadvertently obligates bringing a sacrifice, it is not a uniform case. The Torah extends dispensation to those too poor to pay for an animal offering: "And if he is poor and cannot afford...."[47] However, when it comes to the thirty-six categories of offenses carrying *karet*, an unintentional transgressor brings a *chatat*. If he is doubtful about his act (not sure he actually misbehaved), then he brings an uncertain guilt offering or *asham talui* (אשם תלוי).

In normative cases, what are the animals that transgressors must bring for these egregious sins? The Rambam writes that the matter must be closely analyzed and scrutinized. If a sinner inadvertently committed idolatry, he brings a one-year-old goat as a sin offering. This is the case whether the offender was royalty, a commoner, or the High Priest. However, if the sin included profanation of the Mikdash, his remedy is to offer a ewe or she-goat. That is so when the transgressor can afford the expense, but where he cannot bear the cost, he will suffice with two doves or two turtledoves. One acts as a burnt offering, the other a sin offering. If the man is really hard up, then it is enough for him to bring one-tenth portion of flour dough, as a verse spells out.[48]

In situations where his accidental sin concerned other offenses, the Torah takes the offender's social status or role into account. Categorically, this is not to say that what is wrong for a pauper may be acceptable for a prince—or vice versa. Rather, an error in deed for a man belonging to the rank and file, or as the Torah calls him an *am ha'aretz* (עם הארץ), lacks the weight of a misprision committed by a leader. Thus, a simple man brings a female goat or ewe for a sin offering. If he is a tribal chief or *nasi* (נשיא), or even a king or *melech* (מלך),

---

46. Vayikra 4:2.
47. Vayikra 5:7.
48. Vayikra 5:11.

he must bring a male goat. A High Priest is required to bring a bull for a sin offering, and it gets wholly consumed by flames on the altar.[49]

This concludes the Rambam's opinion. The Ralbag fundamentally differs in his commentary on the Torah, but it is sufficient here to maintain the Rambam's opinion.

Another instance that requires a man to bring a sin offering is when he has sexual relations with a woman who is part maidservant.[50] Here, regardless of whether he had foreknowledge of her particularly ambiguous status, he must bring a ram for a guilt offering, called *asham vadai* (אשם ודאי) or *asham shifchah charufah* (אשם שפחה חרופה). An additional case arises when a man derives benefit from Mikdash property. Misappropriation carries with it an obligation to bring a ram for a guilt offering, called *asham me'ilot* (אשם מעילות). This is true if the affront was accidental. However, if it was willful, he does not bring any sacrifice. This is because consecrated objects are not profaned when the act was intentional, but instead the object remains in its proper state; it hasn't been compromised or profaned. This is further elaborated in Talmud Bavli.[51]

There is another instance concerning false oaths (שבועת העדות ושבועת הפיקדון). Whether one lied on purpose or not, he still needs to bring a sacrifice. It is similar to cases where a man soiled the Mikdash or its sanctity. When it comes to falsifying affidavits regarding security deposits, an offender brings a ram for a guilt offering. So too when a man steals an object and lies under oath about absconding with it, his remedy is to bring a ram guilt offering. Those are all of the cases where individuals are required, as a result of speech or conduct, to bring sacrifices.

This concludes type 1, and now we proceed.

2. A miscellany of matters concerning a man's body. This category will be further subdivided into five.[52]

>   (a) *Zav* or *zavah* (זב או זבה). When a *zav* (a man who has had an abnormal seminal emission) or *zavah* (a woman who has had

---

49. BT *Horayot*, chapter 2.
50. This can occur when a woman was initially owned by two owners but later one owner manumitted.
51. BT *Kiddushin*, chapter 2.
52. Abravanel indicates that there will be five categories, however he proceeds to enumerate six.

abnormal vaginal bleeding) completes the required spiritual cleanliness procedures, he or she is commanded to bring two turtledoves or two doves. One is a burnt offering, the other a sin offering.

(b) *Metzora* (מצורע). A *metzora* (a Biblical "leper," that is, a person who is suffering from *tzaraat*, an impure state resulting from uttering forbidden speech) brings two sheep. One is a burnt offering, the other a guilt offering. It is called an *asham metzora* (אשם מצורע), and in addition he must bring one ewe for a sin offering. Impecunious perpetrators satisfied their obligations by bringing two doves or two turtledoves—one for a burnt offering and the second for a sin offering, plus one sheep for a guilt offering.

(c) *Korban niddah* (קרבן נידה). This resembled the sacrifice brought by a *zav*, namely two doves or turtledoves—one for a burnt offering, the other for a sin offering.[53]

(d) *Korban yoledet* (קרבן יולדת). The sacrifice brought by a *yoledet* (a woman who has given birth) is a one-year-old sheep brought as a burnt offering and either one male dove or a turtledove for a sin offering. If she was poor, she brought two turtledoves—one a burnt offering and one a sin offering.

(e) *Korban nazir* (קרבן נזיר). This governing law, particular only to nazirites, does not distinguish between willful and unintentional acts, and it is likened to the sacrifice brought by a *metzora*. Namely, an offender brings two turtledoves or two doves—one a burnt offering, the other a sin offering. A one-year-old sheep serves as his guilt offering.

(f) *Korban hager* (קרבן הגר). Converts wishing to adopt Heaven's ethos adhere to these three steps, after which they are fully integrated Jews: circumcision, *mikveh* (ritual bath), and sacrifice. A convert's sacrifice consists of two turtledoves or doves—both offered as burnt offerings. See also the *Sifrei*, Parashat Shelach Lecha, "And when a convert will dwell with you."[54] The sages

---

53. This was not a *korban* brought for the usual seven days of *niddah*; it was brought only by a *zavah gedolah*, one who sees blood for three days in a row during the eleven days of *zivah*.

54. Bamidbar 15:14.

elucidated that just as the original Jews had joined the Sinaitic covenant by performing the three deeds (circumcision, *mikveh*, and sacrifice), so too all converts desiring to assume the heavenly mantle under Judaism's banner must conform to those same acts. They continue and bring the example of Jews who underwent circumcision and brought sacrifices. Should converts follow those same rigors? That same verse continues and teaches, "And he offered a fiery sacrifice."[55] They derived that bird offerings were to be totally engulfed by flames. In this way bird offerings are unique, because when animals are burned upon the altar, at least part of the animal (its hide) gets distributed to Kohanim.

3. Obligations due to matters concerning his property. Type 3 covers sacrifices that man brings as a result of his property. Two examples are the *bechor* (firstborn) or *maaseh behemah* (animals brought as tithes). They resemble peace offerings, except that tithe animals must be eaten by their owners in Jerusalem, like *maaser sheni* (מעשר שני). If the firstborn animal is unblemished, then he is sacrificed and eaten by the Kohanim. Details are outlined in Talmud Bavli, *Bechorot*. Also when a man brings firstborn animals, they are accompanied by peace offerings, as is elaborated there.

4. Obligations incurred by calendric considerations. Type 4 deals with sacrifices that are time-sensitive, functions of the Jewish calendar cycle. For example, Jews must ascend to Yerushalayim three times annually for the major festivals. The sacrifice brought by one who ascends—called an *olat re'iah* (עולת ראיה)—is a burnt offering. During those occasions, in addition, he must bring a peace offering or *chagigah* (חגיגה): "And you shall celebrate to Hashem your Almighty."[56] A second peace offering besides the *chagigah* is the *shalmei simchah* (שלמי שמחה), a reference to the verse "And you shall rejoice on your festival."[57]

The sages have elucidated the many ramifications of those three sacrifices, such as: Who is obligated to offer them? How is the obligation discharged? When are they offered?[58] Without a doubt, these three sacrifices (*re'iah*,

---

55. Ibid.
56. Devarim 16:15.
57. Devarim 16:14.
58. BT *Chagigah*, first and second chapters.

chagigah, and *simchah*) are compulsory. The *chagigah* was brought on the day of the fourteenth; it is a peace offering. This refers to the fourteenth of Nissan, the day before the onset of Pesach, as a verse states, "And you shall offer a *pesach* to Hashem your Almighty—[from the] flock and herd."[59] These are optional, as is explained in Talmud Bavli.[60] Though the Talmud characterizes *korban chagigah* as a public or communal sacrifice, this is only because so many individuals are obligated to bring it. A better classification of *chagigah* is among personal and not public sacrifices. Support is taken from the fact that it does not have the power to push off Shabbat observance, as is the case with communal offerings.

5. Incurred on account of oaths or goodwill. These are sacrifices that a man obligates himself to do arising from his oaths or out of goodwill. One example is a man who opts to become a *nazir*. After the standard thirty-day stint, he brings a one-year-old sheep for a burnt offering, a one-year-old ewe for a sin offering, plus a ram for a peace offering. Or take a situation where a man verbally takes an obligation upon himself by saying, "I vow to bring a burnt offering," or "I promise to bring a peace offering." Alternatively, he might walk over to a particular animal among his herd or flock, place his hand on it, and pronounce, "This is a burnt offering," or "This shall be a peace offering."

Halachah draws clear lines of distinction of obligations arising from a *neder* (oath) or *nedavah* (free-volition utterance). Simply put, oaths have a greater stringency. Namely, if a man pledges to sacrifice a certain animal and then something happens to it—say, it dies or runs away—the animal owner still must make good on his promise. This he does by appointing a substitute animal. This would not be the case if his pledge were one of free volition, in which case he would not have to make restitution. Deduce from here that a man is not permitted to take an oath or volunteer to bring a sin or guilt offering. However, he is allowed to promise or volunteer to bring a burnt or peace offering—either from animals or birds. Parenthetically, one may not commit to bring a peace offering using a bird.

This concludes the second category of sacrifices that individuals bring. Recall that personal sacrifices lack the urgency to supersede Shabbat or set aside *tumah* (טומאה).

---

59. Devarim 16:2.
60. BT *Pesachim*, sixth chapter.

Communal Sacrifices That Mimic Private Ones

Here we address communal sacrifices that mimic private ones. When the Great Sanhedrin issues law that is later discovered to have been promulgated in error, and it results in misleading the nation, remedial steps must be taken. More to the point, following a ruling by the Great Court, people purposefully performed an act punishable by *karet*. That is, had folks accidentally blundered of their own accord, they would be required to bring a sin offering. In this case, they unwittingly acted upon the ill advice of the Sanhedrin. These laws are promulgated in the Talmud.[61] In such cases, the Sanhedrin must atone for their offense by bringing a sin offering. If their flawed decision misled Jews to unknowingly perform idolatry, the public brings a bull as a burnt offering and a he-goat for a sin offering. Actually, each tribe brings these two types of sacrifices on behalf of their co-tribesmen. Atypically, however, this goat is totally burned on the altar, since it is a tribal sacrifice. The Torah commands that the bull be completely consumed, too. It is called a *chatat hakahal* (חטאת הקהל). The *Sifra*[62] derives a *binyan av* (general principle) from this case applying to all situations arising from public sin offerings. Namely, it is completely burned on the altar. The *se'irei avodah zarah* (goat sin offering) is so called because the Great Sanhedrin's ill counsel wrought this undesirable outcome.

What if the Great Sanhedrin caused the nation to sin in other ways? They must bring a bull for a sin offering. This offering is known as *par he'elem dvar shel tzibbur* (פר העלם דבר של ציבור). Its name is on account of the verse's phrase *v'neelam mimeno* (and the matter escaped them). Occasionally it is known as *par haba al kol hamitzvot* (a bull that comes for the commandments). The Torah requires that it be wholly burned, a requirement that each and every tribe performs. For this reason, this category belongs under the heading of public sacrifices, since it is written, "And the congregation offers it."[63] A second verse states, "And all of the congregation of Bnei Yisrael will be forgiven."[64] These offerings also resemble personal sacrifices in that they do not supersede Shabbat nor may they be offered if the people are *tamei*.

---

61. BT *Horayot*.
62. *Sifra*, Vayikra, chapter 4.
63. Bamidbar 15:24.
64. Bamidbar 15:26.

Summation

Distinct patterns emerge when we enumerate the sacrifices as we have done. Thus, observe that all the animals used for public sacrifices are male—even for those public sacrifices that have aspects in common with privately brought ones. No public sin offerings are burned except for the goat on Yom Kippur (a matching goat to the one sent to the desert), goats brought in repentance for idolatry, and the bull used when the congregation erred. Other sin offerings are eaten by male Kohanim. We also note that female animals are brought for individual sin offerings, with the exception of three sin offerings for which male animals are used despite their being private sin offerings. We refer to

1. the goat that a king offers if he inadvertently sinned in a matter that would land him *karet* had he done it willfully and been required to bring a sin offering for standard sins
2. the bull brought by the Kohen Hagadol for *karet* violations
3. the goat and bull are brought by the Kohen Mashuach for unintentional sins, as well as
4. the bull for Yom Kippur

The following halachic parameters tend to confuse, so we will digress a moment to explain. Generally speaking, sin offerings that individuals bring (as opposed to communal offerings) do not get wholly burned on the altar. Recall that such a requirement would deprive officiating priests of their fair due. Now, the sole exception to that rule occurs when the animal in question happens to be a bull (i.e., not a goat or a bird). In rare cases, though, the bull does totally go up in smoke. Specifically, we label the bull either a *par haba al kol hamitzvot* or a *par Yom Hakippurim*.

In sum, whenever rank-and-file sinners bring their sin offerings, that animal is a female and is culled from the flock (not the herd). In contrast, when chieftains sin, they bring a he-goat. To elucidate, cases involving a bull or *par haba al kol mitzvot* and the *par Yom Hakippurim* are both, to restate the obvious, males. They get reduced to ashes and smoke. The reason the Torah calls the former category *par haba al kol mitzvot* reflects a prefatory verse:

"A man who sins inadvertently [and transgresses] any of Hashem's negative precepts…"[65]

Our overall statement takes into account all sacrifices brought upon the altar. The things in common are that only Kohanim without blemish may officiate and that the animals designated as sacrifices must also be free from imperfections. Animals are only slaughtered during the day, as it says, "On the day that I commanded it to Bnei Yisrael to offer their sacrifices."[66] The sages deduce this from the Torah's word choice, "day," in contrast to night. A final point is that sacrifices were only carried out in the Mikdash in Yerushalayim, or more specifically Mount Moriah, as the verse alludes.

4. Why Sacrifice?

This final section seeks to investigate meanings or rationales behind why Jews brought sacrifices. The Rambam writes that sacrifices should be viewed, in the main, as a concession of sorts.[67] Put differently, the practice of bringing sacrifices lacked the soulful component inherent in other Torah commandments.

In broad strokes, let us overview Hashem's universal plan, focusing on His people's role in it.

God sent Moshe to forge out of the Hebrews a nation of priests, a holy nation. The prophet's goal was teaching them to attain an intimate knowledge of the Maker: "And you have been shown to know."[68] Another verse captures this same inscrutable expanse: "And you shall know today and etch it in your heart."[69] Intimacy with the Infinite One must be viewed as the national mission statement: "And to serve Him with all of your hearts"[70] and "And you shall serve Hashem your Almighty."[71]

Let us contrast those heady aims with a far less otherworldly one, ubiquitously present in the ancient world. Pagan practices, as a matter of habit, featured steady streams of assorted sacrifices. This was the chief way pagans related to their gods. Temples were meeting spots to gather and offer different

---

65. Vayikra 4:2.
66. Vayikra 7:38.
67. Rambam, *Moreh Nevuchim* 32:3.
68. Devarim 4:35.
69. Devarim 4:39.
70. Devarim 11:13.
71. Shemot 23:25.

animals on their altars. Burning incense amidst prostration and so on was all acted out with due deference. Pagodas or shrines were built by votaries while their priests gazed to the stars, worshipping the celestial bodies and galaxies as far as the eye could see.

Here is where Heaven's operation needed to tread gingerly. Canceling or voiding these forms of religious practice may well have met with popular grumbling within the Jewish camp. Is it not part and parcel of the human condition to defend the status quo? Marriage to conventionality is hard to decouple or decondition. Might Jews not have fiercely resisted a modern religious system that, well, bucked all contemporary religious systems and trimmings? To fully comprehend the ancient mindset, a little role playing is in order. Imagine if a prophet were to ascend a dais and pronounce from Jerusalem:

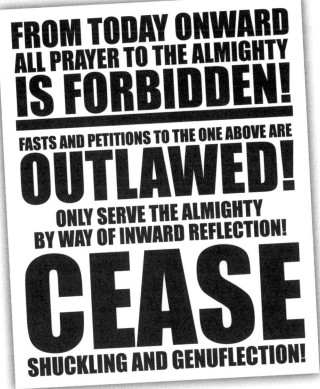

FROM TODAY ONWARD ALL PRAYER TO THE ALMIGHTY IS FORBIDDEN!

FASTS AND PETITIONS TO THE ONE ABOVE ARE OUTLAWED!

ONLY SERVE THE ALMIGHTY BY WAY OF INWARD REFLECTION!

CEASE SHUCKLING AND GENUFLECTION!

Outcries—if not out and out calls for the prophet's ouster—would ring out in vehement unison. For this reason, Heaven kept many ancient religious institutions intact, though with salient alterations. First and foremost, paying homage to God's creations was banned. Similarly, it was forbidden to honor notions bereft of truth and authenticity. In a word, all devotion was directed to the Almighty's holy name—exclusively. Furthermore, rites and rituals were centralized to the Mikdash, and to an altar dedicated to His name. God commanded the Jews to construct a sanctuary, consecrate it, and build an altar of earth to His holy name. When it came to sacrificial service, new rules and regulations were put into effect but the upshot was, again, homage to the one God.

Bowing, incense, and animal offerings all shared an address in common—and the Almighty stood at the very epicenter of all religious sentiment and impulse. Pious convictions and crafted instruction effectively wiped out all vestiges of the old guard. Corralled into a cul de sac, idolatry would become a dead letter. Judaism turned a new leaf and new corner as its major credo blossomed. God returned to center stage in the Hebrews' hearts and minds. Gradualism made it all possible, advances the Rambam. Die-hard pagan opponents' objections had been preempted, derailed. By increments, Jews came to their senses.

This concludes the Rambam's approach. Crossing foils with him, the Ramban cuts a diametrically opposed opinion.

Few topics in Judaism and Tanach riled and fired up the Ramban against the Rambam as much as the subject of sacrifices. His blistering attack calls the Rambam's words "prevaricated." The notion that the Mishkan's holy altar was conceived in pagan sin—born a bastard before being "sanitized"—simply does not wash. A steady onslaught of Scriptural support bolsters the Ramban's assault.

The Ramban's first salvo was "For it is a fiery meal to Hashem."[72] One of righteous Noach's first acts after his ark grounded was to erect an altar: "And Hashem smelled the sweet aroma."[73] Where, the Ramban baits, were idolaters at that juncture of human civilization? Earlier in the Chumash, Hevel had offered to Hashem the firstborn of his flocks, "And Hashem heeded Hevel."[74] No lurking pagans at the dawn of man. Bilaam said, "Seven altars I have dedicated, and I offered a bull and ram upon the altar."[75] He had no interest in propitiating gods with these religious gestures.

Turning to etymology, the Ramban would have us examine the Hebrew word for sacrifice or *korban* (קרבן), meaning "to approach," beginning with the verse "And My sacrificial meals [are for] My sweet aroma."[76] Could Heav-

---

72. Vayikra 3:11.
73. Bereshit 8:21.
74. Bereshit 4:4.
75. Bamidbar 23:4.
76. Bamidbar 28:2.

en's professed sentiment be nothing more than trifling phantasm or puerile babbling? The Ramban's disapproval certainly reads as a philippic.

After the Ramban's polemic, the Narbonne[77] charged to the Rambam's defense. He deflected criticism, essentially, by saying that the attack was unfounded. The Rambam did not intend his words to be construed to imply that God's command to offer sacrifices smelled of apologetics to primitive beliefs. Instead, the correct reading of Rambam points to the fact that the sacrificial service was the climax of the Temple worship. In fact, the Narbonne's words ring quite hollow and do not get at the meat, as it were, of the matter.

We submit that this is what the Rambam really meant to say on the commandment incumbent upon Jews to bring sacrifices. He holds that the Torah delineates several commandments in order to instill proper thought and beliefs. Thus prayer, petitioning, learning Torah, fasting and supplication, tzitzit, tefillin, mezuzah, and the like are specifically designed to inculcate within the soul deep, heartfelt service to the Creator. These mitzvot, pure and without ulterior motive, Hashem considers worthy in the first order. As such, they are compulsory bill of fare regardless of time or place; they are always rich and poignant. By contrast, the commandment to offer sacrifices is of a different ilk. "Watch yourselves lest you shall offer sacrifices anywhere that you see."[78] Besides restricting venues, Hashem also cautions Jews from sacrificing at indiscriminate times. Forestalling this undesirable abuse, Hashem limited the practice to only one place which was earmarked for His service—the Mikdash. In addition, the job was taken out of the hands of the uninitiated and placed exclusively with Aharon's descendants.

Do these restrictions not suggest that Heaven had reason to regulate and supervise sacrificial service? Does it not appear plain that the Mishkan mitzvot stand lower than those cited above (prayer, petitioning, etc.)? No less than the Ramban, the Rambam bases his evaluation of the Mishkan upon Scripture as well. He hears the exasperation of the prophets. After all, much anger and vituperation is leveled at the Jewish people by the hoary visionaries.

Maddened, prophets rebuked the people on account of their overzealousness to bring sacrifices. To illustrate, an exasperated Shmuel vents, "Does

---

77. Rabbi Moshe Narboni, called the Narbonne due to his residence in the French city of Narbonne. A philosopher, Jewish commentator, and translator, he was born in Perpignan, France, around 1300 and died sometime between 1362 and 1368.

78. Devarim 12:13.

Hashem desire *zevachim* (burnt offerings) as much as He wants [Jews] to listen to Him?"[79] Yeshayahu laments, "Why the abundant quantity of your sacrifices? says the Almighty."[80] Incensed, Yirmiyahu slams backsliders: "For I did not address your forefathers on the day when I took them out of Egypt concerning the matter of burnt offerings and *zevach* but rather regarding this matter I commanded them, saying: Listen to My voice and I will be for you God."[81] In no uncertain terms, the psalmist chides, "Not for your *zevachim* do I reprove you, and [as for] your constant burnt offerings before Me, I will not take from your house a bull."[82]

Let us shed more light on the Rambam's position regarding sacrifices. He holds that incorporating the ancient rite into Judaism came as an "afterthought," a concession that Heaven dispensed with reluctance and apprehension. His opinion represents a repository of no fewer than six Talmudic/Midrashic sources, as follows.[83]

1. In *Menachot* it is written that whoever delves into Torah does not need a sin, burnt, guilt, or meal offering.[84]

2. *Makkot* quotes from Tehillim: "For one day in Your courtyard is better than one thousand."[85] The Talmudic sages adduced from the psalmist's sentiment that one day immersed in Torah learning superseded the thousand sacrifices that Shlomoh would eventually bring.

3. *Shemot Rabbah* melds a medley of three Scriptural sources.[86] In this third rabbinic source, an allegorical conversation takes place between the collective body politic of the Jews and Hashem. From our *midrash*, we hear a desperate complaint lodged by the people after the Temple was destroyed. "When the Jews will reflect on their dismal post-Temple state, they will ask: When the *nesiim* sinned, they brought sacrifices and gained atonement. Or when a Kohen Mashuach transgressed and brought a sacrifice, he too achieved catharsis. We who live in the post-Temple period, what shall we do to remedy

79. I Shmuel 15:22.
80. Yeshayahu 1:11.
81. Yirmiyahu 7:22–23.
82. Tehillim 50:7–8.
83. BT *Menachot* 110a; BT *Makkot* 10a; *Shemot Rabbah* 38:4; a second, distinct reference to BT *Menachot* 110a brought in *Sifrei* on Bamidbar 28:8; BT *Temurah* 29a; and *Vayikra Rabbah* 22:8.
84. BT *Menachot* 110a.
85. Tehillim 84:11, cited in BT *Makkot* 10a.
86. Shemot 29:1, Hoshea 14:3, and Tehillim 26:6–7, cited in *Shemot Rabbah* 38:4.

our sins? Hashem calmed the people and said: I desire words and not sacrific-es.... I appreciate and hold you in good stead on account of words of Torah."

4. In a separate Talmudic statement,[87] we find that Rabbi Shimon alerts us: "Come and see what is written in the Torah section dealing with sacrifices. God's name is not written there as 'Kel' or 'Elokim,' but rather the four-letter ineffable Name. Why? It nips snide comments in the bud. How? When smart alecks crack jokes about sacrifices being brought in order to satiate Heaven's "hearty appetite," there is a ready response. God did not request, to put it squarely, sacrificial scraps from man. "Do I eat the meat of bulls? Drink the blood of goats?"[88] Of course not! How ludicrous! Instead, He commanded Jews to sacrifice for their own welfare, as the verse attests, 'For your benefit offer sacrifices.'"[89]

We need to digress a moment to address the Ramban's tirade against the Rambam's position on sacrifices. Note, the Ramban brings the *Sifrei*[90] in the beginning of his words, yet curiously omits the Midrash's concluding remarks. This is bizarre in that the *Sifrei*'s conclusion fully supports the Rambam's approach. Also, Rabbi Shimon ben Azzai's opinion regarding why the Torah employs Hashem's four-letter appellation is further support for the Rambam. According to him, sacrifices come to wean the ancient Jews from nagging, primitive influences and instead serve to steer the people's hearts to adhere to their Maker, as evidenced by the four-letter name of God. Underscoring this crucial point, the Torah does not use other names of Hashem ("Kel" or "Elokim"), but instead uses God's appellation of honor. Importantly, the two aforementioned ways of identifying God have been associated with Hashem's angels. This is not the case with God's ineffable name. It always, inalterably, refers to the Almighty. Hence, there is laced within those verses a powerful caution: Don't sacrifice to other deities—only the Holy One, blessed be He.

5. Let us review another passage in the Talmud.[91] Tovia son of Matanya said in the name of Rabbi Yoshiyahu: What does this verse convey? "You should observe to sacrifice to Me at the appointed time."[92] The sage stresses

---

87. BT *Menachot* 110a. This *aggadah* is restated in one of the Ramban's sources (*Sifrei*, Bamidbar 28:8).
88. Tehillim 50:13.
89. Vayikra 22:29.
90. BT *Menachot* 110a, cited in *Sifrei*, Bamidbar 28:8.
91. BT *Temurah* 29a.
92. Bamidbar 28:2.

that the Torah orders Jews to serve Him and not other lords. He asks: And who might be those other masters to whom sacrifices might be directed? He provides the answer: pagans.

6. Clearly, these Talmudic sages concur with the Rambam. Even more resounding proof follows, from *Vayikra Rabbah*.[93] It is written, "When any man slaughters."[94] Rabbi Pinchas shared a parable in the name of Rabbi Levi. Once there was an arrogant and pompous prince. He developed a taste for unsavory and uncouth foods. The king commanded his servants to make sure that the royal table was filled to the brim with those detestable dishes. This he did in order for his son to grow so nauseated that he would eventually foreswear the abominable fare. Herein lies the lesson. So entrenched were the Jews—so absolutely enamored with idolatry to the extreme of obsession by obsequiously serving sacrifices to idols—that the Almighty needed to apply radical intervention. And that explains, concludes the sage, how Jews were commanded to build an altar and offer sacrifices exclusively to Hashem—"When any man slaughters."

This rabbinic saying provides ironclad support for the Rambam. Jews in that milieu had been fatally hooked. Worship of demons and other "harmful spirits"[95] dropped deep roots, and sacrificing to them was a way of life. Attempts to downplay their unpardonable sin simply won't wash. Nor will ascribing it to a mere predilection to only offer peace sacrifices to forces of evil. This is bald falsification, a transparent coloring of truth.

In fact, the problem was widespread and did not discern between the various kinds of sacrifices. "So that when Bnei Yisrael will bring their sacrifices which they offer at large and they bring them to Hashem…and they should no longer sacrifice their sacrifices to demons after which they whore."[96] Again concerning this phenomenon, a verse reiterates, "Any Jewish man or stranger residing among you who offers a burnt offering or *zevach* but did not bring it to the entrance of the Tent of Meeting should not bring it, [for] to do thus to Hashem results in that man being cut off from his people."[97]

---

93. *Vayikra Rabbah* 22:8.
94. Vayikra 17:3.
95. Abravanel pokes fun at superstitious beliefs, hence the quotation marks.
96. Vayikra 17:5–7.
97. Vayikra 17:8–9.

More particulars emerge, and they demonstrate to what depths Hebrews stooped when it came to old sacrificial habits: "Any man who eats [even] traces of blood..."[98] Fresh evidence shows that Jews had not just developed a fetish for peace offerings, but in fact the scourge included burnt offerings, *zevachim*, and all other categories. For that reason, the Torah's prohibition against sacrificing to demons casts a much wider net. Not only did Heaven caution against drinking the blood but rather outlawed all vestiges of sacrificial service.

These strong arguments in favor of the Rambam give one pause—especially as portrayed in the eyes of the Ramban, his chief detractor on the subject of sacrifices. Fairly, students nod in disbelief: Given that the Ramban was thoroughly versed in Talmud, how did he miss these rabbinic writings? Sources are replete. From Chumash, from Prophets, from Writings, and well into rabbinic literature, the case seems to be open and shut. And they bolster if not nail down support for the Rambam. Quite the contrary to the Ramban's stinging censure suggesting that the Rambam's words were "contrived," actually they were rock solid and spot on.

In this light, we will briefly overview the topic of sacrifices from a Biblical perspective. The first man, Adam, and his sons offered animal sacrifices to Hashem. Through them, they served their Maker. Specifically, as they burned animal parts on an altar, they internalized the experience so that they felt as if their own body parts and organs ascended with those flames. That is, they utilized sacrifices in order to promote pious impulses from deep within them. They took this exercise to great existential heights, assigning each anatomical animal body part to a corresponding human one. Thus, animal innards represented their innards; animal kidneys, their kidneys; animal front and hind legs, their arms and legs. When the first men flicked animal blood on the altar, they saw their own blood—nay, souls—engulfed by the holy flames.

Humbled, they offered thanksgiving to their Maker. They offered their life's breath. Fully acknowledging that their sin should have resulted in forfeiting their lives, they praised the Almighty for His compassion and kindnesses. It was Hashem Who accepted animal sacrifices in place of extracting due punishment from man. Divine mercy translated into a sacrificial quid pro quo. To this the Ramban openly acquiesced.

---

98. Vayikra 17:10.

What had motivated Noach to offer sacrifices after the flood? In essence, his sentiments echoed those of Adam. Namely, he beheld a generation mowed down by a deluge as a result of a colossal theological disconnect. Really, toxicity snowballed precipitously from the days of Noach's ancestor Enosh, as it says, "And the land was corrupt before Hashem."[99] Noach's noble act should be seen in a wider context. He desired to stem evil winds so prevalent in mankind's convoluted calculus. In essence, he hoped to rekindle belief in God and dispel atavistic pulls to paganism.

Bilaam's design, when he commissioned multiple altars to be built, was pure. Instead of kissing up to idolatry, he wanted to gain God's good graces.[100] There it is written that he built seven altars in order to conjure up the seven righteous men who had done so before him.[101]

In his brouhaha with the Rambam, the Ramban makes this observation: there is an aspect of sacrifices that must be seen through an altruistic prism. On occasion, the Torah refers to sacrifices as "fiery, pleasing aromas to Hashem"[102] or "divine repast."[103] No question that the Rambam would respond based on his general approach and fundamental principles. Applying them, he would advance that the Torah often speaks in terms of how a man who sacrifices relates to his act. In our context, then, the Rambam would say that the phrases quoted above must be seen from man's perspective. Man imagines sacrifices to be pleasing to Hashem, imagines that they are worthy of a divine repast.

But for the Rambam, sacrifices are, in a sense, dicey business. And the Jewish people's checkered history with them cannot be denied. "And they shall no longer sacrifice to devils after which they whore."[104]

The Ramban finds support for his position from two verses we find in Divrei Hayamim. "For our forefathers acted treacherously and did what is evil in God's eyes. They closed up the foyer doors, extinguished the lamps. They neither burned incense nor offered burnt offerings in the holy place to the God of Israel."[105] This indicates that in some sense, God derives satisfaction from incense and burnt offerings.

---

99. Bereshit 6:11.
100. See *Bamidbar Rabbah*, chapter 20.
101. Adam, Hevel, Noach, Avraham, Yitzchak, Yaakov, and Moshe.
102. Vayikra 1:9.
103. Vayikra 21:6.
104. Vayikra 17:7.
105. II Divrei Hayamim 29:6–7.

Still, the Rambam would answer that those verses do not mean that the absence of offerings itself is what incurs God's wrath. Rather, the desolation of the Beit Hamikdash is an indication that the entire nation had turned to idolatry. Disuse of the Mikdash is what angers God. If they could turn their backs on it, something symptomatic was at work. That is, locking up the Mikdash pointed to an overall level of Torah observance reduced to nubbins. Vice, then, stoked God's fury.

See *Shir Hashirim Zuta*.[106] Quoting the verse "Behold, you are beautiful, my beloved [רעיתי],"[107] the Midrash understands the word *rayati* to mean "my provider." On that verse the sages record an allegorical conversation between the Maker and His beloved Jews. "You Jews are My providers," as derived from a verse that refers to "My fiery bread offering."[108] Separately but relatedly, the Midrash queries: Does the Almighty really partake of food? Eat and drink? A poetic answer follows. Hashem responds that Jews offer and He consumes fire. While the allegorical realm may allow for a romantic representation of God ingesting fire, still a question remains. That is, why is the fiery offering specifically identified as bread? Implied is that Hashem accepts bread (and not only fire) as His own. Here is the Midrash's upshot. Even though Jews offer only fire to Heaven, God reckons it as if they provide for Him—akin to loyal sons who dutifully attend to their father. We offer categorical proof here that Hashem does not have any need for sacrifices.

This whole topic of fiery flames atop the altar with the concomitant offerings has been discussed by the *Kuzari*. In that dialogue between the king and the wise Jew, the king asks in astonishment: What is the import of "My fiery bread offering"? For the incorporeal Almighty, utterly devoid of physicality, what should readers make of this phrase alluding to Heaven's seemingly robust appetite? The sage responded that the key can be found in the phrase "My fiery bread offering." Of course, Heaven derives not a whit of benefit from the altar's flames, let alone from animal parts.

Here is what transpires. The fire on the altar is, not unlike all fires, a consuming one. Atop that fiery energy, Kohanim placed animals for burnt offerings per the verse's designation "for My fiery bread offering." Note how the language bespeaks fire, real flames. That is the intent of the verse. Although

---

106. *Shir Hashirim Zuta* 1:9.
107. Shir Hashirim 1:15.
108. Bamidbar 28:2.

Jews arrange fiery flames, God views it as akin to doting children providing for their father.

Until this point in the discourse, we have portrayed the Rambam's position, which looks somewhat askance at sacrifices. For him the main operative was damage control. But here is a huge qualifier to his remarks. While he concludes that Heaven conceded sacrifices to the Jews as an afterthought, this does not imply that there is not a higher calling to them. In reality, there is. Sacrifices afford man an opportunity to self-reflect in a most experiential way. Taking this deeper message properly to heart is what humbles a Jew before his Maker; it provides a tool to enhance faith in the One Above.

God's unity and divine providence are two other real-life, take-home lessons. Those timeless values served as Adam's and Noach's lode star. Even the Rambam would not deny sacrifice's potential and ability to revolutionize man's ethos. Those early, upright devotees followed their intuition. Animal sacrifice effectuated intimacy with God in a way heretofore unchartered.

Let us make another inroad regarding the Rambam's position. He acceded that those lofty religious values, to be sure, avail themselves through animal sacrifice. However, the more conventional way to internalize and achieve those key fundamentals would be through prayer, reason, and intellectual analysis. Indeed, performance of several commandments inculcates these all-important principles just as effectively as (if not more so than) roasting animal innards and sprinkling a hint of blood.

In sum, the Rambam understands God's command to offer sacrifices as a way for Jews to attain closeness with Him. If we delve into these commandments' rationale, we discover a common root and expose humanity's longtime infatuation with the practice. The fact that man models his ancestors' behavior makes clear that Jews needed to continue that conduct, albeit with considerable calibration. Hence, Heaven's directives called on the nation to build a Mishkan, but pointedly demanded restraints to curb this form of atonement's wretched former associations. More than just a defensive ploy, the commandment dovetailed both intents. Precision guidance (read: centralizing sacrificial practice, officials, and locale) galvanized the Jews' chances that they would be spiritually elevated as a result of their rich Mikdash experience.

Coming full circle, we advance that with the proper checks and balances, what was a questionable proposition turns into a first-rate commandment geared toward some of the religion's most inspiring moments. Hence, we have blended the Rambam and the Ramban's outlooks. Consequently, the Ramban's verbal attack against the Rambam has not only been defanged, but now they mesh as one. Here is another thing: we have obviated the need to seriously entertain the Narbonne's answer.[109]

Until now our discussion has neatly categorized and theorized what may be behind Hashem's command for Jews to sacrifice animals. This has assumed very broad strokes, as if one single rationale fit each of the four kinds (burnt, sin or guilt, peace, and meal offerings). Since this would be overly simplistic, this section will propose distinct reasons behind each type of sacrifice. Our working assumption and premise is predicated upon logic: content or *tachlit* (תכלית) closely tracks form or *tzurah* (צורה). Given that their respective forms differ, it follows that their content will too.

- Why are peace offerings partly consumed on the altar, with some being eaten by Kohanim and the remainder going to the animal's proprietor?
- Why are sin and guilt offerings not offered to their proprietor but instead shared between the altar and the Kohanim?
- Why should the animal owners and Kohanim be deprived of any edible part of the burnt offerings?

It is preposterous to advance that these vital differences should not bespeak vast variance with regard to their purpose or meaning. Furthermore, review must yield answers to the following questions.

- Why are burnt and peace offerings both brought with a meal offering consisting of flour mingled with oil, with *levonah* and wine libations? And without these holy garnishes, burnt and peace offerings are not brought.
- Why doesn't a sin or guilt offering follow the same model and require a meal offering—not even a token part of it such as flour, *levonah*, wine, or oil?

---

109. For brevity, we have omitted other commentaries that Abravanel rejects.

Burnt Offering, Meal Offering, and Wine Libation

Beginning with a premise that there must be underlying insights to glean, this section sets out to discover them. Before doing so, we set down that for our purposes there are three kinds of sacrifices (and not four as delineated above). One is the *korban olah* and its auxiliary meal offering and libation. Two is the sin or guilt offering category. Clumping them together highlights their commonality; both imply that a sin was done. Having noted their shared base, the fact is in one case a man is certain that he inadvertently sinned (sin offering), whereas in the second case he is unsure. At any rate and as mentioned, sin or guilt offerings do not have meal offerings. The third type is the peace offering with its meal offering. Accordingly, we seek out three significances—each with its unique message.

Burnt offerings are an expression of a Jew's rational soul yearning for intimacy with its Maker, yearning to cleave to God. The simile works like this: Souls are eternal. The duly designated animal is slaughtered. After its death some of its body parts burn. This catalyzes transformation, a change that takes place upon the divine altar. Physically, those parts become one with their engulfing flames. Sweet aromas waft ever pleasantly heavenward. Likewise, there are certain postmortem realities for man—or collectively for men. After death, man's essence ascends God's holy mount. There in Heaven's sacred chamber his soul cleaves, communing with the Creator under His throne of glory. Is God not likened to a consuming fire?

Continuing with the animal sacrifice motif, a man's soul climbs in the form of a pleasing aroma to Hashem. Man is called a burnt offering, as the instructive term suggests his soul's upward spiritual mobility. Just as animal parts ascend in billowing smoke from the altar, so too does man's intellectual spirit return to the lofty place from whence it came.

These areas of esoterica have been discussed or at least alluded to by the sages.[110] They relate that a man brings a burnt offering as a result of his fantasies or machinations. Along those lines, Rabbi Levi reveals an explicit verse in Sefer Iyov. "And he awoke early in the morning and he

---

110. *Vayikra Rabbah*, chapter 7.

offered burnt offerings…for Iyov said: Perhaps my sons sinned and cursed God in their hearts."[111] On this verse, the sages adduced that a man who brings a burnt offering expunges his debased dregs and dross.

Through dedication, he renews his relationship with God and himself. Reaching higher consciousness, he coaxes his soul to climb new heights. Of course it is no coincidence that the daily offering was a burnt offering—a male without blemish. Consider how formats make a difference: daily sacrifices were male, while the raw material is female, as mentioned in the Rambam. To elaborate, that which gives a thing its especial identity relates to the masculine. The container that holds this essence relates to the feminine. The officiating Kohen placed his hand on the burnt offering's head. This reminds man that the animal's body parts will be walked up the altar plank in man's stead. Astride the altar, Kohanim will sprinkle the burnt offering's blood in a veiled allusion to man's fate—man's soul taken to Heaven.

More clues abound. Insofar as a burnt offering figuratively interweaves with man's rational soul (a man's true essence), the verse says, "Man, when he steps up to offer a sacrifice to Hashem."[112] Understand that this idea of a man stepping up is another way of saying he delves deep into his inner being. It is that innermost being, like a burnt offering, that is at the heart of the matter. He lays himself—his desires and will—before the Maker. *I am here now willing to serve You, Almighty God*, he utters. *I want to strengthen my resolve for You, scale the highest spiritual places.* He fully acknowledges and silently proclaims as much through his sheep, his agent: a holy soul climbing the altar in Jerusalem's Mikdash, the planet's most sacred haunt. Can the Master demand anything more? Is there any greater satisfaction for Him? Atonement practically becomes a foregone conclusion, albeit a personally gruesome one.

Yet there is another tremendous benefit wrought by the burnt offering. Paving the way for personal (and national) intimacy with God, the process harnesses divine bounty for the benefactor(s). The sacrifices of Kayin and Hevel hoped to achieve material gain. The sages note that Adam also brought a burnt offering, as did Noach after the flood. The three patriarchs and Moshe each brought burnt offerings on their own altars for the express purpose of meriting bounty and bountiful prophecy.[113] And it was Bilaam who ordered

---

111. Iyov 1:5.
112. Vayikra 1:2.
113. See *Bamidbar Rabbah* 20:18.

that altars be erected so that he could offer bulls and rams. He said to King Balak, "Stand here adjacent to your burnt offerings and I will go. Perhaps God will go forth to me."[114] To Bilaam's thinking, burnt offerings held out the best hope for bagging a spiritual boon.

Now we will develop ideas regarding meal offerings and wine libations. Recall, these are part and parcel of the whole burnt-offering story. This element of Mishkan service undergirds Judaism's belief in the soul's eternity as well as its inherent pull to remain wired into its Maker. Getting man to place his life's focus on nurturing the timeless, intellectual soul finds traction in this meal-offering aspect of the burnt sacrifice.

Acknowledgment of just how different man is from non-speaking animals is, perhaps, an excellent starting place. Using refined flour, then, is an object lesson. Animals do not grind their flour finely; only man does. Consider two other salient points:

1. On the second day of Pesach, an *omer* consisting of barley is brought to the Mikdash. Why not wheat flour? This grain choice suggests that humanity does not yet attain equipoise until counting forty-nine days of the *omer*. At the end of that period, two loaves are offered from wheat flour. That period, not surprisingly, coincides with the Festival of Shavuot celebrating the Law-Giving event.

2. The *minchat hasotah* was made from barley. The sages point out that this particular grain reflects the concupiscence of a *sotah*, a wife who has been accused of committing adultery.[115]

Conclusively, grain type matters. Thus, when the wheat flour meal offering joins with the burnt offering, a statement is being made about a lot more than health foods or the relative nutritional benefits of waving kindred golden stalks. It is no less than an epic lifestyle choice facing man. The Torah intimates that to develop a soul properly requires graduating beyond human conventions. Intellectual and character refinement steady his climb.

Actually, flour alone isn't sufficient. Oil mingles with it. Pure olive oil adds an important dimension, as it represents intellect. Moreover, added to

---

114. Bamidbar 23:3.
115. BT *Sotah* 14a.

untainted olive oil is *levonah*—an exquisite aromatic. Taken as a whole, the smell wafts irresistibly. From a deeper perspective, this meal offering can be likened to a man in harmonious sync. Pleasantness as a Jewish ideal emphasizes erudition and probity.

How do wine libations fit into this picture? Fruit of the vine conveys a quality unique to the Jew. Wine symbolizes Torah. Commonly, prophets likened the nation to vineyards. Yeshayahu writes, "For the House of Israel is the Lord of hosts' vineyard."[116] And Yechezkel notes, "What is the vine tree more than any other tree?"[117] The psalmist adds, "Look from heaven and see and remember this grapevine."[118]

Seeing that the burnt and meal offering convey this most eloquent Jewish clarion call regarding the true, invincible nature of the soul, there can be no questioning that it is the choicest of all sacrifices. At the pinnacle of Mikdash service stands the daily burnt offering with its meal offering and wine libation. Accordingly, in Parashat Tetzaveh, it gets top billing: "And this is what you shall sacrifice on the altar."[119] The verse sounds as if burnt offerings were not only brought on the altar but were the altar's raison d'être.

Burnt offerings were brought twice daily—morning and evening. Man's main mealtimes conform to that schedule. In a spiritual way, those two intervals are apropos because they provide sensible guidelines to when man should nourish his soul. Sunrise and sunset are propitious opportunities to contemplate the universe's Maker. More details on this point of better appreciating peeping or waning sunrays will emerge in Parashat Pinchas.

In addition to those twice-daily sacrifices, all *musafim* (מוספים) without exception were burnt offerings, meal offerings, and wine libations. This vouches for the fact that Jews during their holidays attain heightened awareness. Animal sacrifices and the driving message they embody assure this. When dire financial circumstances dictated, a man would bring a *minchat olah* (מנחת עולה) without *minchah v'zevach* (מנחה וזבח); then the essence of his sacrifice exclusively zeroed in on the burnt offering, as discussed when talking about man's soul. Destitution gave him respite so far as enhancements of the offering were concerned.

---

116. Yeshayahu 5:7.
117. Yechezkel 15:2.
118. Tehillim 80:15.
119. Shemot 29:38.

In summary, the matter is straightforward. The main thrust behind bringing burnt offerings to Hashem, together with meal offerings and wine libations, has been amply explained. Neither animal proprietors nor Kohanim partook of its food. Is the soul not sole property of the Holy One? Does God have a partner who can claim credit for creating man's soul?

More about burnt offerings consisting of bulls, sheep, and birds will be discussed later in this volume.

Sin and guilt offerings[120] are brought as a result of a man committing a sin, as discussed above. A sin offering comes about when a man sins unintentionally, whereas a guilt offering results when a man is uncertain whether he violated a negative commandment. It has been ascertained that when it comes to bringing burnt offerings, peace offerings, or meal offerings, there is no distinction regarding the purveyor of the offering. That is, the basic law does not take into account the man's social status—be he a king or cameleer, a High Priest or a lowlife. However, sliding scales do play a role for sin or guilt offerings. The main determinant is what function the offerer plays within Jewish society. For instance, if the inadvertent sinner was a Kohen Mashuach, he was required to bring a bull, and the entire thing was burned essentially the same as a burnt offering.

Yet there are two important differences between a Kohen Mashuach's bull for a sin offering and a burnt offering. One, a burnt offering is burned entirely on the altar, but not so with the Kohen Mashuach's bull.[121] Only the bull's innards made it to the altar; the remainder was shunted beyond the Mishkan's confines.[122] There it was set aflame. Two, blood from burnt offerings was not carried into the holy chamber and dashed on the *parochet* or on the incense altar.[123] In contrast, the blood of the Kohen Mashuach's sin offering was brought in and sprinkled seven times before Hashem and upon the holy *parochet*.[124]

If the sin offering expiated for the Jewish congregation collectively, it followed the same model as presented for the Kohen Mashuach.[125] What if

---

120. Abravanel groups these two together for the sake of simplicity.
121. See Vayikra 1:9.
122. See Vayikra 4:8–12.
123. See Vayikra 1:5.
124. See Vayikra 4:6.
125. See Vayikra 4:13–21.

the inadvertent sinner was a *nasi* (tribal chieftain), a king, or even one of the *shoftim* (judges)? They brought a male goat, but its blood was not dashed upon the *parochet* inside the Mishkan. Only the innards were incinerated on the altar, with the other body parts given to the Kohanim to eat.[126] In the event that the sinner was a Jew from the ranks or that he was asked to testify to something he had witnessed, but falsely swore that he did not witness it, or if he was a man who touched anything *tamei* or experienced an event that rendered his person *tamei* and then entered the Temple grounds, or if he verbalized a lie under oath, then in all of these cases, his offering consisted of a ewe or female goat.[127]

Sin Offerings

In the paragraphs above, we have outlined a remarkable versatility surrounding burnt offerings. To recap, consider some of the similarities and differences between them.

- In what way is a Kohen Mashuach's bull like a burnt offering?
- Why is a burnt offering completely burned upon the altar, yet a Kohen Mashuach's bull has two designations?
- Why the different treatment with their respective obligations concerning the animal's blood?
- Why should a bull be brought for both the Kohen Mashuach and the congregation?
- For what reason does a *nasi* bring a male goat and not a bull?

This sampling of queries plus many others will be answered in Parashat Vayikra. But before proceeding to the *parashah*, there is another matter that draws our attention. At the end of Parashat Vayikra, we read of a case where a litigant causes or forces a potential witness to take a solemn oath. This request prompts the party in question to comply. In fact it becomes a mitzvah that he must perform.

Then things get tangled. Instead of testifying on behalf of the litigant, he tries to toss aside his religious obligation. Brazenly, he swears falsely to the court that he has no testimony to provide.

---

126. See Vayikra 4:22–26.
127. See Vayikra 4:27–5:6.

What can be gathered, in a general sense, regarding the Torah's attitude toward sin? Logically and as far as the Torah is concerned, Hashem laid out clear warnings before the nation cautioning against sin. Performing positive commandments and steering away from doing negative ones assumed urgency.

A divine system established strata by which to deal with offenders. Take an example of a man who erred unwittingly and did that which he ought not have done. Heaven dictates that, as a first line of consequence, a man must pay monetarily for his misdeed. Assessments call for pecuniary payments. This would sufficiently deter him from perpetrating similar thoughtless acts.

Translating this into practical terms meant that the sinner would be fined a *korban chatat*, in essence a monetary fine. This ordeal is designed to prevent repeat offenses. A similar rationale can be stated for what are called *korbanot hateme'im* (קרבונות הטמאים). Their shared aim was to warn those who were lax in contracting *tumah*. It was largely assumed that a man could do a lot more to prevent association with *tumah*. Righteous-minded men kept up a high guard and thus fended off the undesirable consequences of *tumah*.

Therefore, a *nazir* brought a sacrifice if he was derelict, since he let down his vigilance and betrayed his high principles and noble commitment. To streamline and paraphrase the sages: Alacrity brings vigilance, vigilance purity, and purity leads to sanctity.[128]

We can also add to this category of watchfulness (or lack thereof) when it comes to the *zav*, the *metzora*, a man who is *bo'el niddah* (impure from having engaged in relations with a *niddah*), *tamei met* (impure from having touched death), or a man who eats swine flesh or insects or rodents. All the more so, a man needs to be mindful not to accidentally do an act which if done on purpose would warrant *karet*. Dishonest is the man who commits these most heinous infractions, excusing them as unintentional.

Lame rationalizations are more aggravated when the man perpetrating them is someone in a position of authority. Take a Kohen Gadol who issues a false dictum causing people to sin by doing something that the Torah explicitly forbade. Either ignorance or superficiality brought him to mislead the congregation. How egregious is his offense! An officer entrusted to teach law and preserve the integrity of the commandments is found negligent in his duties. Practically revered among the people as a *malach* (angel) due to

---

128. Mishnah *Sotah* 9:15, BT *Avodah Zarah* 20b, JT *Shekalim* 14b.

his high office, he nevertheless floundered. He not only betrayed his station but brought down his people, people who looked up to him for God's word.

The *parashah* discusses his case first, specifically because of the great travesty involved. If strict law were to be applied to him, he would deserve capital punishment—a forced early retirement, if you will. However, dispensation is granted to him on account of the accidental nature of his misleading of the people. He must bring a bull to gain absolution, and that serves in his stead. Placing his hand upon the bull's head, he readily acknowledges the gravity of his act. Sprinkling blood upon the holy *parochet* and on the incense altar are his pleas for divine pardon.

Note further symbolism. The bull's innards ascending upon the altar's flames attest to his steadfast ideals and moral compass. While not denying that sin had transpired, the Kohen Mashuach's offering intimates that the sin was not on purpose. Moreover, when the remainder of the animal parts was transported outside the Hebrews' camp and burned there, this spotlighted a dichotomy. That is, the top official's clean intentions versus his sordid physicality: the body bears the lion's share of the misdeed.

Unmistakably, there is a wide separation between the Kohen Mashuach's sin offering and burnt offering. For the burnt offerings bespeak divine reward and spiritual attachment between man and Maker. Incinerating the burnt offering invokes these truths. However, the Kohen Gadol's sin offering hints at divine punishment due to him on account of his having erred. Errors committed by ranking public officers are treated severely and chalked up as if done deliberately. Broken down by percentages, the minority of the bull is brought to the Mishkan's sacred altar, whereas the overwhelming majority of it gets ignominiously carted out beyond city walls. Location reveals so much about the two sacrifices' contrasts. Namely, the disparate locations for burning the two sacrifices indicate varying levels of holiness. An *olah* ranks higher than a priest's *chatat* (sin offering).

What can be said about the discrepancy concerning the respective animals' blood? When it comes to the sin offering's blood, recall that the reason it is dashed inside the Mishkan's holy chambers is to effect atonement—either owing to the severity of the Kohen Gadol's misdeed or to the fact that the nation transgressed. For this reason we will learn in Parashat Acharei Mot's section dealing with Yom Kippur that Hashem commanded that the bull's and goat's blood be dabbed on the front of the *parochet*.[129] It further says, "And it will atone for the sacred [objects] from the *tumot* of Bnei Yisrael and their ill acts for their sins."[130] Yet another verse from that section draws parallels: "And Aharon offered a bull for a sin offering for his misdoings and to atone for himself and for his family."[131]

The point is made. Clearly, the sin offering's blood had been sprinkled inside the Mishkan for the purpose of attaining forgiveness. In contrast, the burnt offering—unassociated with sin—had not needed to accomplish the same aim as the sin offering. Blood, therefore, played no part in its ritual.

Addressing the question of why the Kohen Gadol's sin offering had been unceremoniously burned "on the outs" reveals this. Had the bull been offered on the altar, it would have been accorded a certain mark of distinction inappropriate given his misprision. This stands in contrast to the sin offering brought on behalf of the congregation whose accidental misdeed if done on purpose would have necessitated a punishment of *karet*. That is offered on the altar as a show of its greater intrinsic value.

Coincidentally, there is a corresponding sacrificial requirement in the event that the Great Sanhedrin errs and misleads the congregation. Since the men of the Great Assembly had been entrusted to faithfully guide the Jews, their proclaiming a law incorrectly results in damage—not only because they flubbed but also in terms of their direct role in causing others to stumble. Details surrounding the Kohen Gadol's sacrifice are therefore identical to that of the Sanhedrin.

To keep matters straight, remember that we are comparing the sin offerings of the Kohen Gadol, Sanhedrin, king, and the *nasi* or tribal chieftain. When reviewing the verses, note that both the Kohen and Sanhedrin bring a bull, but a king and *nasi* bring a goat. Why do those latter two get off easier? In a word, the Torah does not equate them, since their respective jurisdictive responsibilities differ. The king and *nasi* are not enjoined to teach and spiritually guide the people to the same degree as their colleagues.

Far from it. To put it in more analytical terms, understand that it is a question of quantifying damage or culpability. The priest and Sanhedrin members, by dint of their infelicitous pronouncement, fail and cause failure

---

129. See Vayikra 16:14–15.
130. Vayikra 16:16.
131. Vayikra 16:6.

to others. Hence, their punishment entails the bigger animal sacrifice (bull), whereas a king's or tribal chief's error reflects a personal misstep but not that of misguidance of others. They must bring a goat for atonement, essentially the same requirement for a man of the rank and file who transgresses. Parenthetically, a tribal head should have been requested to bring a she-goat, as was the case with common folk, but out of respect to his station, the Torah bade him bring a male goat. In a pyramid structure, below the top-tiered bull is a male goat. Underneath that is a she-goat, ruminants subservient to bucks.

Regarding the blood of these various sin offerings, another difference emerges. The blood of a *nasi*'s offering is not dashed inside the Mishkan's holy chambers, in contrast to that of both High Priests and the Sanhedrin. This underlies the fact that a *nasi* had not erred as seriously as the other two categories. In other words, sprinkling blood is seen as a drastic measure in order to attain divine forgiveness. A chieftain's mistake is assessed as much less offensive than that of a High Priest or Sanhedrin.

A High Priest's or Sanhedrin's sheep is completely incinerated upon the altar because of the correlating sin's extreme disruption to society. Misleading the population rips away at the national fabric. In contrast, no comparable prevailing damage can be attributed to a *nasi*'s sin. His animal is only partially burned in the Mishkan. When discussing the common man's sin offering, recall that it is a nanny goat and not a buck. Female goats, in this manner, symbolize everyday folk and everyday folly, as recorded in the Rambam's *Moreh Nevuchim*.[132] Deference to the High Priest, Sanhedrin, and tribal chief played a part in securing their need to bring a male goat. Barring such a dispensation would have brought undo attention to their sin, underscoring their signal failures.

The blood of a private individual's sin offering is not ushered inside the Mishkan's holy places. Simply, such a person's misdeeds don't merit it. With a Kohen Gadol or the congregation, though, their esteem does warrant that treatment. In accordance with the average Joe's moderate standing within the community, his sin offering is not totally burned. His transgression is very much a localized affair, hardly impacting those around him.

---

132. Rambam, *Moreh Nevuchim* 3:8.

Consider the following verse: "And when a soul sins by hearing a solemn desecration."[133] Hearing a curse invoking Heaven's name is a serious offense. Let us better explain. When the Torah uses the cognate identifying a guilt offering (*asham*), this is not to be taken literally. Instead, the verse speaks of sin offerings. Emphasis is on the pangs of guilt experienced by the man who perpetrated the wrongdoing.

This section deals with *tumah* and *asham*. Despite the man being aware of a prohibition of touching certain objects and entering certain places in a state of *tumah*, he acts frivolously. For this he is commanded to bring an *asham* to Hashem. Implied is that the fellow experienced pangs of wrongdoing by flouting this area of the Torah's prohibitions. Essentially, according to the Ramban's explanation, he turns himself in and in so doing is required to bring an *asham* sacrifice. Furthermore, according to the Ramban, he understands that the term *asham* instructs about the severity of the misdeed. Learning from the word's etymology, the Rambam studied the cognate and derived its implication from a verse in Sefer Hoshea: "Shomron will be laid waste, for she has sinned against her God."[134] Compare *asham* with *chatat*. The latter conjures up a man who veers from the straight and narrow pathway, as a verse says, "To the gate and do not sway."[135]

Let us look at *asham gezelot* and *asham shifchah charufah*. These are two transgressions that require offenders to bring sacrifices even if they committed their acts willfully. The same is said about the *asham nazir*. These are in marked contrast to *asham me'ilot*. Misappropriating Mishkan property is, of course, despicable. For that reason, an offender must bring a guilt offering even for inadvertent acts.

Upon reflection, sin offerings are a function of negligence regarding commandments in a general sense. Root causes have to do with an overall devil-may-care attitude. The basic premise holds that if a man cared or thought more about consequences, he would conduct himself with probity. From Hashem's perspective, the offender gets slapped with a guilty verdict despite his sin being accidental. No free passes for inadvertency, because the bottom line is that a red line was crossed. "And it [knowledge] avoided him."[136]

---

133. Vayikra 5:1.
134. Hoshea 14:1.
135. Shoftim 20:16.
136. Vayikra 5:3.

Implied here in the verse is that there had been prior knowledge and awareness before he had his "lapse" of memory. Read: guilt=sin. Importantly, though, guilt in the present context does not mean uncertain guilt or *asham talui*. In the Torah, the word *asham* takes on different shades of meanings depending on its context, as will be developed.

"And if he cannot afford it."[137] Leniency when it comes to sin offerings has limited applications. That is, no dispensation is made for a poor Kohen Gadol, impoverished congregation, or indigent *nasi*. Those three categories of sinners can afford to pay full restitution. That is not the case when talking about run-of-the-mill folks. For them, special dispensation will be considered per a person's financial situation.

Let us review the operative verse regarding poor transgressors. "If the man who sacrifices is poor and cannot afford to bring a ewe or she-goat, then he brings two turtledoves or two doves."[138] Torah instructions are explicit that both birds get burned on the altar, as it says, "to Hashem." Obviously, after these birds are toast, as it were, nothing remains to give over to officiating Kohanim.

"Whether it be a sin offering or whether it be a burnt offering."[139] Fairly, one wonders why the two disparate kinds of sacrifices are mentioned in one verse. Two points are conveyed. One has to do with an error he committed, as it says, "Whether it be a sin offering." Two is taken from the perspective of intent. When it comes to a man bringing a burnt offering, he is motivated by the very highest religious desires. "Whether it be a burnt offering": sacrificing a ewe or she-goat translates as part of the animal (its innards) taken to the altar and put to the flame. Some edible parts, however, are distributed among the Kohanim. This is not the case when a sin offering consists of two birds, because the altar's fire devours down to the last morsel. Though in theory it might have been a good idea to burn one bird and feed the other to Kohanim, in practice it won't work. Both birds are to be treated identically despite the fact that the first one on the altar gets called a sin offering and the second one a burnt offering. That order is significant. It is only after a man's sins have been exonerated that he may graduate to offering exalted gifts to Heaven.

---

137. Vayikra 5:7.
138. Ibid.
139. Ibid.

To the extent that a man is so needy that he can't even afford to buy two birds for his sin offering, the Torah allows for an easier payment plan. "He shall bring a sacrifice consisting of one-tenth of an *eifah*."[140] In efforts to distinguish this sacrifice, the Torah commands the Kohen to cup his hands and take a measure somewhat similar to a pinch. In Hebrew that amount is called a *kamitzah* (קמיצה). Some part is burned on the altar, while the remaining part is shared with Kohanim. "And the Kohen will atone for his sin which he committed from one of these sins."[141] Look closely at this passage's verses and note the sliding scale or progressive nature of a sin offering's costs.

It says in Parashat Shelach Lecha, "And if you err and commit."[142] The sages explain that the verse is to be construed narrowly.[143] Specifically, it refers to violating prohibitions associated with idolatry due to the Sanhedrin's misleading directive to the people. In such a case, a bull must be brought for atonement. However, if the sinner was a Kohen Gadol, a *nasi*, or a common man, the violation requires them each to bring a goat. Interestingly, animal sacrifice types depend upon the particular sin perpetrated. Consequently, for practically all of the Torah's prohibitions, the priests and people fall into a uniform grouping. This underscores how people are human and liable to make mistakes with Torah commandments. Heaven displays zero tolerance, though, when it comes to paganism, which is different on account of its particularly odious nature. Recall how Mount Sinai's unequivocal proclamation outlawing the primitive practice got top billing: "I am Hashem your Almighty…you shall not have other gods before Me."[144] Compelling logic paints each and every Jew with the same brush so far as punishment and sacrifice for paganism are concerned. Claims of ignorance just do not wash.

This concludes discussion of the *chatat*, and we now move to *asham*.

Asham Offering

Etymologically speaking, the term *chatat* stresses that a man knew with certainty that he accidentally violated a Torah commandment. *Asham* emphasizes something else. The man lacked clear-cut knowledge and is unsure

---

140. Vayikra 5:11.
141. Vayikra 5:13.
142. Bamidbar 15:22–31.
143. BT *Horayot* 8b.
144. Shemot 20:2.

whether he veered from Torah pathways. In frustration, he accuses himself of being unfocused. Furthermore, he berates himself for being ignorant. Did he transgress a Torah directive or not? Was the deed permissible or prohibited? Plagued by doubt, the man brings an *asham talui* until he gains clarity. Note that in our present context, the word *asham* takes on a different meaning from the one provided above. Earlier we said that *asham* was so called from the reference point of Hashem, but here the mood and flavor is reflexive. That is, a man incriminates himself because he lost control and acted in an oblivious manner, and therefore lays blame on himself.

In fact, there is an important observation to be made here concerning the sages' sensitivity to nuances in the Hebrew language. When Chazal coined the term *asham talui* or uncertain guilt, they imparted great insight.[145] In that predicament, a man blames himself. That is reflected in the true sense of the word *asham* or "guilt." Indeed, the Torah's use of the term *asham* without the word *talui* is borrowed terminology.

For that reason, the verse brings various types of *asham talui*. "When a person grossly misappropriates [holy items] and sins accidentally with regard to that which is consecrated to the Lord."[146] This verse describes a man who derived personal benefit—though unwittingly—from property belonging to the Mishkan. The assumption is that he lacked knowledge that the object he used was sacred. Confusion clouds his mind. Did he or did he not err? Does the Torah demand restitution for those in his situation? When is an offender required to bring a guilt offering to Hashem consisting of an unblemished ram?

Accosted by unpleasant accusations, the man indulges himself by covering up for all possible wrongdoing. That is, he dodges blame. Ignorance, he convinces himself, is not a crime. Only transgressors who act willfully must be punished. Coming to quell these self-serving rationalizations and nip them in the bud, the Torah demands of laissez-faire and cavalier sinners to take responsibility for misdeeds. Actually, punishment goes to the other extreme for the sake of instilling fear of Heaven. Instead of getting away with a sheep offering, he must bring a more expensive ram. And just in case Mr. Deadbeat thought he could show up with a scrawny ram and by so doing fulfill his moral obligation, the Torah stops him in his tracks. "Full retail price," the

---

145. Abravanel does not cite a source for Chazal having coined this term.
146. Vayikra 5:15.

verse demands. An interesting side note is order. In the desert, rams were a rare commodity and thus fetched a hefty sum.

The Torah similarly demanded a steep restitution for a man who absconded with property belonging to the Mikdash. Creating a deterrence to those who might make light of taking liberties with sacred property, the Torah slapped the transgressor with a minimum damage of 120 percent. This is computed by adding to the value of the object a fine of 20 percent: "And add one fifth."[147]

Add-ons are less punitive than they appear. Here is why. The Torah asserts that misappropriated hallowed objects or *hekdesh* (הקדש) need to be restored at market or replacement value. In efforts to forestall a man from under-assessing that object and thus shortchanging the Mikdash, a 20 percent surcharge was tacked on. This guaranteed that the Temple's balance sheet would not suffer decline. Kohanim received the surcharge from the offender: they were chosen to officiate in the Mikdash, and their livelihood depended on it.

"If a soul sins by accidentally transgressing one of the negative commandments."[148] Recall this verse concerns a man who is unsure whether he committed a prohibited act. By illustration, a man had two pieces of meat in front of him—one (*shuman*) permissible and the other (*chelev*) not—and he knows that he ate one. He doesn't know whether he ate the kosher or the *treif* one. Furthermore, he was never warned or cautioned that one piece was problematic. He is commanded to bring a male ram valued at the price mentioned above. An officiating Kohen helps him achieve atonement for his accidental offense.

Stress is laid on the fact that he did not know whether he transgressed or not. If he knew with certainty, he brings a sin and not a guilt offering. "A guilt offering to Hashem."[149] In fact the sacrifice is called an *asham talui*, signifying that he does not know whether he erred. Of course Hashem harbors no such doubts, since all is for Him an open book. Thus Heaven holds the sinner accountable, and the man is liable to bring an *asham*. After the man offers his sacrifice, he is absolved of wrongdoing.

---

147. Vayikra 5:16.
148. Vayikra 5:17.
149. Vayikra 5:19.

Similarly, a verse teaches, "When a person sins and misappropriates and denies that he absconded with a deposit or a stolen object."[150] This case describes a man sinning on purpose. "And if a man sins and is guilty."[151] Understand this to refer to a man plotting to sin against his God. Though he originally perpetrated the act with the aim to steal, he later had a change of heart. Confession or self-incrimination allows the opportunity for full repentance. Apropos, he returns the stolen object or vessel that his friend placed in his charge or a lost item he stumbled upon and took home. Next, he pays the owner for the value of the object. In addition, he tacks on a fifth of that principal amount. The victim is the recipient of those amounts of money. When does all of this transpire? It happens on the day when he feels remorse for his ill-begotten behavior and confesses his sin.

Another case concerns a false oath or *shevuat sheker* (שבועת שקר). Here, too, repentance includes bringing a ram offering to the Kohen. Lying by invoking God's name is a severe offense, and for that reason he must pay for his crime by bringing a costly ram.

This wraps up our discussion of guilt offerings, and we conclude this discourse with the topic of peace offerings.

Peace Offerings

Important points need to be developed regarding peace offerings. These will come to the fore after the following introductory suppositions. Two subheadings of peace offerings include *zevach todah* (זבח תודה) and *neder* (נדר) or *nedavah* (נדבה). Note that for all intents and purposes *neder* and *nedavah* are treated as one. Details of these different types will be brought in Parashat Tzav.

On occasion a man will be moved to give thanks and praise to Hashem as a result of receiving special divine compassion, favor, and grace. Take for example when a man inherits landed property or experiences other miraculous happenings: "If he sacrifices a thanksgiving offering."[152]

Consider the second type of peace offering. A man prays to Hashem for material bounty. Thereafter, the farmer's prayers are answered in ways that can only be described as blatant supernatural intervention.

---

150. Vayikra 5:21.
151. Vayikra 5:23.
152. Vayikra 7:12.

Of these two types of peace offerings, the first one is motivated by a past event, whereas the second one stresses beneficial future outcomes. When the recipient ascends to Yerushalayim, he basks with his family in religious repose. If this head of family is bringing a thanksgiving, it means that part of the sacrifice is offered on the altar (animal innards and internal organs). Those enflamed body parts represent a man's inner workings or his thought processes. Medically speaking, since those parts play key roles in a healthy organism, the man professes that with this sacrificial act he pours out his soul to the Maker.

Another point: the peace offering brought to the altar is among an animal's fattiest parts, and so far as the altar's fire is concerned, the easiest to burn. Strikingly practical, those specific animal body sections are the least edible parts for man's nutrition. Thus there is no real loss to either the animal owner or the Kohen. Delicious and nutritious morsels are distributed to the Kohanim. More of this will be explained in the germane *parashah*.

After the altar receives its due, the Kohen takes his portion. In effect, this enhances religious fervor, because instead of just the animal owner rejoicing over Hashem's blessing, the Kohen does too. Not immaterial, the officiating Kohen bestowed his own blessing upon the man with whom he broke bread. There was a miscellany of other animal meat distributed to the Kohanim as good cheer reverberated throughout.

Until now there was emphasis on thanksgiving offerings. If the peace offerings came as a result of an oath or free-volition utterance, a similar model followed. Namely, some of the animal was burned on the altar, other parts handed out to Kohanim. Merriment positively permeated the Mikdash. Brimming goodwill went forth from Zion.

Appreciation of material success was expressed in many ways. Jews took stock of the goodly land that the Almighty had gifted them. Herds and flocks delighted in luscious fields and pastures. Raw ingredients for the staple products bread, oil, and wine grew prodigiously. God wrought all this blessing. Consisting of either animals of the herd or flock, peace offerings further included gift offerings of wheat flour as well as oil and wine, since these were considered the two most valuable liquids.

When we get to the appropriate *parshiyot*, there will be more in-depth discussion regarding the deeper significance of peace offerings, according to their particular kind. Furthermore, we will provide explanation as to why they were always accompanied by meal offerings and wine libations. "Be it a male or a female, sacrifice without blemish."[153] Unlike burnt offerings, which must be males, or sin offerings, which had to be females, the Torah did not dictate the peace offering's gender. This is because the underlying rationale for peace offerings differed from that of burnt or sin offerings. Peace offerings ushered in and fostered a feel-good mood of brotherhood. Etymologically, peace offerings do just that—they stoke *shalom*.

Kohanim were entitled to take from the animal's breast and thigh. Clearly, these gifts were given to them because they are the tastiest parts. Breast meat is delectable to man's palate, thigh meat coming in second place. In Parashat Tzav, it says regarding peace offerings, "If a man brings a thanksgiving."[154] Thanksgiving offerings are accompanied by unleavened *challot* or *challot matzot* whose dough has been mingled with oil, plus unleavened wafers or *rekikei matzot* that have been smeared with oil. *Challot* include leavening substances. This sacrifice needed to be eaten on the day it was offered on the altar, but extended "until the next morning's dawn" if some of it was leftover.[155]

A second subcategory of peace offerings is brought as a result of a man taking an oath or free-volition utterance. Unlike a thanksgiving sacrifice, this one is not associated with *challot matzot, rekikim*, or any other kinds of bread mentioned above. Another difference in the two types of peace offerings is that for this one an extra, second day of eating is granted. Thus, for a man bringing a sacrifice arising out of an oath or free-volition utterance, his time frame begins with the day the animal was slaughtered and includes that night plus the following daytime period. However, for thanksgiving sacrifices, the animal owner does not have the second-day grace period.

The sages did not ascertain that all peace offerings were accompanied by meal offerings.[156] It is significant to note that the wide array of breads served with the thanksgiving offering were not part of the oath or free-volition utterance sacrifice. Still, even for this latter peace-offering category there was a token meal offering brought to the altar. That is, an officiating Kohen took a *kamitzah* of refined wheat flour, oil with *levonah*. This mixture was then

153. Vayikra 3:1.
154. Vayikra 7:12.
155. Vayikra 7:15.
156. See BT *Menachot* 59a; Rambam, *Mishneh Torah*, Maasei Hakorbanot 2:2–5.

set aflame on the altar as an incense aromatic. When it came to the breads or wafers brought with thanksgiving offerings, they were eaten by the Kohanim and the owners. "Together with *challot lechem chametz*."[157] Concerning the meal offering part of the thanksgiving sacrifice, a verse instructs, "Do not make *chametz*."[158]

Thanksgiving offerings included a wide selection of breads because this is the owner's expression of appreciation for an auspicious event that has already occurred. The logic is that the owner's joy has been enhanced by a favorable outcome. By contrast, when a man makes an oath or free-volition utterance, he has not yet merited seeing the fruit of his reaching out to the Maker.

Consider a crucial verse that is in the section dealing with the Festival of Succot. "And you shall rejoice over all of the good that the Lord your God has given you."[159] Stress falls on expressing gratitude for what has already been given and received in the past, highlighting that a farmer inspecting his harvest experiences a high, if not euphoria. The Torah has no such command on the holiday of Pesach. Agriculturally speaking, the farmer's heart is filled with apprehension in the springtime: Will the upcoming harvest season bring blessing or blight?

As stated above, both types of peace offerings come with separate time limitations so far as eating the meat is concerned. The oath and free-volition sacrifice was given wider berth. Why? Since he eyes a future event, his prayer is longer and more drawn out than that of a man whose prayers have already been answered. The latter's supplications will tend to be abbreviated sentiments of praise and blessing.

This wraps up our mini-discourse aimed at providing greater understanding of the burnt, meal, sin or guilt, and peace offerings. *Neder* and *nedavah* sacrifices were offered in a spirit of generosity and open-handedness, and indeed this is a benefit of all sacrifices, as they foster these qualities. The *olah* sacrifice engendered faith in fundamental areas such as belief in the soul's eternity, potential to attain intimacy with the Creator, and prophecy. Finally, *chatat*, *asham*, and *shelamim* sacrifices facilitated better clarity regarding divine providence and reward and punishment. Heavenly succor extended hope to sinners for atonement. Without this lesson about compassion, transgressors

---

157. Vayikra 7:13.
158. Vayikra 6:10.
159. Devarim 26:11.

would likely fall into despair, thinking that sin spells hopelessness. All that would proceed from such feelings of inadequacy is a rut, grinding deeper until cynicism egged the sinner on to more inappropriate behavior.

After this critical introduction, readers are better positioned to understand the running commentary on the Torah's verses presented below. Authoritative principles have been laid down. They will serve students in good stead.

The Parshiyot

VAYIKRA

Sacrifices: A Primer

TZAV

Sacrifices: A Retrospective

SHEMINI

On Day Eight

TAZRIA

On Leprosy

METZORA

Moral Meltdown

PARASHAT VAYIKRA

SACRIFICES: A PRIMER

First *aliyah*

"And He called to Moshe.
And Hashem said to him from the Tent of Meeting, saying:
Speak to Bnei Yisrael and you shall say to them:
[When] a man from your midst sacrifices to the Almighty,
if [it shall be from] an animal—from the herd
or from the flock you shall offer your sacrifices."

Classic commentators take the position that this verse which opens Sefer Va-yikra must be read in sequence with a concluding verse in Sefer Shemot: "And the glory of Hashem filled the Mishkan."[1] They posit that there is an implicit understanding that God's glory departed from Mount Sinai and planted itself above the ark covering or *kaporet*. Specifically, it dwelled in between the two cherubs or *keruvim*. They further opine that since Moshe was not admitted to the holy of holies without express permission from Above, God called out to him.

Those expositors further explain that the Mishkan's sanctity assumed that selfsame high-water mark of holiness which had been associated with Mount Sinai when the Law was transmitted to the Hebrews. Recall that at that momentous event, a grave alarm cautioned, "Watch yourselves from climbing the mountain...for whoever ascends the mountain will die."[2] A similar prohibition applied to the Mikdash: "And a stranger who approaches will die."[3]

Finally, these writers further claim that other parallels existed between the two sacred places. Regarding Sinai it is written, "And also Kohanim who

---

1. Shemot 40:34.
2. Shemot 19:12.
3. Bamidbar 18:7.

come near to Hashem will become sanctified lest He lash out at them."[4] No dispensation had been granted to the Kohanim, even though they are deemed worthy enough to work in the Mikdash. And also to Aharon it was issued: "And he shall not enter at any time to the holy [place]."[5] Just as with regard to Mount Sinai a verse teaches, "And Hashem called to him from the mountain,"[6] so too here it is written, "And He called to Moshe. And Hashem said to him from the Tent of Meeting, saying."[7]

We advance that there is a more accurate interpretation of our *parashah's* opening verses. The term "Ohel Moed" (Tent of Meeting) refers back to the first words, "And He called to Moshe." Also, there is a connection to the ensuing words, "And Hashem said to him." Rejiggering, here is how Sefer Vayikra begins: "And Hashem called to Moshe from the Tent of Meeting and He said to him, saying."

These introductory points lead to an important observation. Some of the Torah commandments were given to Moshe on Mount Sinai, while others were propounded from the Mishkan. Getting to the gist of the matter, all mitzvot pertaining to sacrifices emanated from the Ohel Moed.[8]

Note how the Torah employs two distinct terms here: "He called" and "Hashem said." What is the difference? "Calling" implies an initial separation or distance between two (or more) parties, and the action verb's goal is to close that gap by bringing the invitee to the inviter. By contrast, the verb "speaking" is used when both parties are already in close proximity to each other.

"Speak to Bnei Yisrael and you shall say to them." Jews had toiled to put together the Mishkan and its vessels. In wistful anticipation they waited for Torah to flow forth from the hallowed compound. When Hashem's word did come from the Mishkan, they rejoiced over His commandments to offer sacrifices and serve Him. In great measure, the Mishkan's maiden message to the people was Heaven's way of acknowledging the people's faith and worthiness.

"From the Tent of Meeting." God rolled out His program of sacrifices. The financial onus fell squarely upon the people's shoulders. Underscore: this

---

4. Shemot 19:22.
5. Vayikra 16:2.
6. Shemot 19:3.
7. Vayikra 1:1.
8. The all-important topic of the origin of the divine commandments—whether Mount Sinai or Ohel Moed—is a classic one which Abravanel develops throughout Chumash.

first command was directed toward the people. Contrast it to a later section in the *parashah* in which Aharon and his sons were told first about animal blemishes. Here the people feature before Aharon. But in the next *parashah* (Tzav), it will be Aharon and his sons' turn to get first billing. They were notified at the outset of commands that pertained to Mishkan activity.

"[When] a man from your midst sacrifices."[9] The term "man" does not suggest a gender preference, implying that men offer sacrifices but not women. In fact, both men and women brought sacrifices. A similar construct is found in Sefer Bereshit, teaching that the verse specifies "man" but actually refers to both man and woman: "And He called their name Adam."[10]

"If [it shall be from] an animal—from the herd or from the flock you shall offer your sacrifices."[11] Strict limitations were placed upon a man desiring (or required) to sacrifice. Either herd or flock animals—that was their Spartan choice. Later it is explicit that "flock" includes both sheep and goats.

"[When] a man from your midst sacrifices to the Almighty."[12] No exclusionary rule is being conveyed to suggest that Gentiles may not offer sacrifices in the Temple. According to some commentators, the words "from your midst" outlaw Jewish heretics from making sacrifices. Here is how their a priori logic works. Since the commandments take aim at Jews, the words "from your midst" appear redundant. In order to derive meaning, those writers determined that the subject must, perforce, be renegade Jews. Gentiles, on the other hand, do not commonly get addressed by God, and hence there is no reason to exclude them. All Jews, however, are in the mitzvah loop. Lapsed Hebrews lose their original, inherent privilege.

There is another rationale behind the Torah preventing renegade Jews from offering sacrifices. Sacrifices afford a man an opportunity to get closer to his Maker. If the owner of the animal removes himself from the fold, should he now feign association with the nation? Such divine scrutiny or attention from Heaven puts him in an extremely compromising light. In effect, he makes a spectacle of himself. The prepositional phrase "from your midst" (מכם) teaches this law, as it presents a potentially lethal boomerang. To be clear, even should an apostate repent, his sacrifice does not accord him comprehensive

---

9.   Vayikra 1:2.
10. Bereshit 5:2.
11. Vayikra 1:2.
12. Ibid.

atonement. Instead, it repairs those limited or specific invidious act(s) relating
to his apostasy.

We return to an earlier point. May Gentiles sacrifice? The answer is yes,
as long as their animals are not blemished.

"[When] a man from your midst sacrifices." With regard to sacrifices, the
very first command takes up burnt offerings which a man brings either as a
result of a vow or out of free volition, the point being that it is not compulsory.
Since that is so, it will assuredly be brought good-heartedly and in a spirit
of altruism. This is deduced from an early verse brought in our *aliyah*: "If he
brings a burnt offering from the herd, it must be a male without blemish. He
offers it in the Tent of Meeting's courtyard, sacrificing in a spirit of goodwill
before the Almighty."[13] In our verse, the term "goodwill" has multiple applications that are positive, as we demonstrate.

"from the herd"	Herd animals are the preferred sacrificial type.
"male without blemish"	Only choice animals make the grade.
"He offers it in the Tent of Meeting's courtyard, sacrificing it in a spirit of goodwill"	The donor's mindset is marked by a spirit of volunteerism.
"before the Almighty"	The individual seeks intimacy with God, obviously a religious ideal.

This book's prolegomenon has already stated why the Torah limited animal
sacrifices to bulls, sheep, or goats. Additionally, it was clarified there that the
main purpose behind burnt offerings concerned Judaism's belief in the eternal,
rational soul's pining to stay attuned with its Maker.

"And he rests his hand on the burnt offering's head. And it is accepted
on his behalf to atone for him."[14] The involvement of the man's hand alludes
to the parallel fate shared by an animal and its owner. Now, consider an officiating Kohen who oversees and expedites the burning of sacrificial animal
parts upon the altar, creating a stirring aroma that ascends heavenward.

Waxing philosophic, what awaits man on his final journey? Judaism
posits that man's everlasting soul climbs upon high, where it is reunited with

---

13. Vayikra 1:3.
14. Vayikra 1:4.

God. Recall that often in Tanach, Hashem is likened to a consuming fire. Are not the souls of the righteous sweet and pleasing before the Holy One?

King Shlomoh observed, "No man on earth will [only] do good and not sin."[15] Axiom: All men's minds meander along forbidden recesses, some more and some less. "And it is accepted upon his behalf to atone for him." Burnt offerings are not about remedying sins. They are about curbing fantasies. The Mikdash is the ideal venue to offer sacrifices because of the inspiration it engenders and evokes. In such holy places, a man's mind can concentrate without clutter.

Burnt offering services were not necessarily the sole domain of Kohanim. In fact, non-priests did participate. With regard to some of this *aliyah*'s verses, ambiguity arises. The following points lay out crisp parameters and delineate which activities were within the purview of Kohanim and which were not. We spell out five tasks that were attended to by non-priests.

1. **Hand leaning.** "And he rests his hand on the burnt offering's head." The sages teach that when the Torah calls for "hand leaning," it must be with both hands.[16] They deduce this from the text "And Aharon placed his two hands on the goat's head."[17] Rashi derives his source for this law from the section dealing with conspiring and lying witnesses. Namely, just as when the Torah specifies "witness" or *eid* (עד), it equals two witnesses, so too in our verse. Thus, "He rests his hand" creates an obligation for a Jew to place his two hands upon the animal's head at the time of slaughter. This requirement elicits confession and repentance.

2. **Slaughtering.** "And he shall slaughter the bull before Hashem."[18] A man who brings this sacrifice may slaughter it. "Before Hashem" implies that he slaughters the burnt offering while the animal's head and face are angled toward the holy of holies (located to the west of where he stands).

3. **Skinning hide.** "And he shall skin the burnt offering's hide."[19] Animal owners tan hides.

---

15. Kohelet 7:20.
16. BT *Menachot* 93b.
17. Vayikra 16:21.
18. Vayikra 1:5.
19. Vayikra 1:6.

4. **Cutting and quartering.** "And he shall cut it into [other] pieces."[20] Carving up sacrificial bulls into twelve sections by animal owners made subsequent sacrifice steps easier for Kohanim, as they could hoist the prerequisite beef slabs upon the altar's pyre. The officiating Kohen then rotated the meat with great facility. This allowed for quicker consumption by the altar's eager flames. For accuracy's sake, there were twelve bull body parts (main organs and chief anatomical sections), as the verse suggests, "And the head and the fat."[21] Dicing up the bull into smaller pieces was deemed inexpedient.

5. **Rinsing.** "And you shall wash its innards and legs in water."[22] Preparation such as this was done out of respect for the Mikdash's sanctity. The sages teach that the fat or *pader* (פדר) was placed on the *beit hashechitah*, but not lesser anatomy parts such as intestines or hooves.[23] In fact, parts deemed inferior did not get burned but rather were discarded to predesignated refuse run-off sites. So prioritizing a bull's body parts spared the sacred compound from noisome smells. Parenthetically, animal owners assumed responsibility for that unwieldy job.

Dispensation was not forthcoming for any of these acts, including this last one of sanitation disposal. Such work simply could not be shirked, even if the animal owner was a king. Of course, a regent would be assisted by his attendants. Still and all, since the king presides over his retinue, he might justly be called a "hands-on monarch."

The following areas are where the Torah requested the Kohanim's actual input when it came to burnt offerings.

6. **Collecting blood.** "And Aharon's sons the priests offered the blood."[24] This referred to their gathering blood in a specified vessel at the time the sacrifice was slaughtered.

7. **Sprinkling blood.** "And they dashed blood all around the altar."[25] Exclusive to Kohanim, this deed is explicit in the Torah. "All around"

---

20. Ibid.
21. Vayikra 1:8.
22. Vayikra 1:9.
23. BT *Yoma* 26a.
24. Vayikra 1:5.
25. Ibid.

clues priests in that this demand could be met efficiently by sprinkling twice at opposite corners. Aim for blood flicking was directed toward a particular spot along the altar's base. By targeting one corner (first to the northeast), the Kohen actually hit that corner's right (north) and left (east). Next, he lobbed another blood sprinkle at the opposite corner (southwest). Perforce, hitting those two remaining sides of the altar meant that, in effect, blood reached all four directions. Residual blood not used in the manner just described was poured upon the altar's southern base, a suitable place for its disposition because there the blood dashing concluded. In sum, "all around the altar" was another way of saying that a bit of blood made its way to each of the four sides of the altar. All of this was standard procedure for burnt offerings. However, for sin offerings a different blood-dashing model emerges. Namely, there the Torah stresses that blood was sprinkled on the horns of the altar.

Four altar protrusions, or "horns," as they were known, contained rich symbolism. They represented four primordial elements.[26] So established, the Torah conveys that these four elements foment sin. How? When a man's lifestyle is out of kilter, the imbalance is manifested in an abundance of one element to the detriment of another. Disequilibrium dulls his conscience, resulting in behavior inappropriate to his station. In the extreme, he displays animalistic exuberance. Note that outright sin, however, did not enter the picture. Had the case been one of blatant iniquity, it would be beyond the jurisdiction of a burnt offering. Reflecting this, the officiating Kohen need not dash blood on the altar's four horns but rather on its base. As stated above, burnt offerings taught about man's finitude and the soul's interconnectedness with the Maker. That fusion played out when blood intermingled with Hashem's altar. A union between man and God was produced. In terms of this underlying, exalted message, all of the altar's sum components are equal. For that reason there was no need to trouble the Kohen to sprinkle blood high upon the altar, since the base accomplished the same end goal.

8. **Fire on the altar.** Kohanim kindled and made sure fire on the altar never extinguished. "And Aharon's sons the priests placed a fire on the

---

26. These elements (fire, air, earth, and water) are per Aristotelian philosophy.

altar."[27] Distinctly associated with the altar, this job devolved upon the Kohanim.

9. **Arranging altar wood.** "And they set wood upon the fire."[28] As in item four of the first list above, this too was an activity closely connected to the altar. Consequently, only Kohanim could take care of it. Something important about this task must be clarified. The verse is not speaking about the altar wood arranged each morning when a fire was kindled atop the altar. Instead, our verse describes the Kohanim adding wood to the fire as animal parts were laid on the altar. The sages add that this commandment took into consideration two measures of wood.[29] Two Kohanim were needed to carry the wood when placing burnt offerings' animal parts in their proper burning spot on the altar. To be exact, this job employing two Kohanim was needed for the daily evening burnt offering. For the morning's daily offering, one Kohen sufficed to complete the work of bringing two measures of wood. In sum, the Torah lays out different human resource requirements for the evening versus morning services.

10. **Arranging animal parts.** "And Aharon's sons the priests shall arrange the [other] pieces—the head and the fat."[30] This informs readers that animal neck fat was not surgically separated from the head. Had the fat been removed, it would have left behind one gory and grisly neck. Turning the holy compound into a horror show is an affront that will not be abided. "The priests" in the plural connotes that many had to participate in this undertaking. Consider that two took hold of one big animal section; one man grabbed a lighter piece. This showy procedure was followed for public sacrifices. For an individual's sacrifice, no such fanfare was generated. "And they arranged wood upon the altar."[31] In another verse more details about this emerged. "And the priest burned wood upon it every morning."[32] This supplementary verse teaches an important chronology of events. That is, first wood had to catch fire, and afterwards he placed the burnt offering meat upon it.

---

27. Vayikra 1:7.
28. Ibid.
29. BT *Yoma* 26b.
30. Vayikra 1:8.
31. Vayikra 1:7.
32. Vayikra 6:5.

This sums up a total of the ten tasks involving the altar. Half of them could be performed by men who brought animals to the Mikdash, with the other five entrusted only to officiating Kohanim. Insofar as the burnt offering was totally consumed on the altar and an irresistible and prepossessing aroma went forth, the sacrifice was most pleasing to Hashem.

"And if he brings from the flock a sacrifice."[33] The Ramban writes that this section deals with a goat brought as a burnt offering. In fact, there is more than a passing resemblance between laws governing a bull and a goat. For that reason, some aspects are omitted here concerning goats. For example, goat owners also rested their hands on their goats' heads and Heaven accepted these offerings from them, garnering atonement for them.

And yet, it must be assumed that since the Torah added a separate section about goat burnt offerings, there must be something novel about the subject. Apparently, there existed a hierarchy in the two animals' respective value and worth. Bulls were a head above goats. The Torah accedes as much by beginning this *parashah* with bulls, followed by this present section about goats. Lower down beneath goats come bird sacrifices, and after that meal offerings. Delineations make this point clearly. Had the Torah simply listed a potpourri of animals in a single breath, a wrong impression would have been created. People would gather that all carry the same weight. Independent coverage prevented this mistake from cropping up. Men of means and generosity, therefore, brought bulls for their burnt offerings. If that proved beyond a fellow's budget, he brought a goat, and so on and so forth, until the case of a good-hearted chap who was moved to bring a burnt offering but lacked funds and therefore brought birds or perhaps even a meal offering.

Something else is at work, too.

A separate paragraph about goat burnt offerings introduces certain laws that were not included in the verses concerning bull burnt offerings. One is as Rashi deduces from our verse: "And if he brings from the flock a sacrifice… or from sheep or goats."[34] Itemization conveys that not all herd animals are fit for the altar. Specifically, old, sick, or infected ones do not make the grade. Two, again Rashi makes a point on the verse above with bulls: "And they shall sprinkle the blood." He asks, "Blood—what does this imply?" It is permissible

---

33. Vayikra 1:10.
34. Ibid.

to dash blood on the altar even if the blood of one type of animal gets mingled with that of another type of animal. Rashi then probes further, asking what is the law if blood of a kosher animal is mixed together with that of an animal ruled disqualified for altar use. Or what about when a sin offering's blood gets mingled with a burnt offering's blood—is that permissible? In one verse the generic word "blood" is used, but here with goat burnt offerings it is modified with a possessive case: "its blood." Building on Rashi, it is posited that had the Torah not written a separate section concerning goats, these laws would not have come to the fore based on a Scriptural underpinning.

Other crucial commandments are traced to our verses here concerning flock animals (goats or sheep). "And he slaughtered it on the north side of the altar before Hashem."[35] The bull burnt offering verses above mention "before Hashem," however omit precise location references zeroing in on the altar's northern exposure.

Here is why. Above with bulls, verses did not need to divulge details about the north, because the Torah relied on that information being imparted with goats: "And Aharon's sons the priests sprinkled its blood."[36] As stated, that verse taught about certain issues with comingling blood from different animals. Stressing the proper sequence of events, before talk of blood sprinkling, there needed to precede clear-cut instruction to slaughter the sacrifice. Hence, "And he slaughtered it,"[37] to lay down a rule. No dashing of blood may be performed before ritual slaughter has been completed. The Torah holds back one detail from the description of the slaughtering procedure for bull burnt offerings in order to provide it in this section concerning goat burnt offerings, obviating the need to repeat the same *halachah*. When it came to other laws, a given section's juxtaposition shed light on germane laws concerning burnt offerings.

"And the internal organs and the legs shall be rinsed in water."[38] This instruction always follows after directives to arrange sacrificial animal organs upon the wood. Why? It is imperative to first place specific organs or *nitchei ha'eivarim* (נתחי האיברים) on the wood. On top of those designated organs, a Kohen piles innards and legs. During the Mishkan inauguration ceremony, we

---

35. Vayikra 1:11.
36. Ibid.
37. Vayikra 1:5.
38. Vayikra 1:13.

also note this sequence: "And you shall dissect the ram and wash its innards and its legs and place them [together] with *netachav* (its [other] pieces) and with its head."[39]

Reviewing this paragraph about the goat burnt offering, recall that the animal owner took upon himself three areas of activity: slaughtering, rinsing, and quartering the animal. Why are the last two spheres of the goat owner's participation—hand placing and skinning its hide—omitted here? The bull verses spell out how the owner places his hands on the animal's head. By extrapolation that rule is extended to all instances of burnt offerings. Put differently, certain operatives were put into place at the beginning of this *parashah* dealing with burnt offerings. And the directive to skin an animal's hide was also derived from the bull verses' "And he skins the burnt offering."[40] By deduction, all animal owners must skin their burnt offerings. However, when the Torah gets to slaughtering, note the language: "And he shall slaughter a male from the herd."[41] No explicit mention is made regarding burnt offerings. A similar observation is made concerning specific animal organs or *netachim* (נתחים): "And you shall cut it into [other] pieces."[42] Lest one get the wrong impression that this instruction is only an issue for the bull burnt offering on account of its prestige, but that perhaps a man who brings a goat is not so enjoined, another verse set the record straight. That is, even though a man brings a second-tier burnt offering (a goat), he still must cut and quarter its flesh.

Now let us review the five activities that priests performed. Out of the five, two are mentioned in the goat verses. That is because the other three can be learned from them. Take for example "And Aharon's sons the priests sprinkled its blood."[43] It was understood that animal blood could only be dashed on the altar if it had been collected in a Mishkan vessel. Also, with regard to the goat burnt offering cut into pieces, it is written, "And the Kohen shall set them upon the wood on the fire."[44] That verse had subsumed within it "And the sons of Aharon the Kohen placed a fire on top of the altar." An additional, legal application was also derived from here. "And they arranged the wood on top

---

39. Shemot 29:17. We translate *netachim* as [other] pieces. Understand that these are very specific animal organs.
40. Vayikra 1:6.
41. Vayikra 1:5.
42. Vayikra 1:12.
43. Vayikra 1:11.
44. Ibid.

of the fire." This is because when it is written "And the Kohen arranged them," it was clear that wood and fire directions were implied.

An unwritten yet understood principle emerges from these *parshiyot*. Namely, in the absence of explicit mention of an officiating Kohen, animal proprietors take the initiative. This is so since normative behavior dictated that he would attend to these aforementioned tasks with aplomb and without a trace of hubris. King David writes in Sefer Tehillim, "You, Hashem, do not despise a broken and contrite heart."[45]

Here is another telling observation in the verse concluding with the prepositional phrase "before Hashem." Missing here is the expression about it being "accepted by Heaven on his behalf" as was the case with the bull verses above. This is in keeping with the burnt offering hierarchy previously established. Since bulls cost the owner more money, acceptance is closely associated with that valuable offering. Invariably, the more cash a man expends, the more it distresses him. Heaven frowns upon gifts brought begrudgingly and therefore cautions a skinflint, in so many words, to shrug off the bull's high-end price tag. Concentrating on the big picture, namely that the Torah gives him the distinct privilege to extend a gift to God, helps him focus. But for the grace of Hashem, a proprietor's own blood and soul might have been beckoned to the altar. Hard feelings as described are more likely when a man purchases a bull. Given the smaller outlay of buying a goat, the likelihood of emotional backlash is lessened. Consequently, the Torah did not have to caution a man who gives away his goat to eke out an inward smile.

In the bull verses, it is written that the animal was carved up and quartered. "And Aharon's sons the priests arranged the head and the fat."[46] Note how there is no possessive case modifying a sacrifice's head or fat. The goat verses do, however, employ a possessive case: "And he cut it into [other] pieces—its head and its fat."[47] In an apparent inconsistency, when the Torah comes to writing about the animal's innards and legs, its style abruptly reverses. The bull verse states, "And he shall rinse its innards and its legs in water,"[48] but for the goat it says, "And he shall rinse the innards and the legs in water."[49]

---

45. Tehillim 51:19.
46. Vayikra 1:8.
47. Vayikra 1:12.
48. Vayikra 1:9.
49. Vayikra 1:13.

Why are there these discrepancies? Arranging animal parts on the wood was within the purview of priests, whereas rinsing had been carried out by animal owners. Bulls, owing to their size, necessitated the cooperation of many Kohanim. "And Aharon's sons the priests arranged the head and fat"—no possessive case. A large staff implies faceless anonymity. In contrast, since animal owners did the rinsing, the Torah stresses singularity.

Before concluding this first *aliyah*, we bring more halachic distinctions between bull and goat burnt offerings. This time, grammatical nuances elicit comparison and contrast. In bull burnt offerings, those parts offered on the altar are not referred to with their possessive pronouns. Thus, "And Aharon's sons the priests arranged the morsels—the head and the fat."[50] In contrast, a later verse featuring animals of the flock does use possessive pronouns. "And he shall cut it into its [other] pieces—and its head and its fat."[51] Styles flip when we get to verses speaking about an animal's innards or legs. Hence, the bull verse states, "And its innards and its legs he shall rinse in water."[52] We observe the inclusion of possessive pronouns. Yet the herd verse says, "And the innards and the legs he shall rinse in water."[53] Sans pronoun.

What do these grammatical inconsistencies reveal? Arranging animal parts upon the wood atop the altar is the purview of the priests. Animal own-ers, on the other hand, rinse the animals' innards and legs. Therefore, when bulls were offered for burnt offerings, the job called for the participation of many Kohanim. "And Aharon's sons the priests arranged the animal parts—the head and the fat." No one priest got the nod to handle it. No singular possessive pronoun. Instead many priestly hands were called on deck to assist. Stressing the innards and legs, however, the verse does utilize a singular possessive pronoun: "And its innards and its legs."[54] One man attended to it, and that man was the animal proprietor.

Now let us turn our attention to a sheep or goat burnt offering. "And the Kohen arranged them on the wood."[55] Since the priest worked this animal alone, the Torah teaches "and its head and its fat."[56] A single priest sufficed.

---

50. Vayikra 1:8.
51. Vayikra 1:12.
52. Vayikra 1:9.
53. Vayikra 1:13.
54. Vayikra 1:9.
55. Vayikra 1:12.
56. Ibid.

Again, this is in contrast to an expanded priestly labor force when tackling the bull burnt offering.

Our passage steers folks away from misconstruing. That is, readers should not think that the Kohen who offered up parts of the goat on the altar was the same priestly attendant who rinsed the innards and legs in water. Identical textual construct could mislead. Preempting the whole issue, the Torah changes stylistic tack. "And its head and its fat." A singular pronoun hints at the involvement of the Kohen. "And the innards and the legs" without a pronoun suggests a role for the animal owner. No mention is made of the Kohen. Our position receives support from verses describing the inauguration of the Mishkan. We learned there that Moshe served as the acting High Priest. Among his tasks were rinsing animal parts and offering incense. In those verses, pronouns abound.[57] Each one bespoke Moshe's vital roles and multitasking.

Second *aliyah*
"And if his burnt offering to Hashem is from birds— then he sacrifices turtledoves or doves as his sacrifice."

After bulls and goats, birds trail in third place so far as burnt offerings go. This second *aliyah* opens with instruction to sacrifice either one turtledove or one dove. Ibn Ezra corroborates and brings support for his position from Yaakov: "And he took from the rocks of that place."[58] The patriarch took one rock. An additional Scriptural source is "And Elazar the son of Aharon took for himself a wife from Putiel's daughters."[59]

As explained in this book's prolegomenon, these two types of birds were the only ones deemed appropriate. Unlike those comparable introductory verses applying to bulls or goats, only in regard to bird burnt offerings does the text spell out the sacrifice's designation "to Hashem." The bull and goat verses begin, "[When] a man from your midst sacrifices to the Almighty, if [it shall be from] an animal—from the herd or from the flock you shall offer your sacrifices." Here is the reason. Since God is mentioned at the outset, the

---

57. Shemot 29:14, 17, etc.
58. Bereshit 28:11.
59. Shemot 6:25.

Torah does not need to repeat the Addressee with each and every particular type of sacrifice. However, no such prefatory statement was forthcoming with birds. For that reason, the Torah needed to set the record straight. "To Hashem" provides requisite clarity.

"And the Kohen sacrifices him on the altar and cuts off his head."[60] When it came to bulls and goats, slaughtering had been the conventional method of killing them. After ritual slaughter, some of their blood was collected and dashed on the altar. If cutting off a bird's head without a knife is equated to slaughtering mammals, certain problems arise. For instance, non-priests were permitted to slaughter bulls and goats, but they were not able to pop off a dove's head. Also, slaughter took place north of the altar, and a fair distance from it. Logistics necessitated that a Kohen collect and transport the Mishkan vessel containing blood before dashing it on the altar. Snapping off a dove's head transpired next to the altar in order to facilitate dabbing the bird's blood on the side of the altar. Perforce, Kohanim exclusively needed to perform the decapitation of the fowl. Clear demarcation lines existed in the Mishkan for non-priests. Animal owners were even forbidden to stand too close to the altar, as a verse cautions, "And a stranger who approaches shall be put to death."[61]

In sum, burnt offerings went according to different standing orders depending on whether they were bulls and goats or birds. In the case of birds, Kohanim brought the sacrifice close to the altar before cutting off its head, but when it came to bulls and goats, even non-priests could slaughter. Bear in mind that this had been done a ways off from the altar.

Note an ambiguity in the verses discussing the bird offering. Until now, the Torah talks about birds in the masculine: "sacrifices him on the altar and cuts off his head." That changes as the verses continue: "And he removes his crop with her feathers. And he casts her beside the altar."[62] Seemingly slapdash grammar is not problematic, as occasional syntactical flexibility has precedence in Sefer Bereshit: "Behold he ripped off an olive tree leaf in her beak."[63] Apparently, verses discussing the bird's gender (as expressed in possessive cases) lack cohesion. Similarly here, sacrifice or *korban* (קרבן) is masculine, whereas fowl or *tor* (תור) and turtledove or *yonah* (יונה) are feminine.

---

60. Vayikra 1:15.
61. Bamidbar 18:7.
62. Vayikra 1:16.
63. Bereshit 8:11.

"And [the Kohen] cuts off his head." The bird's head was severed at the nape of the neck. Pressure brought to bear in that region separated the head from the rest of its body, after which an officiating priest brought the bird's head to the altar and placed it upon the fire. The bird's body, then, had been pressed against the altar's side. Squeezing caused blood to drip down the altar's side. To be graphic, the bird's blood oozed from the altar's upper part to the altar's mid-point, called in Hebrew *chut hasikra* (חוט הסיקרא), before dripping down lower.

"And resulting was his blood on the altar's side."[64] Birds' bodies do not contain much blood. They certainly don't have enough to fill a Mishkan-sized vessel to splash on the altar. For that reason the Torah commanded Kohanim to smear some along the side of the altar. A similar procedure was followed when a man brought a bird sin offering, as it says, "And he dashed from the blood of the sin offering."[65] Observe that an intermediate step of collecting bird blood in a Mishkan vessel is omitted. To accommodate this exigency, Kohanim performed bird decapitation while standing on top of the altar. This maximized utilization of the bird's limited blood supply.

"He shall crop it by its wings. He shall not separate [it entirely]."[66] A deep laceration or tear had been carried out between the bird's wing and the nape of its neck. Cropping had been performed by bare hand at the rear side of the bird. In this way, the effect was similar to the procedure used to kill bull and goat burnt offerings. Recall their body parts had been cut up and quartered.[67] Given a bird's petite size and insufficient body mass to cut up, this instruction had been issued. "He shall not separate [it entirely]." The bird, though cloven, still was left tenuously whole. Having to deal with one body as opposed to two body parts allowed Kohanim greater alacrity in performing their tasks.

"And nip off its head and offer it on the altar."[68] Compare this bird burnt offering verse with those concerning a bird sin offering: "And he shall cut off its head at the nape of its neck but not sever it [entirely]."[69] Missing here is the detail of separating the head from the body. This underscores a difference

---

64. Vayikra 1:15.
65. Vayikra 5:9.
66. Vayikra 1:17.
67. See Vayikra 1:6.
68. Vayikra 1:15.
69. Vayikra 5:8.

between burnt and sin offerings. Namely, with burnt offerings, the Torah prohibits complete decapitation, and should it occur, it is a sin. The same cannot be said should a Kohen take off the head of a burnt offering, as the sages have written.[70] The bird's head was burned separately from the body; it had to be cut off of it. Bird sin offerings shed light on bird burnt offerings. How? The verse regarding the sin offering states that the cut was "at the nape of its neck"[71] to imply that the head was not cut off entirely but remained tenuously attached at the neck.

However, a bird burnt offering's procedure resulted in a different outcome. Since the aim was for the bird to more closely resemble big animal burnt offerings (which had been carved up into head and fat), so too splitting the dove and turtledove necessitated a clean cut. Hence, no Torah instruction needed to add here the sin offering detail "at the nape of its neck."

Why were directives different for a sin versus burnt offering? It was because part of the sin offering was eaten. Keeping a sin offering intact better guaranteed that the bird's head would not be misplaced or lost. Together with its body, the head could be eaten. In contrast, burnt offerings were completely put to the altar's flames. Hence, a clean cut does not fundamentally detract from its purpose.

"And he removes his crop with her feathers. And he casts her beside the altar."[72] Why did the Torah provide these details, and what do they convey? Rashi notes regarding animals used as burnt offerings that these beasts only eat that which their owners feed them. Consequently, the Torah instructs, "And you shall wash its innards and legs in water."[73] However, birds by their roaming nature peck and eat whatever comes their way. Since these feathered fellows are unscrupulous and show no compunction about "stealing," their fate reflects this. "And he casts her beside the altar."

If Rashi's words were designed to be authoritative, a question arises: Why not discard the whole bird, the entire "thieving" culprit? Zoologists' knowledge can provide an answer. They posit that an animal's foods go through four stages of digestion: (a) via the stomach, (b) via the liver, (c) via the veins and

---

70. BT *Zevachim* 65a.
71. Vayikra 1:17. Abravanel understands "by his wings" to mean at the nape of the bird's neck.
72. Vayikra 1:16.
73. Vayikra 1:9.

arteries, and (d) via the limbs. If we retrieved food from an animal's stomach, we would observe that it had not been altered from the time of ingestion.

Now, here is where the Rambam derives a *halachah* concerning interpersonal monetary damages. It covers the case of a thief who pilfers and then subsequently dies. The Rambam opines that if a stolen object's form did not alter, then even if the original owner had despaired of retrieving it, and even where the thief died and the thing was in his offspring's possession, still and all it must be returned. However, if the object's shape did change while in the thief's possession, then even had the owner not despaired, the law is different. Namely, the thief retains possession of the thing and pays the owner its value (assessed as of the time it was stolen). This is the law as far as the Torah is concerned, since it says, "And he shall return the stolen object which he stole."[74] Jewish tradition determines that if it is the same as when stolen, the thief pays for it. But if the thing had been altered, the thief pays its value. Applying the Rambam's ruling, the Torah obligates priests to dump the bird's innards because "stolen" food sits in the bird's liver unchanged. However, by the time "stolen" contraband makes its way further along the digestive process (veins, arteries, and limbs), it is unrecognizable. This feathered felon now "takes possession." Its vile body is casually discarded, cast aside.

"And he removes his crop with her feathers." A bird's crop refers to its digestive organ and the plumages covering it. Razor-sharp precision guided Kohanim to the bird's exact anatomy, saving them time and effort to pluck the feathers of the sacrifice.[75]

"And he casts her beside the altar." A question arises as to where Kohanim dumped the bird. "East to the place of the ashes."[76] Some authorities understand that it had been tossed from where the officiating Kohen stood—or in other words, to the east of the altar. Others say that the lifeless bird's body began there before being shunted along until it came to the altar's ash heap.

As an aside, the altar dustbin was cleaned daily. Only in Parashat Tzav will more details be revealed about work associated with the altar. There it is recorded, "And heaved the ashes."[77]

---

74. Vayikra 5:23, cited in Rambam, *Mishneh Torah*, Hilchot Gezeilah 2:2.
75. Abravanel states that Ibn Ezra and Saadiah Gaon provide alternative explanations, but their interpretation of Scripture need not be viewed as authoritative.
76. Vayikra 1:16.
77. Vayikra 6:3.

Now we return to our passage. "Into the place of the fatty ashes."[78] The Torah provides a foretaste of a place whose designation is yet to be revealed. Compare this with another verse that presages a future event. "Half a shekel based on a holy shekel equal to twenty *gerah*."[79] That is, the Torah foreshadows that the currency will be twenty *gerah*.

Upon deeper reflection, something here in our verse is amiss. It is impossible that the crop and bird intestines are sent to the altar's ashes just for them to rot and smell. Imagine a congested day at the Mikdash where one hundred decomposing bird carcasses littered the area. Could solid waste engineering inefficiencies and hare-brained notions about bird dispositions allow the altar to deteriorate into a fetid garbage bin? Is this what *Pirkei Avot* counted as a Mikdash miracle?[80] Certainly not. Rather, understand that bird gizzards did not spend day upon day there. They were removed together with the altar ash beyond the Mikdash compound. Even outside the Mikdash, like other sacrifice waste product, bird remains did not produce effluvium.

"And when a [Jewish] soul will offer a gift offering to Hashem, his offering shall be fine flour and he shall pour oil on it and put frankincense in it."[81] Shimmying lower on the burnt offering spectrum of sacrifices is this gift offering. It is brought as a result of a man uttering an oath or *neder* (נדר) or of his free volition or *nedavah* (נדבה). This is the gift or meal offering.

The verb in this verse is inflected in the feminine gender (נפש כי תקריב). In mid-verse, the gender switches to masculine (את קרבנו). Grammatically, the term *minchah* is not gender sensitive and may be either masculine or feminine. The Hebrew word for camp, *machaneh* (מחנה), is a similar case. Many examples of Hebrew nouns whose declension switches between masculine and feminine appear in our *parashah*.

There are two reasons the Torah discusses gift offerings before peace offerings. One has to do with the Torah desiring to teach about a hierarchy within the overall burnt offering rubric. Since gift offerings fall well beneath the most prestigious bull sacrifice, goat gift, or bird present, they are appropriately placed here. To the point, fauna trump flora. Peace offerings belong in a

---

78. Vayikra 1:16.
79. Shemot 30:13.
80. *Pirkei Avot* 5:5.
81. Vayikra 2:1.

separate heading altogether, and hence are treated only after all four distinct types of burnt offerings are listed.

The second reason is that when the section began with optional sacrifices (cf. obligatory sacrifices), it relayed sliding-scale burnt offerings similar to the obligatory offering model. For that reason, verses provide sacrifice levels to suit every budget. Thus if buying a bull or goat proved too expensive, cheaper gifts could be arranged in the form of bird or flour presents.

Technically, a man only obligated himself when he proclaimed a clear-cut willingness. This could be gauged, for example, if he said, "Behold, I undertake to bring a gift offering to the Almighty." Words such as these represent bona fide pledges to the Mishkan. Should a man express sentiments to bring a gift offering in vague terms, it is understood that he is obligated to bring the following ingredients and recipe: *isaron solet, log shemen,* and *milo kometz levonah* (עשרון סולת ולוג שמן ומלוא קומץ לבונה).

There is, however, a catch. There are five different gift offerings, meaning that a donor must specify which one he has in mind at the time of his pledge.[82] "And he brought it to the Kohanim, sons of Aharon, and he shall take from there his handful."[83] Perhaps more properly pedantic, the verse's wording could have reflected what actually happened had it said, "And he brought it to the Kohanim, sons of Aharon, and his taking." Still, the verse's structure conveys that donors brought this gift to one of Aharon's sons.

What happened next? The donor, on the instruction and example of an officiating priest, took his handful of gifts. This model was strictly enforced by the sons of Gershon as they worked their shift overseen by the line of Itamar. In other words, there was a two-tiered chain of command in the Mishkan leadership. First Aharon directed a given Mikdash service, and then one of his sons oversaw activities.

Note here a difficulty with the plain grammatical reading of the verse. It says that "he brought it to the Kohanim, sons of Aharon," yet later in the same verse it is written in the singular: "and he shall take from there his handful." The explanation is that a man brings it to a group of priests, but when it comes to executing the offering, only one priest actually performs the cupping. This

---

82. See "Categories of Sacrifices" in Abravanel's Prolegomenon to Sefer Vayikra for a listing of the five types of *minchah* offering.
83. Vayikra 2:2.

is supported by the verse "at the hand of Aharon."[84] Yet the meaning is "his son" (בנו)—only one of his sons.

Rashi stresses what the two words "from there" mean, explaining that the location from which the donor brought his handful had been a permissible standing area for non-priests. The emphasis is that this task could be performed by anyone—anywhere in the Mishkan's courtyard. Included in the permitted area, yet still considered sufficiently holy, was an eleven-cubit pedestrian platform at the courtyard's entrance set aside for Hebrews (non-Leviim and non-Kohanim).

Ramban takes a different perspective but first quotes Rashi, who writes that certain gift offering acts required a priest's input. That is, Kohanim exclusively attended to the gift offering service from the time it was cupped in the palm of the hand and thereafter. It can be adduced that up to that stage, even non-Kohanim fully participated. Ramban questions Rashi's position, saying that prior to cupping or *kamitzah* is presentation or *hahagashah*. Categorically prohibited in the Torah would be a non-priest's inclusion in that task: "it shall be presented to the priest, and he shall bring it to the altar."[85] Finally, a verse in the next *aliyah* commands, "And the Kohen lifts the memorial part of it."[86] This refers to the act of grabbing the offering. Thus, this sacrifice's order begins with it being brought to the southwestern part of the altar, where the Kohen then cups the mixture in his palm.

This opinion of the Ramban needs to be probed further. How is it acceptable, for example, to grab the meal offering anywhere in the courtyard? Had it not already been presented to the altar? Does this imply that the grabbing took place there, as is implied in Parashat Tzav: "And this is *Torat haminchah* which Aharon's sons brought before Hashem in front of the altar, and he picked some of it up in his grabbing."[87] Note how this is consistent with what is written in the third *aliyah* of this *parashah*: "And he approached the altar, and the Kohen lifted up some of the gift offering as a memorial offering to Hashem."[88]

Here is a key point. Had the Torah not specified "and he shall take from there his handful," a misunderstanding might have surfaced. That is, it could

---

84. Bamidbar 4:27.
85. Vayikra 2:8.
86. Vayikra 2:9.
87. Vayikra 6:7–8.
88. Vayikra 6:8–9.

have been deduced that had the offering grab not taken place atop the altar, then it was disqualified, as is the case when Kohanim cut off a bird's head for a burnt offering. This is, after all, the Ramban's opinion. However, now that the verse states, "and he shall take from there," ambiguity has been avoided. The law is that grabbing is permissible anywhere in the Mishkan courtyard.

To review the various steps, let us write plainly.

☑ **Step one.** A Kohen takes the meal offering and presents it at the corner of the altar.

☑ **Step two.** A Kohen removes the same, dedicating it to Heaven.

☑ **Step three.** Note two options. If a Kohen desired to pinch or grab the mixture anywhere in the Mishkan courtyard, he was permitted to do so. If the proprietor had been moved to bring the gift offering by means of his direct participation, he would have to inform the Kohen of his decision. At that point, the Kohen would direct him to stand in a designated place. We can well imagine how an impassioned and inspired donor approached the matter, riveted by a sense of the sublime. His soul is afire.

See the Rambam's comments on Talmud Bavli's tractate *Zevachim*. There he equates the performance of cupping a gift offering with an act of slaughtering a sacrifice. Consequently, it is acceptable everywhere [in the Mikdash], as is the case when a sacrifice is slaughtered. Moreover, it is similarly prohibited for non-Kohanim to carry it out, just as non-Kohanim may not cut off a bird offering's head.

"And the Kohen shall offer up its memorial offering upon the altar."[89] No mention is made of the memorial or *azkarah* (אזכרה) being placed upon the altar's burning wood, as is the case with the burnt offering instructions. We shall soon see how that was also the modus operandi for peace and sin offerings. The explanation has to do with the modest size, quantity, and volume or mass of the meal offering plus *levonah*. Altar wood does not come up in our section in order to teach that even altar coals or *gechalim* (גחלים) sufficed to burn the meal offering—without utilizing any wood.

"The remnant of the meal offering belongs to Aharon and his sons. Out of Hashem's fire sacrifices, it is most holy."[90] In Hebrew, the term "remnant" or *noteret* (נותרת) is feminine and stands in contrast to other verses that use the masculine form of the word, *notar* (נותר).[91] The reason for this discrepancy is that in Parashat Tzav, we find that only a small quantity of the peace offerings remained unconsumed by the Kohanim on the day of sacrifice. This reflected their determination, which militated heavily against leaving leftovers. Thus, if by chance they could not perfectly fulfill their task, only insignificant traces remained. That remnant was irretrievably lost. Utilizing the masculine form of the word conveyed that point.[92] Meal offering leftovers were not a negligible quantity but rather a significant portion of it. A little palmful of meal was set aside, and the rest was ready to be eaten. Writing in the feminine gender alludes to a sizable amount of the overall offering available for consumption.[93]

"The remnant of the meal offering belongs to Aharon and his sons. Out of Hashem's fire sacrifices, it is most holy." Distributing meal offerings to Aharon and his sons is spelled out here and repeated in the next *parashah* (Tzav). "Every meal offering which is oven baked and each one done in a pan...goes to the Kohen who offered it...and every meal offering mingled in oil...belongs to Aharon's sons..."[94] Taken together, these verses instruct that some meal offerings go exclusively to the officiating Kohen. They are the oven-baked meal offerings or *maafeh tanur* (מאפה תנור), those prepared in a frying pan or *marcheshet* (מרחשת), or deep fried or *machavat* (מחבת). The officiating

---

89. Vayikra 2:2.
90. Vayikra 2:3.
91. E.g., Shemot 29:34, Vayikra 7:16.
92. Abravanel's reasoning on the significance of grammatical gender here is not clear, but he establishes this as a given in Parashat Tzav.
93. See previous footnote.
94. Vayikra 7:9–10.

Kohen has claims on them. However, meal offerings mingled in oil or *belulot ba'shemen* (בלולת בשמן), as well as dry ones or *charivah* (חריבה) needed to be distributed among all Kohanim.

Since divvying meal offerings did not follow one uniform procedure, the Torah needed to write out instructions separately. "The remnant of the meal offering belongs to Aharon and his sons. Out of Hashem's fire sacrifices, it is most holy." Rashi writes that Aharon's name is meant to give him first dibs. Also, he keeps his share, whereas assistant priests must divide up their meal's remainders.

According to Ramban, oven-baked meal offerings, those fried in a pan, and those deep fried are different from regular meal offerings of fine flour or *minchat solet* (מנחת סולת) and the meal offering that accompanies the first fruit, both of which are mixed with oil, and from meal offerings of a sinner or a *sotah*, which have no oil at all. The first three go to the officiating Kohen, for he put much work into their preparation, while the latter types (involving less work) are divided among the entire group of Kohanim on duty at the time.[95]

But Ramban is wrong, because the Kohanim did not do the work of preparing the offering. That was done by its owner before he brought it to the Beit Hamikdash. According to the sages,[96] all meal offerings were shared by the entire priestly group on duty, as Ramban notes in his comments.[97]

In the last several verses that we have been covering, the Torah treats the flour offering in far greater detail than it does the oven-baked, pan-fried, and deep-fried ones. Why? Notice how when it comes to these latter three, a single phrase is repeated: "The remnant of the meal offering..."[98] To wit, there is not a word about pouring in oil or *levonah*. Simply, since the Torah laid out the rules and regulations regarding the flour offering, it is understood that the identical arrangement was employed for the oven-baked, pan-fried, and deep-fried meal offerings too. This makes sense because all four gift offerings are written about in uninterrupted sequence. Consistency dictates that all four are subject to the same laws. "The remnant of the meal offering..." This phrase, a repeating refrain, lends weight to the shared traits of the three meal offerings with the flour one first broached.

---

95. See Ramban, Vayikra 7:9.
96. *Torat Kohanim.*
97. Vayikra 7:9.
98. Vayikra 2:3, 2:10.

Though the fact is somewhat queer and curious, it appears as if a stir was created when a man arrived to bring his gift offering. Due to the large number of competing priests attending the Mikdash, when someone came with his oven-baked, pan-fried, or deep-fried present, a free-for-all-ensued. Blithely, they snatched it away from the owners. This practice of wrangling was sanctioned by the sages.[99] Moreover, they legislated that all gift offerings were to be equally divided among the officiating Kohanim. With the exception of the Kohen Gadol, that is. His share came off the top. In fact, rabbinic powers allowed intervention, especially because the Kohanim had been forthcoming with their blessing in the matter. Reviewing these verses in this light provides a smoother grounding than the forced one advanced by the Ramban.

A total of ten chunky *challot* and matzot had been oven baked. They gave off the appearance of leavened wheat flour baked goods. Probably the dough lacked much moisture, since no oil had been added to the flour mixture; only after baking was it dipped in oil. Perhaps oil had been layered in the dough before baking.

Concluding this second *aliyah*, a verse says that [a Kohen] brought ten "thin matzah wafers daubed in oil." Coats of oil came after they baked. Pan-fried gift offerings consisted of a large, oil-coated matzah. After its baking, it was formed into thin strips. These were placed in a peculiar-shaped frying pan best described as a double-decker bowl functioning as a cooking vessel. On top of the open-faced matzah, oil was poured. Small, thin slices cooked in oil. In this manner, a delectable dish was readied. "It is a meal offering."[100] Skimping on oil and bringing it dry was not an option.

Third *aliyah*
"And if your sacrifice is deep fried, it shall consist of sifted flour in oil."

The deep-fried offering began as finely sifted flour dotted with oil. One-tenth of a measure, *isaron* (עשרון), of flour was emptied into an oil-greased deep pan or *marcheshet* as cooks are wont to prepare. In Hebrew the term *marcheshet*

---

99. Though Abravanel writes that the sages sanctioned the priest's behavior, he does not quote his source.
100. Vayikra 2:6.

relates to simmering, hissing, or boiling noises produced by oil cooking on top of a fire.

"And you shall bring the gift offering which is made by these [ingredients] to God."[101] All three kinds of gift offerings are being referenced here (oven baked, pan fried, and deep fried). Chronologically, here is the order: First, the owners prepared their gifts in their homes, closely paying attention to predetermined recipes. Next, they carried them to the Kohen with the requisite flour, oil, and *levonah*.

"And when it is brought to the Kohen, he shall serve it on the altar."[102] It was the owner who brought the makings of the offering to the Kohen. Then the Kohen laid it upon the altar. Actually, only a portion of the offering was laid there. That part is known as a memorial or *azkarah*. "And he shall burn it upon the altar—a sweet aroma to the Almighty."[103]

Afterwards, the Torah records, "Each of the offerings that you shall bring to Hashem may not contain leavening, for all rising agents and all honey you may not offer as a fire offering to Hashem."[104] Learn a generalization from this particular gift offering to all of them. They must all be matzot and not leavened bread. According to the sages, the verse is conveying something universal to gift offerings.[105] Namely, this extends to all gift offerings that accompany individual or communal sacrifices.

Why did Heaven forbid the inclusion of leavening agents and honey? The Land of Israel, the Torah teaches, is endowed with seven types of produce.[106] Furthermore, consider how the Torah already incorporated many of these species into the sacrifices. For example, Jews offered sacrifices (gift offerings previously mentioned) using wheat dough, jealousy and *omer* offerings of barley, wine libations, and oil as an important ingredient in gift offerings as well as in *challot* and wafers. Since many of the seven made the Mikdash grade, if you will, it would be easy to err and say that the remaining special and indigenous produce may be utilized too. To forestall this undue liberty, Heaven issues an unequivocal directive: "all rising agents and all honey you

---

101. Vayikra 2:8.
102. Ibid.
103. Vayikra 2:9.
104. Vayikra 2:11.
105. BT *Menachot* 57a.
106. "It is a land of wheat, barley, grapes, figs, and pomegranates—a land of olive oil and [date] honey." Devarim 8:8.

may not offer as a fire offering to Hashem." Writing explicitly "all rising agents" sets limits. Since wheat and barley were permitted in the making of matzah, folks should not get the wrong impression and expand this permission to include leavening agents. This is forbidden.

Why doesn't honey appear in Mikdash recipes or services? Also curious is that this prohibition extended to sweets made by grape, fig, pomegranate, or date honey by-product. Rashi goes further. He learns that any fruit sweetener is out of the question, including bee honey.

In any event, there are disparate reasons that the Torah prohibits rising agents and honey. Leavening agents are off-limits so that infelicitous time delays will not occur. That is, all Temple offerings have time limits within which they must be eaten. Were the Torah to have required some or all meal offering to be leavened, the time required for the leavening process would have eaten into the window of opportunity during which the offering may be eaten. This is especially true during autumn and winter, when leavening takes longer. Hence, the prohibition against leaven.

There is a second reason that leavening agents were forbidden. Basically, leavening ferments flour dough. Though inedible by itself, when put into dough the sticky blob can be eaten. Rennet enzymes work on this same principle with cheese manufacturing. Thus, leavening agents retard a swift running of the sacrifice timetable and are unfit for human consumption.

Honey and other sweeteners are prohibited for other reasons. Consider this premise: Sweet condiments would render sacrificial meat humanly irresistible. Insuppressible gusto would overcome people partaking of their holy repast. To be sure, there is something wonderfully special about ingesting sacrificial meat. However, if officiating Kohanim knew that delicious dressing was to be added, it would serve to hustle their pace beyond the requisite dignity. Ebullience might even cause Kohanim to jump the gun and offer animal sacrifices prematurely.

A second problem with candied honey sauce was that it could be eaten independently of other food. Unwittingly, officiating priests' fingers might just make their way over to the honey jar, resulting in an awkward raiding of the Mikdash pantry. Stumbling blocks, even if made out of luscious honey, are stumbling blocks all the same.

Briefly summing up, we have shown that both leavening agents and honey were prohibited, albeit for opposite reasons. The former would stall Mikdash service while the latter risked disrupting its proper decorum and pace.

The Torah outlawed leavening enzymes for a third reason. It urges Jews to distance themselves from distracting, evil annoyances during Mishkan services. Man's pesky, evil inclination is likened to leavening agents, as Rabbi Alexandri murmured to God: "Master of the universe—the matter is clear before You that I yearn to do Your will. What places stumbling blocks in my way? Is it not man's evil inclination?"[107]

Honey was likewise prohibited in the Mishkan for another reason. It disturbs man's reasoning ability. As noted by Avicenna,[108] honey's pungent smell and properties cause man to lose control of his faculties, ultimately rendering him imbecilic. Other symptoms include breaking out in cold sweats. He further writes of terrible effects associated with honey. Evidently, honey contained potentially lethal compounds injurious to human health. Inhaling poisonous substances in concentrated honey impairs man's mental dexterity. Given these deleterious consequences, this sweetener should be spurned by pious priests employed in the Mishkan. In fact, Heaven issued stern warnings to them.

"You shall offer them as first breads to God, but do not bring them up to the altar as a pleasing aroma."[109] Here, instruction is given which permits a man to bring leavening agents or honey as first fruit offerings, but caution must be taken not to burn them on the altar by themselves.

"You shall offer them as first breads." This verse contrasts *menachot* with breads of the first fruit offering or *korban reishit* (קרבן ראשית). Unlike *menachot*, the *korban reishit* may be leavened and may contain honey. "They shall be baked as *chametz*."[110] Continuing, the verse's subject moves to *lechem bikkurim* (לחם ביכורים). "But do not bring them up to the altar."[111] Even though leavening agents and honey are part of the *lechem bikkurim*, it had not been burned on

---

107. BT *Berachot* 17a.
108. Persian philosopher, 980–1037 CE, author of *The Book of Healing*.
109. Vayikra 2:12.
110. Vayikra 23:17.
111. Vayikra 2:12.

the altar. Rather it was eaten by the Kohanim. "It shall be the portion of the Kohanim, though holy to Hashem."[112]

"And add salt to every meal offering. [Use] salt on your meal offering so as not to void a covenant with your Almighty [which requires] salt on every sacrifice."[113] Typically, bread ingredients always include wheat flour, leavening, and salt. Seeing that the Torah prohibits using leavening agents in bread sacrifices, people might have assumed that salt was similarly verboten. Assuaging such jitters, the Torah states explicitly that salt is a must.

Here is solid proof that salt may be added when making matzot for Pesach. Those halachic authorities who prohibit its use don't do so on the basis of concern over *chametz*, but rather for another reason. That is, the commandment is to bake bread of a poor person or *lechem oni* (לחם עני), denoting bread made with barebone ingredients and taste.[114]

Though the verse requires using salt, it does not mention the amount of salt to add. Simply, any cook will tell you that salt is added according to an individual's personal taste. "[Use] salt on your meal offering so as not to void a covenant with your Almighty [which requires] salt on every sacrifice." This commandment is conferred upon all meal offerings. Even gifts that are not meal offerings need salt. Thus, for example, it was put on meat. Salt keeps meat from putrefying, preserving it. "A covenant with your Almighty [which requires] salt." Furthermore, salt flavors meat agreeably.

But that's not the half of it. Salt is part and parcel of established culinary seasoning. Withholding it betrays a maladroit chef, a sophomoric valet who sets a shabby dining room table.

Let us examine why the Torah spells out four types of meal offerings requiring flour.[115] Four types of meal offerings correspond to man's four main body fluids. They are blood or *dam* (דם), red fluid or *adumah* (אדומה), white fluid or *levonah* (לבונה), and black fluid or *shechorah* (שחורה).[116] There

---

112. Vayikra 23:20.

113. Vayikra 2:13.

114. *Orach Chaim* 405.

115. *Minchat choteh* (מנחת חוטא) or *chatat* (חטאת), *minchah* (מנחה), *minchat Kohen Mashuach* (מנחת כהן משוח), and *minchat nedavah* (נדבה מנחת). A fifth type of *minchah, minchat hasotah* (מנחת הסוטה), uses barley rather than flour. See the prolegomenon to Sefer Vayikra, where the subject is broached in "*Menachot*: Grain Sacrifices," within section 2, "Categories of Sacrifices." Here, our discussion dives deeper.

116. Abravanel is borrowing from Aristotle and other ancients who believed man's body fluids were four.

is another rationale for these four distinct meal offerings. Social Man may be classified into one of four kinds. One is a group comprising righteous and upstanding individuals. For upright people in this class, sin or transgression doesn't come into play. A mirror opposite, the second type of character wallows in moral squalor. Perhaps predisposed with unbridled libidos, they openly acknowledge their sorry plight. Third is typified by those self-aware folks who admit their ethical shortcomings to themselves, yet others in their social milieu relate to them as being wholly righteous. Finally, the fourth set are clueless as to their self-worth while their cohorts brutally label them as the louses they honestly are. An example of this last grouping can be found in Sefer Shmuel. King Shaul believed himself to be innocent until Shmuel called him out for his considerable misdeeds.

Type of person	Offering to be brought	Characterization
Righteous	*minchat hasolet*	their deeds are refined without blemish
Sinners	*minchat maafeh tanur*	combustible passions are a blazing furnace
Self-aware	*minchat hamachavat*	generally check their outbursts
Moderate sinners	*minchat hamarcheshet*	simmering and hissing surround him

After delineating these aforementioned four subcategories of gift offerings, a fifth one emerges and concludes this third *aliyah*. "And if you shall offer a first grain offering to Hashem, it shall be brought as soon as it ripens on its stalk, consisting of first fruits roasted by fire and ground. Fresh kernels shall be your first fruit offering."[117] Our verse teaches that when first fruits comprise a gift offering of an *omer*, it is brought in the springtime. During that season, it is

---

117. Vayikra 2:14.

basically ripe but not yet of a sufficiently dried composition. Consequently, the grain's natural suppleness makes it difficult to ground up or pulverize into flour. Agriculturally speaking, this verse stresses the grain's budding youth, signified by spring or *aviv* (אביב) and the quality of being soft and full or *rach u'malei* (רך ומלא). At this blossoming juncture, conditions are not yet ready for pounding. Fire's heat hastens the maturation process by roasting the grain's kernels, which results in the creation of coarse meal or *geresh* (גרש). Essentially, popped grain occurs when heat expands kernels, causing them to break open.

Starting with a coarse grain meal base, other ingredients must be added. "And you shall put oil on it and place frankincense upon it. It is a meal offering."[118] Characterizing this as a meal offering emphasizes how these preparation steps hit the mark, crowned as a most fit presentation.

Profound meanings concerning this gift abound, especially in light of what ancient naturalists noted regarding flora's biological passages in the course of a calendar year. In autumn, their growth is suspended. For example, fields and vineyards lie still and motionless. Springtime witnesses bio life's flowering, cascading vibrancy. This is especially observable with blood. So much so that Avicenna writes about certain infirmities that affect man at certain seasons of the year. He writes, "The illnesses of spring include a surplus of blood, which leads to burst blood vessels." Afflictions of springtime cannot be alleviated with standard medical intervention,[119] such as bloodletting or ingesting laxatives.

When blood production exceeds normal levels within the body, passions run amok. Body temperature rises. Performing certain Mikdash activities combats these phenomena. Thus in the spring, the Torah demands that Jews bring *minchat bikkurim*, corresponding to human development noticeable at that time of year. Namely, spring is the time of youth, a season marked by the ripening and fullness of the human body. Emotionally and intellectually, man's mind expands concurrent with these growth spurts.

Developmental jolts associated with spring also usher in perfervid fits and bouts. Thus, people are ablaze with flames reminiscent of ripe grain roasting in fire. Man is best served, at this juncture, by redoubling efforts to harness galloping hormones. The rabbis worded their sage sentiment this way. "Son,

---

118. Vayikra 2:15.
119. "Standard," of course, refers to Abravanel's fifteenth-century standards.

if you feel yourself overcome by urges, drag them to the study halls. For if it [base impulse] is comparable to stone, Torah study will melt it. And if it is like metal, Torah will obliterate it, as a verse teaches: Behold, My words resemble fire, says the Almighty, like a sledgehammer shattering a rock."[120] In our verse, the term coarse meal or *geresh* suggests a process of breaking or popping, as Rashi explains. How appropriate, then, that the word's nuance tends more to a fracture than a pulverization. Rabbinic counsel advises man against waging utter war on his nettlesome urges. Exaggerated zeal in neutralizing these desires threatens to upset if not totally upend our natural world's order. The sages address this point squarely, stating that if it were not for human impulses, a man would not have the gumption to build a house or marry.[121] This is the underlying message behind this sacrifice. Ripening stalks consisting of first fruits are roasted by fire and ground. Moderation is being preached and indoctrinated. Tempering and not obliterating man's physical needs is the goal.

"Fresh kernels shall be your first fruit offering." In Hebrew fresh kernel or *karmel* (כרמל) alludes to young adulthood. In agricultural terms, it connotes grains that are tender, supple, and full-bodied, encased within a pod or stalk. This definition and description are derived from the verse "And fresh kernels in its pod."[122] A second nuance takes into account a period of development associated with adulthood.

Taking these interconnected ideas and binding them together teaches an important lesson. When spring rolls around, a man's soul is best served when he proceeds with caution and balance. Discipline over his natural inclinations is critical—perhaps especially so when he enters manhood. For this reason, the Rambam steers young men away from certain esoteric studies and philosophy.[123] He asserts that this particular age grouping, being bombarded with hormonal changes and so on, is highly vulnerable. Young people cannot handle topics possessing potentially charged content matter.

---

120. Yirmiyahu 23:29, quoted in BT *Succah* 52b.
121. *Bereshit Rabbah* 9:7.
122. II Melachim 4:42.
123. Rambam, *Moreh Nevuchim* 1:34.

Fourth *aliyah*
"And if your sacrifice is a peace offering, then if it is unblemished cattle—either a male or female— they may be offered before the Almighty."

Recall that we answered above why the Torah discussed the subject of gift offerings after the section dealing with burnt offerings, and by so doing effectively pushed this present topic of peace offerings down a notch. It had to do with the Torah's interest in arranging a hierarchy of sliding-scale burnt offerings insofar as these were obligatory.

There is a second explanation for the Torah's sequencing of sacrifices. A donor who brings gifts to the Mikdash mulls three options. If his desire is to give an entire animal, he will take the route of bringing a burnt offering. A second choice would be to have his donation shared between the altar and officiating priests. That is known as a gift offering. However, if he wants to see his sacrifice split three ways—altar, priests, and animal owner—then he is looking at peace offerings. Judging a man's gift to the Mikdash in this light reveals a clear-cut hierarchy. Highest on the chart are burnt offerings, as he designates Heaven to be the sole recipient. Next come gift offerings. Both are referred to as most holy sacrifices or *kodshei kodashim* (קדשי קדשים). In third place are peace offerings known as gifts of lighter sanctity or *kodashim kalim* (קדשים קלים).

Viewed from a different perspective, there are three distinct and varying platforms or venues for the consumption of sacrifices. The first one is the altar or Hashem's table. Yechezkel puts its specs as follows. "The wooden altar stood three cubits in height, two cubits long. There were corners and its length and breadth consisted of wood. And he [a *malach*] said to me: This is the table which is before Hashem."[124] Conclusively, "Hashem's table" refers to the altar, because there Heaven's portion is burned.

The Ohel Moed's courtyard is the second one. That area was set aside for Kohanim to eat their share of sacrifices. "And the remainder of it shall be eaten by Aharon and his sons. Matzot you shall eat in a sanctified place—in the Tent of Meeting's courtyard. There they will eat it."[125]

---

124. Yechezkel 41:22.
125. Ibid.

Finally, the third, expanded platform took in the municipal borders of Yerushalayim. Sacrifice proprietors partook of their portion of peace offerings in the Land of Israel's holy capital. "And its breast as a wave offering and its leg offering—you shall eat it in a pure place."[126] Rashi explains "And its breast as a wave offering" is talking about public peace offerings, meaning that they must be consumed "in a pure place." He continues with a rhetorical question: Shall we advance that the first, earlier portions had been eaten in smutty venues? Absurd. Rather, those first-choice sacrificial parts known as "most holy" certainly were consumed in a sanctified spot. However, these latter portions need not be eaten inside the Mishkan compound. It was sufficient to partake of them within the Jewish encampment, since it was pure. (Ritual lepers or *metzora'im* were placed in quarantine outside the camp's parameters.) By deduction, lesser sanctified meat was eaten anywhere within the Holy City.

The three platforms for consumption of sacrifices	Supporting verse
Altar—"Hashem's table"	"This is the table which is before Hashem." –Yechezkel 41:22
Courtyard of the Tent of Meeting—priestly table	"Matzot you shall eat in a sanctified place— in the Tent of Meeting's courtyard." –Yechezkel 41:22
Municipal borders of Yerushalayim— owner's table	"And its breast as a wave offering and its leg offering— you shall eat it in a pure place." –Vayikra 10:14

To reiterate and sum up, burnt offerings were wholly consumed on Heaven's table; gift offerings had two platforms—some burned on the altar while other parts became priestly domain eaten in the Mishkan courtyard. Lastly, peace offerings were divvied up three ways between the altar, the priestly table in the courtyard, and a table at the owner's discretion anywhere inside Yerushalayim.

---

126. Vayikra 10:14.

Type of offering	Associated platform
Burnt offering or *olah* (עולה)	Wholly consumed on the altar
Gift offering or *minchah* (מנחה)	Some burned on altar, others eaten at priestly table in Mishkan courtyard
Peace offering or *shelamim* (שלמים)	Divided up three ways between the altar, the priestly table in the courtyard, and any table in Jerusalem

Peace offerings may be male or female animals, so long as they are sans blemish. This underscores the very nature or rationale behind this offering—it brings pleasure, enjoyment, and happiness to the donor and to his social circle.

"And he slaughters it at the Tent of Meeting's entrance. And the priestly sons of Aharon dash the blood around the altar."[127] Emphasis is placed on the fact that slaughtering need not take place in the shadow of the altar, as was the case for slaughtering burnt offerings. Much more leeway is allowed. Note that no explicit mention is made regarding priests collecting the blood of peace offerings. Our verse only states, "And the priestly sons of Aharon dash the blood." Still, that point is understood. How can blood be sprinkled had it not been collected first?

Better, this verse aims at something else. Which animal innards from peace offerings were to be offered upon the altar? If the animal was from the herd, the Torah demands "from the fat or *chelev* (חלב) that covers its innards and all the fat that is on the innards. And the two kidneys as well as the fat upon them and along its flanks and the lobes of its liver."[128] Reasons that Hashem directed certain animal anatomy to be offered on the altar while shunning other parts have been discussed. Another possibility is that innards when shown fire become engulfed in flames suddenly. Afterwards, they create an orderly and pleasing fire. Kidneys were thus chosen because of the considerable fatty layers surrounding them. Liver lobes, too, are attached to lots of blubber.

This section concerning peace offerings twice repeats the phrase "And he shall sacrifice a peace offering before the Almighty." The first time states

127. Vayikra 3:2.
128. Vayikra 3:3–4.

that "You shall offer unblemished ones before the Almighty"[129] and the second "And he shall offer from the peace offering a fire before the Almighty."[130] Why this redundancy? The first verse tells how the sacrifice is earmarked for God and not the priests or proprietors, though they also share its meat. The entire animal belongs to Heaven, but Heaven reciprocates the generosity, if you will, by granting others (priests and proprietors) shared enjoyment. In effect, this catapults them into regal guests at His table. So that readers do not mistakenly assume that peace offerings are fully consumed by Heaven like burnt offerings, a second verse relates, "From the peace offering a fire before the Almighty." Read: not the entire animal is dedicated to the One Above; rather, some of it is.

Interestingly, the Torah does not say here to whom the remainder goes after the choice part ascends the altar. An identical lacuna exists when it comes to the permissible part of sin offerings. This stands in marked contrast to gift offerings, which are divided among Aharon and his sons. How can this seeming lack of evenhandedness regarding the recipients be explained? An important answer and principle follows.

Parashat Vayikra is only concerned with listing sacred sacrifices that merit a place on the altar. In the following *parashah* (Tzav), pointed discussion will earmark recipients (priests and proprietors). The exception to this rule is gift offerings, from which Aharon and his sons were informed in our *parashah* that they will receive their due. This is a concession to still uneasiness in the wake of our *parashah's* very first opening section dealing with burnt offerings. It had not gone unnoticed that these sacrifices were burned completely, leaving not so much as a crumb for anybody else. This *parashah's* second section talks about gift offerings. Again, it was observed that only a few meager finger pinches were offered on the altar. Interested parties grew edgy, wondering what would be the fate of the rest of it.

Commotion churned in the people's hearts. Calming verses quelled unrest by stating unequivocally that Aharon and company were slated to share gift offerings with the altar. Even though that detail had been imparted, other particulars had not been, and they are taken up in the following *parashah*. Thus, for example the locale where priests and people would partake of their

---

129. Vayikra 3:1.
130. Vayikra 3:3.

holy repasts had not been divulged here. Since the Torah had needed to broach certain points regarding gift offerings, such as the priest's right to some parts of them, there was no reason to reveal more. The storm, in a manner of speaking, had passed. Donors reasoned that since gift offerings were parceled out, it stood to reason that this would be the case for peace and sin offerings too.

Verses now discuss what happens when peace offerings are not cattle, but rather sheep or goats. Practically these two subcategories of peace offerings are identical, though sheep-tail fat sticks out as an additional body part that needs to be brought to the altar. "Its fat of the whole fat tail he shall remove up to the backbone."[131] Much fat sits there, as can be observed in sheep that battened in Far Eastern lands.[132] In contrast, neither cattle nor goats have blubbery tails. Anatomically speaking, this verse means that the entire rump area was lopped off and offered.

Another slight variation between cattle and sheep can be derived through a close, comparative read of the respective verses. That is, in the case of cattle the Torah specifies, "And the sons of Aharon offered up,"[133] but here it states, "And the Kohen offers it upon the altar."[134] The former is plural, but for sheep the statement is written in the singular. Further note that the upcoming verse regarding goat peace offerings resorts back to the singular: "And the priest shall offer them on the altar."[135]

Here is the import. From the perspective of the altar's fire and concomitant pleasant meat-roasting aroma, priests needed to improvise. Since cattle and sheep body parts were plump, officiating priests placed their innards in one concentrated pile upon the pyre, thus producing the desired effect. An irresistible smell wafted far and wide. However, when it came to a goat's anatomy, yielding scrawny and slim pickings, Kohanim had to spread measly innards around the altar's fire to produce adequate aromatic smoke cooking.

By utilizing scant differences in wording, the Torah alludes to these varying altar procedures. Initially in the first two cattle and sheep sections, the root קטר (as in "they shall offer by smoke" or *hiktiru* [הקטירו], or "smoke offering" or *haktarah* [הקטרה]) conveyed how offering their respective body

---

131. Vayikra 3:9.
132. Abravanel supplies this interesting tidbit.
133. Vayikra 3:5.
134. Vayikra 3:11.
135. Vayikra 3:16.

parts had been accomplished through a one-time placement upon the altar's wood. But the third section dealing with goats moves to the plural for the reason just stated. Not surprisingly, a similar construction can be found in the laws governing bird burnt offerings. "And he cropped him by his wings, [but it] had not been separated [entirely]."[136] Rashi learns that the verse should be understood differently. That is, instead of "by his wings," it should be "with his wings." He meant that sufficient bird meat needed to be burned on the altar along with the bird's wings; additional fowl meat guaranteed that even a poor man's burnt offering would produce a titillating effect.[137]

Here is a general rule for Sefer Vayikra's first two *parshiyot*. Concerning regular sacrifices using cattle, the Torah never adds the possessive case when discussing its blood. Therefore, verses state "blood" or *dam* (דם), but not "its blood" or *damo* (דמו). Yet if the animal is a goat, the principle is to always write "its blood." Perhaps this has to do with their respective quantities of blood. Since cattle's blood consisted of substantial volumes, the commandment to collect its blood could not be achieved without some of it spilling from the designated Mishkan syringe. But when it came to collecting goat's blood, given that its quantity was manageable, priests did a more fastidious job.

Rashi asks about the verse "And the priests offered and spilled the blood,"[138] what is meant by "the blood"? He categorically rejects the possibility that the Torah's usage of "blood" lacks a possessive case in order to intimate that even disqualified blood may be dashed on the altar. This he asserts by bringing a proof from verses concerning goat's blood, where a possessive case is the rule of thumb.

Following is another guiding principle. In the section above concerning cattle peace offerings, it says, "And Aharon's sons offered it on the altar, [on the same spot as] the burnt offering atop the wood upon the fire as an offering—a most pleasant aroma for the Almighty."[139] Compare this with our section of sheep peace offerings: "And the Kohen offered it on the altar—a sacrificial offering for the Almighty."[140] Now, to present goat peace offerings,

---

136. Vayikra 1:17.
137. The Ramban emphasizes how Kohanim were extremely particular when it came to which animal parts were brought upon the altar. Additionally, they took great precaution not to mingle permissible innards with impermissible ones.
138. Vayikra 1:5.
139. Vayikra 3:5.
140. Vayikra 3:11.

it says, "And the Kohen offered them on the altar—a sacrificial offering for a pleasant aroma. All the fat is for the Almighty."[141]

What does each of these textual nuances teach? In the first instance (cattle), the verse conveys a halachic ramification when there is a sacrifice surfeit—a bottleneck on the altar. Thus, if when attempting to sacrifice the peace offering upon the altar there are still residual burnt offering parts that have not yet been consumed, it is permissible to place peace offering animal fat on the fire even though it results, perforce, in a mélange. Second, a law is transmitted whereby if a peace offering needs to be sacrificed but there is no meat present on the altar, it is still permissible to offer its innards. Finally, there is a third detail that concerns peace offerings, too. Namely, when priests sacrifice peace offerings and the altar has a backlog of other animal fats or fats from sin or guilt offerings, it is fine to pile on the peace offering's blubber as well in order to put them all to flame together.

"And if his offering is a goat, and he offers it before the Almighty."[142] With this verse, students are drawn to a textual inconsistency. From the beginning of this *parashah* until now, when a given section delineates the type of offering (burnt, gift, or peace offering) along with its type of animal, bird, or grain, the Torah repeats that offering's heading. But here, there is no mention that the goat is earmarked as a peace offering. Returning to the heading of the previous section yields an answer. "And if your sacrifice is a peace offering [taken] from the flock before the Almighty..."[143] Flock denotes both sheep and goats. For that reason it is not necessary to repeat goats in conjunction with peace offerings. To be picayune, really even sheep had not initially been tied to peace offerings. Note that that section's opening line did not read, *And if a sheep be offered as his peace sacrifice.* Only three verses after the paragraph's introduction does the Torah say, "And he offers for a peace offering—a sacrifice for the Almighty."[144] And to split hairs even more, the only reason that sheep and peace offerings are mentioned in the same breath here is that the Torah desired to introduce a new law regarding a sheep's fatty tail being burned on the altar. A requisite quality of being without blemish does not even get broached directly with those verses about sheep and goats. The prefatory

---

141. Vayikra 3:16.
142. Vayikra 3:12.
143. Vayikra 3:6.
144. Vayikra 3:9.

verse suffices: "And if your sacrifice is from the flock...an unblemished male or female it shall be."[145]

A severe prohibition is issued now via this verse which closes this fourth *aliyah*. "An eternal statute for all time and place: Do not eat any fat or blood."[146] Why are blood and fat offered to the Almighty on the altar yet considered *treif* for Jews to eat? Several reasons follow.

1. According to the Rambam, **primitive pagan priests drank** the blood of cattle, sheep, and goats. By so doing, these devotees **believed they could join the coterie of demons** and other "harmful spirits." Besides, the Torah issues a rationale for why blood is prohibited to imbibe, yet no such reason for outlawing fat has been forthcoming.

2. The Ralbag explains according to the lines of then accepted medicine and science. **Nutritionally speaking**, both blood and unacceptable fats are **injurious to a man's health**. This explanation is flawed. Actually, blood is healthier than animal flesh. It is most certainly preferable to animal bones. And the Torah did not cast aspersion on eating them. Clearly, fat cannot be claimed as harmful to man's diet.

3. Mystics find meaning in King Shlomoh's description of Hashem, as it were: "My Beloved is pure and ruddy."[147] The Almighty is depicted with a florid countenance. This lines up with God's stern judgement bringing to bear a strict letter of the law, or *middat hadin* (מידת הדין). The Torah suggests how this can be tempered. Hashem instructs the Hebrews to tame, as it were, Heaven's ominous trait by placing blood on the altar. When it is offered with animal fat or *shuman* (שומן), amelioration or temperance results. This **defuses potential backlash, facilitating a calmer and safer world**. Symbolically, white fat of animals hints at Hashem's trait of compassion.

---

145. Vayikra 3:6.
146. Vayikra 3:17. Note that the term "fat" or *chelev* referred to here is a halachic concept referring to a very specific internal fat designated for the altar. The prohibition of consumption does not refer to ordinary fat typically found in beef.
147. Shir Hashirim 5:10.

4. High living and alluring looks, it is said, cause and contribute to man sinning. Health is a function of blood. Fat makes beauty. **When blood boils, man sins**. This all-too-human reaction is closely associated with youth's impetuousness. Excessive indulgence also pushes man to sin, as a verse in Sefer Devarim says: "And Yeshurun waxes fat and kicks."[148] Acceding to these popular notions, Hashem commanded that both of these surpluses be obliterated on His altar. Underscoring blood and fat's sinister part in fueling man's errant ways, proper caution dictates that he **immolate those self-destructive tendencies**.

5. Homiletic Talmudists arrived at this conclusion.[149] A man's **abstention from food and drink is paramount to offering a sacrifice**. They deduce this on account of the end result of fasting—a man reduces his blood volume as well as his body fat. Rav Sheshet was accustomed to fast after praying, at which time he uttered: "Hashem, it is revealed before You that when the Mikdash stood, a sinner had a ready remedy: he offered animal sacrifices consisting of its blood and fat. Through this means, a transgressor **attained atonement**. But now there is no Mikdash, and so I sit and fast. My blood and fat diminish. Please accept my personal sacrifice **as if I stood in Yerushalayim and offered an animal sacrifice** before You. Please let there be divine appeasement."[150] These teachers' moral lesson is certainly correct.

6. Metaphorically, one may draw transgression in the color red and forgiveness in white.[151] The prophet Yeshayahu borrowed this color-schemed imagery: "If your sins shall be [colored] crimson, they shall turn as white as snow. If they are red, fleece white they will become."[152] Utilizing this **color coding**, Hashem

148. Devarim 32:15.
149. BT *Berachot* 17a.
150. Ibid.
151. Abravanel interjects this thought on the subject.
152. Yeshayahu 1:18.

commands Jews to dash blood on the altar. This underscores a contrite people professing confession for their sin. "I will admit my wrongdoing to Hashem."[153] Here is more Scriptural support: "And my guilt grew to the highest heavens, and that they offered to Him."[154] As stated, animal fat conveys forgiveness and pardon. "For with You is forgiveness."[155] Based on these two symbols, sacrificing blood and fat is quite enlightening. Just as man's sins are recorded before Him, so too does his exoneration come from Above. Unequivocally, rich imagery plays a part in Hashem's decision to have blood dashed in the Mikdash and fat burned on the altar. Hebrews may not ingest it.

For all of these diverse aforementioned rationales, God deemed it fit to have blood sprinkled in the Mikdash in addition to being offered upon the altar. We also gained understanding as to why Hebrews may not consume it.

Moreover, we have broached the subject of prohibited animal fat. In a word, incompatible biochemistry stands at odds with a Jew's dietary needs. Returning to the issue of blood, it too is incompatible, although for other reasons.[156] Suffice it to say that for a nation aspiring to be wise and discerning, both of these animal by-products cross forbidden lines.

Admittedly, until now discussion has not been comprehensive or conclusive. However, passages in Parshiyot Acharei Mot and Re'eh promise to reveal substantially more. Ultimately, we will better grasp the Torah's prohibitions against eating blood and fat. For now, take it as axiomatic that ingesting blood incalculably damages a man's exalted soul and unsettles its highly attuned inner harmony.

Now we turn to another question. Why do these two prohibitions (fat and blood) straddle sections dealing with sacrifices? Talking about the various other offerings helps solidify a position. Namely, had a man not dedicated those particular ingredients, be they meat or flour, as an offering, he would be permitted to enjoy and eat them. But at the end of the passage about offerings, the Torah points out that the contrast between the sacred and the

---

153. Tehillim 32:5.
154. Ezra 9:6.
155. Tehillim 130:4.
156. Abravanel propounds medical and nutritional theory of his day, all of which has been omitted here.

profane is not black and white. Even within the domain of the profane there is restriction. "Do not eat any fat or blood."[157]

How might things get sticky? If people attributed these prohibitions to the fact that their status had been defined by dint of their having been consecrated for holiness, then a major blooper might surface. Faulty logic might lead people to believe that had those key ingredients not been consecrated, then they would be fine to eat. Such a mistake is unconscionable. For example, in conjunction with other major altar diet staples (animal meat, refined white flour, loaves of bread, crackers, and matzah), that is the case. Status as altar-dedicated food puts them beyond the pale. Hence when they are not holy, Jews may freely eat them. Enter the Torah's verse to inform Hebrews that blood and fat are different. Irrespective of their role in Mikdash service, they are roundly prohibited for all times.

That is the approach adopted in Parashat Tzav, where burnt, gift, sin, and guilt offerings are fully discussed (though peace offerings receive a more limited treatment). At that juncture, the Torah pronounces its caution for Jews to refrain from ingesting fat and blood. By contrast, the Torah here warns against eating fat and blood, though no punishment for the offense is explicit. In Parashat Tzav, the prohibition is repeated together with its dire punishment, namely spiritual excision or *karet* (כרת).[158] In Parashat Kedoshim, another mention regarding contraband fat and blood is broached.[159] And before that in Parashat Acharei Mot, during the section delineating illicit sexual relations, the punishment is explicit.[160]

---

157. Vayikra 3:17.
158. Vayikra 7:25.
159. Vayikra 19:26.
160. Vayikra 17:10–14.

Fifth *aliyah*

> *"And Hashem spoke to Moshe, saying:*
> *Speak to Bnei Yisrael, saying:*
> *When a soul sins inadvertently—*
> *violating any of Hashem's negative commandments—*
> *and does any one of them."*

When complete, this discussion will consist of four separate divine communications to Moshe.

The first prophecy [161]

This first divine communiqué detailed a whole host and array of information regarding burnt offerings, made up of cattle, sheep, goats, and fowl. It also addressed gift offerings. Note two shared observations. Each was brought of the owner's free volition, and they were entirely consumed upon the altar.

The second prophecy [162]

With this fifth *aliyah*, discussion turns to sin offerings. These, too, are obligatory offerings. Four distinctions are recorded, depending on the seriousness of the offense and the offender: (a) the Kohen Mashuach, (b) the nation, (c) a *nasi*, and (d) the rank and file. When a common man sins, he is commanded to bring either a sheep or goat. As an illustration, take the example of a man who had the ability to testify in court on behalf of his friend but didn't. Sin clouds his soul. Other instances include when he accidentally touches something ritually impure or he utters a curse invoking God's name. Assuming that

---

161. Prophecy 1 corresponds to Vayikra chapters 1, 2, and 3.
162. Prophecy 2 is revealed in Vayikra 4:1–5:13.

he could afford to bring a ewe or she-goat, he must. However, if his budget cannot handle that high cost, he may opt for a less expensive remedy. Two doves or turtledoves suffice. If even that outlay stretches him beyond his means, he may bring a one-tenth *eifah* flour offering. All of these subjects broadly labeled under Moshe's second prophecy will be clarified.

The third and fourth prophecies[163]

These deal with guilt offerings. Itemizing them, the third prophecy addresses a man who confiscated property belonging to the Mikdash and must bring an *asham me'ilot*. But when guilt cannot be established with certainty, then he brings an uncertain guilt offering or *asham talui*. Both of these are not, technically speaking, money matters or *dinei mamonot* (דיני ממונות). By contrast, the fourth prophecy, about the *asham gezeilot* (אשם גזילות), an offering for one who stole and denied it but then repents and confesses, highlights monetary misdoings.

We have shown how these commandments all fit neatly within their four respective compartments.

Why does the Torah lay out this particular hierarchy when it comes to these prophetic passages teaching about sacrifices? The ordering conveys an important principle when dealing with Heaven's modus operandi. God begins things on the positive side of the spectrum and then (if need be) continues with less savory stuff—to wit, sacrifices man must bring to atone for his sins. See Sefer Bamidbar's section on the *sotah* (Parashat Naso): "And if a [strange] man did not lie with you because you did not betray your husband's trust, then you shall be acquitted...but if you did act adulterously, impurely..."[164]

---

163. Prophecies 3 and 4 line up with Vayikra 5:14–19 and 5:20–26 respectively.
164. Bamidbar 5:19–20.

Similarly in those Torah chapters that proclaim blessings and curses,[165] the former always pave the way. Later, horrors associated with execrations follow.

BURNT OFFERINGS
GIFT OFFERINGS
PEACE OFFERINGS
voluntary expressions
of love, goodwill,
and altruism

SIN OFFERINGS
obligatory expressions
of penance after wrongdoing

GUILT OFFERINGS
obligatory expressions of penance for certain or
uncertain guilt (*asham me'ilot* or *asham talui*)

ASHAM GEZEILOT
obligatory offering for one who stole money and denied it
but then repents and confesses

So too this pattern and model is adhered to here. When it comes to listing sacrifices, the Torah begins with burnt, gift, and peace offerings, since these are expressions of love, goodwill, and altruism. Only after that spiritually idealistic category is depleted do verses delve into obligatory sacrifices incurred as a result of man's darker side. Fear of God is the operative remedy when it comes to addressing man's baser behavior. These sacrifices assume a different tenor, tonality, and dynamic.

---

165. Bamidbar 26:3–46; Devarim 28:1–69.

Moreover, when the prophets extolled sacrifices, they gave across-the-board praise for burnt offerings. See Sefer Tehillim: "Then You desired sacrifices of the righteous—burned completely."[166] From God's perspective, King David asserts, Jews will only offer those types which connote affection. Foretelling future rosy happenings, a period that will not witness Hebrews sinning, thereby obviating a need to atone with sin and guilt offerings, the prophet Yeshayahu presages, "And they will bring their burnt offerings and sacrifices to the Holy Mount and be joyous in the House of My prayer—all in good cheer upon My altar."[167] Verily, the Almighty only yearns for burnt and peace offerings.

Now commentary will return to explaining the verses in this fifth *aliyah* of Parashat Vayikra.

"If the anointed Kohen sins and brings guilt on the people, then he shall offer a bull for the sin that he committed—an unblemished young bull—to the Almighty for a sin offering."[168] Interestingly, this is the exact prescription given to patch things when the nation transgresses. To wit, when a Kohen Gadol sins, he must bring a bull sin offering. Its blood is collected in order to dash it seven times toward the front of the holy *parochet*. In addition, it is sprinkled on the corners of the golden incense altar located in the Ohel Moed. All remaining blood is spilled on the second altar's base. He must also burn its innards, its flesh and hide, and any other part of it outside the encampment. Ditto for sacrifices brought on behalf of the people. Rationale for this twin arrangement has been outlined in the prolegomenon. It takes into consideration how the two misdeeds are equated: that of the Kohen Gadol and that of the people.

Let us backtrack and consider a fuller picture. Accidentally, the Kohen Mashuach permitted to the nation that which really should have been prohibited. Specifically, he passed judgment on a negative commandment, ruling that a given act was acceptable to do. More to the point, his misguided advice caused people to perform heinous deeds which, had they been done willfully, would have resulted in spiritual excision (*karet*). Identical causes

---

166. Tehillim 51:21.
167. Yeshayahu 56:7.
168. Vayikra 4:3. In our passage, Abravanel uses the following three designations synonymously to refer to the anointed Kohen or High Priest: Kohen Hagadol, Kohen Mashiach, Kohen Mashuach.

brought the nation to transgress. Don't read "nation" to mean the congregation as a whole; rather, it refers to the Great Sanhedrin. Proof for this interpretation comes from the verse "And the thing was concealed from the eyes of the congregation."[169] That supreme halachic body instructed the people to perform an act which had they done it purposely would have carried *karet*.

To state the obvious, we are not talking here merely about a minor blip or faux pas. Far from it. Adhering to the Sanhedrin's counsel, the people perpetrated a baleful deed. The verses teach parity between the Great Assembly's versus a High Priest's blunder. Accidentally, both badly misled their constituents. Most senior authorities entrusted with being repositories of Jewish law floundered, resulting in mass confusion and chaos. Making amends means that both must bring bulls, as the Torah spells out.

Why couldn't the Torah economize by writing both laws about the High Priest and Great Sanhedrin in a single passage? Why do both need separate and expanded Scriptural treatment? At root lay a prescient approach. It is that Hashem wanted to facilitate the return of sinners to their flock. Repentance or *teshuvah* stood at the heart of the matter. How? Regardless of whether transgressors are individuals or part of a multitude, the Torah wanted to go on the record, if you will, that the Kohen Mashuach—a man of wisdom, sagacity, and halachic acumen par excellence—as well as the greater Jewish congregation are beckoned to return to Hashem.

When it came to wisdom, knowledge, and judicial prowess, the anointed Kohen was considered the most endowed advisor among all of his co-religionists. Repentance follows a redemptive process designed to cleanse bodies and souls. Every Jew is bidden to take a close look at the unfortunate events—focusing on individual and collective transgression. Bulls have been designated by the Torah as a vehicle by which the Kohen may right his wrong. Why? Leading these lumbering bovines to the Mikdash's courtyard was quite the to-do. Slaughtering them and offering those choice parts could only be accomplished with great commotion; the event resounded most emotively, striking deep human chords.

Strain and tension kept at feverish pitch when the Torah topped matters off with a further demand. Residual bull parts were transported out of the Mikdash and camp confines, ultimately burned beyond the pale. The import

---

169. Vayikra 4:13.

of the High Priest's and the people's penance for their transgression had been designed to maximize effect.

Man, woman, and child witnessed, empathized, and shuddered at their sin. In turn, this triggered an outpouring of repentance and catharsis on a monumental scale. By writing two separate paragraphs, the Torah assures that this mega-event will have double-barrel firepower. Only one thing is better than a passage all but assuring comprehensive *teshuvah* among the people, and that's two passages aiming at that same desired target.[170] Repristination.

Apropos, the Talmud quotes Rabbi Yehoshua ben Levi. He says that when the Jews in the desert sinned with the Golden Calf, it was not a simple matter of lapse due to an inherent moral shortcoming. Rather it was for posterity to gain something by their misstep. That is, when Jews throughout history would sin, they would recall how Hashem forgave the Jews who prostrated themselves to the calf. Encouraged, they would find the inner strength to do *teshuvah*. "It should only be so that their hearts will always fear Me and they will keep My commandments."[171]

The just-quoted Chazal is reminiscent of Rabbi Yochanan in the name of Rabbi Shimon Bar Yochai. He teaches that it was well beyond King David's moral character to sin in that particularly notorious circumstance. Similarly, Bnei Yisrael had no business getting embroiled in their moral imbroglio. Attesting to King David's sterling character is a verse in Tehillim: "My heart shuddered within me."[172] As for the Jews' part, it was well out of character too, as the verse attests: "It should only be so that their hearts will always fear Me."[173]

Why, then, did those scurrilous events transpire? David's experience opens up dialogue and opportunity for sinners. Should a man trip, fellow Jews will comfort him. How? They will tell him that surely King David was but an individual and yet the gates of repentance availed him. So too can you, a mere individual, heal yourself through *teshuvah*. Now, if a sizeable crowd stumbles and wonders whether positive transformation can occur, well-wishers will extend them comfort by illustrating the example of the Jews sinning by worshipping a golden calf.

---

170. BT *Avodah Zarah* 4b.
171. Devarim 5:25.
172. Tehillim 109:22.
173. Devarim 5:25.

The Talmud raises a valid question.[174] Why did the passage need to relate stories about an individual and about a community? Could not that same inspiring and lofty message have been relayed just as efficiently with either one of the two cases (King David or the Jews in the desert)? Actually, the Talmud answers, it couldn't. Had Tanach written only about King David's act, then scoffers might taunt: Teshuvah *works for single individuals since their misdeed transpires behind closed doors.* In other words, the misdeed was contained. But should a community all partake in forbidden fruit, contrition is not a theological proposition, since the matter snowballed. A full-blown, veritable spectacle proliferated. On the other hand, consider the possible shortcoming had the Tanach only recorded the Golden Calf debacle. Cynics would have a field day discouraging individual sinners from reaching out to Heaven. Why? *God forgave them,* they sneer, *because He has compassion for the masses. But for peons and menials, He has no time.* Thus, the sages conclude it was compelling for Tanach to relate both events. Jointly, they thoroughly expose and squelch the cynics' folderol and venomous skepticism.

Another sage, Rabbi Shmuel son of Nachmani, said something similar in the name of Rabbi Yochanan. It says in Sefer Shmuel, "The saying of David the son of Yishai, and the saying of the man most high."[175] The psalmist (David) refers to an enlightened man who offers burnt offerings as a means of attaining *teshuvah.*

In review and after having brought the insightful words of the sages, the matter of the Torah's seeming redundancy has been addressed. Note the repetition of the term "bull" in the verses quoted here: "And he shall bring his sin offering[176]...and lean his hands on the bull's head and slaughter the bull.[177] And the Kohen Mashuach shall take some of its blood[178]...and all the bull's blood...[179] and all the sin offering bull's fat...[180] and the bull's hide...[181] and take out the entire bull."[182] As stated, it is for good reason that these two pas-

---

174. Quoted above (BT *Avodah Zarah* 4b).
175. II Shmuel 23:1.
176. Vayikra 4:3.
177. Vayikra 4:4.
178. Vayikra 4:5.
179. Vayikra 4:7.
180. Vayikra 4:8.
181. Vayikra 4:11.
182. Vayikra 4:12.

sages reiterate the High Priest and Great Sanhedrin's sin offering. Moral lessons abound, as does the Torah's purposeful use of bulls brought as sin offerings.

An alternative explanation presents itself. The Torah suggests that the Kohen Gadol's bull sin offering as well as that of the congregation alludes to the flagitious Golden Calf. Recall, it was Aharon, serving as Kohen Gadol, who inadvertently participated in the affair. Unwittingly, his act caused the congregation to commit one of its greatest blunders. In effect, all successive High Priests' accidental sins in performing prohibited Torah commandments serve as a constant dig. Indeed, they reflect ungainly atavism, a throwback to that original heinous, idolatrous travesty. Imperative, too, was for the High Priest to burn the bull's fat and blood. By the Torah so obligating, it conveys an important personal fact and observation concerning Aharon's true religious bent. That is, his inner being reverberated with proper probity. His life's blood, his life's breath, and his life's work—all identified with those parts offered on the altar to Hashem—gravitated to holy meditations. Aharon, at heart and in deed, was a faithful man of God. Now consider the disposition of the bull's other body parts. Its hide and bowels, representing Aharon's physical deed and offense, though unintentional, were burned outside the camp's confines.

Indeed this fits for that despicable transgression. If Aharon's role is put into perspective through analysis of the bull sin offering, how should students evaluate the act of the participating Hebrews? Understand that the Jews had not intended to descend to the depths of depravity by dancing around a golden calf idol. Unconscionable. This assessment has been advanced in Sefer Shemot.[183] Briefly, they thought that it was a useful expedient to create such a mascot or concrete representation. Queerly, it was supposed to act as a substitute for their absent leader Moshe, a golden lightning rod to channel harvest bounty from celestial bodies. Again and as with Aharon, analyzing disposition of the bull's body parts, a picture emerges regarding Jewish sin associated with the Golden Calf. Internally, the people's gut was in a good place. God was foremost on their minds, but their odious deed reeked. Accordingly, the bull's innards were sacrificed upon the altar, while other anatomical sections were junked beyond the encampment.

Fairly, Aharon and the congregation shared religious headspace, though there was a major divergence too. "If the Kohen Mashuach sins, foisting guilt

---

183. *Abravanel's World: Shemot, vol. II*, Parashat Ki Tisa, second *aliyah*.

upon the people…" When measured, the High Priest's sin exceeds that of his co-religionists insofar as he causes a nasty thing through his instruction, which in turn points to faulty training of the High Priest himself. Due to his high station, inadvertence, the sages declared, is tantamount to intentional error. The Great Sanhedrin's erroneous decisions are, similarly, viewed the same way. Bluntly, something flunked. This caused a nation to veer from walking in Hashem's ways. Appropriately, they personally absorb all costs of the sin offering. Collectively too, they press on the bull's head as they utter confession for their sin and for that of their fellow Jews.

Practically speaking, the bull sin offering that the Great Sanhedrin brings is just like that which the High Priest brings. Pay close attention to the verse's language: "And the Kohen Mashuach takes…and he brings it to the Tent of Meeting…and he dashed some blood…before the Almighty in front of the *parochet hakodesh.*"[184] Delegating to subordinates was out of the question. The High Priest collected the bull's blood before transporting it to the Mishkan's holiest chamber. Generally reserved for Yom Kippur, this ritual was reenacted on this most solemn occasion.

"And the Kohen dashed some blood on the horns of the incense altar before Hashem."[185] Omitted from this passage, however, is a phrase that declares forgiveness as is encountered in the narrative of the congregation's,[186] *nasi's,*[187] and rank-and-file citizen's[188] catharsis. One need not adopt the approach of the Ramban, who states that due to the High Priest's station, atonement is not achieved via his sacrifice. Hallowed tradition posits unequivocally that nothing (read: nothing) stands in the way of any man's rehabilitation and forgiveness. Instead, understand that the High Priest's and Great Sanhedrin's laws concerning their bull offerings form a single section. Underpinning this unity is the message that what is true of one is true of the other. Since the Torah states the Great Sanhedrin's *teshuvah,* it also implies the same for the Kohen Gadol. To wit, see Parashat Tzav, where it is written regarding the case of the

---

184. Vayikra 4:5–6.
185. Vayikra 4:7.
186. Vayikra 4:20.
187. Vayikra 4:26.
188. Vayikra 4:31.

community inadvertently sinning. "As he did for the sin offering bull [פר העלם הצבור] and the Kohen wrought their atonement, and they were forgiven."[189]

Axiomatic is that the term "their [atonement]" or *v'nislach lahem* (ונסלח להם) refers to the congregation plus the Kohen Gadol—each one receives divine dispensation by and through their respective sacrifices. Paying close attention to sentence structure in this section yields interesting finds. In particular, we note how a word here or a word there requires analysis, as do the variations of the placement of phrases within the sentences.

Let us illustrate. On occasion "and it will be forgiven" follows "and they will take the bull out of the camp." And yet other times, notably in the passage featuring the congregation's offering, those phrases change order. Why? It is because the Torah wants to draw similarities or parallels between the people's collective sacrifice and the Kohen Gadol's offering. "And they were forgiven." This teaches readers of an overlap between the congregation and the Kohen Gadol.

Probing deeper into this section's message of the sin offerings provides layers of insight. Jewish tradition points to four crowning glories.[190] Rabbi Shimon counts three. They are the crown of Torah, the crown of the High Priest, and the crown of kingship. However, the crowning glory of a man's integrity bests them all. This sage asserts that if a Kohen Mashuach sins, he gives all priests a bad name. "And if the entire congregation of Israel errs and a matter of Jewish law escaped them"[191] corresponds to the crown of Torah. That diadem's patina, too, dims.

Rashi explains that this is speaking about the Great Sanhedrin. "Jewish law escaped them." These erudite and saintly men blundered in a matter of grave consequence, in a matter of punishment calling for *karet*. On their watch, a law was bungled. They permitted a thing that was forbidden. And their co-religionists thereby stumbled. "When a *nasi* will sin."[192] He represents kingship, and thus the Torah describes a regent who fumbles.

Finally, foraying temporarily into the *parashah*'s sixth *aliyah*, "And if an individual's soul sins from within the community."[193] Here we come to the

---

189. Vayikra 4:20.
190. *Pirkei Avot* 4:12.
191. Vayikra 4:13.
192. Vayikra 4:22.
193. Vayikra 4:27.

fourth crown depicted by Rabbi Shimon. It adorns forthright men of valor. And yet they, too, fall and dent their once shiny crowns.

"And the congregation offers a bull from the cattle for a sin offering."[194] Missing in this bull's traits is the fact that he is without blemish or *tamim* (תמים).[195] This hints at a uniformity between both cases of the bull. The Torah connects these two cases in a single broad paint stroke, as it adjures both the community and the individual to repent. Characterizing the bull in one of those cases (Kohen Mashuach) as unblemished reflects that same high standard for the second one (congregation). "And he shall do to the bull just as he does to the sin offering bull; thusly shall he do to it."[196] Neither offering sanctioned anatomical flaws.

Order matters in the Torah. First, this section began with the case of the Kohen Mashuach's offense before verses dealt with the congregation. Why? Morality dictates a man setting right his own affairs before preaching to others. Standing apart from the common folk, the Kohen Gadol is viewed as a messenger or *malach* of Hashem. Eyes are trained upon him to take charge, guide, and lead. Exemplary in piety, the priest is watched and emulated. He and members of the Great Sanhedrin were observed, their words and edicts sought after. Mentors of the first rank had toiled long and arduously. Indeed, they were a cut above the rest, inspiring untold multitudes. See Parashat Shemini, in which Moshe says to Aharon: "Approach the altar and perform your sin offering and your burnt offering and [thereby] attain your forgiveness and that of the people. And he performed the people's sacrifice and he achieved their atonement as Hashem commanded."[197] Moshe taught that only after Aharon cleansed himself was he in the position to cleanse others.

"When a *nasi* will sin."[198] Sequentially, this section about *nesiim* follows cases involving when a Kohen Gadol and the congregation transgress. Recall that "congregation" in this context refers to the Great Sanhedrin. Unwittingly, they sinned. Later verses will take up the subject of other strata of offenders, but they do not play a public role within the nation's judicial hierarchy. Common, however, to this broad topic of sin offerings is this: an individual

---

194. Vayikra 4:14.
195. See Vayikra 4:3.
196. Vayikra 4:20.
197. Vayikra 9:7.
198. Vayikra 4:22.

sinned by accident or by mistake, with no premeditation or intent. Also, this category of private citizens takes into account that their wrongdoing has not caused others to stray.

In essence, there are two classifications. The first comprises men of renown. Atop this list is the *nasi*. During certain historical periods of Jewish life, *nasi* meant king, as the Ramban has written. "And he transgressed one of Hashem your Almighty's commandments."[199] A regent is, of course, the apotheosis and paragon of power; he fears no man. Yet strikingly, the Torah teaches that kings must fear Heaven. Parenthetically, while each king served as *nasi*, the obverse is not so. Prophetically, Yechezkel confers, "And David My servant will forever be their prince."[200] This observation is seconded here. "When a *nasi* will sin"; read: a king. By the same token, the verse noted in the case of a Kohen Mashuach's sin that no Kohen ranked higher than he. Also, the Torah designates the Great Sanhedrin, peerless when it comes to legislative bodies. Can there be a question, then, that *nasi* means king? Is there a citizen who wields more might?

"When a *nasi* will sin…or when he becomes aware of his sin."[201] This matter has been well explained by Ibn Ezra. The first case describes a king who knew of his misconduct but he had perpetrated it unwittingly, whereas the second case transpires without his knowledge. Another person witnessed the king's slip-up and reported it to him.

The Ramban provides rationale for a case whereby somebody brought the news to the king. Guilt occurs when a regent commits an act prohibited by the Torah, a punishable one. In the second instance, where the king is apprised of misdoing, spiritual rehab transpires as a result of his offering a sacrifice. Likely, the Ramban's approach is too literal. When the verse says "and he is guilty [אשם]," it doesn't mean that the king must bring a "qualified guilt" offering or *asham talui*. Rather, this is another way of indicating inadvertent sin. Either the monarch admits to his accidental sin or a third party brings it to his attention.

"And he shall bring an unblemished male goat for his sacrifice."[202] Why wasn't the *nasi* obligated to bring a bull? As stated, the Torah had not entrusted

---

199. Ibid.
200. Yechezkel 37:25.
201. Vayikra 4:23.
202. Ibid.

a regent with the task of teaching or instructing his subjects to the same extent as a High Priest or Great Sanhedrin. Consequently, his personal affront lacks impact. As if to underscore leniency, the Torah's fine amounts to the cost of a less expensive he-goat and not a more costly bull. Bringing a bull sin offering is the sole domain and reserve of the community's mainstay halachic authorities (High Priest and Sanhedrin). Their misjudgment, perforce, directly impacts the Hebrew myriads, almost surely leading them astray.

The question of the *nasi's* sacrifice now takes a different angle. Seeing that he is an individual, why does the verse set him apart from all other individuals who sin inadvertently? A citizen's sin offering is a she- and not a he-goat. Hebrew etymology tips off readers and provides an answer. The term *se'ir* (שעיר) carries a double entendre, connoting a he-goat as well as the evil inclination or *satan*. Thus, a *nasi* was thrown off Hashem's path due to an encounter with his overwhelming inner impulses. Satanic machinations, if you will, gobbled him up. Regarding demons or *shedim* (שדים), a verse later in Sefer Vayikra says, "And they shall cease sacrificing their offerings to satanic demons."[203] A *nasi* bringing a he-goat is deemed more dignified than the hoi polloi offering a she-goat. Just as female goats are dominated by males, so too the Jewish people collectively defer to their royal ruler.

Besides being a he-goat, another requisite trait is that it must be blemish free. This attests to the *nasi's* and people's inadvertency in their sin. In a sense their piety is pure, unquestioned. Sin came about innocently enough, certainly without prior knowledge or intent.

After the *nasi* presses his hands upon the goat's head, the verse states, "And he slaughters it in the place reserved for burnt offerings."[204] That same venue was used when rank-and-file Jews brought their sin offerings. No such instruction was issued to the Kohen Mashuach or the congregation when they brought their bull. Instead it says, "And he slaughtered it before Hashem."[205] Why the discrepancy?

As stated, the sin of the High Priest or Great Sanhedrin registered as intolerably egregious. "Simply inexcusable" is the Torah's reaction to this cascading chaos stemming from their misapplication of Jewish law. Although accidental, it is judged and treated as if gravely injurious. Compared to it,

---

203. Vayikra 17:7.
204. Vayikra 4:24.
205. Vayikra 4:15.

the *nasi*'s and folk's inadvertent misdeed barely scores a blip on a morality chart. How different is their fault when measured by that one committed by a priest or the Sanhedrin. Moreover, the venue next to the burnt offering spot suggests that when they repent their action, Heaven promises them a positive reevaluation. Instead of having been seen as sinners, they are viewed as if they brought the more prestigious burnt offering. This step-up explains why no blood is collected before the sacrifice is taken to the Mikdash's inner sanctum. That heavy remedial exigency only needed to be performed when the High Priest or Great Sanhedrin sinned. A lighter request demanded that an officiating priest need only dash some blood "on the horns of the altar."[206] Furthermore, "And all its fat he shall burn upon the altar."[207] This hints at their souls' spiritual level which practically glosses over their unintentional transgression. "And the Kohen shall atone for him, absolving him of his sin and granting him forgiveness."[208]

Sixth *aliyah*
"And if a soul from out of the rank and file
will accidentally sin
by doing a negative commandment of Hashem
that he ought not have done, and is guilty."

This section concerns itself with a man from any walk of life who sins by accident. Specifically, this transgression is the type whereby had a man done it on purpose, he would suffer *karet*. Since he acted accidentally, he atones by bringing either a sin or guilt offering. The idea here is that he realized his mistake on his own, owing to the feeling that he sensed his conduct was amiss. Shame gnawed at him as he contemplated the enormity of his misdeed.

"Or his sin which he did was made known to him."[209] Others observed his misstep and reported it back to him. In both of these cases, his remedy is to bring a fixed sin offering or *chatat kavuah* (חטאת קבועה). It consists of a she-goat. His mistake stemmed from carelessness, and thus it befits him to

---

206. Vayikra 4:25.
207. Vayikra 4:26.
208. Ibid.
209. Vayikra 4:28.

bring a female goat. As stated, the term *se'irah* (שעירה) connotes demons and other "harmful spirits," or something coarse, crude, and uncouth. In any event, both connotations conjure up satanic machinations and man's ubiquitously capacious and ever-stalking evil streak. Nevertheless and in all fairness, his blunder was not mean-spirited. For that reason, his sacrifice must be without blemish, for that best matches his inherent innocence, as noted above.

"And if his sin offering consists of a ewe, it must be free from blemish that he brings it."[210] Females are stereotypically associated with crude superficiality, as the Rambam has acceded.[211]

Notice that a new phrase is added in this section dealing with rank-and-file folks: "by doing one of the commandments of Hashem [that He specified not to do]" (בעשותה אחת ממצות ה').[212] Yet with the High Priest and Great Sanhedrin, the language reads, "from any negative precept" (מכל מצות ה').[213] In the section dealing with the congregation when they sin without intention, the verse is somewhat general and vague. "And they did...when a soul sins inadvertently by doing any of the prohibited commandments."[214] And this is the language the Torah uses for the *nasi*: "And he did any one of the negative precepts."[215] No mention is made of his lack of intention, which does figure into the section talking about the average Joe (or Yossi).

In the Tanach, locution differences are significant. All of the souls, collectively, must adhere to all of the commandments. An individual, however, has no practical way to scrap each and every Torah directive. Being neither a priest nor a king automatically rules out his flouting laws incumbent upon them by dint of their prominent station within the Jewish national fabric. Theoretically at least, the margin of error is higher for a High Priest or Great Sanhedrin members. Within their legislative scope and powers, they wield broad authority. If they are derelict, it is possible for them to improperly instruct the masses to violate each and every Torah prohibition carrying a punishment of *karet*. To a lesser extent, a king's executive order may mislead subjects in a way that a private citizen cannot.

---

210. Ibid.
211. The Rambam and Abravanel put forth gender stereotypes prevalent in the Middle Ages.
212. Vayikra 4:27.
213. Vayikra 4:2, 13.
214. Vayikra 4:2.
215. Vayikra 4:22.

Let us illustrate. A Jew from the ranks (read non-Levite, non-Kohen, or not born to royalty) has virtually zero access to Mishkan vessels or accoutrements. Thus the likelihood of him anointing another Jew with consecrated oil or *shemen hamishchah*—a prohibited act—is remote. Likewise, the chance of his making any other forbidden usage of that oil or incense is very slim. (*Karet* is meted out to offenders for this serious misappropriation.) But those prohibitions are facilitated as a result of a High Priest, regent, or Great Sanhedrin's misruling or mishandling. It is in the realm of possibility that a Kohen will err or abuse anointing oil privileges. And the same goes for a king. Recall that Davidic kings were anointed.

Again the question of likelihood arises for sacrifices. Who is most liable to mislead the people to perform untoward activities with sacred Mikdash rites? It is within the purview of kings to enter the holy courtyard, as was the case with King Uziyahu.[216] That courtyard is totally out of bounds to commoners, however.

Summing up, we have demonstrated that High Priests, Great Sanhedrin members, and kings are far better positioned to cause their co-religionists to err than are rank-and-file citizens. That explains why the Torah words things differently for these different societal classes. Thus the verse specifies "by doing" as opposed to "from any negative precept."

Now discussion turns to another category of sins. "And if a soul hears the voice of an oath, and he is a witness or saw or knew of it, if he does not relate it over, he bears onus."[217] The Torah uses the term "soul" for the people bringing the *asham* offerings, for anyone who possesses a soul must bring them—both men and women. Now, when it comes to giving testimony, of course, even simple Jews must avail themselves of the opportunity to testify. They too must follow prescribed guidelines or face dire repercussion. Specifically, the verse describes a case whereby a man must swear under oath that he saw or heard nothing of material substance with regard to a legal proceeding. The Torah makes explicit that if a man is privy to vital testimony but fails to share what he saw or heard, sin will eventually entangle him. The matter will weigh heavily upon him.

---

216. II Divrei Hayamim 26:16–20.
217. Vayikra 5:1.

"Or when a soul touches anything that is ritually unclean—whether it is the carcass of a nonkosher animal, regardless if it was non-domesticated or domesticated—or any carcass of a ritually unclean creeping animal, but he does not recall touching it. Still, he is ritually defiled and he is culpable."[218] Clarifying, the verse teaches a gradation of wrongdoing and gives a basis for evaluating the severity of defilement. The first case mentioned is that which is most lenient on the spectrum, when a man sullies himself by contact with a *sheretz tahor* by swallowing it. Alternatively, this low-level tumah occurs when he touches an impure animal or beast carcass. Included is when he comes into contact with a *sheretz tamei*.

Note the pyramidal ordering of *tumah*. "Or when a soul touches a *tamei* thing." This refers to swallowing a carcass of a *sheretz tahor*. Next, when the Torah lists "or carcass of a *tamei* beast," it refers to *tumah* that is more stringent—a carcass of something inherently *tamei*, be it wild beast, animal, or *sheretz*.

"He does not recall having done it. Still, he is *tamei* and is culpable." When our verse describes the man as blameworthy, it means something broad. That is, judges will rule that he must come to court and testify. It also means that our verse ascribes *tumah* to him, since he either inadvertently ingested or touched things that trigger defilement. In those two cases he had a vague misgiving. At a later juncture, clarity knocked. *Yes*, he recalls, *I erred when I touched something tamei. I erred when I was not forthcoming with admissible evidence.*

Scrolling higher on the chart of *tumah*, the verse states, "Or when he touched a man's corpse."[219] This form of uncleanliness is the granddaddy of them all. "For any of his *tumah* by which he sullies himself."[220] This catch-all includes cases whereby a man touches a *zav*, *zavah*, *niddah*, or *metzora*. It may possibly refer to someone who eats sacred food or enters the Mikdash without having adequately ritually prepared himself—in all instances sin had been unintentional. Namely, at the precise time of his blundering, he was completely unaware of what was transpiring. Later, his revived memory revealed his mistake, leading to his self-incrimination. "And he knew and was guilty."[221]

---

218. Vayikra 5:2.
219. Vayikra 5:3.
220. Ibid.
221. Ibid.

"Or a soul when he utters an oath."[222] The Torah speaks about either a man or woman here. To fall into the category of this type of offense, it is insufficient to have thoughts, meditations, or murmuring. Actual words must be pronounced. Thus for example, a man may mention Hashem's name or attribute with his positive or negative statement.[223] To illustrate, he said: "I swear by God that I will eat this," or "I will refrain from eating that." This he had clearly voiced, adhering to the technical grounds for sin proscribed by hallowed tradition. Afterwards he forgot what he uttered. "He does not recall having done it."[224] Initially drawing a blank with regard to the solemn oath invoking a divine name, he eventually came to his senses. "And he knew and he was culpable."[225] Simply, the Torah reveals how he gained knowledge of his transgression and felt acute pangs of guilt.

In all of the cases mentioned above, the verse pronounces punishment. "And when he will admit his shame to any of these [offenses] and confess his sin."[226] Cover-up never entered his mind. "And he brings his guilt offering to the Almighty for his sin which he sinned. From a flock, it is a ewe or she-goat used as a sin offering. And the Kohen shall gain exoneration for him [the transgressor]."[227] A little confusingly, the verse calls this sacrifice a "guilt offering" or *asham*, but it really is his sin offering or *chatat*. Recall in this volume's introduction, we stated that a true guilt offering was referred to by the sages as a "provisional guilt offering" or *asham talui*. This delineation is significant because it characterizes differences between a guilt versus a sin offering. Misunderstanding arises because the word *asham* bears two meanings or shades of nuance. It can refer to a man's anguish or feelings of guilt, and it can also mean a "provisional guilt offering," underscoring his uncertainty over a given event. Had he or had he not transgressed? On still other occasions the term *asham* in a verse may express a man's feeling that he let down his Creator by misbehaving. Other times, *asham* might convey that an accident is a form of guilt. Had he been more vigilant, he would not have been derailed from the straight and narrow path.

---

222. Vayikra 5:4.
223. See *Torat Kohanim*.
224. Vayikra 5:4.
225. Ibid.
226. Vayikra 5:5.
227. Vayikra 5:6.

In order to avoid confusion with the verse's word *asham* here, potentially misleading readers to chalk up the thing as meaning a "provisional guilt offering" and not a sin offering, the Torah adds, "And he knew and he was culpable for having done one of these."[228] Sobering reality had, at last, made inroads, and the sinner no longer labored under earlier doubts. Replaying his act brought lucid recollection. Hence this sacrifice—a sin offering—swept away the last vestiges of this verse describing a "qualified guilt."

"And when he will admit his shame." He confronted his act, his inadvertent sin. It led him to conclude that no doubt remained. Unreservedly, this verse describes a sin and not a guilt offering.

The Torah did not go into the details of how this offering was sacrificed on the altar because they are identical to those of the sin offering described above.

"And if he cannot afford a lamb, then he may bring for his guilt which he sinned two turtledoves or two doves to the Almighty. One serves as a sin offering, the other a burnt offering."[229] Sins for which these guilt offerings needed to be brought are common. And poor people certainly were among those who committed them, try as they might to avoid sin. The Torah therefore provides relief for them: "And if he cannot afford a lamb."

Though dispensation is available on a limited basis to someone who interfered with due process and the courts, or for cases involving *tumah* or for those who compromised solemn oaths, the reality is different. In fact, this topic has been broached in this volume's prolegomenon.[230] There we explained that financial leniency was extended to all cases where a man from the rank and file sinned. This is deduced by noting that only after a list of qualified sins is recorded, the Torah instructs "And if he is unable to afford a lamb."

"Then he may bring for his guilt which he sinned two turtledoves or two doves to the Almighty. One serves as a sin offering, the other a burnt offering."[231] By so commanding the sinner, the Torah assures that a portion is dedicated to Kohanim and a separate one to the Almighty's altar. Specifically, Kohanim eat that bird designated as a sin offering, whereas the altar's fire consumes the burnt offering.

---

228. Vayikra 5:4.
229. Vayikra 5:7.
230. See section 4, "Why Sacrifice?" in Abravanel's Prolegomenon to Sefer Vayikra.
231. Vayikra 5:7.

This bird sacrifice follows a prescribed sequence. "And he shall offer the sin offering first and clip off its head at the nape, yet not sever it."[232] The sin offering affords man atonement. After he attains forgiveness, it is appropriate to follow up his clean-slate status with a burnt offering, a gesture that gains him further closeness with his Maker. Taken as a whole, dedicated efforts serve to reunite man and God.

Technically, an officiating Kohen must sever the bird's neck in a spot at the nape or back of the neck. Special care is taken not to decapitate the head from the bird's body, as the Torah cautions. This concludes the sixth *aliyah*.

Seventh *aliyah*

"And if a man cannot afford
to buy two turtledoves or two doves,
then his sin sacrifice shall consist of one-tenth eifah
of refined flour. [This] his sin offering shall be.
He may not use oil, nor shall he use frankincense,
for it is a sin offering."

The Torah pities indigent Jews. If dire straits are his lot and he lacks funds to scrap together payment for two birds, there is still a way out. His sin offering will suffice when he brings a modest amount of refined flour. This bare-boned offering lacks oil and spice, reflecting both the man's shoestring budget and the Torah's distinction between sin and gift offerings. Recall that gift offerings are flour mingled with oil and frankincense. Sin offerings are bereft of both. "For it is a sin offering."[233] Insofar as this is a sin offering, it is deemed inappropriate to adopt the more lavish recipe used for gift and meal offerings.

Though a modest dish, still a part of it is earmarked for Kohanim to enjoy after an obligatory quantity or *kamitzah* is brought to the altar. "And he is forgiven, and the remnant shall be the Kohen's as a gift and meal offering."[234]

This wraps up discussion regarding all aspects of sin offerings.

Following is the Torah's treatment of men who sin inadvertently yet lack clarity about whether they in fact did sin at all. Uncertainty does, however,

---

232. Vayikra 5:8.
233. Vayikra 5:11.
234. Vayikra 5:13.

plague them. This next category of sacrifice is called a provisional guilt offering.

Several subcategories of wrongdoing are covered in this type of sacrifice, as the coming verses illustrate. First, "a soul when it sins unintentionally
by misappropriating sacred property, he should bring his guilt offering to
Hashem—an unblemished ram of the flock, its value set at two silver shekalim according to the rate of the holy [Mishkan] for a guilt offering."[235] This
verse implicates a man who inadvertently derived enjoyment from property
belonging to the Mikdash. His Torah obligation had been to forestall such
oversight. Thus, his error is chalked up as a misappropriation, requiring him
to bring a ram to attain forgiveness. Rams are larger than other animals of the
flock. Furthermore, he is required to bring an unblemished male. To avoid
confusion, the Torah spells out just how much this ram should cost. Understand this price tag as a minimum amount (two shekalim). Of course, if he
desires to purchase a pricier one, that's fine. Supply and demand, as always,
come into play. In the desert, rams were rare and no trifling bill of fare.

"And that which he enjoyed, for his having sinned [by taking] holy things,
he shall pay—its value plus he adds one-fifth—and he gives it to the Kohen.
And the Kohen will garner his atonement with the ram guilt offering, and he
will be forgiven."[236] A twenty-percent add-on was designed as a deterrent. Cal-
culate as follows. If a man consumed sacred property valued at five shekalim,
then his fine totals six shekalim (five plus twenty percent of five). This amount
he transfers to the Kohen. Note, however, that this payment is apportioned.
The fine of one shekel goes to the Kohen. But the principal of five shekels
goes to the fund of the Beit Hamikdash, from which the misappropriated
holy property was taken. Comprehensively, this fine of six shekalim is called
a provisional guilt offering concerning sacred property, or an *asham me'ilot*.
Finally, the verse calls on the offender to offer a ram for the sake of gaining
forgiveness. Such an expensive sacrifice draws attention to the gravity of the
sin. Deriving benefit from holy belongings is unquestionably heinous.

It is important to stress that two distinct transgressions are being discussed in these concluding verses of the seventh *aliyah*. As already written,
the first one is called an *asham me'ilot*, whereas a second one is known as an

---

235. Vayikra 5:15.
236. Vayikra 5:16.

asham talui. "And a soul when it will sin and perform one of the negative precepts of Hashem that ought not to have been done, yet he lacks knowledge thereof. Nonetheless he is culpable and bears responsibility."[237] The Torah captures this situation's dual nature. On the one hand the man lacks mental clarity with regard to his act—hence the deed was an accident because "he lacks knowledge thereof." Yet at the same time it appears as if he acted purposely, willfully. The latter sentiment is evidenced by the phrase "nonetheless he is culpable and bears responsibility."

The sages describe the following case.[238] A man has before him one piece of meat that is kosher, the other not. He knows that he ate one of the pieces, but he doesn't know from which category he partook. Thus, he brings a qualified or conditional guilt offering, pending further probe into the matter. Guilt is a strong word, yet appropriate owing to the fact that the man was not more careful. Fittingly, "he brings an unblemished ram from the flock according to the value of a guilt offering."[239]

"And he did not know and will be forgiven."[240] Pardon is granted since the man lacked full knowledge of his deed. An *asham talui* serves that purpose. However, by deduction, had he ample awareness, then his sacrifice would have to be a sin and not guilt offering. This point raises a question. Namely, if a man was clueless about having sinned, why is he obligated to bring even a conditional guilt offering? The Torah's answer is forthcoming. "It is a guilt offering. He definitely offended the Almighty."[241] God knows that the man transgressed. Consequently, his ram offering is warranted.

It should be noted that this second section called *asham talui* does not make note of a financial fine of paying for the principal plus one fifth. Since this matter only concerns a Jew and his Maker regarding whether he ate or did not eat prohibited food, there is no point to assessing damage by valuing and then adding a twenty-percent penalty.

Having concluding our remarks about these two types of guilt offerings, there is one outstanding passage to explain. It concerns monetary matters.

---

237. Vayikra 5:17.
238. Source could not be located.
239. Vayikra 5:18.
240. Ibid.
241. Vayikra 5:19.

"And Hashem spoke to Moshe, saying: A soul when it sins and acted treacherously by God's name…"[242] Specifically, these are cases whereby a man deceitfully invokes the Lord's name for the purpose of evading or obstructing legal proceedings. This undermines his fellow Jew's desire and pursuit of evidence or testimony. Several instances of treachery are recorded in the verses. "And he denies [possession of] his fellow's property or kept lent money or stolen goods or wronged his fellow or lied about finding a lost object. And he swore in vain about any one of the aforementioned social and commercial things."[243] To better understand, examples of these cases follow.

Denying possession refers to a man lying by claiming that he never held his friend's property which was given over to him to watch or guard. Significantly, that transfer had been a private affair and had not taken place in the presence of witnesses. Keeping lent money means that duplicity occurred as a result of having borrowed cash from his friend. Stolen goods here represent a departure from the first two modi operandi of the unsavory person. This is where a man violently grabs property belonging to another. It may also include scheming or scamming, whereby goods were obtained deviously. Importantly, utilizing cockeyed accounting practices fits this bill. Continuing, there is the case of a man who found a lost object and had a Torah obligation to return it to the rightful owner, yet failed to do so. Instead, he swore under oath that he didn't find it. In any of those cases or similar ones, a man willfully lied under oath. Crucially, if he inadvertently lied, he would not be liable for punishment.

If a man is guilty of any of the crimes recorded, the Torah says, "He must pay the principal" to the owners "and add one-fifth for the one to whom it belonged, restoring it on the day of his guilt."[244] The timing teaches that the thief returns ill-gained property when he comes to seek atonement for his malfeasance.

Additionally, reparations are due to Hashem. "And his guilt offering he brings to the Almighty."[245] Lying under oath which tagged God's name to it brought his character shame and calumny.

---

242. Vayikra 5:20–21.
243. Vayikra 5:21–24.
244. Vayikra 5:24.
245. Vayikra 5:25.

"And he shall be forgiven for any offense that he committed."[246] This clarifies that in the event that he denied and lied to one hundred victims, he must bring one hundred offerings in order to attain atonement. We learn from this a special law that governs business matters. That is, where false oaths and cover-up are included, it is called a willful and not an accidental act. A separate and distinct verse corroborates that key point.[247]

---

246. Vayikra 5:26.
247. Abravanel does not specify what that verse is.

PARASHAT TZAV

HASHEM'S ALTAR: A BRIDGE

First *aliyah*

> *"And Hashem said to Moshe, saying:*
> *Command Aharon and his sons, saying:*
> *These are the laws concerning burnt offerings.*
> *It is the burnt offering [placed] upon the pyre*
> *on top of the altar for the entire night until the morning.*
> *And an altar fire constantly burns on it."*

Recall that in Parashat Vayikra, Moshe addressed the Hebrew general assembly. That was because the *parashah* dealt with and focused on categories of the populace needing to bring sacrifices. In contrast, here the Torah highlights Aharon and his sons, as Moshe instructed them in proper procedures. After all, they were entrusted with officiating in the Mishkan. Some tasks were performed by Aharon the Kohen Gadol, while others were done by Aharon's sons. They were subordinate to him. "Command Aharon and his sons."[1]

"These are the laws concerning burnt offerings."[2] Beginning this *parashah*'s discussion with burnt offerings makes eminent sense. Most sublime and exalted are the teachings they invoke. Indeed, they capture man's profound religious yearning and potential. Apropos, Parashat Vayikra also began its discussion on sacrifices that way. Our *parashah* validates burnt offerings' prominence as if Heaven goads man: *If only Jews reached proficient spiritual levels so that they only brought burnt offerings—but not sin or guilt offerings—to the Mishkan!*

By no means is this *parashah*'s discussion of sacrifices simply a replica of the previous *parashah*. One example of the divergence of the two *parshiyot* is the order in which sacrifices are listed. In Parashat Vayikra, verses take up the topic of peace offerings before sin and guilt offerings. Here, however, sin and

---

1. Vayikra 6:2.
2. Ibid.

guilt offerings precede peace offerings. Why? There logic dictated that order, as written in Parashat Vayikra's fourth *aliyah* as well as our prolegomenon. Presently, verses speak about those sacrifices designated as holy of holies or *kodshei kodashim*. In this way, burnt offerings as well as sin and guilt and gift offerings share that prestigious appellation. Peace offerings are categorized as "lesser" or "lighter" sacrifices, or *kodashim kalim*.[3] Later in this first *aliyah* when dealing with gift offerings, the Torah is explicit. "It is holy of holies— like a sin or guilt offering."[4] In sum, this *parashah*'s modus operandi begins discussion with those most holy sacrifices before moving on to those known as lighter or lesser ones. Textual juxtaposition of burnt, gift, sin, and guilt offerings followed by peace offerings effectively conveys the point.

Alternatively, there is another rationale at play to explain a seemingly inconsistent treatment of the various sacrifices. This we can deduce through a close examination of the Ramban's commentary on the verse "And the Kohen who offers a man's burnt offering."[5] In fact, this passage's law applies to some sacrifices mentioned above (e.g., burnt and sin offerings), to the exclusion of others (peace offerings). Note how the priest's role appears sandwiched between various sacrifices (after sin and guilt offerings and before peace offerings). Our earlier question resurfaces there. Namely, for style consistency the Torah should have written about peace offerings after burnt, sin, and guilt offerings. By rearranging the various types of offerings, our verses allude to a sharp division. Priests' activities consist of one set of procedures for burnt, sin, and guilt offerings and yet another set for peace offerings. Highlighting the priests' angle, then, is crucial. Punctuating their role provides pivotal clues to accurately portray the different natures of sacrifices. That is, the Torah lists one set of sacrifices (burnt, sin, and guilt offerings) followed by priestly instruction ("And the Kohen who offers"). Trailing afterwards are verses dealing with peace offerings.

"These are the laws concerning burnt offerings."[6] This verse is not introducing definitive rules and regulations concerning burnt offerings. Instead, what follows is a set of specific, tailored laws for the public daily afternoon

---

3. Abravanel notes here that Ramban takes a similar approach to this issue in his comments to 6:18 below.
4. Vayikra 7:6–7.
5. Vayikra 7:8.
6. Vayikra 6:2.

sacrifice. For the duration of the entire night, it burns upon the altar. Readers need to view this verse as one that supplements and complements the section on burnt offerings that we find in the first chapter of Parashat Vayikra. That is, the Torah expects readers to go back to the earlier *parashah*, study the applicable laws on the burnt offering, and apply them here in our *parashah*. These *parshiyot* are the main body of literature surrounding all burnt offerings.

"It is the burnt offering."[7] After generalizations, our verse sheds light on particulars. Namely, divine direction calls on priests to make sure that the afternoon communal burnt offering roasts throughout the night. It lays down permission to allow flames to lick the afternoon burnt offering all night. This detail had not been broached in Parashat Vayikra. Moreover, no discussion whatsoever regarding public burnt offerings—neither the morning nor afternoon animal—had been elucidated in this *sefer*'s first *parashah*. "It is the burnt offering." By so referencing, this verse further propounds laws introduced in Sefer Shemot: "And this is what you shall do on the altar...you shall do one sheep in the morning and one in the afternoon...a burnt offering forever."[8] Because of those verses in Shemot, our verse here highlights, "It is the burnt offering." These and all Tanach verses must be constructed in a comprehensive and integrated fashion.

The Torah tells us explicitly that meat of the afternoon burnt offering may burn on the altar for the entire night. An allowance for burning the morning sacrifice all day is conspicuously missing. Why? Because the fact that the meat of the morning offering may burn all day is obvious. Why shouldn't it? But night is a succeeding calendar day from the previous afternoon's burnt offering. Hence we might have thought that the Torah put a limitation on how long into the next day the afternoon offering may stay on the altar. This is why it is only regarding that offering that the Torah needs to state explicitly that it may burn on the altar throughout the night.

Establishing that the whole night was within an acceptable time frame provided that textual assurance. Thus for example, our verse clarifies that a Sunday morning burnt offering roasts on the altar all day. That Sunday afternoon a second public daily offering is made well before sunset. Sundown, the verse spells out, does not require priests to remove the animal from the altar,

---

7.   Ibid.
8.   Shemot 29:38, 39, 42.

but rather teaches that residual animal body parts may burn continually until Monday sunrise.

"And the priest dons his linen garment—his linen trousers he shall wear on his body."[9] The Ramban writes that the removal of the altar ashes or *terumat hadeshen* (תרומת הדשן, literally raising of the ashes) must be performed while a Kohen wears his official clothing, and moreover, this activity requires him to be fully decked out in his priestly wardrobe. Note that the Torah here only lists two of his four priestly articles, as it says, "his linen garment…his linen trousers." Students should not erringly conclude that officiating Kohanim need remove altar ashes with partial ceremonial dress. Only two are written explicitly because that affords readers an opportunity to glean a clearer understanding of the priest's strict dress code. Divine demand not only requires priests to wear trousers, but his trousers must correctly fit his frame. Hence, if a Kohen's linen pants are too short and do not reach his feet, it impinges upon his Mikdash work. More than that, ill-tailored clothing disqualifies that work. The Ramban winds up his remarks by saying that no undergarments may interpose between a Kohen's official clothing and his flesh.

Essentially, there are two steps to ash removal, and both are explicit in this passage. First is *terumat hadeshen*, which declares the obligation to remove ashes. It refers to charred sacrificial remains on the top section of the altar. Daily, those remains get raked or removed from the top of the altar before being placed near the altar's ramp. "And he places it next to the altar."[10] Phase 2 is when a priest carries out excess ashes, a process called *hotzaat hadeshen* (הוצאת הדשן), as it says, "And he removes the ashes beyond the encampment to a pure place."[11]

The Ramban's words certainly ring true. But why are these two laws (no undergarments and well-fitting garments) promulgated here as opposed to in other Torah passages? The reason has to do with this particular form of Mikdash activity—removal of altar ashes. Some readers might frown upon the apparent menial drudgery of carrying away charred ashes for interment near the ramp. By wearing knee-length knickers instead of normally tailored linen pants, an officiating priest might preserve cleanliness. Additionally, undergarments could keep soot from sticking to his person and thus maintain

9.   Vayikra 6:3.
10.   Ibid.
11.   Vayikra 6:4.

his personal hygiene. To forestall these potential misunderstandings, the verse writes two important laws at this juncture.

Targum Onkelos comments that the words "and the priest dons his linen garment" are meant to be read in a general sense, intimating all articles of a priest's clothing. The *Targum's* approach has three flaws. One, if his linen garment or *mido bad* (מדו בד) is all-inclusive, then how does one single linen material convey other raiment consisting of different fabric? See Sefer Shemot, which states, "and the *avnet* was made of *shesh, mashzar*, and *techelet* and *argaman* and *tolaat shani*—all embroidered."[12] This was the prescribed material for "Aharon and his sons." Second, if "linen garment" points to additional clothing, then at a minimum the Torah should have utilized the plural form of the word "linen" (מדיו and not the singular מדו). And third, if "his linen garment" signaled more vestments, then the verse would not have had to specify that the priest wore his linen pants directly upon his flesh.

Though these three points seem to present difficulties for the *Targum's* commentary, they don't. Here is a way to reframe and restate his comments. Perhaps the term *mido* is in singular owing to Tanach style, which often refers to objects or categories of things that way. Two examples are "this that is glorious in his apparel" or *zeh hadur bilvusho* (זה הדור בלבושו)[13] and "for my vestment they cast lots" or *v'al levushi yapilu goral* (ועל לבושי יפילו גורל).[14] In that light, let us reexamine our verse, "his linen trousers he shall wear on his body" or *u'michnesei bad yilbash al besaro* (ומכנסי בד ילבש על בשרו). This latter phrase stresses that no garment may come between a priest and his bare flesh. But moving forward in the verse, although it says *mido bad* in the singular, the singular refers to a category of people and not to one individual; this verse teaches that removal of altar ashes may be performed by subordinate priests. This clarification is important, since another verse may confuse readers: "Command Aharon and his sons [*banav*/בניו]."[15]

Perhaps someone might erringly submit an interpretation whereby ash removal to the ramp is the sole domain and responsibility of a Kohen Gadol, but that ash removal beyond the Mikdash confines may also be performed by an associate Kohen. For a false proof, this speculation continues, they would

12. Shemot 39:29.
13. Yeshayahu 63:1.
14. Tehillim 22:19.
15. Vayikra 6:2.

bring an upcoming verse: "And he removed his clothes."[16] Surely this refers to the Kohen Gadol taking off all of his eight articles. "And he puts on other clothing."[17] Are not, the misdirected fellow professes, the four garments worn by subordinate priests?

Such misinterpretation of Torah is swiftly dispelled. "And the priest dons his linen garment—his linen trousers he shall wear on his body." In fact, all aspects of ash removal may be done by Kohanim wearing white linen. To conclude, ash removal is not the sole purview of a Kohen Gadol. Though this reading is helpful in providing an alternative understanding of the *Targum*, Rashi's explanation is better. He says that the word "his linen" or *mido* (מדו) means his tunic or *ketonet* (כתונת).

"He shall wear on his body." It is likely that this instruction has two applications. Both the Kohen's linen and his linen pants must rest on his body without any interference.

"It is the burnt offering [placed] upon the pyre on top of the altar for the entire night until the morning." One might presume that after the Torah specifies that the burnt offering burns all night, it is superfluous to conclude with the words "until the morning." Actually, that phrase adds two things. First, these words convey that an animal's innards may continue roasting even after the sun rises. Still, those crispy innards do fall into the prohibited category of leftover sacrificial meat or *notar* (נותר) and as such become strictly forbidden to eat or enjoy. Textual proof: "In the morning it must be burned."[18] Second, removal of the ashes may not be done at night, since the Torah requests that they smolder until daybreak. Now, if the verse had stopped short and had not spelled out "until the morning," it would imply that priests should scoop up the ashes that night. "Until the morning" sets the priestly instruction right.

"And he shall pick up the ashes that were consumed by the fire—the burnt offering upon the altar."[19] The following is what the Ramban explains on the verse "when a *nasi* sins."[20] In Hebrew, the term *asher* (אשר) is versatile and has several nuances. Sometimes it means "when"; an example is "when Yosef came

---

16. Vayikra 6:4.
17. Ibid.
18. Shemot 12:10.
19. Vayikra 6:3.
20. Vayikra 4:22.

to his brothers,"[21] or later in Bereshit, "when they finished eating."[22] Examples of that definition abound in Tanach. This is how we explained "when a *nasi* sins," even though the Hebrew letter *kaf* (כ), usually found in the expression *ka'asher*, meaning "when," is missing. Often a *kaf* is dropped, though its meaning is not affected and must be understood as if it had been written.[23]

This grammatical point brings us to our verse. "And he shall pick up the ashes which (*asher*) were consumed." These particles of speech (which, who, that, etc.) are called connectors or relative pronouns. Conventionally and for our purposes, commonly in Tanach, letters get dropped or omitted from certain words, though students are advised to read those seemingly truncated words as if prefixes or suffixes appeared.

Priests removed ashes from a burning altar pyre. Scripture conveys as much in one verse that states, "And he shall pick up the ashes."[24] Another verse reads, "and the fire shall continually burn upon on the altar."[25] Thus, we must deduce that even while ashes were being removed to the altar's ramp, the altar's fire burned.

Unlike Ramban, who understands it as "when," Rashi's commentary to our verse understands the word *asher* as "which." The literal sense of the verse is "He will remove the ashes which the fire has consumed the burnt offering." It means, "He will remove the ashes which are the result of the fire consuming the burnt offering." According to Rashi, the verse tells us that a Kohen removes ashes from the part of the offering that has been most consumed by the fire. Which part? The part toward the interior of the altar's surface which has already been consumed. Obviously, the outer parts or those further from the fire would still be burning. But this is so only because, as we have pointed out, the altar fire does not burn meat evenly. The interior parts, closer to the heat, begin to ashen while the outer parts only later begin to show the effects. Hence, our interpretation of "He will remove the [inner] ashes" conveys this practical Mikdash information. Our explanation is pleasing. We need not resort to Rashi's forced reading of the verse. To conclude, by translating the

---

21. Bereshit 37:23.
22. Bereshit 43:2.
23. E.g., Devarim 11:27, Shemot 34:18.
24. Vayikra 6:3.
25. Vayikra 6:5.

term *asher* as "at which time" or "when" (i.e., as the Hebrew word *ka'asher* [כאשר]), we read how ashes were relocated at the time they came into being.

Moving on, let us make another point. Lacking here is a descriptive term found in Parashat Vayikra (though in the context of a bird offering's crop and feathers). "And he tosses it beside the altar—eastward" or *kadimah* (קדמה).[26] This does not represent a difficulty, because Heaven's directive had previously been issued. "And he tosses it besides the altar—eastward—next to the place where the ashes were."[27]

Fairly, students wonder why location is learned by deduction here, but explicitly when discussing bird burnt offerings. Surely this is where the Torah should have chosen to impart that key piece of information. Should Scripture have sufficed to give vague instructions with the bird offering, it would have been adequate to write along the lines of "And he tossed it next to the altar, to the place where altar ashes lay." What was important about specifying the altar's eastern exposure for the bird's crop and feathers?

Here is the answer. Mentioning the altar's eastern flank served in a manner of speaking to deride the eastern direction as a whole. This disparaging dismissal of one of the world's four directions (north, south, east, and west) had in mind a silly notion then prevalent among ancient pagans, those religiously impaired primitives. Moral troglodytes bowed down to the sun, treating it as a deity. In deference to the great ball of fire's emergence on the horizon, they prostrated themselves to the east as if that particular direction on a weathervane portended power.

The Ralbag corroborates this idea. He writes that the ashes were put on the east side of the altar, adding that they were on the bottom, for that was where day's first sun rays shone. In order to forestall folks from attributing the placement to sun worship, the preponderance of prominent activities took place in the west. Only relatively second-rate, lesser tasks were relegated to the Temple's eastern wing. That explains why the bird offering's nape and feathers were deposited there.

"And he removed his clothes and donned other garments and he removed the ashes beyond the encampment to a clean place."[28] This verse clarifies that a Kohen may not skip steps by taking ashes directly from the altar to the

26. Vayikra 1:16.
27. Ibid.
28. Vayikra 6:4.

designated spot beyond the Mikdash confines. Proof of this is the fact that the first leg of the ashes' journey, if you will, must be to the altar's base, while an officiating priest dons his finest raiment. Contrast that law with another that dictates a priest need not put on fancy vestments to march ashes out of the Mishkan.

Note that should a priest sidestep both prescribed directives, a fallout ensues. One, he will have taken out ashes in his most elegant priestly garments, or two, he may have performed the first removal in inappropriate "work clothing." Both outcomes are best avoided, since they are undesirable and inappropriate.

"And he removed the ashes beyond the encampment to a clean place." Significantly in the passage dealing with the bird burnt offering, the Torah does not say that priests carried out its crop or feathers. This piques our curiosity as to whether or not there were remaining crops and feathers in the first place. However, when it came to leftover ashes, no such doubt ever surfaced. Ashes most certainly did remain over. Also, it is likely that the bird's nape and plume had been soiled with dirt or debris. In that case, gnarly body parts were mixed with altar's ashes and were removed in toto.

The altar ashes, the Torah says, were removed "to a clean place." Our verse is vague. Was there a designated ash heap somewhere? Was that suggested by "a clean place"? Similarly unclear is whether or not a bird's crop and feathers were ignominiously dumped for ravens, buzzards, or other scavengers to wolf down.

To gain perspective and focus, let us recall the means of disposition commanded in the case of the High Priest's bull offering: "And he removes the whole bull beyond the camp confines to a pure place—where the ashes are spilled—and burns it on the wood in a fire. Where the ashes are spilled they shall be burned."[29] Rashi learns the words "and he shall remove the ashes" to mean that a pile or bulge of ashes formed, essentially overcrowding the altar's limited workspace.

Let us clarify. Rashi holds that although *terumat hadeshen*, removal of the ashes, was a daily mitzvah, it was not incumbent upon priests to do a spic-and-span cleaning. Detailed debris removal occurred on an as-needed basis.

---

29. Vayikra 4:12.

In order to alleviate ash buildup upon the altar, it was decreed an obligation to thin out the pile daily. Ash debris was placed near the east exposure of the altar's ramp. Of course with time, an ash hill not only filled a cavity specifically dug for this purpose, but even began to mount higher and higher. At the priest's discretion, he would scoop it all up before carrying it outside the Mishkan confines. Undoubtedly, that cavity contained an admixture of bird body parts (crop and feathers) plus altar ashes. Also it is understood that an area had been designated outside the Mishkan, serving as a biodegradable composter. Thus, priests always returned to the same spot in order to dump collected bird body parts and ashes. Ultimately, it became mulch prior to reabsorption into the earth's topsoil. The Ralbag states the location lay east of the camp. Later when the Mishkan and Beit Hamikdash stood, the places where these altar by-products were buried lay east of the respective host cities (Shiloh, Nov, Givon, and Yerushalayim).

In a short span of this *aliyah's* first seven verses, we observe a common refrain. "And the fire burned continually upon the altar."[30] Compare this with "And the fire shall continually burn upon the altar—it shall not be extinguished."[31] And yet a third verse has it as "A continual fire shall burn on the altar—it shall not be extinguished."[32] All three distinct expressions are imperative. Here are the reasons.

One, ample wood must be on hand atop the altar every evening so that it will burn an entire night until the morning. At daybreak, that fire must still be ablaze. Two, priests are cautioned to make sure that the fire burns even as they collect altar ashes. This stands in direct contrast to other "institutional cooks" who douse fires from stoves or ovens in the morning. Typically, they extinguish their cooking pits' fires and begin anew when they return to their work. Third, there are two possible instructions that may be either jointly or severally applicable. The wood placed on the altar in the morning likely sufficed to burn all day. That was the case whether or not a particular day had normal traffic (read: standard number of public sacrifices) or if things got particularly hectic on the altar. This is deduced from the verse "and he offered upon it the fatty [parts of the] peace offerings."[33] Rashi elucidates that

---

30. Vayikra 6:2.
31. Vayikra 6:5.
32. Vayikra 6:6.
33. Vayikra 6:5.

Kohanim paid close attention to the altar's calendar or log book. When they anticipated a heavy workload, they arranged for extra wood to burn. This provided assurances that all sacrifices got thoroughly barbequed.

"And the Kohen burned wood upon it every single morning. And he arranged the burnt offering upon it and he offered upon it the fatty [parts of the] peace offerings."[34] The thrice-recurring phrase demanding priests to burn animal parts upon the altar seems redundant: and…burned upon it or *u'vi'er aleha* (ובער עליה), and…arranged upon it or *v'arach aleha* (וערך עליה), and… offered upon it or *v'hiktir aleha* (והקטיר עליה). Here is a possible explanation. When the Torah says, "and he offered upon it," it refers to burnt offerings. This makes sense in light of a peace offering verse in Parashat Vayikra. There it is written, "And Aharon's sons offered a burnt offering on top of the altar."[35]

Note our verse. "And he arranged."[36] Divine directive instructs priests to place burnt offerings on the altar's wood. Regularly in Parashat Vayikra, verses say that the arrangement of the animal's organs is conveyed in terms of placement on the wood but not on the fire. Given that detail, when our verse states, "And the Kohen burned wood upon it every single morning," it stands to reason that placement on the fire is implied. This is borne out by a verse: "And they arranged wood upon the fire and placed the burnt offering upon it."[37] Deduce that this refers to the altar's wood pile, as another verse says, "And the priest arranged them upon the wood and offered upon it the fatty parts of the peace offering."[38] Read that this modified instructions for burnt offerings.

In the following way does Rashi clarify the phrase "And he offered upon it the fatty [parts of the] peace offerings": when people bring peace offerings, priests need to offer their fatty parts on top of the burnt offering roasting on the altar.

Naturally, students ask why our verse limits talk to peace offerings yet seemingly skips over sin and guilt offerings. How striking, especially considering that all three sacrifices share common laws. Here are two reasons. First, it is inappropriate to roast sin or guilt offerings after burnt offerings when

---

34. Ibid.
35. Vayikra 3:5.
36. Vayikra 6:5.
37. Vayikra 1:7.
38. Vayikra 1:12.

they were brought by one man for one situation. Proof of this is evidenced by a verse: "And he sacrifices first on behalf of the sin offering."[39] Second, our verse intended to teach a generality in conjunction with peace offerings. This is due to their designation as sacrifices brought by righteous individuals. Extrapolating a given principle to sin offerings gives a wrong message. Heaven offers a prayer, as it were, that Jews not find themselves bringing sacrifices alluding to unbefitting conduct. This concludes a straightforward approach to our passage.

Talmudic sages relate that Shacharit (the morning prayer service) was established in order to commemorate the two daily burnt offerings in the Mikdash.[40] Scriptural allusions to the evening, morning, and afternoon prayers in this *parashah* give rise to the sages' words. "It is the burnt offering upon the fire on the altar all night until morning"[41] alludes to evening prayers. "And the priest shall burn wood upon it every morning"[42] hints at morning prayers. Immediately afterwards the Torah specifies, "This is the law of gift offerings. The sons of Aharon bring it."[43] This takes afternoon prayers into account.

The *Kuzari* shares these resplendent insights.[44] To paraphrase, it advances that during a man's day, his most sublime moments include those times spent in prayer. Shabbat stands alone among the seven days of the week, thus Shabbat supplication allows man to strive and forge greater connectedness with the Creator. This spiritual template or beckoning models a physical one. Namely, prayer for man's soul may be likened to nourishing food for his body. When he prays at night, it lifts and ennobles his soul, the effect of which persists well beyond the particular deed. In man's physical realm, his stomach remains sated and satisfied long after a good dinner. Will it not suffice him until the morning light? Surely, he is content until breakfast.

What is the *Kuzari* imparting? It teaches that man's love and affection for God remains with him from the time of one prayer service to the subsequent one. In this way, prayer should be viewed as a continuum of man's highest expression of displaying love for Hashem. Fire is an image at the center of the

---

39. Vayikra 5:8.
40. BT *Berachot* 26b.
41. Vayikra 6:2.
42. Vayikra 6:5.
43. Vayikra 6:7.
44. *Kuzari*, chapter 43.

Kuzari's metaphor. To quote, "For love is as intense as death, jealousy as cruel as Hell. Its blaze is flames of fire—divine inferno."[45] In our context, ardent and everlasting love expressed by Jews for their Almighty One gets renewed nightly with evening prayers. Intense passion remains steady in place until the next morning. That is when Jews arise to greet their Maker for morning prayers. In our passage, this sublime message is insinuated. "It is the burnt offering upon the fire on the altar—all night until the morning. And the fire of the altar burns."

Borrowing from the *Kuzari's* grand disquisition, we can insert a marvelous working model for our entire *parashah*. "This is the law concerning the burnt offering." Allusion to an eternal, rational soul is made. Verily, it corresponds to the ever-rising burnt offering. Axiom: Man's divine soul yearns to cleave harmoniously with God. "It is the burnt offering upon the fire on the altar all night." Here, profound religious sentiment lodges by conveying how spirituality works. Piety, then, is pursuit of passion symbolized by the altar. Ideally, man experiences otherworldly fervor during the night, a time metaphorically and generally associated with his baser side. Dark thoughts and machinations, habitués of pitch-black night, escape. But man can develop his altruistic side. When he purges stalking shadows, when he wrestles and subdues lubricious leanings, he rids himself of moral muck. He builds a spiritual altar. Burned in a holy pyre at night, he shimmies free with morning's dawn. Eternity belongs to him.

The Mishkan's altar tells this story of a soul's triumph. Holy sparks fuel man's exploration. An epic love story, this rich imagery captures man's highest aspirations vis-à-vis his bond with the One Above. And this trek takes place deep within a man's breast.

Consider God's altar. Fat burns on it. So too it is with man's heart. Adipose tissue envelopes heart muscles. Just as an altar fire consumes animal fat surrounding organs, so too does proper conduct and *kavanah* desiccate unwanted flab. Service to God offers catharsis to humans' predisposition to perpetuate conventional concoctions.

Still, there is an available antidote and a game-changing bill of fare. Essentially it boils down to a conscious regime of practicing forthright behavior while casting out the kind that Heaven disrelishes. To revert back to the verse,

---

45. Shir Hashirim 8:6.

"And the priest dons his linen garment."[46] This encourages man to officiate and serve the Almighty as a means of retooling character traits. Undesirable personality attributes become attenuated; by wearing priestly breeches, he clothes what had been mercilessly exposed vacuity and bareness.

"And he removes the ashes which the fire has consumed."[47] This affirms how man is ultimately responsible for controlling and reining in base notions leading to exaggerated physical pursuits. The bane of man, these are residual ashes. As man shows more love for God, he sheds those underlying causes of unflattering conduct which are anathema to Him. Analysis of the Hebrew term "ashes" or *deshen* (דשן) reveals as much. See the verse "And he eats, and is satisfied and grows tubby."[48] Clearly, it is a reference to unhinged human libido.

"And the burnt offering."[49] This verse teaches how an innate yearning to bond builds bridges to God. The sentiment may be likened to that altar fire propelling burnt offerings toward Heaven. Again, allusion points to a divine soul climbing ever higher, hoping to break free of the limitations of its physical casings and cling to the Divine.

"And he places it near the altar."[50] Suppression of evil thought and sexual lust is, at least hypothetically, buried at the altar's base. Man's heart functions as his altar, where he identifies and confronts concupiscence. King Shlomoh put it this way: "Living men need to place this upon their hearts."[51] Since the heart is the seat and source of eros, it is that control center which grapples and contends with it and subjugates it. "All the heart's desires dwell on mischief each day."[52]

"And he dons other garments."[53] Faithful servants of the Almighty need to wear fresh clothing. Figuratively, this is not referring to dress but rather to adorning oneself with noble bearing. This presupposes approaching mundanity with a grain of salt.

Until now in our passage, verses highlighted a priest putting on his linen pants. Recall that in a deeper sense, they depicted the attainment of exemplary

---

46. Vayikra 6:3.
47. Ibid.
48. Devarim 31:20.
49. Vayikra 6:3.
50. Ibid.
51. Kohelet 7:2.
52. Bereshit 6:5.
53. Vayikra 6:4.

conduct. In Judaism, this is generally achieved through the pursuit of fair balance or moderation. That can be called step 1. Following that comes a period of contemplation, which leads to recognizing human underpinnings of base desires. Step 2, then, envisions man changing old clothes for new ones as he opts for more otherworldliness. Altar ashes (read: flabby moral fiber and mindless distraction) must not only be carried out beyond the Mishkan parameters but also removed to a clean, designated spot. Tellingly, disposing of the ashes to a filthy area is prohibited.

Life's task is an invitation to seek inner harmony, a wholesomeness associated with love of God. Emphasizing that fundamental, the verse states, "And the fire burns upon the altar—it does not get extinguished."[54] Man's heart, ideally, brims with love for Heaven—twenty-four/seven. Making piety his moral pointer parallels priests preparing a steady wood supply for the altar. Arranging fresh wood every morning is one of the officiating Kohen's routines. Repositories of faith, knowledge, and sage counsel, these embody a priestly caste, a tribe set apart from all others. *Tzaddikim*, like a fresh breeze, breathe inspiration into their co-religionists.

Alternatively, the verse "And the Kohen arranges wood upon it every morning" evokes morning prayers. This is the sage's opinion, holding that when man's love for the Almighty fills his heart, he arises each morning and offers prayer to Him. See *ahavah rabbah* in the daily prayer book.[55] Burnt offerings personify man's spiritual side, his soul. Through this worship, he discovers pathways to the Infinite One.

"And he offers fatty peace offerings upon it."[56] Embedded within this verse's message is this: When a man masters these heady lessons, concretizing them into overt behavior; when he fuses his heart and will in love for God; when he divorces himself from nagging emptiness and niggling smut, then we behold a man girded to approach the altar. This is a man fully capable of offering to Hashem, imbued with affection for the Holy One. His service and his body and his fulfilment in partaking of this world are all healthily in sync.

Interestingly enough, though the *tzaddik* brings peace offerings, and perforce partakes in his share of the meat, we need to qualify something. Hashem's true servant, insofar as each fiber of his being communes with God, does not

---

54. Vayikra 6:6.
55. BT *Berachot* 26b.
56. Vayikra 6:5.

upend or even mildly detract from an intimate relationship with the Divine. The *tzaddik*'s inner fire, ever ablaze and atremble, maintains single-minded dedication; it is his *idée fixe*.

Furthermore, considerable amounts of his divine service consist of timely prayers murmured. They are, according to the Talmudic sage, each evening and morning. "And this is the law regarding gift offerings which Aharon's sons offer before Hashem."[57] Seeing that afternoon prayer services find favor before the Maker, and considering how Tanach records that this afternoon time slot hit the mark on behalf of the prophet Eliyahu, our verse states "before Hashem." Propitious best describes that window of opportunity, as it is written, "And it was when the gift arose and Eliyahu approached."[58] No such special dispensation is recorded for burnt, sin, guilt, or peace offerings. Indeed, afternoon prayers—those median meditative moments between Shacharit and Maariv—curry much favor.

In conclusion, we have provided two poignant approaches for our discerning readers. Powerful insights may be gleaned by dedicated and tenacious thinkers. The first one followed a straightforward model; the latter pierced esoterica's realm. Accept them as goodly gifts from Above.

"And this is the law regarding gift offerings" or *minchah* (מנחה). Notice how this prefatory remark differs from language adopted in those passages discussing burnt offerings. "This is the law regarding burnt offerings. It is the burnt offering."[59] Here, however, no such repetition is found. Similarly, we do not find reiteration in Torah verses concerning sin, guilt, or peace offerings, either. The reason for the extra burnt offering phrase is that this verse pertains to laws concerning afternoon gift offerings, as explained above. For that reason, it adds, "It is the burnt offering." Afternoon public burnt offerings are distinct from both private gift burnt offerings and public morning ones. But when it comes to gift, sin, guilt, or peace offerings, they are the selfsame ones mentioned in Parashat Vayikra. Hence, no verbal marker is needed to draw distinctions. Phrases such as "It is the gift offering" or "It is the sin offering" only make sense when one kind or subcategory of that particular sacrifice is being highlighted to the exclusion of others.

---

57. Vayikra 6:7.
58. I Melachim 18:36.
59. Vayikra 6:2.

For this *parashah*, the Ramban's comments are plain and straightforward. Specifically, he enumerates four commandments concerning gift offerings: (a) matzah must be eaten, (b) it is eaten in the Tent of Meeting's courtyard, (c) Aharon's sons may partake of it, and (d) contact with property belonging to the Mishkan possesses power enough to turn a mundane object into a holy one. A *midrash* on this *parashah* delivers novel insights.[60] For example, a Kohen's gift offering is scooped using three designated fingers. Besides, he must serve it before the Almighty.

Phraseology plays a pivotal role in understanding Mishkan logistics. It has been determined, for example, that "before the Almighty" refers to the altar's western exposure, whereas when a verse states, "And toward the altar," it conveys the southern flank of the altar. However, a combination of both directional phrases conveys the southwest corner of the altar.

Direction-wise, it is understood that Kohanim first gained access to the altar by using the south and west as a starting point. For the record, Parashat Vayikra says, "And a soul when it brings a gift offering…"[61] This is followed by "And he pours oil upon it and places frankincense upon it." That resembles our verse. Then it continues: "And he scoops up its measure consisting of the gift offering's flour and its oil."[62]

Predictably, readers wonder why the grammatical construction of the word "frankincense" or *levonah* varies. Sometimes the word is associated with a possessive pronoun (i.e., "his"); other times it isn't. Compare the following. We reference Parashat Vayikra's paragraph beginning with "And when a man sacrifices a *minchah* offering."[63] There it is written, "And he pours upon it oil and places upon it frankincense."[64] Now contrast our nearly identical verse, "And he lifts from it his *kometz* from the refined flour of the *minchah* and from its oil, and all of the frankincense or *levonah* (לבנה)…"[65] Why doesn't the Torah say "from its frankincense" or *mi'levonatah* (מלבונתה)? In other words, why must the verse call for all of the *levonah* and not simply a dash of it?

---

60. See *Torat Kohanim* on Vayikra 6:7.
61. Vayikra 2:1–16.
62. Vayikra 2:2.
63. Vayikra 2:1–16.
64. Vayikra 2:1.
65. Vayikra 6:8.

Let us return to the words of the sages.[66] They deduce from the words "his filled *kometz*" or *m'lo kumtzo* (מלא קמצו) in Parashat Vayikra the following. If he had secured the cupping in his hand but then a little salt or *levonah* escaped from his grip, then the gift offering is disqualified.

Two more lessons emerge. One is that salt is added to the gift offering (recall that the Torah commands inclusion of salt, as it states, "And each gift offering sacrifice must be salted"[67]) before the officiating priest scoops his *kometz*. It needed to be put in one designated part of the gift offering mixture, just as was the case with the *levonah*. It, too, had a separate use apart from the *kometz*. Contrast that with the oil ingredient of the gift offering. This system of adding the gift offering's ingredients is derived from Rashi's comment on the words "And he pours oil upon it,"[68] meaning that oil is generously poured over the entire contents of the recipe. "And he puts frankincense on it" suggests that the spice is sparingly and gingerly applied. That first point about when the salt was added should be clear, because if it was placed after the *kamitzah*, it would be impossible to make that assertion. This is because of the law deduced that if salt fell from a priest's grip, the whole thing is ruined. The implication is that salt had been placed in the mixture at an earlier juncture. Also consider this: if salt had been liberally sprinkled on the surface of the entire recipe, it would not be possible to take hold of some of those salt granules.

"And the leftover from it shall be eaten by Aharon and his sons."[69] Here is a grammatical point. Whenever an object starts off as being whole—whether in its natural or contrived, artificial state—and then part gets lopped off from the original mass, that newly created sub-unit is called a leftover or remainder—*noter* (נותר). Furthermore, it makes no difference if the leftover is ninety or nine percent of the original. Proof is adduced when considering a gift offering. Though a palmful has been removed, that remainder is thus named. Consider another example from Sefer Bereshit: "Lavan's remaining flock."[70] Here is an instance when a full half has been severed from the original. A verse states, "To Elazar and to Itamar, his remaining sons."[71] And yet another example

---

66. *Torat Kohanim.*
67. Vayikra 2:13.
68. Vayikra 2:1.
69. Vayikra 6:9.
70. Bereshit 30:36.
71. Vayikra 10:12.

when the overwhelming first part has been cut away: "And the leftover until the morning."[72]

"And he offers a sweet aroma upon the altar as a commemoration to the Almighty."[73] It is fitting to analyze what the Torah means when it repeats (or omits) the refrain about how Heaven finds the different types of sacrifices so tantalizing. Count no fewer than four variant phrases. One is pleasing aroma or *reiach nichoach* (ריח ניחוח). It may appear by itself and is another way of saying fiery or *isheh* (אשה). To illustrate, see how the *minchah* is treated in our *parashah*: the term *reiach nichoach* appears alone.[74] Now, in Parashat Vayikra we find "*isheh reiach nichoach*."[75] We may generalize the following. Wherever the Torah says *isheh* alone, it is a substitute for *reiach nichoach*. To wit, we cite "and he offered from it his sacrifice, an *isheh* to God."[76] Afterward it says, "and the priest offered them on the altar—*lechem isheh* for a *reiach nichoach*."[77]

To continue this discussion, we move on to the passage pertaining to leavening and honey. "Do not offer from it as an *isheh* to God."[78] Consistent with our principle, we then read, "And upon the altar do not bring them up for a *reiach nichoach*."[79] Our proof is conclusive. Clearly, the two terms are interchangeable. If the Torah omits *isheh* and *reiach nichoach*, be assured that the offering does not make the cut in Heaven's eyes.

To illustrate the importance these terms convey, in Parashat Vayikra regarding bull burnt offerings, it says, "a fiery pleasant aroma before the Almighty." Similar verbiage goes for sheep, goat, or bird burnt offerings, and for gift offerings. Their commonality is that they all are brought voluntarily, and for the express purpose of fostering greater religiosity. Hence, those sacrifices are choice ones in God's eyes. Barbequed meat wafts irresistibly. Overall, the sacrificial act pleases the Maker.

Let us move to the subject of peace offerings consisting of bulls, sheep, or goats. "A fiery sweet aroma before the Almighty" signals that it is an exemplary

---

72. Shemot 12:10.
73. Vayikra 6:8.
74. Vayikra 6:8.
75. Vayikra 1:9.
76. Vayikra 3:14.
77. Vayikra 3:16.
78. Vayikra 2:11.
79. Vayikra 2:12.

gesture of probity. These too, recall, are brought in a spirit of pure altruism with no traces of fault or misdoing.

Contrast those above-referenced favorable categories with guilt or sin offerings. Since they are tainted and come to remedy ill-deeds, their fiery aspect is readily acknowledged, but not their sweetness before Heaven. This reflects the trying circumstances associated with sin or guilt offerings. God would surely dispense with this sacrificial gift, preferring man to shun sin.

Turning to sin offerings, when the proprietors were the Kohen Gadol, Sanhedrin, or *nasi*, the word *isheh* is omitted, as is *reiach nichoach*. Hashem considers any such situation that gave rise to sin offerings as most regrettable and reprehensible. But when we compare sin offerings of a common Jew, given that his transgression had not rated so rancorous, his sacrifice is described as "a pleasant aroma before the Almighty."[80] This conveys that a simple man's missteps do not cause, if you will, an uproar in Heaven. God acknowledges the comeliness of an individual's sin or guilt offerings.

Concluding, we observe that it is the intrinsic nature of a particular offering or sin that dictates how Heaven relates to its beauty or hideousness. Certainly in the case of our passage concerning gift offerings, Hashem views them in an unequivocally positive light on account of their having been brought in a spirit of lofty volunteerism. Verily, it is "a sweet aroma upon the altar as a commemoration to the Almighty."[81]

Rashi explains how this section must be extrapolated to include all gift offering types—especially gift offerings that Kohanim bring (and other kinds still not covered in the Torah). Let us return to our verse. "And the leftover from it shall be eaten by Aharon and his sons. In a holy place—in the courtyard's Tent of Meeting—matzot must be eaten."[82] These instructions are applicable in all cases of gift offerings, with the sole exception of those brought by priests. There they are wholly consumed on the altar and not by Kohanim, as we will learn in the next *aliyah*.

Our verse drives home two details. They are: (a) "in a holy place" and (b) "in the courtyard's Tent of Meeting." This is necessary because in the context of the Mishkan, a "holy place" is generic and relative. It may even include the holy of holies. To wit, see "With this Aharon must come to the

---

80. Vayikra 4:31.
81. Vayikra 6:8.
82. Vayikra 6:9.

holy [place]."[83] Clarification in the form of a second description, then, obviates uncertainty. Had the Torah only provided direction for Kohanim to eat "in the courtyard's Tent of Meeting," readers would not have gleaned a rationale for why Heaven deemed that venue fitting. Adding the words "in a holy place" gives proper perspective. Note that "in a holy place" is synonymous with another Torah phrase, "a place of holiness." This can be deduced from another verse: "Why didn't you eat the sin offering in a holy place?" or *bi'mekom hakodesh* (במקום הקדש).[84]

"It shall not be baked with leavening agents. Their portion I have distributed to them from My fiery offerings. Most sacrosanct, it is comparable to sin and guilt offerings."[85] This verse sheds light on the earlier one in two ways. When it is written here, "It shall not be baked with leavening agents," it conveys the reason Kohanim eat unleavened bread. Namely, it is considered a divine dish. Given that prestigious categorization, we view the priests as if they partake of food served on God's table. Just as matzah is considered Heaven's food, so too may Heaven's guests (priests) partake of that same bill of fare. Do not servants of royalty share what their royal employers dish out? For that reason but by contrast, first fruits or tithes may consist of either leavened or unleavened breads (e.g., first fruit wheat or barley). Why? They are not served upon a king's dining table (read: on the altar). However, gift offerings were brought, in toto, to the Regent's table (on the altar's southwest flank), and so the bread had to be unleavened per our verse's instruction. After the Kohen's hand-cupped portion had been taken and there were remainders, he ate. Apropos, he ate matzot, since they made up the gift offering brought to the altar.

Now we turn to the second reason gift offerings were eaten in a holy place. That was because "it is comparable to sin and guilt offerings." They too were eaten in a designated holy spot, as it is written, "in a holy place—in the courtyard's Tent of Meeting." Still, while gift offerings do share some halachic guidelines with sin and guilt offerings, they are far from identical. At the end of the day, sin and guilt offerings pull rank, fitting into the category of "holy of holies."

---

83. Vayikra 16:3.
84. Vayikra 10:17.
85. Vayikra 6:10.

Let us acknowledge a textual difficulty. The verse teaches that a *minchah* should be eaten in a holy place—just as is required with regard to sin and guilt offerings. The problem is that the Torah had not yet established that sin and guilt offerings are of the holiest nature or *kodshei kodashim*. Here is a way out of this dilemma. Our verse relies on information that will be imparted in verses below.[86]

Those ideas have been broached in our discussion relating to the half shekel or *machatzit hashekel* (מחצית השקל). That is, the Torah wrote "half a shekel based on a holy shekel was twenty *gerah* per shekel."[87] Yet up to that point, no mention had been made of a "holy shekel."

"Each male descendant of Aharon's sons may partake of it. It is an eternal enactment [because it derives] from God's fiery offering. Whatever touches it rises to sanctity."[88] The Torah stresses that priests' wives and daughters are prohibited from eating gift offerings. Furthermore, this is not an obligation for all of Aharon's descendants to partake of it, but rather those entitled priests who do eat it may only eat that portion allotted to them.

Second *aliyah*
> *"And Hashem said to Moshe, saying:*
> *This is Aharon and his sons' sacrifice*
> *that they offer to God on anointment day.*
> *[It consisted of] one-tenth of an* **eifah** *of gift offering flour—*
> *regularly. One half of it [brought] in the morning*
> *and one half of it in the evening."*

According to Rashi, subordinate priests were entrusted with the job of offering up gift offerings weighing one-tenth of an *eifah*. This occurred on the day of their induction to Mishkan service. In contrast, a High Priest offered this gift offering daily. To emphasize, our verse states that assistant priests brought gift offerings on their induction day. "This is Aharon and his sons' sacrifice that they offer to God." Since this covers the quintessential gift offering, a Kohen Gadol offered it daily beginning from the day he assumed his high office and

---

86. See Vayikra 6:18 and 7:1.
87. Shemot 30:13.
88. Vayikra 6:11.

performed that service thereafter. More exactly, the Torah orders him to bring half of the gift offering in the morning, with the second half in the evening.

Consequently and on the basis of this verse, the sages determined that two distinct gift offerings are alluded to.[89] One is for assistant Kohanim. It is a one-off event transpiring when they commence their Mishkan work. A second deduction concerns only High Priests. For them, it is a daily happening.

"In a pan, in oil, you shall bring it scalded."[90] Technical food preparation laws for gift offerings are being presented here. Those directives had not been imparted earlier. Specifically, these offerings had to be, according to halachic tradition, scalded in boiling water or *murbechet* (מרבכת) before being lightly baked until it becomes "baked pieces of *minchah* offering" or *tufinei minchat pittim* (תופיני מנחת פתים). In other words, baking occurred subsequent to the contents of the dough batter being boiled until jelled. "Brought as bread wafers, you shall offer a sweet aroma before the Almighty."[91] Baking had been done in an oil-greased flat pan.

"And the anointed priest, as his substitute, shall be from among his sons. He shall perform it."[92] The substitute discussed here comes from one of the Kohen Gadol's sons. Permission was granted so far as offering the gift offering upon the altar was concerned. Crucially, though, no cupping had been needed. That was because nothing was given over to the Kohanim to eat. Instead, "And all gift offerings brought by priests had to be entirely burned. None was permitted to be eaten."[93] Gift offerings were fully put to the flame, per the Torah's instructions.

The Rambam has supplied the rationale behind these commandments. Fully charring gift offerings belonging to Kohanim made sense. Had some of it emerged as edible and a Kohen eaten from it, the whole purpose would be defeated, as if no sacrifice had been proffered. Given these stakes, wholly consuming the gift offering was, of course, eminently logical. Metaphorically speaking, when subordinate Kohanim brought their personal gift offerings to commemorate their induction to the Mishkan, it was akin to a servant waiting on his master.

---

89. BT *Menachot* 21.
90. Vayikra 6:14.
91. Ibid.
92. Vayikra 6:15.
93. Ibid.

What can be said about daily gift offerings that a Kohen Gadol was bidden to bring? The following list counts nine reasons for bringing this offering.

1. **Moral rectitude.** Twice daily a Kohen Gadol engaged in soulful introspection, an uplifting constitutional. This dovetailed well with the sages' counsel bidding a man to first reach a considerable level of moral character before sermonizing to others to do so.[94] Of course, no man is a perfect angel. Still, Jews did look to High Priests as their role models. How fitting, then, that the High Priest actuated and personified man's quest for excellence. Daily sacrifices placed him squarely on that road.

2. **Personal example.** Out of recognition of his high profile, a Kohen Gadol grasped that earning the confidence of his co-religionists began at home. Thus, he realized that to best help others achieve their religious goals, he needed to embody sincerity. Two daily sacrifices certainly boosted his godliness. Fellow Jews could not help but observe his efforts. In turn, people sought to emulate him.

3. **Confidence building.** Reticence about bringing sacrifices to the Mikdash was normal. When Jews beheld a Kohen Gadol trudging up and down the holy Temple Mount, not sparing the labor involved, it served as a catalyst for others. In this way, his two offerings acted as solid ice-breakers.

4. **Equalization.** Aside from normal compunctions associated with bringing sacrifices, poor folks had another chip stacked against them. They felt self-conscious that their bare-bones budget only allowed them to bring a smallish gift to God. Seeing their High Priest offer a bare-bones present greatly lightened their heavy hearts.

5. **Humility.** A proper diet of Torah values begins with a heaping helping of humility. The Kohen Gadol's measly gift offerings, in full public view, deflated pomp or showy delusions of grandeur.

---

94. BT *Sanhedrin* 18a.

6. **Moderation.** High Priests and their associates subsisted on gifts that people brought to the Mikdash. As a verse teaches, "The remnant of the meal offering belongs to Aharon and his sons."[95] By ordering a Kohen Gadol to burn his twice-daily offering to a crisp, rendering it inedible, the Torah imparts a lesson. When priests did partake of Mikdash gifts, it had nothing to do with a desire for a free lunch. Fulfilment of divine accords motivated their actions. Had their intent been merely to binge, they would hardly have been able to resist snacking on what they had to bring twice a day.

7. **Gratitude.** A Kohen Gadol's gift offering expressed thanksgiving for all tithes bestowed upon his priestly caste by fellow Hebrews who donated regularly in the Mikdash and beyond (i.e., in the Land of Israel).

8. **Restitution.** Priests regularly grabbed and scooped and cupped in the course of their Mikdash service. Perhaps inadvertently, they overreached their gift offering quota by spooning too much. Bringing daily gift offerings made provisional amends for any possible accidental takings.

9. **Mikdash service.** Hashem desires daily services to consist of public and private components. Communal burnt offerings in the morning and afternoon only partially fulfill that requirement. Commanding High Priests to bring gift offerings, sacrifices which priests are particularly fond of, meets that heavenly objective. Moreover, having the High Priests represent the Jewish community was appropriate given the affection with which they were held in God's eyes. As a result, each morning there was a public and private offering, repeated every evening. Praise—public and private—rang aloud for the Almighty in perfect unison. Had the private offering instead been entrusted to other parties, it could very well have happened that on certain days unforeseeable circumstances might have interfered with this smooth running of affairs.

---

95. Vayikra 2:3.

Another rationale explains why Hashem chose High Priests to bring daily private gift offerings. Remember, Aharon had been implicated in the Golden Calf mess. This proved to be a stubborn moral stain, a constant trial. That sordid affair, like a bone lodged in a man's throat, set off a chronic gagging reflex from generation to generation. "And on My day of remembering…"[96] No calamity befalls the Jewish people without some trace of that sin being drudged up. Substituting for Aharon, High Priests take a proactive stance. Bringing offerings twice daily lessens residual damage caused by the Golden Calf's grievous transgression. Owing to Hashem's method of meting out punishment in regular, small doses, the Torah calls on the High Priest to bring part of his sacrifice in the morning, the other half that evening. It is a slow-release but perfectly regulated anodyne.

Here is another important piece of information to explain certain aspects of gift offerings, things that were only moderately touched upon in Parashat Vayikra. Of the several kinds of gift offerings discussed there, one type was the *minchah al hamachavat* (deep fried). This current *parashah* elaborates. That attests to its qualities differing from the others. Seemingly, it was a composite of all four types of gift offering.

To review, we list those four kinds:

1. fine flour or *minchat solet* (מנחת סולת)
2. oven baked or *minchat maafeh tanur* (מנחת מאפה תנור)
3. deep fried or *minchat machavat* (מנחת מחבת)
4. pan fried or *minchat marcheshet* (מנחת מרחשת)[97]

Note that this last one embodies four traits common to the other gift offerings: (a) it was made from wheat flour, as was the fine flour offering; (b) it shared being cooked in oil in common with the deep-fried offering; (c) it was prepared by first being placed in boiling water, so it had that in common with pan-fried offerings; (d) and finally, our verse stipulates *tufinei* (תופיני), which we defined above as "lightly baked." But according to Rashi the word has another connotation, "baked several times." That is, after it was boiled, it was baked and re-baked before being pan fried. By being baked, it shared

---

96. Shemot 32:34.
97. Also called *minchat hachavitin* (מנחת החבתין).

something in common with other oven-baked meal offerings. Accordingly, it had overlapping qualities with all four other meal offerings.

Why did this scalded and baked offering need to go through so many cooking processes? This assured that each of the four types was duly represented daily at the Mikdash. In this manner, it was as if each one had been offered every day.

"And the anointed priest, as his substitute, shall be from among his sons. He shall perform it."[98] The two most prominent national figures were the king and priest. Scripture equates them: "In indignation of His fury He has spurned king and priest."[99] The former's responsibility was to protect his people's life and limb, whereas the latter watched over and guarded their souls. Mighty and towering were these two national leaders. When they died, their sons inherited their father's positions. In the case of priests, our verse conveys as much. In fact, a second verse corroborates this: "Seven days they shall dress the ascending priest from among his sons."[100]

For kings, the operative Torah source is "so that he shall have longevity over his kingdom—he and his sons among Israel."[101] On the words "he and his sons," Rashi derives a *halachah* that primacy is given to a king's son over other candidates. Stress is placed on the right man possessing humility and fearing Heaven. Taming hubris develops humility. However, adherence to the Torah's commandments marks a truly God-fearing Jew. When selecting contenders for a Kohen Gadol, search committees favored modest and pious candidates. As asserted, a son is considered first for that top job. In any event, the Torah makes it clear that kings and priests leave their posts to their sons. Shortlisted, they inherit the inner track. In sum, we have provided two verses (one here and one in Sefer Shemot) that highly encourage a Kohen Gadol's son to take over for his father.

What are students to understand from the juxtaposition of verses that interrupt a general discussion of sacrifices with those that speak of Aharon and his sons' offerings? Above we learned about gift offerings. Following that idea with gift offerings brought by Aharon and his sons shows consistency. As stated, that verse insinuated two distinct variations: the case of a plain

---

98. Vayikra 6:15.
99. Eichah 2:6.
100. Shemot 29:30.
101. Devarim 17:20.

Kohen during his inauguration or the twice-daily personal gift offerings of a Kohen Gadol.

"And Hashem spoke to Moshe, saying: Speak to Aharon and his sons, saying: This is the law concerning sin offerings. In the place where you slaughter the burnt offering, you shall slaughter the sin offering before the Almighty. It is holy of holies."[102] We noted in Parashat Vayikra that all sacrifices were enumerated to Moshe during four distinct prophecies: (a) burnt, gift, and peace offerings (all nonobligatory sacrifices);[103] (b) sin offerings;[104] (c, d) various guilt offerings.[105]

Interestingly, in this *parashah* we discern five prophecies: (a) obligatory burnt offerings,[106] (b) pan gift offerings,[107] (c) sin offerings,[108] (d) prohibition against eating hard animal fat,[109] and (e) peace offerings.[110] Curious readers ask: Why doesn't the Torah cover all sections of sacrifices in one large, all-inclusive umbrella prophecy? Also, what is this prohibition doing in the middle of prophecies teaching about sacrifices?

Here is the rule. Each distinct topic gets treated in its own separate prophecy. Hence, since new information was gleaned from verses talking about pan gift offerings, a separate prophecy imparted them to the prophet. The same must be said for the Torah prohibition against eating certain animal fat. When Scripture wanted to return to the original subject of sacrifices, it necessitated a fresh communiqué from Above. All told, this is how five prophecies funneled into one section.

This section sets out to discuss sin offerings. Because it wanted to introduce new aspects of them, a separate prophecy was deemed requisite. To illustrate, sin offerings vary. Some of them required ritual slaughter on the north side of the altar. That information had not been gleaned from Parashat Vayikra (with the exception of sin offerings brought by a *nasi* or by a

---

102. Vayikra 6:17–18.
103. Vayikra 6:1–3.
104. Vayikra 4:1, 5:13.
105. Vayikra 4:22–35.
106. Vayikra 6:1–11.
107. Vayikra 6:12–16.
108. Vayikra 6:17, 7:21.
109. Vayikra 7:22–27.
110. Vayikra 7:28, 8:36.

rank-and-file individual). Here all communal sin offerings plus those brought by individuals are broached.[111] This is the Ramban's opinion.

Another example of a heretofore unmentioned law was that Aharon's descendants could eat from the sin offering's meat in the courtyard of the Ohel Moed. Female descendants of priests, however, did not enjoy that privilege. Ensuing verses expand on additional laws. "Whatsoever comes into contact with its meat becomes sanctified."[112] And "If its blood spills on garments,"[113] or "And an earthenware vessel which cooked it."[114]

Note this weighty observation regarding sin offerings. Whenever a sin offering's blood is brought to the Ohel Moed for the express purpose of achieving atonement, that animal's meat may not be eaten. It must be totally burned upon the altar. These are called "internal sin offerings" or *chata'ot hapnimiot* (חטאות הפנימיות). Earlier the Torah issued a command to burn this type of offering, but now it added a separate prohibition on eating from it. This is in keeping with Rabbi Yossi Hagalili's opinion.[115] Summing up, it has been made clear that this latest round of sin offering verses produced a new communiqué to Moshe, shown by the fact that new laws had been revealed to him.

"In the place where you slaughter the burnt offering, you shall slaughter the sin offering."[116] Despite written instruction having already appeared in Parashat Vayikra in the case of a Kohen Mashuach when he caused the congregation to sin, the location of the slaughter did not appear there. In order to prevent misunderstanding, a verse needed to set the record straight. Namely, one should not erringly think that in especially egregious cases the sin offering would not be slaughtered as a burnt offering in the north. This verse poignantly drives home that point: *all* sin offerings are slaughtered on the northern side of the altar.

"All male priests may eat of it. It is holy of holies."[117] This verse sounds redundant in light of an earlier verse stating, "The priest who offers it shall eat from it."[118] In fact, both of these verses are critical. Together they teach that

---

111. Vayikra 4:29.
112. Vayikra 6:20.
113. Ibid.
114. Vayikra 6:21.
115. *Torat Kohanim*, Vayikra 6:23.
116. Vayikra 6:18.
117. Vayikra 6:22.
118. Vayikra 6:19.

any Kohen who is fit to work in the Mikdash and thereby facilitates his fellow Jew's catharsis may eat meat from sin offerings. Had the Torah only brought the verse "The priest who offers it shall eat from it," but not the second verse, "All male priests may eat of it," then confusion would reign. It would imply narrowly that only the actual officiant may enjoy its meat, to the exclusion of all other Kohanim. That is, even the entire team of priests working that shift, those men who contributed to the overall smooth running of the Mikdash's activities, would be excluded.

Now we address the potential mistaken message had the Torah only specified "All male priests may eat of it." This broad generalization would be liable to be interpreted too inclusively. To wit, it would then seem that the only qualification needed to eat from sin offering meat is proven priestly lineage—strictly a matter of DNA. In other words, priestly eligibility or fitness would appear to be waived. To obviate misreading, the Torah had to include both of these verses. Now, taken together as a whole, this proper balance teaches that priests who qualify to serve in a Jew's cathartic service may eat from sin offerings. Conversely, those priests who lack license to perform Mikdash work are prohibited from partaking of the sin offering's sacred communion. Close textual reading affords this deduction: "The priest who offers"[119] sets the bar firmly. Read: only those capable of offering may eat meat from sin offerings.

Discussion on sin offerings should not be looked upon as if it were an isolated ruling. Let us use our newly acquired knowledge and see how it applies to our first *aliyah*'s treatment of gift offerings. Recall the verse "All male descendants from Aharon may eat it."[120] Rashi explains that this means that even those priests possessing physically disqualifying blemishes may eat from gift offerings. This he deduces since there is no contra verse expressing something like "The priest who brings the gift offering may eat of it," as was the case with sin offerings.

"All males belonging to the priestly class can eat from it. It is holy of holies."[121] The import of these two verses requires clarification. Understand that there is not a causal relationship being established. The fact that male Kohanim are allowed to eat from sin offerings is not due to that meat being considered holy of holies. Instead, the underlying message conveyed is a

---

119. Vayikra 6:19.
120. Vayikra 6:11.
121. Vayikra 6:22.

comment on what came earlier. Hence, officiating Kohanim eat sacrificial meat in a predesignated holy area. Specifically, that area was the Ohel Moed's courtyard. Additional verses that taught other instruction regarding sin offerings (laws about other food that touches sacred meat or how to handle blood-stained priestly garments) must be seen in this light. All of those rules and regulations are in place because sin offerings are "holy of holies." Given their grave status, painstaking precautions must be punctiliously practiced.

Explicit proof is found later in this second *aliyah* in those verses dealing with guilt offerings. "All males belonging to the priestly class can eat from it. It is holy of holies."[122] Without a doubt, the descriptive phrase "holy of holies" refers back to and serves to limit those who may eat gift offerings. To the point, male priests may eat it. Second, "holy of holies" teaches that priests must eat it in a holy place. The reason these particular offerings may be eaten by males and not females, by priests and not Israelites, owes to the fact that they rate as holy of holies.

See Parashat Shemini, where it is written, "Take the gift offering...for it is holy of holies. It is your statute and the statute of your sons."[123] Sons are included here but not daughters. This stands in marked contrast to the lesser holy level of other sacrifices, called *kodashim kalim* or lower sanctity. Equally, males and females eat them, as it states, "You and you sons and your daughters."[124]

This line of reasoning enables us to derive another halachic implication on this subject of what it means to designate offerings as "holy of holies." This strictly limits those who may benefit from this hallowed offering, as the verse establishes, "All male descendants eat from it." A priest's female family members are excluded.

"If its blood spills on garments."[125] Applicable only to sin offerings, this law is not germane to burnt, peace, or guilt offerings. Why? The reason is that those internal sin offerings are brought to the Ohel Moed for the purpose of dashing blood on the partition, on the golden altar, and even in the chamber of the holy of holies itself. The officiating Kohen dabbed his finger in blood several times. Given that, it was to be expected that some of the sacrifice's

---

122. Ibid.
123. Vayikra 10:12–13.
124. Vayikra 10:14.
125. Vayikra 6:20.

blood would spill on his garments. However, when it came to those other sacrifices, it was extremely remote to have these "work accidents," since they did not call for him to carry blood into the sanctuary.

"And the earthen vessel in which it had cooked was broken."[126] Rashi learns that since sacred ingredients had been absorbed into the clay vessel's walls, it assumed the stature and status of a leftover or *notar* of the sin offering. This requirement to destroy earthenware vessels carried over to all cases of sacred foodstuffs that had rested in them.

Expectedly, students ponder why this rule—though uniform for all sacrifices—should be introduced here as opposed to in association with cases involving peace or guilt offerings. Here is the answer. Sacrifices characterized as "holy of holies" may be eaten in the day and on a single night. Contrast that with other lighter offerings or *kodashim kalim*. They may be eaten over a period of two days and one night. Expiration, therefore, accelerates rapidly for these *kodshei kodashim*—faster than the longer shelf life of lesser sacrifices. So, when the Torah desires to teach laws about how to dispose of clay vessels, it prefers to attach that requirement to most holy offerings. This is because the vessel that cooked the ingredients was more vulnerable to its contents' sacred nature. An auxiliary question is how sin offerings differ from guilt offerings. Though these two sacrifices share much in common, the fact is that sin offerings were more regularly offered in the Mishkan. Greater leeway exists to bring sin versus guilt offerings.

"This is the law regarding guilt offerings. It is holy of holies." This section[127] on guilt offerings follows on the heels of the discussion of sin offerings. In a real sense, these two categories are parallel and overlap. New details emerge here which better fill in earlier gaps regarding guilt offerings. For instance, they are "holy of holies." As opposed to some other types of sacrifices described as lighter sanctity or *kodashim kalim*, these are listed in the weightier corner as *kodshei kodashim*. Another aspect of guilt offerings revealed here is that their slaughter took place where burnt offerings had been slaughtered. Rashi adds that until now it had not been explained which of the animal's organs were

---

126. Vayikra 6:21.
127. Vayikra 7:1–10.

burned on the altar.[128] Parenthetically, in Parashat Vayikra that information had been supplied for sin offerings.[129]

Given that the Torah spelled out in Parashat Vayikra which animal organs were offered on the altar so far as sin and peace offerings were concerned, an obvious question arises. That is, why was that detail not addressed there? The reason is that sin and peace offerings run the gamut of various animals. Recall, they may be bulls, rams, or he-goats.[130] Which animal to bring was a function either of what the person bringing the offering wished (as in the case of a peace offering) or of the personal status of the person bringing it (as in the case of the sin offering). Now then, some sacrifices required offering an animal's fatty tail or *alyah* (אליה) together with other innards; others did without the *alyah*. Verses spell matters out to avoid making Mishkan mistakes.

This brings us to the subject of guilt offerings, also found in Parashat Vayikra. The Torah there delineates three types of guilt offerings with their corresponding three categories of offenses. Crucially, those guilt offerings do not allow for taking a variety of animals, but instead are quite uniform. There is no differentiation in the ways the various guilt offerings are brought. To the point, if Parashat Vayikra desired to delineate guilt offering animal parts brought to the altar, it would have needed to discuss each of the three guilt offerings separately. Or if verses did not want to go into depth for all three categories, then at the very least they would have had to deal with one or two of them. Still, anything less than a thorough treatment of all three guilt offerings would have appeared awkward and disjointed. Listing one or two guilt offerings to the exclusion of the others simply is not a valid approach. How could it be that one guilt offering has something over the remaining types?

Balance and fair-handedness dictated treating all three guilt sacrifices consistently. Thus in testimony to the multifarious character of this subject, it was deemed preferable to leave details out for successive *parshiyot*. That focus was achieved in this *aliyah*, and a detailed concentration of guilt offering laws emerged. Regardless of guilt offerings being adult rams (as was the case in Parashat Vayikra[131]) or being brought by one who has relations with

---

128. See Rashi on Vayikra 7:3.
129. Vayikra 4:8–9.
130. Devarim 14:4.
131. Vayikra 6:5, 15, 18, 25.

a quasi-maidservant[132] or even if the proprietor was a nazirite[133] or *metzora*[134] whose offering included young sheep and female sheep, one thing was certain: no option to bring other types of animals existed.

Both guilt and sin offerings are considered holy of holies. This is so because they are brought as a consequence of a man's sin. Peace offerings, by contrast, are of lower tier, since their proprietors had not transgressed. Sacrificial nomenclature signals more than simply whether or not a given offering belongs in column one or two. It extends a supportive hand to sinners. Calling guilt and sin offerings *kodesh kodashim* broadcasts a message to them: repentant sinners are not cast aside or marginalized. Nor are they relegated to second-class citizenship so far as Heaven is concerned. In other words, past transgression and sin do not create a stigma. Catharsis fully rehabilitates the sinner, allowing him to again be fully counted among the nation's finest.

A spanking new slate—that is how Hashem views him. Admiration is showered upon him, for he tasted sin, fell, and yet picked himself up. Have the sages not written that where a repentant sinner stands, even a righteous man may not approach?[135] As stated, peace offerings are not brought as a result of sin. Only sin and guilt offerings does the Almighty consider "holy of holies." Indeed, He most highly values those two sacrifice categories. It is the lesser type of peace offering, that type which the unstinting and unwavering individual brings, that gets designated as *kodashim kalim*.

Let us turn to gift offerings. They too are called *kodesh kodashim*. Typically, this modest sacrifice is brought by poor and indigent Jews. Though financially strapped, they yearn with all their hearts for intimacy with their God. See Rashi.[136] He notes that the words "A soul when it brings a gift offering" depart from standard phrasing for those who bring freely to the Mikdash. He asks: Which Jew brings a gift offering to God? Is he not a poor man? Encouragingly, the Almighty recognizes his supreme efforts and promises to view his modest gift as if he laid his very soul and life's breath upon the holy altar.

In sum, three categories comprise the holy of holies. They are sin, guilt, and gift offerings.

---

132. Vayikra 19:21.
133. Bamidbar 6:18.
134. Vayikra 14:12.
135. BT *Berachot* 34b.
136. Rashi, Vayikra 2:1.

"All male priest descendants may eat from them."[137] The Torah teaches here that Kohanim are entitled to partake of these sacrifices. This applies equally to priests who officiated over gift offerings in the same way as it does to sin and guilt offering meat. "And the priest who offers a man's burnt offering—that priest may take [the animal's] hide. It belongs to him."[138] This detail informs us that even though, by definition, burnt offerings are wholly consumed by the altar's fire, care was taken to preserve the animal's hide. Presiding Kohanim may take it. By deduction, an important law is taught regarding other sacrifices. Namely, priests derive enjoyment of some parts of them.

This section started by affording more details regarding sacrifices before following up with verses discussing how Kohanim would divvy up gift offerings. Progressing, this *aliyah* concludes with instruction on how to divide the various kinds of gift offerings. In fact, assorted cooked gift offerings must be shared among the priests. It doesn't matter if the offerings were oven baked, pan fried, or deep fried—officiating priests partake of them nevertheless. When it comes to all other categories of gift offerings, the participant list expands. That is, any male descendant of Aharon eats it. The Ramban offers a justification for Mishkan largesse. Namely, munificence makes sense since priests slaved over food preparations. The sages provide other rationales.[139]

Third *aliyah*
"And these are the laws concerning peace offerings which he sacrifices to Hashem."

This section discusses rules and regulations dealing with peace offerings. In Parashat Shelach Lecha,[140] the Torah teaches that, roundly, peace offerings are accompanied by gift offerings made of refined flour mixed with oil. Additionally, wine libations were part of this service, as a verse apprises: "And they shall perform a fiery sacrifice for Hashem—a burnt offering or sacrifice."[141] Later

---

137. Vayikra 7:6.
138. Vayikra 7:8.
139. See *Torat Kohanim*.
140. Bamidbar 15:1–16.
141. Bamidbar 15:3.

in that passage we learn that gift offerings and oil were offered, as is written, "A fiery offering, a pleasing aroma to the Almighty."[142]

Rashi states that the verse refers only to gift offerings and oil, but wine is not named as a fiery offering. Nor does he opine that it is placed on or poured upon the altar's fire. The Ralbag adds that if wine were to be poured atop the fire, it would extinguish it. That would be counter the Torah, which issues a clear-cut prohibition against dousing the altar's eternal flame.

Yet wine was utilized on the altar. How? The altar had funnel holes. Wine decanted on the altar flowed into those orifices, ultimately making its way underground. This plumbing system contributed to keeping the Mikdash, a place dedicated to honoring Hashem's name, neat and tidy.

Here is a compendium of laws concerning peace offerings. As we shall see later in the *aliyah*, Kohanim did not have free rein to eat all of the sacrifice's meat. In fact, they were only allowed to partake of its breast and thigh. "And the breast goes to Aharon and to his sons. And the right thigh shall be a tithe to the Kohen, from My altar to his sons."[143]

But when peace offerings come as a fulfillment of man's expression of thanksgiving, they are different. They must be brought together with bread. "If they bring it as a thanksgiving offering, he brings this thanks offering together with matzah *challot* mixed with oil and matzah wafers anointed with oil."[144] This means that priests are entitled to meat and bread, but only the breast and thigh parts of the animal flesh. So far as bread is concerned, it may either be leavened or unleavened. It worked out to one portion per sacrifice. That is, one loaf of each of the four types of bread. The remainder became property of the proprietors.

Why did this peace offering come with bread? It enhanced joyous ambience for both the officiating priests and the sacrifice owners. After all, it is commonplace for celebrants to include others in their happy occasions.

Also alluded to here are future good times of redemption. When that era arrives, those extant (and ecstatic) Jews will offer a slew of righteous gifts. These will include peace offerings, as the prophet Yeshayahu foresaw: "And I will bring them to My holy mountain. And I will cause them to be mirthful in My house of prayer. Their burnt offerings and their sacrifices will be pleasing

---

142. Bamidbar 15:10.
143. Vayikra 7:29–34.
144. Vayikra 7:12.

upon My altar."[145] The sentiment expresses how they will offer sacrifices of thanksgiving, and they—priests and proprietors—will rejoice through them. Yirmiyahu stated, "When Hashem ransoms Yaakov and redeems him from hands stronger than him, they shall come and celebrate in Zion, an exalted place. And they will stream to Hashem's goodly places. Upon the garden—and on wine and upon oil and upon flocks and herds. And their souls will be as a fertile field. They will no longer know any pain."[146] It is also written, "Then the maiden will be happy in her dance.... And I will satisfy the souls of the Kohanim with dainties and My people with My goodness. They will be sated. God has spoken."[147]

Building upon these prophecies, we advance the following. Their references to herds and flocks correspond to peace offerings. Images featuring abundant grain, wine, and oil imply accompanying breads mingled with oil. Wine, though not imbibed with sacrificial meats or breads, was enjoyed by Kohanim when Jews gave it to them in the form of tithes. Alternatively, priests drank non-sacred wine or *chulin* (חולין) during the course of their Mikdash repast. This is borne out by a verse, "And you shall offer peace offerings and eat there and be happy before Hashem your Almighty."[148] Another Scriptural source adds, "And wine gladdens man's heart."[149] Similarly, we find that King David sent to all the people wine with meat as part of his peace offerings.[150]

"If they bring it as a thanksgiving offering." This verse is the halachic source requiring those Jews who experienced divine compassion to bring thanksgiving sacrifices for having overcome tribulation or crisis. Such events include: (a) successful ocean crossing, (b) surviving desert treks, (c) freedom from incarceration, and (d) regaining sound health after illness. Obligation to bless the Creator for His kindness is echoed by King David. "Praise Hashem [for] His benevolence and [for] His wonders shown to man, and they shall offer sacrifices of thanksgiving."[151] Specifically, this implies an obligation to bring thanks offerings. These consist of peace offering meat as well as accompanying bread mingled in oil, wafers laced with oil, and fine flour boiled

---

145. Yeshayahu 56:7.
146. Yirmiyahu 31:10–11.
147. Yirmiyahu 31:12–13.
148. Devarim 27:7.
149. Tehillim 104:15.
150. II Shmuel 6:19.
151. Tehillim 107:21–22.

before being pan baked in oil. These are leavened *challot*—all part of a greater peace offering brought for thanksgiving. Rashi corroborates this when he notes that there are four kinds of breads—three are matzah (*challot*, wafers, and crackers) and one is leavened bread.

What did the Torah have in mind with these four peace and thanksgiving sacrifices and their corresponding four different kinds of breads? By breaking down the four breads to three unleavened and one leavened, a moral observation becomes discernable. In man's world, good prevails over evil. Cynics and fools imagine the opposite to be true. See the Rambam.[152] It is a point he unabashedly drives home. Moreover, the Rambam asserts that lurking evils are a result of man's own doing. In essence, there are three subcategories of one main discourse.

First, consider that man is a physical being. Mortality, by definition, means that he is imperfect. His end will, perforce, witness a marked decline in vitality and well-being until death overtakes him. Second, man's struggle with others ultimately results in stronger ones conquering weaker ones. Third, think about man's undoing as a result of overeating, overdrinking, sexually overindulging, plus a foolhardy appetite for tempting high risk. Daredevil activities threaten his life. Quite literally (and quite predictably). King Shlomoh addressed this point when he penned, "Man's folly steers him off the path."[153]

After having presumed these things, let us conclude as we assess matters. Matzah symbolizes contentiousness, as a verse expresses, "he loves strife" or *ohev matzah* (אוהב מצה).[154] Leavening alludes to balance, equilibrium, restraint, and moderation. The sages counsel, "Happy is a judge who lets his court case age and mature or *mechametz* [מחמץ]."[155] As a rule, man is inclined to self-inflict mortal wounds by overdoing the wrong things. Haste often causes injudicious speech. Given to bullheadedness, man engages in antiquated, imaginary, or highfalutin theological babbling. Tinny prattle takes aim at the Almighty, impertinently inveighing against Him. Iyov, the protagonist in the book bearing his name, is a case in point.

In Heaven's efforts to temper man's proclivity toward making wrong choices, the Torah provides Jews with ample antidote. In the context of

---

152. Rambam, *Moreh Nevuchim* 12:3.
153. Mishlei 19:3.
154. Mishlei 17:19.
155. BT *Sanhedrin* 35a.

sacrifices, this means that when a man brings a peace offering of thanksgiving, it must consist of three types of matzah. They correspond to three potential trouble spots that jostle to derail him. Picture this offering as a sharp judo chop designed to shock and invigorate a man's noble sensibilities. *"WAKE UP,"* the matzot clamor to slumbering souls. *"Remember that when temptation strikes, inciting you to battle against your Maker, a trusted remedy is near. Recall His kindnesses and wonders wrought on your behalf. Internalize this lesson."*

A speed bump of sorts, matzah is an object lesson par excellence. It screams, *Take it slow!* Words evoked by its unleavened composition tell a profound lesson. Jews are urged to exert utmost caution before engaging the Lord on swampy theological battlegrounds. Hesitation is healthy. Should a Jew cast that stone? Lift up his hand? Utter that blasphemy? Duel God on the grounds that He does not supervise events? Or worse, that God is aloof or uninterested to show man favor? Matzah's very image sobers man as it communicates messages of moderation.

Torah commands Jews to bring leavened *challot*. Metaphorically, the Chosen Nation needs to live by this instruction. They must sit on their personal vicissitudes, trials, and tribulations for a good, long time. Anguish and calamity are best dealt with after a fair passage of time. "Let it be" is the *challah*'s wise advice. When internalized, a disciplined Jew will recognize that God is the God of perfect faith. A stranger to wrongdoing, He is straight and righteous.[156]

Additionally, we may posit that peace and thanksgiving offerings need to be brought with abundant bread in fulfilment of its key social component. That is, a proprietor invites others to share his joyous salvation and divine deliverance. Had the Torah not required him to have so much food on hand for the occasion, this might force him to cut back on invitees. Sacrificial meat must be enjoyed together with bread. Having sufficient bread assures a celebratory repast among family and friends. It has been noted above that this animal sacrifice was taken from a ram—a midsize animal not exactly known for its mammoth proportions.

The rabbis estimate how much mutton it typically yields. Furthermore, they approximated (or recommended) that one measure of meat goes nicely with two measures of bread. After having made these calculations, one other thing becomes clearer. This particular brand of peace offerings (peace and

---

156. Based on Devarim 32:4.

thanksgiving) must be consumed in one day and one night, despite other peace offerings having been allotted twice that amount of time. Namely, peace and thanksgiving sacrifices have an inherent public face to them, as the host is publicizing a miracle or effecting *pirsum hanes* (פרסום הנס). Given this racing, ticking twenty-four-hour time stopper, a sacrifice proprietor has every incentive to hustle guests to his *simchah*. One literally pictures a mad dash for the dining hall, huddled by a host's loved ones and closest friends. Religious content for the event is manifest, with each participant eager to hear how Hashem bestowed favor upon the host. In turn, he retells the wonder of his salvation to the gathered crowd, and in so doing duly elevates God's name and honor. Imagine had the Torah given its normal quota of two days and one night for this peace and thanksgiving offering. Had that been the case, the proprietor would feel no pinch whatsoever. More than that—he wouldn't have sent even one invite, because a wider time frame makes all the difference in the world.

Another element about sacrifice meat must be interjected here. Scorn greeted proprietors who wasted or squandered time and thereby failed to eat or share their sacred meat. Incinerating holy leftovers as the buzzer sounded, to put it lightly, amounted to a boot in the seat of the animal owner's britches. Bystanders will likely cast invectives, wondering why his closest circle hadn't participated in the festivities.

"And he shall offer from it one out of each offering as a gift to Hashem. For the officiating Kohen who dashes the blood of the peace offering—it goes to him."[157] It is interesting to ponder why Hashem distributed four bread loaves to the priests for their Mikdash work. Why precisely four and not more or less? Here's the calculus. With peace offerings, priests were entitled to take breasts and thighs. Heaven figured that four loaves sufficed for that quantity of meat. Four bread rolls amounted to one-tenth of forty. It stands to reason, then, that the breast and thigh which is the Kohen's portion of the meat also constitute a tenth of the animal. This could be the reason that the sages of truth[158] knew the exact specifications of the breast and thigh. They figured that it had to comprise exactly ten percent of the meat.

---

157. Vayikra 7:14.
158. Though this title is generally associated with kabbalists, it is not likely that Abravanel had them in mind, for he rarely quotes them. It is not clear to whom he refers.

An auxiliary question to the one above may be posed. Instead of pro-viding one bread count (four loaves) per peace offering, why didn't bread get calculated on a sliding scale? That is, would culinary considerations be better served if the meat and bread ratio followed a predetermined equation? After all, that formula was in use elsewhere, as it is written, "And their gift offerings and their libations as per spoken word. [They are] three *esronim* per bull and two *esronim* per ram and one *isaron* per sheep and wine for its libation."[159] Predetermined uniformity might have proved an excellent solution for peace offerings. To illustrate, when peace and thanksgiving sacrifices were bulls, then, say, $3x$ was the bread quantity. If the animal was smaller, then one or two bread rolls would suffice. But this formulation had not been implemented because Hashem did not want to overly burden the donor. He wished to leave him some leeway. Thus for example when the animal he offered was a bull, two options availed themselves to him. One, seeing that there would not be enough bread to go around for the guests at his table (because the bull was so hefty), he simply added more non-sacred bread on his own initiative. Two, he could send portions of meat to people who were not at his table. In this case, he would send meat only. A recipient would provide his own bread.

On the general subject of time limits for eating sacrifices, why didn't the Torah cap one night and one day for all other *kodshei kodashim*? This question is strengthened when we consider that the location where they were slaughtered was provided. And in our section, verses did spell out those time constraints for peace and thanksgiving sacrifices.

To reply, the Torah relied on what had been written explicitly concern-ing ram peace offerings (which were brought by priestly inductees). There it was recorded, "You shall take the inauguration ram and cook its meat in a sacred place."[160] Rashi elucidates "a sacred place" to mean the courtyard of the Ohel Moed. This is so because it is holy of holies. There it is written, "And if meat from the inauguration ram remains or from the bread until morning, you shall burn its remains in fire. It may not be eaten, for it is sacred."[161] We deduce that whatever is eaten in holy places in the Ohel Moed's courtyard is holy of holies. Another *halachah* derived is that the allotted time frame is

---

159. From Musaf prayers on the festivals (based on Bamidbar 15:4–11).
160. Shemot 29:31.
161. Shemot 29:34.

one day and one night. Since those laws were transmitted there, they need not be repeated elsewhere.

"And if he brings a sacrifice for the purpose of fulfilling a vow, or if it is a voluntary offering, it must be eaten the day he offers it. And on the morrow the meat may be eaten."[162] After the earlier section concluded its discussion on peace offerings, it launched this one concerning people who made vows or signaled intent to bring a voluntary offering. Generally, this particular sacrifice type comes about as a consequence of man's fervent prayer or spiritually motivated vow. High religious sentiment, then, translated into his bringing a peace offering to the Almighty. Hoping to curry favor with God, he made a pledge. King David enunciates this mindset. "Please, Almighty...for I am Your servant. I am Your servant, the son of Your maidservant. Unshackle my cuffs. To You will I offer my sacrifice of thanksgiving, and in the name of God will I call out. My vows I will donate to Hashem—even in the presence of all His people in the courtyards in Hashem's palace. Verily—in Yerushalayim. Halleluyah!" See Sefer Tehillim.[163]

There, Sefer Tehillim conveys how priests are recipients of certain parts of peace offerings, and that they were eaten in the Mikdash's courtyards. Besides priests, the sacrifice proprietors also partook of their allotted meat. This they consumed in Jerusalem.

Why does this section begin with peace and thanksgiving offerings, following up with peace and vow offerings? One answer is that the Torah lists the more common sacrifice first. Another response has to do with presenting a logical sequence—holy of holies before lighter sacrifices. Thus, originally verses took up sin and guilt offerings before proceeding to vow and voluntary offerings, lighter ones. Placement of peace and thanksgiving sacrifices works as an excellent middle ground on account of it having some properties of both categories.

Consider what makes these peace offerings similar to holy of holies. Both must be eaten in a time frame of one day and one night. Vows and volunteer offerings share traits with other light sacrifices, too. How? They may be eaten anywhere within Jerusalem's boundaries. As noted above, holy of holies' meat was eaten within the Mikdash walls and permitted for one day and one night

---

162. Vayikra 7:16.
163. Tehillim 116:16–19.

(until midnight). Lighter sacrifices are given more time. To be specific, they are permitted for two days and one night. They may also be eaten anywhere inside the Land of Israel's capital.

Continuing, peace and thanksgiving sacrifices are eaten in Jerusalem for one day and until midnight. This represents a middle ground on the holy and lighter sacrifice spectrum. Why doesn't Scripture peg a specific place for where light sacrifices are to be eaten? True, they may be eaten anywhere in Jerusalem, but there is no explicit Torah source for so doing. In contrast, when it comes to holy of holy meat, several verses lay it out clearly. In response, the Torah relies on deductive reasoning. Location is explicit when it comes to holy of holies. Thus sin, gift, guilt, and inauguration ram offering verses all have "And they shall be eaten in a holy place."[164] No such locale instruction is present for lighter sacrifices. Seemingly this is interpreted to mean that they were eaten throughout the Hebrew encampment or *machaneh Yisrael* (מחנה ישראל).

For all sacrificial meat, including peace offering meat, strict regulations were in force. "And if the meat had contact with something unclean, it may not be eaten. It is to be burned in a fire. But the meat may be eaten by anyone who is ritually clean."[165] Successive verses give more instruction on how to handle sacrificial meat. "And the soul who eats meat from the peace offering which belongs to Hashem and yet he was *tamei*, then his soul shall be cut off from its people."[166]

Torah guidelines require peace offerings to be eaten in a *tahor* venue. This refers to the Hebrew encampment. Halachic lepers or *metzora'im* were forbidden from entering that camp area. In post-desert years and after Yerushalayim was liberated, the capital city had never been allotted to any one of the twelve tribes. Its status resembles the Hebrew encampment. Hence, while Jews trekked in the desert, lesser sacrificial meat or *kodashim kalim* was permitted in the Hebrew encampment. In the Land of Israel, Jerusalem as a whole parallels and assumes the designation as the Jewish camp.

See Parashat Shemini. There it is written, "And Moshe spoke to Aharon... take the remaining gift offering from Hashem's fiery offerings and eat it— matzot next to the altar, for they are holy of holies. And you shall eat them in

---

164. *Minchah*: Vayikra 6:9; *chatat*: Vayikra 6:19; *asham*: Vayikra 7:6.
165. Vayikra 7:19–20.
166. Vayikra 7:21.

a pure place, and the breast that was waved and the thigh that was donated you shall eat in a pure place."[167]

Rashi asks rhetorically: And should we presume that earlier sacrifices that were written about had been eaten in squalor and sordid settings? Obviously not. Rather, this verse teaches that no issue arose regarding permissible eating areas for holy of holies meat. Emphasis is intended to contrast both types of sacrificial meat: lesser versus weightier sacrifices. Lesser meat, treated to more lenient standards than its weightier counterpart, does not have to be eaten in the Mikdash. Jerusalem municipal borders suffice. As stated, purity is defined in terms of the Holy City's rule to keep lepers out.

Why aren't peace and thanksgiving sacrifices categorized just like holy of holies as peace offerings brought during inauguration? After all, they share laws in common. It is because time considerations are not the ultimate arbiter in choosing which column to place a given sacrifice in. Instead, the sole determinant is location. Hence, those sacrifices eaten in a holy place are holy of holies, whereas those permitted to be eaten in the Hebrew encampment at large belong in the lesser sacrifice placement. Peace and thanksgiving offerings are a case in point. Despite their narrow window of permitted time, they enter into the lesser sacrifice category, so to speak.

As advanced above, the entire reason for hastening proprietors to eat sacrificial meat has to do with a concerted effort to publicize Hashem's name and glory. Disallowing that meat to be eaten in the courtyard was a foregone conclusion. Perforce such a stringency would have meant that Israelites would be, per se, persona non grata. In other words, technical considerations ruled out the courtyard as a fitting venue.

"For the officiating Kohen who dashes the blood of the peace offering—it [a portion] goes to him."[168] Note that it is a Kohen who dashes blood, but not the one who attends to the sacrifice on the altar or the one who attains atonement for the proprietor who earns a portion of the offering. To clarify, the Kohen who helps effectuate catharsis is the same one who dashes the blood. For that reason it says in Parashat Acharei Mot, "For the life breath is in the blood, and I have given it to you [to place] atop the altar in order to atone for your souls, because the blood atones for the soul."[169] From here it

---

167. Vayikra 10:12–14.
168. Vayikra 7:14.
169. Vayikra 17:11.

is conveyed that the key element in the cathartic process rests with a Kohen dashing blood on the altar. In our context, this explains why that entitles him to take his rightful portion. Finally, the Torah did not stress the officiating Kohen who offers or the one who garners forgiveness. It is consistent with the principle that a priest who dashes blood on the altar carries the lion's share.

"And the meat of his peace and thanksgiving offering shall be eaten on the day it was offered. He may not leave it until the morning."[170] Straightforward and plain understanding of this verse conveys that this particular sacrifice contains two leniencies.

One, there is no commandment to burn leftovers on the second morning, as is the case with the inauguration sacrifice. Regarding that latter instance, the Torah says explicitly, "And if there will remain from the flesh of the inauguration offering or of the bread until morning, you must burn leftovers in fire."[171]

Two, a phrase shouting warning signals of what awaits a man who does not heed the Torah's time frame is omitted. Commonly, a short caution states that a man's soul will be cut off if he exceeds the allotted opportunity. Take for example a man who eats vow or voluntary peace offerings on the third day. In fact, rationale for this prohibition has nothing to do with some Torah demand to finish the meat on the very day the animal was slaughtered. Instead, Heaven encouraged alacrity so that the offering owner would get organized and send out invitations to the guests in a timely manner. The express goal was to share sacred victuals with loved ones. Still and all, leaving meat over until the second day after its slaughter was also permissible. An outside limit, though, was ordered. "And the sacrifice meat leftovers on the third day shall be burned in a fire."[172]

"And the soul who eats from peace offerings that belong to Hashem, and yet he was *tamei*, his soul will be cut off from his people."[173] Ibn Ezra sensed a redundancy here, for the following verse says essentially the same thing. This led him to explain that the first verse speaks of a man whose *tumah* is the result of something that happened to his body: either he had become a *zav* or a *metzora*. Alternatively, the fellow may have experienced a nocturnal emission or *mikreh lailah*. The Ralbag followed Ibn Ezra's lead.

---

170. Vayikra 7:15.
171. Shemot 29:34.
172. Vayikra 7:17.
173. Vayikra 7:20.

But their explanation is untenable, since a later verse is explicit. "Speak to them for your [future] generations. Any man from your descendants who will approach things that are sacred which Bnei Yisrael sanctify to Hashem, and yet he was *tamei*, his soul shall be cut off from before Me. I am God."[174] That verse employs the phrase "and yet he was *tamei*" or *v'tumato alav* (וטמאתו עליו), just as ours does.

According to Ibn Ezra, that first one should be seen as referring only to people whose *tumah* is the result of their physical state (just as ours does). In that case, someone who is *tamei* because of contact with a corpse should be excluded from the death penalty for eating offerings while *tamei*, which is the subject of this verse. Yet Ibn Ezra did not comment on that verse. However, the Ralbag explains the words "and he is *tamei*" to introduce a leniency. He reasons that the severe punishment of *karet* only applies when a man wallows in his *tumah*. But had he taken proactive steps to alleviate even some symptoms of his compromised spiritual stigma, the Torah grants an attenuated punishment.[175] Rashi learns those words "and he is *tamei*" to mean that they refer to a particular *tumah—tumat adam* but not *tumat basar*.

It is possible to distinguish between these two verses in order to arrive at one construction. By so doing, the end result will allow us to learn that the first verse speaks about *tumah* incurred when a man touches a spiritually contaminated object or *tumat masa*, while the second one refers to *tumah* incurred when he carries such an object or *tumat maga*. Indeed, this is consistent with Scripture, which compartmentalizes these two separate kinds of *tumah*. "Whoever touches a carcass will be *tamei* until evening…and whoever carries a carcass shall clean his clothing and is *tamei* until evening."[176]

Generally these two actions (carrying versus touching) do closely track and follow each other, causing the sages[177] to force an explanation on another verse: "And he sprinkles purifying water."[178] They contend that a Kohen who is responsible for carrying purifying water must cleanse his personal garments. This he does in order to be of one accord with his colleague who administers the water treatment. What results is that a man who touches purifying water

---

174. Vayikra 22:3.
175. The punishment is lashes and not *karet*. See BT *Makkot* 13a.
176. Vayikra 11:27–28.
177. BT *Yoma* 14a.
178. Bamidbar 19:21.

needs to cleanse his garments just the same as a Kohen entrusted to bring the water. Rashi follows the sages' lead on the phrase "And he sprinkles purifying water." In a related idea, the sages said that the Kohen who sprinkles the water is *tahor*. This teaches that the priestly water bearer contracts a severe form of *tumah*, evidenced by the fact that he must clean his clothes.

Ironically, it would seem that a Kohen charged with dashing the cleansing water does not become *tamei*—despite the fact that he touched it. The sages derived this *halachah* due to their analysis of the verb "sprinkle" or *mazeh*. How? *Tumah* does not transpire unless there is an adequate cumulative measure of that water in which to purify a recipient.

Extrapolating from this assumption, let us better understand the words "And he is *tamei*." Narrowly, this refers to *tumat masa*. Recall, he had contracted it in the course of carrying the water container. In contrast, an officiating Kohen who administers the water does not succumb to *tumah*. Why? This is because *halachah* judges him differently than his colleague. Understand that his physical contact with the water is limited to that amount which his fingers touch. Assuredly, his exposure is quite negligible. Therefore *tumah* does not have an avenue by which to invade and ultimately contaminate him. Verses allude to both types of *tumah*. Moreover, they convey a general rule that a man who contracts *tumah*—either *tumat maga* or *tumat masa*—may not eat sacred meat. If he does, then his soul is cut away from his co-religionists.

Alternatively, it is possible to interpret these two verses as speaking about only one form of *tumah*. The reason two verses are utilized is that each contributes to the other. Between the two of them, clarity is achieved. How? The first verse conveys that a *tamei* man may not eat sacred meat, however he is not subject to his soul being cut off unless that compromised spiritual state reaches its zenith. In other words, he had not cleansed himself of *tumah*. Enter now the Torah's second verse. It states that even if his particular *tumah* was minor or secondary—name it *tumat maga*—he still is liable to the severe consequence of having his soul cut off. Applying a priori logic, a man surely incurs *karet* if he had contracted the more serious *tumat masa* and yet ate from sacred meat.

Though plausible, all prior attempts at getting to these verses' plain meaning have fallen short. Following is a better approach. The first verse speaks of a *tahor* man who eats meat of an offering that has become *tamei*.

This can be derived by examining the preceding verse. "Whoever is *tahor* may eat the meat."[179] That is immediately followed by the verse "And the soul who eats peace offering meat from the altar and it is *tamei*."[180] The difference between the two verses is that in the second verse, a *tahor* person isn't just eating meat. He's eating *tamei* meat. Having established that, let us move to the second verse.

"And when a soul touches that which is *tamei* and he ate from peace offering meat belonging to Hashem."[181] This discusses a case where a *tamei* man eats *tahor* meat. When that occurs, the perpetrator is deserving of his soul being cut off from his people. This, then, is the straightforward explanation. Classic commentators learn that there is no Scripture that mandates the punishment of *karet* for a *tahor* man eating *tamei* meat, although it is forbidden. Taking all of these comments as a whole, we have addressed all outstanding issues.

"And Hashem said to Moshe, saying: Speak to Bnei Yisrael, saying: All prohibited fat of a bull and sheep and goat, you may not eat."[182]

The Torah needed to interject its injunction against eating animal fat in this section, which broadly discusses sacrifices. In the absence of a warning, readers may likely have misconstrued earlier verses commanding priests and sacrifice proprietors to eat sacrificial meat. "Whoever is *tahor* may eat meat."[183] Another verse states, "If a soul touches something *tamei*."[184] Based on those verses, it certainly would have been reasonable for readers to conclude that as long as priests, proprietors, and sacred meat were *tahor*, then fat was fair game, too. In instances when the animal fat was *tamei*, its status was akin to other sacred meat that had contracted *tumah*, meaning that whoever touched it became *tamei*. Given its textual context and sequence, our verse's insertion makes perfect sense. Animal fat and blood, regardless of their holiness or commonness, may never be eaten by Hebrews.

Recall that these two prohibitions were outlined in Parashat Vayikra. "You may not eat any fat or any blood."[185] Why did the Torah have to essentially

---

179. Vayikra 7:19.
180. Vayikra 7:20.
181. Vayikra 7:21.
182. Other common names for prohibited fat are tallow or suet.
183. Vayikra 7:19.
184. Vayikra 7:21.
185. Vayikra 3:17.

repeat these proscriptions? Is anything novel conveyed? The short answer is yes. The verses here come to highlight and add new, important details as mentioned.

Another aspect of this commandment that came to light was the particular location Hashem chose to impart this heavenly directive. Also significant is that both blood and fat prohibitions were transmitted at this conclusion of discussions regarding peace offerings. Officiating priests may work with blood and fat despite their being off-limits for Jews to eat, and this does not render them *tamei*. The importance of this clarification warranted separate, self-contained verses.

Sandwiched in between passages teaching about peace offerings, fat and blood prohibitions are pivotal. They provide parameters of which parts of peace offerings may be eaten and which parts may not. Moreover, crucial laws of *tahorah* and *tumah* were elucidated. Tellingly, in actual Torah scrolls written on parchment, students will observe that these verses do not begin new paragraphs. Torah scribes must keep this *parashah* open or *petuchah* (פתוחה), as is the case when there is an intrinsic connectedness between preceding and succeeding verses.

"All prohibited fat of a bull and sheep and goat, you may not eat."[186] This verse relates how despite meat from these animals being *tahor* and of choice quality ("Whoever is *tahor* may eat meat")—still some animal parts are off-limits, such as fat. To qualify, the Torah forbids eating fat but does not outlaw getting benefit from it. "But fat of an animal improperly slaughtered or fatally wounded may be used for other activities."[187] Thus, deriving benefit is fine, "but it shall surely not be eaten."[188] Despite marginalization of eating the fat of a bull, sheep, or goat, their fat may be useful in countless other ways. In fact, not just kosher animal fat is permitted for non-gustatory uses, but the same leniency applies to nonkosher animal fat. Namely, fat extracted from all animals is fine to use.

The Ramban writes that since the Torah forbids only the fat of animals offered on the altar but not that of animals not offered on the altar, a nagging doubt may arise in people's heads.[189] Perhaps they will get it wrong and

---

186. Vayikra 7:23.
187. Vayikra 7:24.
188. Ibid.
189. Ramban, Vayikra 7:25.

determine that animals improperly slaughtered or *neveilah* (נבלה), or fatally wounded or *treifah* (טרפה), fall into a lenient category like animals that are not offered on the altar. Maybe their fat is permissible, as is the case concerning non-domestic, kosher animals such as deer or gazelles. Forestalling erroneous conclusions, our verse states, "but it shall surely not be eaten." Yet for other uses, the sky is the limit. Why? Fat derived from kosher animals is not *tamei nevelot* (טמא נבלות).

In sum, fat does not cause defilement (is not *metamei*) when a man touches it, as is the case with nonkosher animals or *tamei* reptiles. Here is the crux of the matter. The verse's main thrust cautions Hebrews against eating fat. Reiterating: whoever eats fat of those animals sacrificed on the altar to the Almighty has his life snuffed out prematurely. This radical consequence is due to that fat having been earmarked for the altar. How can a servant be so audacious as to pilfer and eat food designated for his master? Are these fatty animal parts not offered to the Master of the universe?

In Parashat Vayikra it is written, "All fat and all blood you shall not eat."[190] In halachic parlance, that verse cautions Jews to refrain from eating the stuff. However, no punishment or consequence is laid down there. Our verse pronounces its ominous verdict: *karet*.

"Do not eat blood in any of your habitations."[191] It is patently false to narrowly construe this verse as meaning only that blood may not be eaten within the Land of Israel. Since the Torah lists blood and animal fat in one verse, this verse needs to be seen as inclusive. Without exception, both of them may not be eaten in the Land of Israel or outside of it. These commandments devolve upon Jews regardless of their living quarters and are not geographically sensitive to the Land of Israel.

"Do not eat blood in any of your habitations, including [the blood of] birds and animals." The prohibition's net widens to take in the blood of birds or animals. But Jews may eat fish or [permissible] locust blood. Since Parashat Vayikra had not spelled out punishment for this transgression, it does so at present. "And that soul will be cut off from his people."[192] Summarizing, Jews

---

190. Vayikra 3:17.
191. Vayikra 7:26.
192. Vayikra 7:27.

may not eat fat or blood. This applies in the Land of Israel or outside of it. A truncated lifespan is handed down for offenders.

After the Torah outlined twin prohibitions against eating the fat or blood of peace offerings, another limitation was put forth. Jews may not eat peace offerings' innards or *me'emurei hashelamim* (מאמורי השלמים). In particular, this refers to those organs that were brought and burned on the altar. Animal breast and thigh meat falls to the Kohanim and too may not be eaten by Hebrews. These laws, it is self-evident, all provide instruction to officiating priests.

"And Hashem spoke to Moshe, saying: Speak to Bnei Yisrael, saying: He who sacrifices his peace offering to the Almighty shall bring his sacrifice to Hashem from his peace offering."[193] This is a directive to a man bringing his animal sacrifice to God. A lesson about priorities is imparted. Namely, even though priests are entitled to enjoy the animal's breast and thigh, those Kohanim are not the main beneficiaries. God is. This nonobligatory sacrifice is not just first and foremost a gift to Him. It is only for Him. A Jew must never lose sight of this fundamental truth. God's grace allows officiating priests to partake, to be sure, but that permitted meat must be considered a gift from the altar, Heaven's holy table.

"His hands shall bring Hashem's fiery gifts—they brought fat which lay on top of the breast—the breast was brought to motion before Hashem."[194] Outstretched arm motions convey that God is the intended Recipient. Taking and motioning with the animal's chest parts further exemplifies how a Jew adorns or bejewels his gift.

At that juncture, the officiating priest sacrifices the animal fat on the altar and takes the breast meat for himself. Similarly, the animal proprietor gives the priest another section, as it says, "And they give the right thigh as a donation to the Kohen—from your peace offerings."[195]

Rashi elaborates on the sequence of events, explaining the meaning behind the strange-sounding images the verse evokes. When a man brings his animal, he places the fat on top of the breast, and when he takes these body parts to hand over to the priest who performs arm motions, then he flips the slab of meat. Now it is the breast's turn to sit on top while the fat is placed on the bottom. This is the import of our verse. "The thigh of the upraising

---

193. Vayikra 7:29.
194. Vayikra 7:30.
195. Vayikra 7:31.

and the breast of the waving, over the fire offering of fats, they shall bring to wave."[196] Namely, the breast shifts on top of the fat. Providing more sequence, after those slabs of meat finished their loop-the-loop twirling, meat was given over to officiating Kohanim. As a result of this roller-coaster ride, breast meat settled on the bottom. "And they placed the fats on top of the breast meat, and he offered the fat upon the altar."[197] According to the sages, three priests participated: the one who put the meat on the owner's hands, the one who waved the meat, and the one who put it on the fire.[198]

On this ceremony, the Ramban advances a plain approach. Namely, a priest waved breast meat together with its fat but not the thigh. Notice that only the breast and fat gyrated, but not thigh meat. Assuming that, it is important to understand why some part (breast) did get waved but not the other part (thigh). "They brought fat which lay on top of the breast—the breast was brought to motion before Hashem.... And the breast went to Aharon and his sons."[199]

Clearly, there is no explicit instruction with regard to waving thigh meat. But here is what the Torah does say concerning it: "And you shall give the right thigh for a donation to the priest—from your peace offerings."[200] This is followed by "He offers the blood of the peace offering and the fat—designated descendants of Aharon are entitled to the right thigh as their portion."[201] Significant differences separate the way these two parts of the animal are treated. Questions and implications practically jump off the page.

Why doesn't the Torah demand taking and waving the breast and thigh together, allowing priests to partake in both of them? They are, we understand, payment for priests offering blood of the peace offering. This entitles them to eat both the breast and thigh meat (or divide them among other priests). In fact, as we will soon learn, this was the case. It involved both of them jointly. "For I took the chest waving and the thigh donation from Bnei Yisrael from out of their peace offerings, and I gave them to Aharon the Kohen and to his descendants for an eternal statute from Bnei Yisrael."[202] We find another

---

196. Vayikra 10:15.
197. Vayikra 9:20.
198. BT *Menachot* 62a.
199. Vayikra 7:30–31.
200. Vayikra 7:32.
201. Vayikra 7:33.
202. Vayikra 7:34.

verse stating, "And Aharon motioned movements with the breast and the right thigh."[203]

Indeed, Scripture is chock full of verses that link both the breast and thigh together. The Ramban's explanation, though plain enough, lacks substance. On what basis does he advance that officiating priests took the breast and thigh separately and not jointly? Here is an answer to the question posed above. The reason Hashem conjoined the peace offering breast and thigh meat is that they reflect and draw upon two fundamental pillars of Jewish creed.

The first one pronounces that God has perfect knowledge of all existence—nothing occurs without Hashem's full awareness of the tiniest details or major trends. The second establishes that God's providence tracks all men. He rewards them all according to their deeds.

Breast meat represents God's perfect knowledge. How? The Hebrew word for breast is *chazeh* (חזה). Conjugated as a verb, it means to see or visualize, as verses prove. "Look upon Zion, the city of our solemn convocations."[204] And another one is, "And let our eye gaze upon Zion."[205] Regarding this subject Hashem declares, "His eyes behold. His eyelids test the children of men."[206] This underlies the Torah's motivation for linking breast motions. In symbolic super shorthand, watchful providence's vision darts all over the world's four corners just as God's eyes continually rove to and fro. Verily, He always glances to the east, west, north, and south.

And what does the fat on the breast convey? Offered on the altar, it suggests the Creator's attuning to man's inner thoughts. Take it as an article of faith: God does see and know man's notions, his heart's impulses.

Thigh meat, too, is a metaphor for divine providence. An officiating Kohen raised and lowered this piece of meat. Additionally, he rotated it. In simple terms, divine providence raises a man from his doldrums or cuts the feet from under one who is toplofty. The sages alluded to these gesticulations' meanings. Breast meat's revolutions are horizontal, whereas thighs follow vertical lines.

Taken as a whole, the joint messages of the peace offering meat make eminent sense. Furthermore, we understand why breast and thigh meat become property of Kohanim. This amounts to nothing less than a testament

---

203. Vayikra 9:21.
204. Yeshayahu 33:20.
205. Michah 4:11.
206. Tehillim 11:4.

to Hashem's all-encompassing knowledge. Another news flash among our verses is how Hashem's providence penetrates as it watches over and lifts up the downtrodden.

Our discussion thus far centered on only two of the priest's meaty gifts. And in fact, there were no more. Three other animal parts that were not designated for priests included the front leg, jaw, and intestine. They were not presents for priests, nor did they assume sacred character. They are termed "mundane" or *chulin*. From both types of sacrificial meat—holy of holies or the lighter sacred type—priests were only allowed to take breast and thigh meat. If, however, the meat was not sacred but rather *chulin*, the Torah commands that proprietors donate to the officiating Kohen a greater variety of meat. In payment for their slaughtering services, priests took front legs. Jawbones were given for the priest's blessing over the slaughtered animal. Finally, he received the intestine as reward for examining the health status of the animal. In any event, those three gifts never rose to a level of holiness.

To reiterate, the Torah commands that the animal owner bring fat which is on top of the breast. This alludes to the knowledge of God, Knower of man's most intimate self and thoughts. Although the acts of raising and waving were done to both the breast and thigh portions, the Torah uses waving with reference to the breast and raising with reference to the thigh to allude to the ideas we have mentioned. Motions of breast meat and donation of thigh meat assume major theological proportions, too. One need not be put off or misled by the gawky-appearing motioning of these two pieces of meat; they are rife with otherworldly symbolism. Afterwards, verses regarding the inauguration or *miluim* (מילואים) convey how "he places fat over the right thigh...and waves them, motioning them."[207]

What is behind the Torah linking Aharon and his descendants with breast meat? Why is thigh meat reward for a Kohen who oversees the blood and fat of the peace offerings? Breast and thigh meat clearly must be viewed singularly so far as priests were concerned. But here is where we move from abstract ideas to particulars regarding Aharon and his sons.

All of those gifts earmarked for priests were divvied up. Not only did the Kohen Gadol take his portion off the top, but he also did not share it. "The officiating Kohen offered the blood of the peace offerings and the fat—to Aharon's

---

207. Vayikra 8:26, 27.

descendants the right thigh meat shall be for a portion."[208] This verse flashes a green light for any qualified priest to dash blood on the altar and offer fat on it. In remuneration, they are entitled to eat meat from the animal's right thigh. The key here is "qualified priest." This disqualifies those priests who are sidelined due to their *tamei* state or elsewise. They may not share this sacred repast. Rashi adds that thigh meat is from the joint at the bottom of the lowest section of the animal's leg up to its knee. The Torah emphasizes the animal's right (but not left) thigh because that side is considered more prominent.

"For I took the chest waving and the thigh donation from Bnei Yisrael from out of their peace offerings and I gave them to Aharon the Kohen and to his descendants for an eternal statute from Bnei Yisrael."[209] This verse spells out to the animal proprietors that officiating priests are acting within their rights when they eat sacred meat. No misappropriation has taken place.

Technically speaking, here is what transpires. Animal proprietors donate their sacrifice to the Mikdash, to God. Hashem accepts possession and then gives some part of it to the party of His choice. Here, it is the priestly functionary who is the beneficiary of Hashem's largesse. Indeed, but by Hashem's grace do His Mikdash servants receive their daily bread.

"This is the gift that Aharon and his descendants receive from the fiery offerings brought to Hashem. [Transfer duly occurred] on the day that Hashem appointed them to serve to Hashem."[210] Conveyed here is that the animal's breast and thigh meat has been eternally reserved by Torah law for the priests. Transfer of this sacrificial meat became effective immediately and in perpetuity upon Aharon and his sons' induction to the Mishkan.

After this section completed a comprehensive treatment of sacrifices, it sums up. "This is the law for burnt offerings, for gift offerings, and for sin offerings, and for guilt offerings, and for inauguration offerings, and for the sacrifice of peace offerings."[211] Note that Aharon and his sons' inauguration sacrifices are thrown into the mix. This is because the laws of gift offerings stated in this passage applied to those they personally brought, as well, on the day of their inauguration.

---

208. Vayikra 7:33.
209. Vayikra 7:34.
210. Vayikra 7:35–36.
211. Vayikra 7:37.

Succeeding the previous verse which outlined halachic aspects of sacrifices, this third *aliyah* concludes: "...which Hashem commanded Moshe on Mount Sinai."[212] Reiterating what has been stated, this verse continues: "on the day when He commanded Bnei Yisrael to offer their sacrifices to Hashem in the Sinai Desert." The body of laws dealing with sacrifices was given while the Hebrews were in the Sinai Desert and after the Mishkan had been erected.

To be thorough, here is the broader picture. Since the Jews stood encamped adjacent to Mount Sinai when God commanded Moshe these laws, the verse specifies, "which Hashem commanded Moshe on Mount Sinai." It is false to assert that Moshe received the tablets and these laws on sacrifices while he stood on Sinai. "On the day when He commanded Bnei Yisrael to offer their sacrifices" conveys important details. When the Jews were in the Sinai Desert, Moshe received divine directives in the Ohel Moed. Moshe had long descended Mount Sinai and was hearing commandments via the Ohel Moed apparatus. There Hashem broached the subject of sacrifices to His prophet.

Fourth *aliyah*
"And Hashem spoke to Moshe, saying:
Take Aharon and his sons with him
and the clothes and the anointing oil and the bull sin offering
and the two rams and the basket of matzot."

Hashem informed Moshe that the time had arrived for him to convene Aharon and his sons, together with their priestly vestments, for the express purpose of having them anointed. Furthermore, Moshe heard instructions to daub the Mishkan and all of its vessels. An extended collection of items on Moshe's list included those things which were written about in Parashat Tetzaveh. Essentially, the prophet Moshe was requested to gather all of his co-religionists to the Ohel Moed so they could be on hand to witness while personnel and equipment were inducted into God's service in the Mishkan. This mega-event would lend dignity and honor to Aharon's prestige and standing among the people.

---

212. Vayikra 7:38.

It accomplished something else. "And Moshe said to the congregation: This is the thing which Hashem commanded me to do."[213] Moshe set the record straight. People should not draw the wrong impression and arrive at false conclusions. That is, the seer had no part in creating what amounted to a socioreligious hierarchy. Unconscionable. Moshe had not promoted his brother or nephews, singling them out for prominence. All had been finely orchestrated from Above.

"And Moshe brought forward Aharon and his sons and bathed them in water."[214] For Aharon and his sons, induction to the Mishkan commenced with self-cleansing and anointment. They were gathered together for that purpose, duly washed, and anointed for all to see.

First clad was Aharon. "And he put the tunic on him."[215] Verses describe how he donned all of the High Priest's clothing and accoutrement. Actually, one piece of clothing is not mentioned—Aharon's pants. Of course, it is preposterous to assert that he walked around exposed. The point is that he always wore his trousers and therefore there was no need to make special note of it here.

After Moshe completed Aharon's dress ceremony, he turned to the Mishkan's needs. "And Moshe took the anointing oil and he anointed the Mishkan and all that was in it. And he [thus] sanctified it."[216] Oil daubing solidified and concluded the sanctifying process. According to the Ramban, Moshe was commanded to erect the Mishkan on the twenty-third of Adar. This he accomplished posthaste. Immediately thereafter, Moshe was apprised of the various types of sacrifices to be offered. Later, the Torah takes up the subject of Aharon and his sons' inauguration. Included in the induction ceremony will be sin, burnt, and peace offerings. However, particulars regarding them are disclosed in earlier *parshiyot*.

Here is the overall picture that emerges when Hashem tells Moshe to have Aharon step forward. Recall that a similar instruction is found in Parashat Tetzaveh.[217] It is repeated here since this was the moment of truth, as it were.

---

213. Vayikra 8:5.
214. Vayikra 8:6.
215. Vayikra 8:7.
216. Vayikra 8:10.
217. Shemot, chapter 29.

Aharon's position became official even though the subject had been broached earlier in Parashat Tetzaveh.

Note that Moshe had not anointed the Mishkan until he first assisted Aharon and his sons to put on their priestly garments. Timing, in fact, proved crucial. Why? Hashem commanded, "And you shall anoint the Tent of Meeting."[218] There a verse commands, "You [Moshe] shall anoint Aharon and his sons."[219] Therefore, Moshe attended to dressing Aharon first so that he would anoint him immediately after having done so to the Mishkan. In other words, he did not want any time to elapse between the Mishkan's and Aharon's anointing. Aharon and his sons should have been anointed together, but a concluding verse in our *aliyah* mentions only Aharon's anointing—immediately after the anointing of the Mishkan—with no reference at all to the anointing of his sons.[220] This is because Moshe wanted to have an anointed Kohen Gadol ready as soon as possible to officiate in the services of that day. Anointing the sons of Aharon together with their father would have delayed that. So Moshe anointed them some time later.

After our verse roundly describes how the Mishkan and its vessels were dashed with anointing oil, the Torah provides particulars. "And he sprinkled seven times from it on the altar. And he anointed the altar and all of its vessels and its laver and its stand in order to sanctify them."[221] Classic commentators attempt to better grasp the nitty-gritty.

Rashi asks what is the source for performing the seven sprinklings. Answering, the Ramban brings a verse: "And you shall sanctify the altar—holy of holies."[222] Moshe understood that the altar needed to be sanctified time and again. Lavish oil sprinkling made eminent sense. In another context, a verse was more forthcoming. Among the activities taking place on Yom Kippur, the Torah teaches, "you shall dip with your finger seven times, and you will purify and sanctify it from Bnei Yisrael's *tumah*."[223] Seemingly, enhanced Mishkan sanctity occurred via profuse blood dipping and oil sprinkling.

218. Shemot 30:26.
219. Shemot 30:30.
220. See Vayikra 8:12.
221. Vayikra 8:11.
222. Shemot 40:10.
223. Vayikra 16:19.

After the Torah describes how Moshe anointed Aharon, it mentions the treatment that his sons received. "And Moshe brought forth Aharon's sons and dressed them with tunics."[224] A question arises whether or not Aharon's sons were anointed. According to the Ramban, they were, but the actual commandment is subsumed in the verse "Just as Hashem commanded Moshe."[225] Likelier, though, they were not anointed. Only Aharon received especial cosseting. Rationale will be provided at the end of this *parashah* when verses discuss two anointings.

Fifth, sixth, and seventh *aliyot*
"And he brought a bull for a sin offering.
And Aharon and his sons placed their hands
on the head of the bull sin offering."

The Torah now describes how Moshe was commanded to deal with the bull sin offering and ram burnt offering.[226] Verses will also detail how the inaugural ram—a peace offering—was handled. The Ramban writes that a second ram was designated as the inaugural ram on account of it being the last on this roster of sacrifices. In Hebrew the term "inaugural" or *miluim* connotes that which is filled or *malei* (מלא). In our context, the idea is that this inaugural ram concluded services by which priests took up their official posts.

Why did Hashem demand priests to offer up these three types of sacrifices: sin, burnt, and peace offerings? One approach has already been advanced in Parashat Tetzaveh.[227] The Ramban explains that the sin offering atoned for the altar besides fulfilling a joint purpose of sanctifying it. This is written explicitly. As for the burnt offering, it came to bring forgiveness to the priests for any inappropriate intentions or thoughts the men may have had. This is in keeping with its general value to attain atonement. Finally, the peace offering was an expression of thanksgiving to Hashem. He gave them an everlasting memorial in His House and by extension, within His walls. Exclusively, peace

---

224. Vayikra 8:13.
225. Vayikra 8:9.
226. Abravanel treats this *parashah's* final three *aliyot* together.
227. Shemot, chapter 29.

offerings marked the priests' transition from inductees or cadets to full-fledged Mikdash officials with full standing.

A similar point was made when we discussed why Hashem commanded blood to be put on each priest's right earlobe, right thumb, and right big toe. To clarify, this part of the inauguration only required blood from the peace but not burnt offering.

Let us further analyze some fine-print details of the ram inauguration ceremony. Apparently, its fatty tail and other internal organs were taken, as was its right thigh. They were waved in accordance with other motions discussed earlier. Subsequently, they were offered on the altar. If so, priests did not partake of their traditional meat—the animal's right thigh. Even with regard to the breast meat, a verse in the sixth *aliyah* records, "And Moshe took the breast, performing a wave-like motion with it before Hashem…and the portion went to Moshe."[228] He received the breast meat since he served as an acting Kohen Gadol. This is also stated in Parashat Tetzaveh.

A fundamental discrepancy is hereby raised concerning the fate of the inaugural mutton (its breast and thigh meat). Simply stated, the matter runs contrary to an earlier section dealing with the laws of the peace offering.[229] There it is explicit and unequivocal that the chest waving and thigh donations are Heaven's sole domain, but that Hashem gifts them to Kohanim. Yet here, a queer reversal is noted. Breast meat was eaten, while thigh meat was wholly burned.

Rashi picked up on these textual difficulties. He writes that "other than here, we do not find anywhere that the thigh of the peace offering gets offered."[230] While he does note the problem, he does not offer a solution.

Here is an approach. Apparently, the right thigh and breast were both prohibited to the animal's proprietors. This was because Hashem divided them among the priests, as it says, "And I do give them to Aharon the priest and to his sons for an everlasting stature from Bnei Yisrael."[231] However, in the case of the inaugural ram, Moshe served as Kohen Gadol. Hashem saw that the breast and thigh constituted a large quantity of meat and that there was no way Moshe could finish it by himself, especially given the prescribed time

228. Vayikra 8:29.
229. Vayikra 7:34.
230. Rashi, Vayikra 8:28.
231. Vayikra 7:34.

restraints. Therefore, the right thigh was burned on the altar simultaneously with the ram's other internal organs. Remaining was breast meat. It went to Moshe. And it sated him. But in normative cases, meaning when a staff of priests worked, it was decreed that both the breast and thigh meat were to be distributed to those officials.

"And Moshe took from the anointing oil and from the blood which was on the altar and he sprinkled it on Aharon and on his vestments."[232] Seeing that earlier verses (see above, fourth *aliyah*) apprised readers of Aharon having been daubed with ointment, what does the repetition add here? It is also worth asking why the first time around consisted only of oil, but this second time was oil and blood.[233] See what we have written on this subject.[234] Briefly, Aharon's investiture necessitated two sprinklings, and they took into consideration two distinct priestly attributes. Originally, anointment established him as Kohen Gadol—a position he held without a mandatory retirement age. Additionally, Aharon's anointing provided his sons and descendants with everlasting tenure, too. Utilizing anointing oil conveyed a permanence of position and actually helped accomplish these things. A second round of anointing witnessed the infusion of blood with the oil. Tellingly, that blood had been removed from the altar. This suggested that Aharon and his descendants' workload centered on the altar. By it, they and their garments became sanctified, as a verse attests, "And he sprinkled it upon Aharon and on his garments and upon his sons and on his sons' garments, and Aharon became sanctified, and his clothing and his sons and his sons' clothing with him."[235]

"And Moshe said to Aharon and to his sons: Cook the meat at the entrance of the Tent of Meeting, and there you shall eat it."[236] This expresses the idea that in terms of inaugural sacrifices, the priests were considered the animals' proprietors—as if they had brought peace offerings to the Mikdash. Recall that this type of sacrifice is apportioned. After the altar and Kohanim take their allotment, the animal proprietor eats his share. Clearly, Aharon and his sons were accorded owner status and rights when it came to inaugural sacrifice meat. Actually, Aharon's sons were entitled to more than meat. "And

---

232. Vayikra 8:30.
233. Shemot, chapter 29.
234. *Abravanel's World: Shemot, vol. II*, Parashat Tetzaveh, fifth *aliyah*.
235. Vayikra 8:30.
236. Vayikra 8:31.

the breads which were in the basket of inauguration as I commanded, saying: Aharon and his sons shall eat from it."[237]

Inauguration ceremonials and events lasted for seven days and limited the priest's movements. "And from the entrance of the Tent of Meeting you shall not depart for seven days, until the day of your completion of your indoctrination, for in seven days your consecration is complete."[238] For that weeklong period, the priests' haunt was the Mishkan. Day and night found them there, though it would be inaccurate to assert that they did not take short leaves of absence from it. The Torah's instruction simply meant that while they were actively engaged in a particular Mikdash activity, they could not interrupt and leave the hallowed compound. This position was shared by the sages as evident when they discussed parameters for the priests' coming and going.[239] In fact, they alluded to the fact that Nadav and Avihu were punished precisely on account of having left the Mishkan—while they were in the midst of officiating—to bring fire from beyond the consecrated confines. "That you should not die,"[240] cautions Scripture.

Priests had other reasons for staying put during the weeklong festivities. Intense learning sessions and seminars, on premises, greatly contributed to their knowledge. This, of course, translated into expert quality of service for the community. Kohanim had been apprised that missteps brought grave consequences and punishment. This dire message was internalized and no doubt contributed to their professionalism. "Kohanim are eager and expert," avow the Talmudic sages.[241]

Rashi, quoting the sages, writes that the Mishkan was erected on Rosh Chodesh Nissan. During the seven days of inauguration ceremonies, Moshe assembled and disassembled the Mishkan in order to be adept at it. When our verse says, "And from the entrance of the Tent of Meeting you shall not depart for seven days," it refers to those assembling and dismantling drills. These honed skills came in handy during the forty years of desert trekking.[242]

So concludes this *parashah*—blessings to God's strength!

---

237. Ibid.
238. Vayikra 8:32.
239. *Torat Kohanim*, Vayikra 10:7.
240. Vayikra 8:35.
241. *Torat Kohanim*.
242. *Sifrei*, Bamidbar 7:1.

PARASHAT SHEMINI

ON DAY EIGHT

First *aliyah*

"And it was on the eighth day
Moshe called to Aharon and his sons and the sages of Israel."

The Ibn Ezra opines that the eighth day marks the eighth day of Nissan. He concludes this on the following basis: the Mishkan was erected on Rosh Chodesh Nissan, and that date begins the eight-day inauguration period. Ibn Ezra rejects the sages' time frame.[1] They posit that induction festivities commenced eight days before Rosh Chodesh Nissan and concluded on it. According to them, Aharon and his sons dedicated themselves to their new positions, ultimately becoming quite ingenious at their Mishkan services. Consequently, on the eighth day, the Mishkan had been readied and stood firmly.

Hashem desired Aharon and his sons to take up their respective posts, and He bade Moshe to summon them. Moshe, the Torah tells us, also called forth the elders. This Moshe did in order to proclaim priestly laws to Aharon and his sons in the presence of the sages and community sheriffs or *shotrim* (שוטרים). During the holy convocation and extending beyond Rosh Chodesh for twelve days, each tribe's *nasi* or chieftain contributed generously to the Mishkan's gala opening. Yehudah's *nasi*, Nachshon ben Aminadav, led off on that very day. To describe the day and event as monumental would be an understatement. Glorious, awesome, exalted, and divine still do not capture that moment's jubilation.

According to the Talmudic sages, that particular day bagged ten crowns from the highest heavens.[2] It is recorded that Moshe commanded that the day's workload be shouldered by Aharon alone.[3] This is not meant as a slight to

---

1. *Torat Kohanim* and Rashi, Vayikra 9:1.
2. BT *Gittin* 60.
3. *Seder Olam*, chapter 7.

the High Priest's sons. Without a doubt, they were all worthy men of renown. Further, they would have administered the sin, burnt, and peace offerings on the altar quite admirably. It was deference to the Holy One that mattered most, according to that *midrash*.

Thus, this singular watershed event necessitated Aharon's personal input to inaugurate the Mishkan's grand opening. As support for this position, the *parashah*'s second verse reads, "And he said to Aharon: Take for yourself a one-year-old calf for a sin offering and an unblemished ram for a burnt offering and offer it before God."[4] A command was issued to take a calf in order to absolve his role in the Golden Calf meltdown. As for the ram burnt offering, its placement elicited an intimate relationship with the Maker. After divine forgiveness had been cinched, this second step made perfect sense. Alternatively, the ram evoked Avraham's greatest moment—Akeidat Yitzchak.

"And to Bnei Yisrael you shall say: Take a young goat…and a ram…"[5] Both were "without blemish." By association, the Torah's description of these blemish-free animals refers to Aharon's pure character. By so naming him, Heaven attests to having investigated Aharon's role in the molten calf and absolved him of willful wrongdoing. Intending no evil, Aharon had been duped by unscrupulous scoundrels, seduced by them.

More evidence to Aharon's righteousness: he brought a young bull or *egel*. This untrained animal corresponds to Aharon's comely ways, unversed in idolatrous machinations. "Bring me back and I will return, for You are Hashem, my Almighty,"[6] might have uttered a chastened Aharon.

The ram burnt offering, too, was unblemished. This wholeness reflected Aharon's spirituality. Sacrifices and the immense potential they unleash in man's psyche brought him into sync with the Creator. At this juncture, no ram peace offering was brought by Aharon, because these normally were to be eaten and shared by priests and animal proprietors after innards had been burned on the altar.

This general model changed owing to Aharon being the one to bring the peace offering. As stipulated earlier, whenever Kohanim brought sacrifices, they were fully burned on the altar. This explains why Hashem did not require Aharon to bring a peace offering on the eighth day. As Kohen and proprietor,

---

4.   Vayikra 9:2.
5.   Vayikra 9:3.
6.   Yirmiyahu 31:17.

he could not have derived benefit from it. Under the circumstances, God ordered that he bring a sin offering to be completely incinerated on the altar, as is customary for sin offerings brought by priests. Additionally, the burnt offering was fully burned to Heaven. Aharon and his sons took their generous portions of meat from offerings brought that day on behalf of the people. This obviated the need for the Kohen Gadol to bring his own peace offering.

"And to Bnei Yisrael you shall speak, saying: Take a kid goat for a sin offering and an unblemished one-year-old calf for a burnt offering."[7] Why did Moshe delegate this instruction to Aharon and not issue directives to them himself although they were all gathered before him? Moshe's gesture bestowed honor upon Aharon. People witnessed how Aharon had assumed power, fully capable of taking charge. From here on out, they took their cues from him. Questioning Aharon's authority never arose, because Moshe made it clear that his brother was acting on orders from Moshe, who in turn had heard it from the Source. "And they took that which Moshe commanded in the presence of the Tent of Meeting's entrance, and the whole congregation sacrificed, and they stood before Hashem."[8] In fact, sacrifice orders came to Moshe, who transmitted them to Aharon. The congregation listened as Aharon assumed the helm.

"Take a kid goat for a sin offering."[9] The High Priest commanded the congregation to collectively offer a goat sin offering. It brought atonement for their role in the Golden Calf ignominy. See Parashat Shelach Lecha, which says, "If sin is committed inadvertently by the community [due to their leadership], the entire community must prepare one young bull for a burnt offering...[and] one goat for a sin offering."[10]

This is the prescribed method to attain forgiveness in cases of unintentional idolatry. Punishment for an entire people committing such an egregious crime and then merely bringing a measly goat highlights a key point. Consequence fits the deed. They stooped low by sacrificing to demons and other "harmful spirits," requiring the bringing of a goat to God to make amends. Moral lapse led them to adopt empty beliefs. Remedy came in the form of an unblemished burnt offering—a sheep and an unblemished calf.

---

7. Vayikra 9:2.
8. Vayikra 9:5.
9. Vayikra 9:3.
10. Bamidbar 15:24.

Here is the message. After national catharsis was achieved, an untrained calf was meant to goad folks to redouble their efforts in heeding commandments.[11] Similarly, like chastened sheep are the Jews before the Almighty. "Unblemished" must be viewed as the operative word. It serves as a metaphor for a new slate to describe the nation's clean break from former moral grime.

In sum, Jews brought three sacrifices on the day Aharon called out to them. First was a calf, next came a sheep, and a goat trailed last. Choice burnt offerings and sacrifices pleasing to Hashem made up their gifts. See more discussion in Parashat Vayikra.[12]

The sages[13] explain that the Jews offered a goat in the desert to attain forgiveness for their ancestors having slaughtered a goat after selling Yosef into slavery. They brought a calf to atone for their part in the Golden Calf lapse.

"And a bull and ram peace offering to sacrifice before Hashem and a flour offering mingled with oil, for today Hashem appears before you."[14] Both of these two animals rate as the choicest ones. Our verse does not call them unblemished. Burnt offerings are not described that way. Such modifiers are reserved to evince an emotive comparison, image, or simile.

"And a flour offering mingled with oil." This was the most splendid of all Mikdash offerings. Our verse concludes with a most riveting prospect: "for today Hashem appears before you." A better reading of this phrase is that Hashem will reveal His presence on account of the Jewish people.

We have dealt with and defined the meaning of the words "His presence" in Parashat Pekudei.[15] Briefly, this divine phenomenon appeared as a brilliant light. So intense was it that man's eye could not behold it. Other verses call it a consuming fire. This description is borne out. While it is true that Hashem did appear before the congregation, there is no indication that the Hebrews actually saw that appearance. Recapping, then, the verse means that a divine fire descended to the vicinity of the encampment. Fairly, it can be called God's messenger or *malach* (מלאך). Often in Tanach, an agent of God (or of a mortal) is named as the Almighty because He had dispatched it.

---

11. An "untrained calf" refers to a young one that had not yet been "broken in" and used to do farm work. Abravanel borrows the language of Yirmiyahu 31:17.
12. Vayikra 1:2.
13. *Torat Kohanim* 9:3.
14. Vayikra 9:4.
15. Shemot 40:34–35.

In the prior verse, Scripture relates that Bnei Yisrael performed per Moshe's instructions to Aharon, which he then passed down the chain of Jewish command. They duly offered their sacrifices, "and they stood before the Almighty." A holy convocation took place in the courtyard of the Mishkan. Eyes trained on the holy of holies. Moshe fulfilled what Aharon had promised.

"And Moshe said: This is the thing which Hashem commanded—attend to it. And Hashem's glory will appear to you."[16] Moshe added credence to Aharon's words. They hadn't been fabricated or crafted. Nor had the prophet or the Kohen Gadol scripted it. Instead, the Almighty communicated via His righteous messengers. The Ramban fully assumes that Moshe was commanded with regard to these sacrifices even though the matter is not explicit. Omissions of this sort are not uncommon in Tanach.

Moshe asked the people to lend their trust. They needed to believe in Moshe's promise to make Hashem's honor appear to them in the form of a higher heavenly flash or fire. It was this same image present on Mount Sinai, as described there: "The appearance of the glory of Hashem was like a consuming fire at the top of the mountain to the eyes of Bnei Yisrael."[17] Earlier in this *parashah*, Aharon conveyed the same. "For today Hashem will appear before you."

After Moshe's prefatory remarks, he spoke to Aharon. "And Moshe said to Aharon: Approach the altar and perform your sin and burnt offering. And you shall achieve forgiveness for your sake and for the sake of the people."[18] From the perspective of Torah standards, it is imperative for a man to tend to his personal growth (offer his own sacrifices) before haranguing others to do so (offer their sacrifices). Also, from this verse's context, note how Aharon's personal atonement directly aids in securing the nation's atonement.

Obversely, sometimes a top-down model presents itself. Hence, if a Kohen Gadol commits a sin, it drags down his co-religionists as well, as the Torah states, "If a Kohen Mashuach will sin to implicate the people."[19] Recognizing a symbiotic and organic relationship, our passage establishes that fact of life. "And you shall achieve forgiveness for your sake and for the sake

---

16. Vayikra 9:6.
17. Shemot 24:17.
18. Vayikra 9:7.
19. Vayikra 4:3.

of the people."[20] The fates of the lead priest and the people are inextricably intertwined.

"And offer the people's sacrifice and atone for them as Hashem has commanded."[21] In fact, the nation's sacrifice adds to their attaining forgiveness, allowing them to emerge free of sin.[22]

"And Aharon approached the altar, and he slaughtered his calf sin offering."[23] Declining to delegate some of the Mishkan's daily chores, Aharon was fully there and engaged. Thus, the Torah attests to his slaughtering the sin and burnt offering despite an explicit *halachah* permitting others to do it. He had let his sons offer the blood while he oversaw them, but the actual blood dashing upon the altar had been carried out by Aharon.

"And he dipped his finger with the blood."[24] Rashi writes that the words "on the protrusions of the altar" refer to the outer altar.[25] Alternatively, it is possible that the altar in question here is the inner, gold one. If that were to be the case, then this sin offering has the same law as that brought on Yom Kippur, the *chatat hakippurim*.[26] Thus, like that *chatat*, it was later burned outside the encampment.

Aharon also burned the calf's innards and flesh on the altar.[27] Its hide he brought outside the Mishkan border and burned it there. "And the fat and the kidneys…from the sin offering he offered on the altar, as Hashem commanded Moshe."[28] He repeated the same procedure for the burnt offering. "And they brought him the burnt offering in pieces…and he offered it on the altar." Readers will note that this section on the sin, burnt, and gift offerings is abbreviated. This was due to previous passages providing greater detail regarding them. To better compartmentalize, note that verses concerning the gift offering begin the second *aliyah*.

---

20. Vayikra 9:7.
21. Ibid.
22. Abravanel notes that the Ramban explains the words "and he shall atone for you" to mean that this is accomplished through his sacrifice, and "and on behalf of the people" by theirs. But Abravanel asserts that the Ramban's comments here are not correct, for such a reading of the verses renders "and atone for them" further on in the verse redundant.
23. Vayikra 9:8.
24. Vayikra 9:9.
25. Rashi, Vayikra 9:11.
26. The *chatat hakippurim* was offered on the inner, gold altar.
27. See Vayikra 9:10, 14, 19–20.
28. Vayikra 9:10.

Second *aliyah*
"And he offered the gift offering and he filled his hand with it, offering it on the altar— this in addition to the morning burnt offering."

"In addition to the morning burnt offering" tells us that all sacrifices, whether they personally belonged to Aharon or to the congregation, succeeded the morning public burnt offering. Picture fiery bookends. Just as the public burnt offering initiated altar worship in the Mishkan, so too the public afternoon burnt offering concluded any given day's service. In essence, they mirror each other.

Our verse imparts an important principle. Even though the congregation purchased and donated the communal burnt offering for the altar on the day of its inauguration, it did not replace or precede the daily morning burnt offering.

The Torah does not describe the inaugural sacrifices of the Kohanim as being "in addition to the morning burnt offering." This is on account of their private, individual status. Remember, they were chiefly employed to train Aharon and his sons in their new Mishkan posts. Accordingly, there was no serious thought that they would somehow exempt the two daily sacrifices. *Torat Kohanim* gives another interpretation of "in addition to the morning burnt offering."[29] This phrase appears in a verse dealing with a meal offering. It teaches us that there was a meal offering that accompanied the inaugural offering, and it was "in addition to" the meal offering that accompanied "the morning burnt offering."

"And Aharon raised his hands toward the people and he blessed them. And he descended from performing the sin, burnt, and peace offerings."[30] Ibn Ezra makes a grammatical observation based on the conjunction "and," per the above "and he descended." The connector means "and he already had descended..." Or put differently, he had first descended the altar from where he had offered a sin offering before blessing the Hebrews. Why did Aharon see fit to utter the priestly benediction after giving thanks? Because the verse states, "And Aharon raised his hands..."

---

29. *Torat Kohanim*, Vayikra 9:17.
30. Vayikra 9:22.

Talmudic sages ask: Perhaps Aharon had blessed them prior to offering the sacrifice (and not after it)?[31] That lacks logic, for another verse conveys, "One who brings a thanksgiving will honor Me."[32]

This approach is the most correct so far as the plain meaning of the verse is concerned. The actual, physical place from where Aharon performed his work, perforce, assumes importance as the optimal spot whereby Hashem's favor may be curried. Given that, it makes sense that he blessed the nation while perched on the altar. After he dispensed priestly benediction, he descended. Note the text's sequence. "And he blessed them. And he descended from offering the sin, burnt, and peace offerings." Analyzing verse placement is an accepted tool for Tanach exegetes, and most useful in unearthing truths.

"And Moshe and Aharon came to the Tent of Meeting, and they came out and blessed the people. And Hashem's glory appeared to all of the people."[33] The two brothers entered the Ohel Moed for the express purpose of offering heartful if brief supplication. Both men's words aimed at coaxing Heaven's fire down from above.

Immediately after expressing their fervent yearning, "they came out and blessed the people." This they did in unison. No sooner had Moshe and Aharon blessed the nation than the Almighty's glory appeared. A tight reading of Scripture follows and lends a working definition for the term "Hashem's glory." It opens the third *aliyah*.

---

31. BT *Megillah* 18.
32. Tehillim 50:23.
33. Vayikra 9:23.

Third *aliyah*
"And a fire came forth before the Almighty, and it consumed the burnt offering and the [animal] fat on the altar. And all of the people saw and shouted. And they fell prostrate."

Divine Fire from Above

The previous *aliyah* informed readers that Hashem's glory appeared to the people. Now we learn how that sight manifested itself. It was a rampaging—albeit surgically pinpointed—flame. Based on this verse, Torah students generally assume that the fire was, besides being highly charged and effusive, also ravenous. That dramatic assumption does not provide an inaccurate portrayal. In fact, the fire didn't toast or consume anything other than the meat of the offering itself. The flame descended from Heaven and touched down, if you will, somewhere above the altar's top surface to roast the meat. From that time and place where the fire hovered, God's glory became evident. The Mishkan had been invested with divine holiness, and would be forevermore.

Thus, the nation all saw this divine fire but feared not. Nor did they all run to take cover lest an uncontrollable (and famished) fire gobble them up. What was the encampment's reaction to the marvelous sight? "And all of the people saw and shouted. And they fell prostrate."[34] Huzzas of jubilation rang out. Supplication and submission ensued. People bowed down as a religious gesture of thanksgiving to God, the Almighty One Who answers them and accepts their sacrifices.

In sum, the nation received two blessings on that august occasion. One came exclusively from Aharon's lips and was uttered as he stood on the altar, in the midst of sacrificial animals. The second benediction had been recited by Moshe and Aharon together after the latter descended from the altar. It ensued as a result of their having entered the Ohel Moed to pray. After exiting, they blessed their co-religionists.

The sages write that they entered the sanctuary for the purpose of Moshe teaching Aharon how to perform the incense commandment.[35] Here is what can be garnered from an earlier verse. "And Aharon raised his hands toward

---

34. Vayikra 9:24.
35. *Torat Kohanim* 9:22.

the people and he blessed them." Priests need to lift their hands at the time of giving their benediction.

The formulation of the priestly blessing, as Rashi writes, is as follows: "God should bless and keep you. God should shine His countenance upon you and grace you. God should lift His face upon you and grant you peace."[36] This, then, was the benediction uttered by Moshe and Aharon as they extended their hands high. Understand that Moshe co-dispensed the blessing by dint of his having served as a priest.

Hashem desired to sanctify His altar and His tabernacle by means of sending down a divine fire from Above.

Below are four rationales.

1. **Fire.** Heaven's corps, comprising a host of His *malachim*, is depicted as fiery. "And the vision of Hashem's glory is like a consuming fire."[37] The prophet Yechezkel experienced his prophecy through a pyrrhic prism. "And a combustible fire and from within it [something] as a current of electricity ensconced in the fire."[38] In the book of Daniyel, he records, "His throne was fire flames."[39] These Tanach passages prove a point. God's camp's coat of arms, if you will, is fire. Fire's role in the Mishkan (and Mikdash) should not be viewed as something nominal. And for sure it is not to be construed as figurative. Images of blazing flames hold a key to properly understanding the nature of the mystical Shechinah's essence, a force associated with the Almighty's majesty. "And they fell prostrate." In the presence of a phenomenon possessing that level of sheer magnitude, can a human reaction possibly be otherwise?

2. **Divine providence.** Man's reason and intellect—bundles of smallish ideas mixed with banal notions—fail to accurately define, let alone process, the impact and full brunt of divine providence. Baffled, human beings question how an infinite, noncorporeal God Who lacks sensory faculties can relate to man, who epitomizes the

---

36. Rashi, Vayikra 9:22.
37. Shemot 24:17.
38. Yechezkel 1:4.
39. Daniyel 7:9.

opposite. How can this yawning paradoxical riddle be bridged? Can the mismatch find common ground and language? God's answer is a resounding YES. In order to address uncertainty, and with an eye to implant faith firmly within man, Hashem sent down His fire. The divine flame, crouching atop the altar, hits the mark. Despite a fire's airy chemical properties, the Creator casts it down. More than that. He attaches an anchor to it, per se, and then chains it just a nick above the altar. Fire represents, then, divine providence. Even though combustible flames possess an airlessness, it is Hashem's iron will that dictates reality. Why? God desires a close relationship with man. Providence facilitates it.

3. **Torah.** Fire symbolizes Torah. This is borne out by several sources. "A fiery law indeed."[40] The prophet Yirmiyahu says, "Behold My words are like fire."[41] Given this connection between fire and divine Torah, and insofar as the Mishkan's splendor featured Jews bringing sacrifices, a situation begged for Heaven's flame to descend. In sum, we put forward that inner harmony results when the Chosen People observe Torah, figuratively linked to divine fire.

4. **Divine propitiation.** Among the Jewish camp, scoffers dwelled. Serious scoffers. Jaundiced, they looked askance at sacrifices. "How can God look upon them as a sweet aroma insofar as He is incorporeal?" they carped and caviled. Naysayers got a whiff of God's answer when they beheld a fire descending from Above, a fire that lapped up the burnt offering and fats with gusto. Doubting Hebrews got a taste of Heaven's blaring intervention broadcasting in unequivocal terms: Thumbs up! Hashem enthusiastically approved of sacrifices. "Bravo! Huzza!" a fire exclaimed. Reaction in the encampment was boisterous. "And they shouted." Unchecked expressions of thanksgiving went out to God for having heartily acceded to their sacrifices.

This wraps up four weighty reasons for Hashem's decision to send fire from Heaven.

---

40. Devarim 33:2.
41. Yirmiyahu 23:29.

The Deadly Sins of Nadav and Avihu

"And Nadav and Avihu, Aharon's sons, each took his own incense pan, and they put fire in them and they placed incense upon them. And they brought a peculiar fire before Hashem that He had not commanded them."[42] Likely, this is the sequence of events. While Moshe and Aharon were blessing the people in heartfelt thanks to God for heeding their prayer and bringing down a fire on top of the altar, Aharon's sons took hold of incense pans. That was when they perpetrated a baleful misdeed.

What was Nadav and Avihu's transgression, and how did it justify their incurring the death penalty? The essay below will tie together a single thread, albeit a knotty one. Note five distinct strands (offenses). In the final analysis, it will be demonstrated how their malfeasance encompassed five areas of criminal behavior that fully justified draconian meed.

SIN #1 As written in the Talmud, the matter pertained to the incense service.[43] Despite the fact that a Kohen Gadol was not the only one authorized to perform this rite—any Kohen could have done it—here is a caveat. The Kohen Gadol had first dibs and was able to perform it whenever he so chose. Subordinate priests had to enter a lottery, and once someone won the opportunity, he was not allowed to perform it a second time for as long as he lived. This is the theory in a general sense. However, on day eight of the Mishkan's dedication, Moshe had laid down an order. Only Aharon was to officiate. Specifically, **all altar activity needed to be done by the Kohen Gadol**, paralleling a regulation on Yom Kippur. On that most holy day, work had to be carried out exclusively by a Kohen Gadol. That is why Moshe said to Aharon, "Approach the altar and offer your sin and burnt offering, and offer the people's sacrifice and [thereby] bring about pardon for them."[44] These referred to the burnt, sin, and peace offerings—all of which fell within the purview of any Kohen.

---

42. Vayikra 10:1.
43. BT *Yoma* 26.
44. Vayikra 9:7.

Technically this is all fine and correct; however, Moshe described a flouting of typical protocol at the inaugural event. A solemn occasion such as this one necessitated the direct and personal intervention of Aharon, the Kohen Gadol. If this sensitivity came into play for sacrifices, then all the more so was it true for offering incense. By its very refined nature, this clearly should have been within Aharon's jurisdiction. Moreover, since Nadav and Avihu had not been asked to do the incense rite by Moshe or their father, the matter comes off as most grievous. **They truly played with fire**, if you will. It is possible that Nadav and Avihu erred in their inflated self-estimation, believing they ranked as co-High Priests. Hadn't they been anointed like their father? They failed to take into account, however, that as long as Aharon was alive, they were his subordinates. Now reread the verse with this perspective. "And Nadav and Avihu, Aharon's sons…" That is, seeing that they were Aharon's sons and they did that which had actually devolved upon their father to do on that particular day, in this misjudgment they transgressed. That concludes their first offense.

SIN #2 Nadav and Avihu's second misprision took into account that **they jointly and simultaneously offered incense**. That was inexcusable, since offering incense only requires one man. Yet the verse states explicitly, "each took his own incense pan."

SIN #3 A third demerit came when **they entered the holy of holies without express permission**. Recall that access to the Mishkan's most sacred chamber is only permitted to the Kohen Gadol—and only once a year. This restriction can be found in Parashat Tetzaveh. "And Aharon shall bring atonement for the altar's protrusions once a year."[45] Just as a king's servant dare not enter his master's chamber without obtaining permission, for fear of dire consequences, all the more so when discussing Mishkan etiquette. Will the King of kings tolerate

---

45. Shemot 30:10.

breaches to His inner sanctum? News of Nadav's and Avihu's
indecorous incursion was noted. "And Hashem spoke to Moshe
after the deaths of Aharon's sons when they approached Hashem,
and were killed. Speak to your brother Aharon [saying]: Do not
enter the most holy place at any time…so that you should not be
put to death."[46] Despite the fact that no warning had been previously
issued to prohibit unceremonious entry into the holy of holies, it
need not be characterized as an ex post facto law; the matter should
have been self-evident to them. This third offense had also been
implicit in the verse "And they brought a peculiar fire before
Hashem." Implied is that they trespassed. According to the sages,
they died there and needed to be dragged out by their relatives.[47]

SIN #4 Next, Nadav and Avihu should have procured a fire for the
incense from the outer, bronze altar. "And he took a pan filled
with fire coals from on top of the altar from before Hashem
and he filled his two hands full of incense spices."[48] Aharon's
sons failed to heed this direction, choosing instead to import a fire
from beyond the Mishkan walls. Indeed, such a fire is clumsy. Let
us clarify a well-known *halachah*. Even though the sages have ruled
that with regard to the outer, bronze altar, it is permissible to bring
a **fire whose source is decidedly not sacred**, they
intended this leniency to apply when fire was needed to burn
sacrifices.[49] No similar dispensation exists for burning incense.

SIN #5 On the Mishkan's eighth day, Moshe served as the Kohen
Gadol. He should have been the one—the only one—to burn
the incense. See Parashat Pekudei. "And he placed [it] on the
golden altar…and he burned the incense spices upon it."[50]
According to the sages, Moshe burned incense for each of those

---

46. Vayikra 16:1–2.
47. *Torat Kohanim* 10:2.
48. Vayikra 16:12.
49. *Torat Kohanim*, chapter 10.
50. Shemot 40:26–27.

eight days.[51] Rashi agrees with this assessment, explaining that burning incense was Moshe's work, and Aharon had only been allowed to participate insofar as Moshe commanded him. "Approach the altar and perform the sin offering."[52] Nowhere is it written that Moshe issued such instructions to Nadav and Avihu. Clearly they sinned by usurping this service, an unfilial act that even their father had not been asked to do. "Which He did not ask them to bring."[53] On the eighth day, Heaven nodded at Moshe and granted permission for him—and only him—to attend to the incense rite. That, of course, meant that Aharon, Nadav, and Avihu had been refused the honor. Perhaps this is what the sages meant when they said that Nadav and Avihu had **advanced *halachah* in the presence of their rabbi** (either Moshe or Aharon).[54] Moshe or Aharon were slated to perform the rite on that day, but not Nadav or Avihu. This concludes a discourse which, through a close reading of the text, places guilt upon Nadav and Avihu. Both men acted out of line, proliferating into five grand felonies.

On the subject of Nadav and Avihu's infractions, the Ramban did not note any of these five points. Instead he offers his own explanation. Their transgression transpired when they took incense in pans. On those pans, they placed an improper fire. As proof Ramban brings the verse "And they put the incense upon it." That is, they put the incense on the pan. And it also says, "And they brought a peculiar fire before Hashem which He did not ask them to bring." They offered a fire in the holy of holies but not incense. Let us add the Ramban's sin to the litany of other items on the charge sheet to further discredit them.

---

51. BT *Avodah Zarah* 34a.
52. Vayikra 9:7.
53. Vayikra 10:1.
54. BT *Eruvin* 63a.

Handily and by utilizing a single verse,[55] it is possible to derive all of Nadav and Avihu's misdoings.

Sin #	Verse	Abravanel's comment
1	"And Nadav and Avihu, Aharon's sons, each took…"	Moshe had commanded the day's service be the exclusive domain of their father, and they should have left well enough alone.
2	"…each took his own incense pan…"	The two of them brought the incense simultaneously, reminiscent of what Korach and his cronies will do in Sefer Bamidbar.
3	"…and they put fire in them and they placed incense upon them."	This refers to their third cardinal sin, as the Ramban posited. Reiterating, they put the fire in the pan *after* they had already put the incense in the pan.
4	"And they brought [it] before Hashem…"	They are guilty of breaking and entering God's inner sanctum.
5	"…a peculiar fire…"	They brought an undesignated flame, which did not include incense.
6	"…that he had not commanded them."	This brings their tally to six sins. Hashem had not asked them or their father to offer incense on that given day. The eighth day belonged to Moshe.

Unauthorized act after act cascaded before reaching a climax. "And a fire came forth before the Almighty and it consumed them. And they died before Hashem."[56] A rogue, combustible current broke away and bolted from the main heavenly fire that had descended from Heaven and had hovered above the altar. Targeting Nadav and Avihu, it shot through them, killing them instantly. In the holy of holies—that is where Aharon's sons fell. The Talmudic sages explain that the fire had not seared their bodies or their garments. Entering through their nostrils and mouths, it short-circuited their vital organs. Breathing ceased.[57]

---

55. Vayikra 10:1.
56. Vayikra 10:2.
57. BT *Sanhedrin* 52a.

Aharon Reels

We may well imagine Aharon's reaction. *"Va'yidom Aharon"* (And Aharon uttered nothing).[58]

CON^USION

d u m b s t r u c k

Seeing his cataleptic brother's ashen complexion and speechlessness, Moshe spoke to him. "And Moshe said to Aharon: This is what Hashem spoke, saying: Amidst My beloved I will be sanctified and in the presence of all the people I will be glorified. And Aharon uttered nothing."[59]

Moshe's intervention assayed to coax Aharon out of his catatonic stupor. Aharon heard his brother explain that what had transpired had been anticipated. It came down to this: the more people involved with officiating in Hashem's Mishkan, the greater chance that disaster will strike.

Compare this to war. The more fighters who participate in a military campaign, the greater the likelihood of risk to life and limb. These are unassailable assumptions. Those serving on the front—whether soldiers or senior Temple officials—become mortally vulnerable (due either to enemy fire or contravening Mishkan rule).

---

58. Vayikra 10:3.
59. Ibid.

The rationale for this has been stated. Axiom: Human error cannot be totally eradicated. And when it comes to the righteous making mistakes, Heaven is very strict and metes out condign punishment.[60] Seemingly innocuous events assume great proportions. To illustrate, take an example of a king's servant who unintentionally (but carelessly) brushes up against his master. Though he means no affront, notwithstanding, he has committed one. The consequences are grave. The Torah is forceful when it comes to compromising the Mishkan's sanctity. Regarding an Israelite, it says, "Any who approach the holy chamber will be punished by death."[61]

The sages[62] relate this homily based on a similar verse: "Around Him it is very turbulent."[63] They explain that God is extremely exacting with His righteous ones, even to a hairsbreadth. Since Nadav and Avihu penetrated God's inner sanctum, an area to which they had no prior clearance, they imperiled themselves. "This is what Hashem spoke, saying: Amidst My beloved I will be sanctified."[64]

Caution could not have rung clearer. *Precisely by and through those men who approach My service will I be sanctified.* Furthermore, "in the presence of all the people I will be glorified."[65] No more sober warning could have been proclaimed to the congregation. By dying in circumstances so public, Nadav and Avihu created quite the storm. And it assured future deterrence. God's intimate chamber is wired with high explosives.

Let us analyze what classic commentators have written in order to see where they misinterpreted our verse. We will take it verse by verse. "And Moshe said to Aharon: This is what Hashem spoke, saying." They ask: *Where did Hashem foretell Moshe of this event? Had it been alluded to, let alone written?* This approach is fallacious. On Mount Sinai we find, "And also the Kohanim who come close to Me will be sanctified, lest Hashem blast into them."[66] Heaven had openly issued a warning about the Mikdash to Nadav, Avihu, and all those in their priestly station.

---

60. *Pirkei Avot* 4:12.
61. Bamidbar 17:28.
62. BT *Yevamot* 121b.
63. Tehillim 50:3.
64. Vayikra 10:3.
65. Ibid.
66. Shemot 19:22.

Alternatively, warning was issued during the inaugural days. "And from the opening of the Tent of Meeting you shall not go out so that you should not die."[67] This warning urged them not to leave the Ohel Moed to look for unauthorized fire—on penalty of death. Nadav and Avihu did precisely as they were told not to do. See the end of Parashat Tzav.[68]

Next we focus on Aharon's muted response. "And Aharon uttered nothing." According to the Ramban, Aharon cried and screamed bitterly, uncontrollably. Only in response to Moshe's request did he fall silent and stop crying. His comments are inaccurate. Aharon would not have expressed remorse before Hashem on a joyous day on par with his own wedding.

So how did Aharon react? To put it curtly, his mental faculties froze. A shutdown gripped him, and he went mute as a stone. Silent and soundless. Aharon could not eulogize his sons as fathers are wont to do in similar catastrophes. By the same token, Moshe did not extend condolences. Does consolation avail where the two boys' souls disintegrated?

"And Aharon uttered nothing." Aharon simply lacked the physical or emotional wherewithal to do more than draw air into his lungs. In Hebrew the verb *va'yidom* (וידם) implies utterly still and aphonic.

Now let us examine Moshe's attempt to resuscitate his reeling brother. First, he spoke to Aharon's heart. The Torah records that inspiring message. Second, he switched gears in order to quickly inter the dead. "And Moshe called upon Mishael and Eltzafan, the sons of Uziel, who was Aharon's uncle. And he said to them: Approach your cousins from before the entrance of the holy [chamber] and carry them outside the encampment."[69] Burial plans had been ordered despite the fact that the two men died in the holy of holies. This inner sanctum, according to *halachah*, was strictly off-limits, with entrée barred unless an urgent matter required attention. However, for purposes of maintaining the place's sanctity, purity, or upkeep, access was granted.

Moshe's directive to Mishael and Eltzafan to inter Aharon's sons outside the encampment is instructive. That location had been the designated place where public offerings and the Kohen Gadol's sin offerings were buried. Additionally, note that Moshe did not order Aharon or his two surviving sons to take part, since halachic considerations restricted them. "Do not attend to

---

67. Vayikra 8:35.
68. Vayikra 8:33–35.
69. Vayikra 10:4.

the dead."[70] As for Moshe on that day, he was serving in the capacity of High Priest. Next in kin to Nadav and Avihu were their cousins. Mishael and Eltzafan performed their job as undertakers with dignity and affection, treating the deceased as a sin offering that had wrought atonement.

Aharon and his surviving two sons listened to Moshe as he propounded pertinent *halachah*. "Do not let your hair grow, and do not rend your garments, so that you shall not incur capital punishment."[71] These Kohanim heard that they were not permitted to grow their hair, as is customary among mourners.[72] Aharon and his sons were also told that cutting their hair on the head—making themselves bald as primitive mourning conventions dictated—was similarly prohibited.

Halachah also prevented Aharon and his sons from tearing their garments. That, too, was a sign of extreme anguish prevalent among pagan mourners. Failing to check raw emotions carries horrific consequences: the death penalty. Worse still, their personal transgression would have spilled over and negatively impacted their co-religionists. But now a conundrum arose. Could the death of such princely men of God be glossed over without mourning, as if they were scoundrels? Heaven's response follows.

"And your brethren, house of Israel, shall cry on account of the burning that God has lit."[73] This verse indicates that widespread mourning for these two beloved, priestly scions ensued. In fact, the day's mood had been blighted with the news of the death of Aharon's sons, but Moshe told his brother and nephews that they were prohibited from participating in the general mourning. Additionally, they needed to stay put. "And beyond the Tent of Meeting's courtyard you shall not depart, lest you incur the death penalty."[74] Heaven handed down strict orders that under no circumstances would tragic news be allowed to mar God's jubilant celebration of the Mishkan's inauguration. "For anointing oil is upon you."[75] Aplomb and steely dignity were paramount owing to the unparalleled sanctity of the occasion.

---

70. Vayikra 21:11.
71. Vayikra 10:6.
72. *Shulchan Aruch*, Yoreh Deah 382:1. See also Rambam, *Mishneh Torah*, Hilchot Aveilut 5:2.
73. Vayikra 10:6.
74. Vayikra 10:7.
75. Ibid.

Sober Thoughts

Kohanim heard more laws. "And Hashem spoke to Aharon, saying: Wine and alcoholic beverages you shall not drink—you and your sons with you—on account of your entering the Tent of Meeting, lest you incur the death penalty."[76] Aharon's and his sons' roller-coaster emotions all took a considerable toll, wearying and draining them. Moshe's directives had effectively stifled and hushed their crying, as all outward expressions of distress or eulogizing had been forbidden. Out of concern that they might turn to strong drink as a way to drown their sorrows, Moshe forewarned them.[77] For that reason, Hashem spoke directly to Aharon, insisting that they not lean on alcohol and spirits to cope.

Two reasons for the prohibition are provided. One is derived from a close textual reading of the verse. The Hebrew prefix *bet* (ב) before the word meaning "of your entering" or *boachem* (בואכם) has more than one meaning. Often it is used as an adverbial clause indicating time, but that is not the case here. As we have translated, it means "on account of" or "due to" or "for." An illustration of this construction can be seen in Hoshea. "And Yisrael worked for the woman."[78] Also in Sefer Bereshit, "For he certainly divined on account of it"[79] or "Will You destroy on account of the five?"[80] Many other examples could be listed. Thus, Hashem informed Aharon that since he and his sons needed to frequent the Ohel Moed, it was unacceptable for them to become bibulous.

Many activities required their input, such as lighting the menorah, arranging the table, offering incense, plus an array of other sanctuary tasks. Inebriation would surely have impinged upon their abilities to get the job done right, resulting in their incurring capital punishment. Permanent legislation went into the Holy Book enshrined as "an eternal statute." Specifically, this law forbids priests scheduled to enter the Mikdash or to approach the altar from imbibing hard drink.

---

76. Vayikra 10:8–9.
77. King Shlomoh acknowledged this putative, time-tested method of self-medication for depression. See Mishlei 31:6.
78. Hoshea 12:13.
79. Bereshit 44:5.
80. Bereshit 18:28.

The second rationale for this prohibition centered on the priest's overall communal function to serve as teachers. Deciding matters of *halachah*, to state the obvious, needs sober thinking. Matters such as discerning between kosher and *treif*, *tahor* and *tamei*, holy and profane came before them. The prophet Malachi recorded their grave responsibility to the nation. "Because the lips of the Kohanim pronounce wisdom, and they shall seek Torah from their mouths."[81] Can a drunkard enunciate his own name, let alone intricacies of Jewish law? For these two purposes of doing Mikdash work and disseminating Torah, God forbade priests from boozing. Rashi, quoting the sages, writes that the Torah only forbade particularly potent and strong wine or other spirits containing high alcohol content.[82]

More simply, it appears that the prohibition cautioned them either when they had to work in the Ohel Moed or when they decided law pertaining to *tehorah* and *tumah*. In other words, timing is key here. That is, at work times during Mishkan shifts or during hours when they sat to decide law, they needed to refrain from alcohol.[83]

Fourth *aliyah*

"And Moshe spoke to Aharon and to Elazar and to Itamar his surviving sons: Take the meal offering from Hashem's fiery offerings and eat it—matzot—near the altar, for it is holy of holies."

After the Torah taught Aharon and his sons laws curtailing priestly mourning practices, it zeroed in on how to perform that day's tasks. They heard about work that still needed to be done. No matter that they were considered, at least in normative situations, mourners whose relatives had yet to be buried. Despite that general ban prohibiting such mourners from partaking in holy food or *kodashim* (קדשים), this case was an exception to the rule. "Take the meal offering from Hashem's fiery offerings and eat it."[84] Moreover, Moshe informed them where it had to be eaten. "Near the altar, for it is holy of ho-

---

81. Malachi 2:7.
82. Rashi on Vayikra chapter 19.
83. *Ohr Yitzchak*, Vayikra 10:9.
84. Vayikra 10:12.

lies." Sanctity determined the venue where Aharon and his sons would eat the offering.

Regarding this divine edict, Moshe would not hear of any hesitation that his brother and nephews may have harbored. "For it is your portion and the portion of your sons—it is from God's fiery offerings."[85] Feelings of despair do not justify a slovenly performance of this commandment. Loyal servants cannot very well pass up food placed before them by their Overseer. Can there be a greater slight to the Master?

Of what food did this gift offering consist? It was fine flour that remained after fiery offerings had burned on the altar. Also, it was made up of sacrificial breast and thigh meat from communal peace offerings that had been waved and donated. Interestingly, those meats had not been eaten in the holy place earlier designated for the gift offering. Indeed, the communal peace offering's halachic guidelines are more lenient than those of the gift offering insofar as there was no need to eat the meat within the Mishkan partition walls. As long as it was eaten in a pristine place, anywhere inside the Hebrew encampment sufficed. Recall that those men who were *zavim* or *metzora'im* were not allowed to remain in the camp. Furthermore, Moshe taught Aharon that these communal peace offerings belong "to you and your sons and your daughters with you, for they are your portion and the portion of your sons. They were given from Bnei Yisrael's peace offerings."[86]

Fifth *aliyah*
"And Moshe sought [to better understand what to do with] the goat sin offering. And behold it was to be burned. And he fumed at Elazar and Itamar, the surviving sons of Aharon, saying..."

After Moshe transmitted laws regarding how to deal with the gift and peace offerings, including where to eat them, he sought clarity on another sacrifice class: the communal sin offering. He revealed to Aharon and his sons that

---

85. Vayikra 10:13.
86. Vayikra 10:14.

part of the cathartic process for the congregation meant eating some of the sacrificial meat.

"And behold it was to be burned."[87] Burning the public goat sin offering took place outside camp borders, just as was the requirement for bull sin offerings. An unusual verb conjugation—*soref* (שורף) and not *soraf* (שרף)—conveys that the burning was carried out by others and not by Aharon or his sons. That conforms to earlier warnings prohibiting them from leaving the Ohel Moed.

Interestingly, our verse tells us how Moshe showed deference to Aharon and did not rebuke him, but expressed fury at Elazar and Itamar. The seemingly superfluous description of both sons as Aharon's "surviving sons" begs explanation. After all, Aharon's family tree had been delineated and well known. Likely, this phrase alludes to Moshe's anger, as if to say: "Are you not concerned that failing to heed Mishkan regulations will land you with a heavy-handed punishment? Have you already buried the memory of your deceased brothers?"

Moshe got specific in his exhortation: "Why are you not eating the sin offering in a sacred place, seeing as it is holy of holies?"[88] The sages elucidate that three goat sin offerings were offered that day.[89] One belonged to the community, a second one to Nachshon, and a third one was for the New Moon. Of these three, only the first one was burned. The sages differ as to the rationale for so doing with the public goat sin offering. One school of thought says that it had to do with it having contracted *tumah*. Others attributed its fate to Aharon's and his sons' intense mourning. Seemingly, this was deemed appropriate since goat public sin offerings or *kodshei dorot* (קדשי דורות) are an eternal statute. Contrast that with other sacrifices, which may only constitute ad hoc or temporary status or *kodshei shaah* (קדשי שעה). Moshe told them explicitly to eat the special *minchah* offering de jure, as it states, "And you shall eat matzot."[90] They deduced from that directive that they were to eat ad hoc offerings as well.

More likely, this is a preferable way to understand why Moshe grew indignant at Elazar and Itamar. On account of their profound personal grief, they failed to apprehend the larger picture. Consequently, they packed and sent

---

87. Vayikra 10:16.
88. Vayikra 10:17.
89. Rashi, Vayikra 10:16. See also BT *Zevachim* 101b.
90. Vayikra 10:12.

away the communal goat sin offering to be incinerated beyond the Mishkan walls. Erringly, they treated the goat as if it were a bull sin offering or a ram burnt offering. This, in essence, was their mistake. They painted all of the public sin offerings in one broad stroke. The verse teaches how Moshe applied impressive mental prowess in order to flush out the truth.

As a result of his efforts, Moshe arrived at two realizations answering these two questions. Why was the goat sin offering burned outside the camp, and why were the remaining two goat sin offerings eaten (those of Nachshon and Rosh Chodesh)? To reiterate, what marked this goat sin offering as different from others that were eaten in a sacred Mishkan place on account of their being holy of holies? Recall that Hashem granted permission to the Kohanim to eat sin offerings as part of the congregation's atonement process.

Consider the relationship between priests and their co-religionists. It is predicated upon officiating priests eating in order to attain forgiveness on behalf of the body politic. This was especially important, since the public sin offering service did not consist of dashing blood on the altar (or anywhere else). "Behold, its blood was not brought into an inner holy place. You must surely eat it in sanctity as I have commanded."[91] Moshe's complaint to Aharon's sons was quite cogent.

Aharon relayed a ready response to Moshe on behalf of his sons. "And Aharon said to Moshe: Behold, they offered their sin and burnt offerings before the Almighty. But these unspeakable tragedies have shaken me. And had I partaken of the sin offering today, would it be pleasing in the Lord's eyes?"[92] Aharon defended his sons. They were new at handling communal sacrifices. Only today they offered sin and burnt offerings on behalf of the general population. "Behold, they offered their sin and burnt offerings." They should be excused for unintentional mistakes when it came to this public goat sin offering.

Aharon attributed their error to another cause beyond their neophyte status. They were still reeling from the morning's trauma of having witnessed their brothers' shocking deaths. "But these unspeakable tragedies have shaken me." Is any human being impervious when racked with misfortune? Moshe listened while Aharon continued. Did he expect the devastated family to have

---

91. Vayikra 10:18.
92. Vayikra 10:19.

any appetite whatsoever, let alone sit down to a hearty repast? *Surely,* Aharon concluded, *there is dispensation in such extreme, dire circumstances for forgetting a point in* halachah. *Add this to their beginner status.*

But it seems more likely that Aharon was not giving excuses for his sons' mishandling. He did seek to ameliorate matters, however. Aharon supplied Moshe with two convincing reasons why the goat sin offering meat ought not to have been eaten. One, "Behold, they offered their sin and burnt offerings." The Jews intended that these sacrifices be wholly donated to Heaven. That is why no mention is made here of peace offerings. The very nature of a peace offering is that it needs to be enjoyed by the altar, priest, and proprietor. However, this was the Mishkan's opening day. Desiring to commence things on the right foot, they viewed their sin and burnt offerings as the sole domain of Heaven. The people were certainly aware that some sin offering meat is divvied among Kohanim, but they surmised that day one should be different, otherworldly. In their minds, this particular sin offering needed to follow the example of burnt offerings, albeit as a one-off opportunity.

There was a second rationale. It was based on the verse "But these unspeakable tragedies have shaken me." Anguish at having experienced the death of his two eldest sons felled Aharon. Combining both of these two reasons, he pithily concluded his remarks: "And had I partaken of the sin offering today, would it be pleasing in the Lord's eyes?" Undoubtedly, such flippancy would not have pleased God.

Under the circumstances and given Aharon's substantial arguments, it made immeasurable sense to equate the sin and burnt offerings. Just for that day only, both sacrifices would be completely burned. On successive days, everything would be executed precisely as Moshe commanded. "And Moshe heard, and it was good in his eyes."[93] Moshe accepted Aharon's pleading, duly recording it as a one-time aberration to normative Mishkan law and procedure.

---

93. Vayikra 10:20.

Sixth *aliyah*
"And Hashem spoke to Moshe and Aharon, saying to them."

After the Mishkan had been built, Kohanim learned about the prohibition barring them from drinking alcohol. The ban attested to the high regard priests enjoyed. They served as mentors and educators, responsible for transmitting Torah to the Jewish masses. In that revered capacity, one of their chief tasks lay in determining questions of holy or profane status: they ruled on what was pure and what was impure. In brief, Kohanim were the people's repository of Torah statutes. For this reason, Hashem needed to address both Moshe and Aharon together in order to convey laws of *kashrut*. Which animals were permitted for Jews to eat? Which not? This section covers the whole gamut of animal life, from quadrupeds to winged.

The two prophets heard how *halachah* discerns between fauna deemed pure versus those that were not. Heaven communicated with them both, though for different end goals. Loyal scribe Moshe wrote down the Torah as Heaven had dictated, whereas Aharon learned how to promulgate law to the people. Based upon his judgment, things were declared permissible or not. Another crucial application of this body of laws has to do with ritual cleanliness or uncleanliness. This impact on the Mishkan, its vessels, sacrifices, or people desiring to bring sacrifices cannot be overestimated. Given this, the sequence here follows naturally with the one above dealing with the various laws governing the Mishkan generally and its opening day in particular.

"And Hashem spoke to Moshe and Aharon, saying to them."[94] "Them" here apparently means the Israelites. But this is difficult, for the next verse says explicitly, "speak to the Israelites, saying."[95] We can explain as follows. The first verse refers to answering specific halachic question when posed by an individual. The second verse is a general introductory lesson in the laws of *kashrut*, addressed to the whole people. God requested them to address the Jews before launching a wider disquisition on the dietary laws.

This is how Moshe and Aharon proceeded to educate the Jews on this topic. Quadrupeds were the first order of the day. "Out of all of the animals in the world, these are the animals which you may eat."[96] In fact, the following

---

94. Vayikra 11:1.
95. Vayikra 11:2.
96. Ibid.

criteria are valid for animals and beasts. That is because in Hebrew, the term "beast" covers a wide spectrum of species. Thus read: herein is the list of wildlife permissible to eat. Two desiderata need to be present before a given animal may be ruled as fit for consumption. "Any [animal] that has true hooves that are cloven and chews its cud, you may eat."[97]

Condition number one is for an animal to be cloven-footed. If it is, then it must meet a second condition—chewing on its cud. This describes a digestive tract capable of regurgitating its food, ruminating on it prior to digestion. Animals that fit both of those bills are kosher to eat, as they are deemed ritually clean. Technically speaking, parted hooves or *mafreset parsah* (מפרסת פרסה) are hooves that are split into two distinct parts. Specifically, the top part of the animal's foot or claw is apart from the bottom part.

Etymology of the term can be traced to Sefer Yeshayahu: "Behold, cut your bread with the poor [people]."[98] A clarification is in order. The Torah is not saying that when these two conditions are met, an animal is rendered pure or *tehorah*. The converse is true. That is, an absence of these traits proves an animal is impure or *tamei*.

How do these two characteristics shed light on an animal's essence? Generally, animals possessing these two descriptions have meat that man enjoys eating. In anatomical terms, ruminants do not grind their food by using upper jaw muscles. This hindrance, if you will, prevents them from eating bones. Instead, they are herbivores. Stomach enzymes further break down their food, softening it and preparing it for its next stage of digestion. In addition, ruminants are commonly plump and their meat tasty to man's palate. Another reason they appeal to man is that they find their food easily and in practically every environment or ecosystem. Besides the physical attributes described, their personalities are even-keeled on account of their being grass eaters—wet or dry grass. Possessing an innately gentle disposition, these animals are not ornery, vicious, or aggressive.

Consider this. Split and wide hooves precluded these animals from needing sharp teeth or claws, as is the case with beasts of prey. Carnivores eat flesh, blood, and bones—all foods that breed wild tempers. On the other

---

97. Vayikra 11:3.
98. Yeshayahu 58:7.

hand, herbivores content themselves with roaming on grassy fields, pastures, and meadows.

The prophet Yeshayahu foretold a time in the Jewish people's national redemption from exile when animal natures will mellow. "The lion, as the bull, will eat straw."[99] Radical dietary makeovers will bring corresponding alterations in animal behavior. Former carnivores will turn away from aggression. Wolves will dwell with lambs, tigers with goats. Depiction of pastoral scenes is painted by Yeshayahu. He understood root causes of animal (mis-) behavior. Diet. Diet. Diet. There is simply no way of getting around it. Carnivores are nasty creatures because they subsist on flesh, blood, and bones. Because predators lack a ready food supply, they resort to hunting. Deadly sharp teeth and claws make them formidable, enabling them to compensate for not having a stomach for subsisting on herbs and berries.

Compare this with how nature has provided for kosher herbivores. Flat-footed, split-hooved, these animals lumber along their merry way picking grass and daisy dainties along the way. Dentition-wise, they don't have incisors. Leaves, blades of grass, and berries do not put up too much of a struggle. Also chewing their cud goes along with this idyllic picture. Kosher animals just do not have a mean bone in their bodies.

On the surface, it may seem peculiar that swine rabbits and camels do not make it onto the kosher roster. Here is an explanation.[100] There are certain innate qualities—attributable to particular physiognomies—that disqualify pigs and camels, whereas rabbits presumably possess elevated levels of undesirable traits. Their bodily fluids or humors, being out of kilter, render them unfit for a Jewish diet. Ultimately, Hashem is Knower of nature and the Creator of all flesh. It is manifestly clear that He knows which food is the right fit for man's spiritual needs. By the same token, if Hashem recognized that a given animal's moral DNA lacked the proper backbone, if you will, then He forbade His people to eat it. "However, you shall not eat from those that only chew their cud or have split hooves.... For you it is unclean."[101] Despite being ruminants, camels are prohibited to eat because they don't have split hooves.

---

99. Yeshayahu, chapter 11.
100. Abravanel made liberal use of then-current natural science to explain the underlying rationale for *kashrut* laws.
101. Vayikra 11:4.

As stated, one trait is insufficient to render an animal kosher. Similarly, rabbits fail the twofold test, but for the inverse reason.

Curiously in Hebrew, some animal type's genders are not determinable by their grammatically gendered names.[102] Note that there are three possibilities when it comes to an animal's sex. The first category is animals that may be grammatically inflected in either masculine or feminine. To illustrate, take the example of bull or *par* (פר) or cow or *parah* (פרה). Other animals only get called by a male designation. To wit, the bull or *shor* (שור), the camel or *gamal* (גמל), and the rabbit or *shafan* (שפן); they do not have any female counterpart. Finally, some animals only have female nomenclatures—even the males of that species. Three examples are the hare or *arnevet* (ארנבת), the stork or *chasidah* (חסידה), and the heron or *anafah* (אנפה).

Returning to our discussion of animals with only one of the two crucial traits to make it kosher, we turn to swine. The Torah instructs how it has split hooves, though it does not chew its cud. Therefore, it is prohibited to eat—*tamei*. No exceptions arise to this requirement. Either an animal meets both criteria and is kosher or has only one (or zero), in which case the Torah categorically forbids it.

The sages have given identifying signs to determine an animal's acceptability to those people who lack sufficient knowledge.[103] Essentially, ruminants are horned. Nature compensates those herbivores lacking canine teeth by endowing them with horns. This can be viewed as a trade-off, and horns may be a substitute for sharp teeth. Developmentally, both incisors and horns grow slowly after an animal is born. Neither is born with them in place. Equally observable is that horns enable herbivores to fend off attackers. This serves as a crucial line of self-defense, especially since they do not possess sharp fangs or claws.

Similar qualities are noticeable when it comes to birdlife. Winged predators that have sharp claws do not have an extra upper toe on their legs. Compare that with kosher fowl. Their legs are longer than their clawed cousins. This better enables them to walk on the ground so they can find, hunt, and peck for food. Upper toes steady them and grant good gait. Studying animal

---

102. All nouns in Hebrew are categorized as either masculine or feminine, but as Abravanel points out, this grammatical gender does not necessarily correspond to biological gender.
103. BT *Chulin* 59b. See Rambam, *Mishneh Torah*, Hilchot Ma'achalot Assurot, chapter 5.

anatomy can be viewed in this way, too. Namely, true hooves and cleft feet add to balance and stability.

Consider this physical attribute of kosher birds. They have crops and multiple-serving stomachs. Parallel to a ruminant's digestive tract, which features an ability to chew its cud, the bird's system allows it to eat and then regurgitate its food. Of the *treif* birds, ravens resemble swine insofar as they possess one out of two crucial desiderata. That is, ravens or crows do have an extra toe, though they do not swoop down on their prey. Crops and other stomach parts are, however, lacking in them. Still other *treif* birds share something in common with camels, rabbits, and hares insofar as they, too, have one kosher mark of distinction. As a rule, birds of prey may not be eaten.[104] Their feet mark them as prohibited, even if their crop and other digestive organs exist. Violent banditos are undesirable and disagreeable to the Jewish palate.

Having established the prerequisite of two signs for kosher animals and birds, the Torah now teaches that the same number of requirements is in effect to determine *kashrut* for fish. "These you shall eat of fish life in the water—all that have fins and scales in the water of the seas or rivers—them you may eat."[105] Some people have hypothesized what the underlying rationale may be for kosher fish criteria. That is, fish with fins and scales have a capability to swim regardless of any given aquatic environment. They possess mobility. But those lacking fins and scales anchor to the ocean's bed. Dirt and debris suckers, they have surly temperaments. This theory is, excuse the pun, fishy. More accurately, when fins and scales are extant in fish, those body parts absorb waste product.

Here is the thing. When fish have both fins and scales, their meat is clean and tasty to eat. On the other hand, if fins or scales are missing, their flesh is exceedingly bloated with waste product. To be sure, fins and scales provide an important outlet for the release of unwanted or unneeded food supplies. When fish anatomy stores up its excretion, it causes fish to become *tamei*.

"All that have fins and scales in the water of the seas or rivers." Significant differences can be traced to saltwater versus freshwater fish. That is why this verse covers both types of fish species. "And any [fish] lacking fins and scales in the seas or in the rivers, from any water fauna or living being that is in

---

104. *Shulchan Aruch*, Yoreh Deah 82:2.
105. Vayikra 11:9.

the water—it is abominable to you."[106] It does not matter, the Torah stresses, whether the subject is aquatic or otherwise, one uniform law governs them.

Note that in this section, the term "abominable" appears three times in rapid succession, plus twice when dealing with fins and scales. This highlights a fish fact. Some fish have fins while they are in the water but shed all of them when they leave their watery habitat. Thus, "All that have fins and scales in the water of the seas or rivers" conveys a rule that it is adequate for fish to have possessed fins and scales in the water even if they don't have those signs when they are removed from their environs. Should fins and scales not be evident in the water, then that sea life must be shunned. Creatures devoid of fins and scales are gross and disgusting. Relating to them as "abominable" amply produces recoil, and inculcates in Hebrews the understanding to avoid such tasteless things. The Torah forbids Jews from eating them, and their carcasses may not be touched; they give a man the shivers.

Another thing about banned fish being labeled abominable: the highly emotive term for abominable thing or *sheketz* (שקץ) invokes feelings of dread, as another verse states, "And I dreaded for my life."[107] Some men might wonder if the Torah went overboard. Just because it outlawed eating the meat of an impure sea animal, was it an overreach to prohibit touching its carcass? To forestall such nagging notions, the Torah repeats: "And any [fish] lacking fins and scales in the seas or in the rivers, from any water fauna or living being that is in the water—it is abominable to you."

A message rings clearly and loudly. Man may not indulge in things that are beyond his grasp. Heaven asks man to avert themselves from attempting to rationalize commandments. Axiom: That which does not have fins and scales in the water is sickening. Do not eat it. Do not mess with it.

"And these are abominable so far as birds are concerned."[108] Following treatment of animals and fish, this section continues with birds. Why did the Torah place laws governing fish before those governing fowl? When it comes to ascertaining *kashrut* of fish and other aquatic life, there are two key characteristics, in the same way as two vital or chief signs identify kosher animals and beasts. Having that in common, it is logical that fish verses follow animal verses.

---

106. Vayikra 11:10.
107. Bereshit 27:46.
108. Vayikra 11:13.

Ascertaining *kashrut* for birds assumes a different approach. Actually, the Torah does not provide explicit parameters for fowl whatsoever. The guidelines, it must be stated, are based on rabbinic tradition and not Written Law. Consider that those signs differentiating kosher from *treif* birds are internal (crop and stomach). Hence, stating them would accomplish practically nothing, as being hidden from the eye, they could not be used to identify whether a bird is kosher or not. No such corresponding list is provided for kosher kinds, because there are so many types of kosher birds.

Birds that were not explicitly prohibited are potentially kosher. In Sefer Devarim, Moshe elucidated matters. He dealt with ritually clean animals and those appropriate for eating. Moving to birds, the prophet records, "You may eat whatever bird that is ritually clean."[109] We will elaborate more when we get to that section.

"For you winged creatures that walk on fours are an abomination."[110] Why? It is because sometimes winged things swarm upon the ground, laying their young that swarm on four legs. Other times, they take to the air and fly using wings. "Abomination" signals that only four kinds of grasshoppers or locusts are permissible to eat. More specifically, these permitted types must walk on all fours plus possess hind legs higher than their front ones. This has to do with long lower ankles taller than their legs to give lift when they desire to jump.[111] At a certain launch stage, their legs coordinate with wings, propelling them into the air. Surefire signs that locusts are kosher are when they have ankles, four legs, and four wings (i.e., wings that cover a majority of the head and body). These comprise kosher locusts.

"For you winged creatures that walk on fours are an abomination." This verse cannot be viewed as presenting an iron-clad rule, for preceding verses have said that there are four-legged locusts that are kosher. Rather, it means that *other* four-legged, winged creatures are forbidden.

Having concluded discussions on what constitutes which animals are kosher and *tahor* and those defined as *treif* and *tamei*, the ensuing verses take up the topic of a man touching carcasses, and how that impacts him. "And as for these, they shall render you *tamei*. Whoever touches their carcass will

---

109. Devarim 14:11.
110. Vayikra 11:20.
111. Abravanel had a solid grounding in the anatomy of locusts.

be ritually impure until evening."[112] The following verses delineate creatures whose physical contact with man—directly or indirectly—renders him impure. Specifically, contraction or contagion of ritual impurity comes about when a man either touches or schleps a carcass of a nonkosher animal or beast.

"And any animal that walks on its paws, going on all fours—they are impure for you. Whoever touches their carcass is impure until the evening. They render you impure."[113] Lions and tigers and bears are classic illustrations for what the verse describes.

Successive verses count eight kinds of taboo, slimy creatures. A man who touches their carcasses is "impure until the evening." Purification occurs when man adheres to two steps. He submerges in a *mikveh* and waits until the sun sets. After both events, he may resume eating sanctified food should he so desire. Here is an important halachic distinction when it comes to a Jew's clothing contracting *tumah*. If a man touches a carcass, his clothes are not ritually contaminated. However, if he carries it, then they are.

"And whenever any of these dead ones fall upon him, he is rendered impure."[114] Deduce that when they are alive, no such negative stigma attaches to the involved party. Indeed, an earlier verse conveys as much. "From their flesh you may not eat, and their carcasses are abominable."[115] The Torah singles out eight creatures for especial ignominy.[116] Let us poetically dub them "the BLIGHTED eight."

A Hebrew who comes into contact with any of them becomes spiritually defiled. All other vermin—though related by biological classification to these—fail to bear that grave spiritual consequence.

The Hebrew term "creature" or *sheretz* (שרץ) is so called on account of its constant scurrying, slithering, or running (run is *ratz* or רץ). Of course, since these lowlifes carry enhanced abomination payload, there is no need to spell out that they may not be eaten.[117] All creatures that share this category

---

112. Vayikra 11:24.
113. Vayikra 11:27.
114. Vayikra 11:32.
115. Vayikra 11:8.
116. Vayikra 11:29–30. There is little consensus among Bible translators as to what these eight critters are. Some identify them as: (a) weasel, (b) mouse, (c) ferret, (d) hedgehog, (e) chameleon, (f) lizard, (g) snail, and (h) mole.
117. Next *aliyah*, Vayikra 11:41.

are forbidden to eat. "And whenever any of these dead ones fall upon him, he is rendered impure."

Contributing to the blighted eight's deplorable disrepute is this. They score top marks in a hierarchy of pests that generate spiritual defilement among Hebrews, triggering proactive steps to remedy the highly undesirable state of affairs. Thus, topping the totem pole, if you will, we place them in the "father of impurity" or *avot hatumah* column. Supercharged classification for these belly crawlers comes on account of the fact that when dead, they transfer *tumah* to vessels that they touch. "Into water is it brought, and it remains *tamei* until evening."[118] Instruction is hereby issued to fully dunk the afflicted vessel in water. After submersion and sunset, it is purified.

Seventh *aliyah*
"And any earthen vessel into which one of them falls shall render impure anything inside that vessel. And you shall break it [the vessel]."

Tamei Animals

More laws follow regarding the blighted eight listed above by name in the sixth *aliyah*. This verse speaks of any one of them coming in contact with earthenware vessels. In *halachah*, there are three applications. One, the dead animal does not have to actually touch the inside wall of the vessel. It suffices if its lifeless frame suspends in midair anywhere in the vessel. Two, the animal does not have to be complete, meaning that even a tiny part of it defiles the whole vessel. And three, contagion reaches the vessel and any of the contents therein—even if the carrion did not make physical contact.

"And you shall break it [the vessel]."[119] No remedy exists to fix or otherwise tamper with a clay vessel that has been tainted. That is, the normative methods of cleansing through water or fire are unable to budge this stain, which has penetrated and lodged within the clay vessel's walls. In a word, it is too disgusting and hence beyond repair. In theory, if there were a way to

---

118. Vayikra 11:32.
119. Vayikra 11:33.

extract the air from inside the vessel and extricate it, that air too would be impure and have the capability to transmit its malaise.

The balance of this seventh *aliyah* explains how to discern between things that contract impurity or *tumah*. It begins with an evaluation of food. "Any food that is edible and that is touched by water—it is [thereafter susceptible to becoming] *tamei*."[120] This law teaches some parameters. Consider food that has become detached from its branch (such as an apple from an apple tree) and is reasonably ripe enough to be eaten. Upon that piece of food, water has been sprayed. It is now in a readied state to become *tamei*, meaning that should an outside thing defile it, it is ritually contaminated. Thus, there are various variables which must be in place before food becomes defiled. In fact, a majority of food products are rinsed in water *before* they are edible to man, widening the net of vulnerable foodstuff.

"And all liquids fit for man to drink in a vessel shall be unclean."[121] The number of such liquids is seven. They include water, wine, oil, and the like. Water, though, only prepares food for *tumah* if it is removed from its source, such as water in a barrel. But if it is river water or in an underground aquifer, it does not. These liquids themselves, when not found in their natural state above ground or underground, may become *tamei*. All vessels are automatically capable of contracting *tumah* from the moment of their manufacture, as opposed to produce of the land, which can only contract *tumah* after it has undergone some form of preparation, such as being dunked in water.

The sages interpret the verb infinitive "to be unclean" or *yitma* (יטמא) in our verse as if it were also vowelized differently than it is pronounced in the Torah: *yitamei* (יטמא).[122] The variation between how the Hebrew word is spoken versus how it is written alters the meaning to the causative. That is, the verse is to be read as a causative if the liquids in question are among those that have an ability to transmit *tumah* to other objects—in other words, the specifically mentioned seven liquids that convey readiness for *tumah*. Liquids other than water are liable to contract *tumah* without any preparation.[123] It is

---

120. Vayikra 11:34.
121. Ibid.
122. BT *Pesachim* 18a.
123. For example, if one of the blighted eight is found floating on top of a glass of milk, the milk is automatically *tamei* no matter where it had been stored.

similarly true that liquids must be carefully guarded from contracting *tumah* for those who drink them.

"Whatever is inside it will become *tamei*."[124] This verse teaches that only food or drink contained in the vessel becomes defiled, for a vessel itself becomes *tamei* only from a primary source of *tumah*. The verse "And anything upon which their carcass falls shall become *tamei*"[125] refers to a vessel. Direct contact with a carcass is required to make it *tamei*.

In sequence, the Torah now discusses the ramifications of a cooking range or stove and *tumah*. What happens if one of the eight blighted creatures lodges inside these cooking appliances and dies (or dies and then gets suspended inside there)? As a preface, in Tanach times, ovens and stoves were large and made of earthenware. And of course, their main feature was that they were constantly fired. "And upon anything which their carcass falls—it will become *tamei*. Ovens and stoves shall be destroyed. They have become defiled. And they shall be impure to you."[126] For all intents and purposes, these major appliances are fire machines. The Torah teaches that even though fire—like water—is a cleansing agent, that does not extend dispensations to ovens and stoves. "They have become defiled" and consequently no remedy presents itself other than destruction—forever. In other words, here time will not heal or mend matters. Should a man resist and attempt to preserve his oven, the halachic presumption remains: that oven is defiled.

"On the other hand, a spring or cistern of gathered water shall be ritually pure. And someone who touches their carcass will be ritually impure."[127] This verse provides a counter-position to that which the Torah advanced above. That is, even though water inside an earthenware vessel becomes impure, this is not the case when water is in a spring or cistern. Springs and cisterns are different, because the water rests upon ground. Thus, even if one of the eight creatures falls to its death in a spring or *mikveh*, the water remains unaffected; it is untainted.

Let us provide working definitions for three Hebrew terms associated with collected water. A *maayan* (מעין) is a freshwater spring; a cistern or

---

124. Vayikra 11:33.
125. Vayikra 11:35.
126. Ibid.
127. Vayikra 11:36.

bor (בור) suggests a housed place of stored or gathered water, and *mikveh* (מקוה) connotes water on an outdoor ground surface.

The sages teach the following on our verse's closing words, "shall be ritually pure."[128] A man who submerges in spring or cistern water becomes ritually pure. In contrast, he is not cleansed should he dip into a tub of drawn spring water.

"And someone who touches their carcass will be ritually impure."[129] Having established a halachic fact that spring water purifies man, this verse qualifies that assumption. If a man submerges in a spring while gripping one of the carcasses, all the spring water in the world does not undo his defilement.

"And when one of their carcasses falls on any seed earmarked for planting, and it has been planted, it remains ritually pure."[130] Above it was written that edible foods that have had contact with water are readied to receive *tumah* (and contract defilement providing that other factors are also present). One might erringly presume that the *tumah* clock, in a manner of speaking, begins ticking when seeds are sown in a field and get irrigated. "It remains ritually pure." Since seeds are in the ground, that freezes or neutralizes contagion. No amount of hosing will change that, for "it remains ritually pure."

Matters change under these following new circumstances. "But if water is put on an [unplanted] seed and one of the creature's carcasses comes upon it, it shall be ritually impure for you."[131] This means that if a seed has been uprooted from the ground, potential for *tumah* readiness is reactivated. In this context, sprinkling water on a detached seed prepares it for succumbing to defilement at a later juncture. Really, this law has been advanced earlier, and there is nothing new about the fact that water is a major catalyst casting a potential state of defilement.

But here a new element is introduced. It needs to be determined how that water got there. If water touched food inadvertently, that does not count. It must be a man's conscious desire to water that motors the irrigation act. "But if water is put." Read: water is put there on purpose. [132]

---

128. BT *Pesachim* 16:1.
129. Vayikra 11:36.
130. Vayikra 11:37.
131. Vayikra 11:38.
132. BT *Bava Metzia* 22b.

This wraps up this present section dealing with *tamei* animals and crea-tures; we now continue with discussion regarding kosher animals.

Kosher Animals

"And when any kosher animal for eating dies, whoever touches its carcass will be rendered ritually impure until the evening."[133] This verse imparts a law governing when a kosher species of animal dies of natural causes. Had it been ritually slaughtered, it would not have caused defilement to a man who touched its carcass. Our verse depicts, however, a natural death of an animal that was potential food. The sages derive a distinction between cases involving a man touching the flesh of a carcass versus coming into contact with other specific animal parts.[134] If a man touches an animal's bones, tendons, horns, hooves, or hide while he is *tamei*, he does not transmit his *tumah*. Seemingly, it is a man touching the edible part of an animal (its flesh) that triggers *tumah*. The animal parts delineated above, though, are not fit to be eaten (bones, tendons, etc.) and hence fail to defile.

Genuine authorities of Jewish law, the sages must be viewed as unim-peachable and, of course, their opinions are unquestionably accepted. Howev-er, according to our verse's straight and plain reading, an animal's body frame and body components are included in the term "carcass" or *neveilah* (נבילה). *Tumah* is contracted by touching a carcass or any part thereof. Consider this logic. While an animal is alive, it does not cause a man to contract defilement (i.e., when he touches it). Similarly, when it is slaughtered for the purpose of providing man with food, it does not cause or exude defilement. This is be-cause ritual slaughter does not detract one iota from its former healthy state of being. In other words, it was healthy before being slaughtered—slaughtered while healthy.

Compare this to an animal that becomes sick or diseased. Its tempera-ment or nature has been altered prior to its death. Deterioration had set in and undermined the animal's vitality and well-being. It is that deterioration that causes man to contract defilement. In a manner of speaking, poison exudes from the dead animal, injecting toxins into anyone who touches or handles it. Quickly, these pathologies invade every organ and system of the

---

133. Vayikra 11:39.
134. *Torat Kohanim*, Vayikra 11:39.

ailing animal, eventually reaching cells in the muscles, tissues, bones, tendons, horn, hooves, and hide. At odds with rabbinic exegesis, the straightforward explanation contends that the animal's carcass and every fiber are diseased. Meltdown transmits *tumah*.

"And whoever eats from its carcass—he shall launder his clothes. And he shall be ritually impure until the evening."[135] Ingesting meat from a carcass, the Torah makes clear, causes defilement in the same way as had a man handled it. This verse teaches that when a man eats tainted flesh, he passes it down from his mouth to his stomach. It is his intestines that are now "handling" contaminated meat. The Torah establishes that as a result of eating or handling an animal's carcass, a man must clean his clothes. He is defiled until the evening.

"And every creeping crawler that scoots along the ground is abominable. It may not be eaten."[136] At first glance, this verse appears redundant. An earlier section prohibited such creatures. In fact, that aforementioned source only discussed the blighted eight. This verse outlaws creepers not previously mentioned. Additionally, we learn here that *tumah* results from eating them, but there is no defilement from touching or handling them.

"All belly crawlers and all those walking on all fours including the gamut from centipedes to creepers along the ground—you shall not eat them, for they are an abomination to you."[137] Belly crawlers propel themselves that way because they do not have legs. Centipedes take into account creatures with more than four legs.

This section concludes its treatment of fauna whose carcasses defile Jews. Whether the dead object is an animal or creepy crawler, these are the pertinent laws. "Do not make yourselves contemptible through any of these creepers. And do not handle them to become defiled. And you will become ritually impure on account of them."[138] A blanket statement forbids Hebrews to eat, touch, or otherwise handle them. Boilerplate gets followed up with detailed substance. Different types of creatures are named, joined by an explicit caution against eating them.

---

135. Vayikra 11:40.
136. Vayikra 11:41.
137. Vayikra 11:42.
138. Vayikra 11:43.

"Do not make yourselves contemptible through any of these creepers." A Jew's essence—his soul—is held in contempt when he eats these abominations. "Creepers" give size or other organic developmental considerations. That is, prohibition to eat these lowlifes begins when they reach an ability to propel themselves along the ground. As far as the prohibition to touch them, the key phrase is "And do not handle them to become defiled." Finally, when it comes to picking them up, "And you will become ritually impure on account of them." The Talmudic sages strike a perfervid chord. Forebodingly, they understand these words to mean that if a man defiles himself in this world, the Maker will defile him in the next one. The heavenly tribunal will hold him in contempt of Court.[139]

Rationale for this rash of injunctions is explicit. "For I am God your Almighty. And you shall sanctify yourselves and be holy because I am holy. You shall not defile yourselves with any means of crawling lowlife that bellies along the earth."[140] Jews are God's servants and attendants. They are meant to observe His example, emulating Him. Insofar as the Creator is holy and apart from all things physical and material—because those physical trappings are a hindrance—so too it is apt for Jews to adopt pathways of holiness. Removing *tumah* and filth elevates. There can be no doubt that when a Jew's life is a cancatenation of one sacred mission after another, the result will be an embracement of holiness. Right action generates refinement. Truthfully, it etches nobility.

The verse reiterates, "You shall not defile yourselves with any means of crawling lowlife that bellies along the earth." Is this verse different from the one above, "Do not make yourselves contemptible through any of these creepers"? To be sure, this is not a warning to stay clear of self-inflicted *tumah*. Instead, it is testimony that since the Torah asserts above "And you shall sanctify yourselves and be holy," when a man toils to preserve his pure soul, he will thereby acquire great things—he will attain holiness.

More promises follow. Commitment to a high degree of spirituality and detachment effectively assures a man that he will not defile his soul by eating crawlers. Vigilance precedes detachment or separation. Separation leads to holiness. A verse in Sefer Bamidbar captures these sentiments: "And you shall

---

139. BT *Yoma* 39a.
140. Vayikra 11:44.

don *tzitzit* and see them and remember all of Hashem's commandments."[141] That verse establishes a positive commandment: "So that you will remember them."[142]

Here is Heaven's promise to His people. Habit tends to create established patterns. Patterns, then, burrow deeply into a man's psyche, until a thing becomes second nature. At that point, a pious man's mode of behavior acts effectively to insulate him while keeping sin at bay. Just as true, consistency self-perpetuates. Positive Torah momentum comes about when practiced and reprised. Ultimately, a Jew becomes holy to his God. What is conveyed with the illustration of wearing *tzitzit* applies to this *parashah*'s concluding section.

"Do not make yourselves contemptible through any of these creepers," and consequently "And you shall sanctify yourselves." No finer exercise does the job. A man who is attuned to holy endeavors will refrain from contracting *tumah*.

Finally, another reason to observe commandments is written: "For I am the Lord Who brought you out from the land of Egypt so that I will be your God and you will be sanctified because I am holy."[143]

Holy God → HOLY PEOPLE

Origins of Kashrut

Why does the Torah prohibit certain foods? Classic commentators tackle this very question. Our treatment shall be thorough, including a critique of major thinkers, as well as an excellent guide to a sorely misunderstood subject.

Some commentators, notably the Ramban, write that health lay at the heart of the matter. Injunctions are designed, they claim, to prevent a Jew from ingesting unhealthy food. *Treif* products cause medical difficulties. See the Ramban's comments on the verse "And these are abominations so far as birds are concerned."[144]

Heaven forfend! Placing health concerns front and center for commandments, making this the raison d'être for keeping commandments, is

---

141. Bamidbar 15:39.
142. Bamidbar 15:40.
143. Vayikra 11:45.
144. Vayikra 11:13.

tantamount to saying that the divine Torah is a desultory medical guide. Holy Writ contains much more than a few sporadic health and fitness tips. Besides, all one has to do is look at Gentiles the world over to refute such reckless speculation. Heartily, they dine on pig, bugs, slugs, rats, cats, dogs, plus every bird in the book. In addition, some eat *tamei* animals and fish—even raw—and yet these folks are cast-iron hale. Radiating stamina and vitality, they show no signs of chronic shortness of breath, let alone illness.

Here is another point to discredit those who will have us believe this section reads as a good health column. Consider the planet's vicious animal species. King cobras, killer bees, and scorpions—about them and a host of other man killers we read nary a word. Similarly, the Torah gives the silent treatment to hemlock or tobacco, while the medical establishment screams bloody murder. Commentators, reducing *kashrut* to a fad diet, are sorely mistaken. Bold and underscore: the Torah is not a medical guide, nor was it transmitted to heal man's body.

Torah is the antidote and elixir for the soul. Verily, it is the cure to what ails man, the prophylactic for what is commonly called the human condition. Prohibited foods are outlawed because they sully a Jew's soul, turning him into something vile. Violating the laws of *kashrut* unhinges the delicate nature of man's pure *nefesh*. Put differently, ingesting forbidden fruit throws off man's natural inner harmony, resulting in a general malaise or clouding of his innate goodness. Moral blindness and turpitude come with each bite. Checkered thoughts and deeds defile man until purity is replaced with prurience, holiness with hideousness.

King David beseeches, "And Your holy spirit do not remove from me." Pleadingly he begs, "God has created me with a pure heart and a new, resolute spirit within me."[145] Returning to our last verses, we read what Hashem deplores: "Do not make yourselves contemptible through any of these creepers." An unquestioned correlation arises. Ingesting defiled food dulls man's heart. When it comes to numbing a Hebrew's honest religious impulse and motive, opiate has nothing over forbidden (read: *treif*) fruit. Both cast a pall of stupor.

Note that the Torah does not refer to prohibited food as something damaging or disease-ridden. Instead, modifying terms include defiling and disgusting. This is instructive insofar as such words drive home a major point:

---

145. Tehillim 51:13.

the Torah cautions against corrosive damage to the soul, not the body. By implication at least, there is a body-soul relationship. When a Jew eats kosher food, it stabilizes natural bodily harmony. A healthy soul assures a pure, rich blood composition that is neither too coarse nor too granular. Forbidden food rocks proper balance.

In medieval times prohibited foods were often the mark of pagan society. The Rambam notes that in India, for example, kosher meat (from cows or goats) was strictly banned. Other countries serve their gods by gulping *treif* smorgasbords. In sum, Torah-forbidden food is contemptible. Consider another angle to this discussion. The fact that the Torah proscribes a crass diet attests to the excellence of man's soul and to the great lengths the Creator goes to foster its well-being.

Having determined the importance of good eating, why didn't Hashem demand His nation to go vegetarian or raw vegan? Was not Adam forbidden from eating meat? Only in a later development and dispensation to Noah and his sons did God allow meat. We hold this question in abeyance until Parashat Re'eh in Sefer Devarim.

Tumah

Level (in descending order)	Ramifications	Remedy
Type 1 (*avei avot hatumah*) Most severe: a human corpse	*Tumah* spreads to people, vessels, clothing, and/or food by touching, handling, or even sharing a common roof. A Jew who has had contact (per above) with a corpse, in turn, is *tamei*. His *tumah* is called *av hatumah*, with its own governing rules. Contaminated persons or objects also transmit *tumah*.	Release from this status takes seven days.

Level (in descending order)	Ramifications	Remedy
Type 2 (*av hatumah*) Second most severe: a *metzora*, one afflicted with *tzaraat*	Passes on *tumah* to those who touch, handle, or treat him and when he enters a residence or *biah*. Transmits *tumah* to any chair, pillow, or rug upon which he sits or lies. (But one who pays a visit to a *metzora* is not defiled by simply being in his presence.)	People or objects that are recipients of contracting this second, type 2 layer of *tumah* are named *vlad hatumah* but are not categorized as type 3. Remedy from this affected grouping necessitates time to elapse— he waits until the evening.
Type 3 Mundane ritual impurity resulting from ordinary life events ranging from menstruation to childbirth.	Not specified by Abravanel.	Not specified by Abravanel in our section.
Type 4 A carcass of a *treif* animal.	Contagion is contracted by touching or carrying it.	Ritual impurity remains with him until that evening.
Type 5 The blighted eight creatures, when dead. Even on a horizontal bar with them is a man who ejaculates.	Transmit ritual impurity to other people or vessels, via physical contact. Mere carrying or handling of the object fails to pass on contagion. Clothing need not be laundered; defilement stops at the man's person.	Not specified by Abravanel in our section.
Type 6 A carcass of a kosher animal (mammal) that died of natural causes.	Whoever touches the carcass is *tamei* until the upcoming evening. The man who transports the carcass (but doesn't touch it directly) defiles the clothing that he's wearing.	Ritual impurity lasts until evening.
Type 7 When a kosher bird dies.	A man sustains impurity when he swallows it. But should he touch or carry it, the man does not become *tamei*.	None needed.

This discussion aims at providing an excellent framework to better understand *tumah* and its hierarchical implications. In descending order, the most severe form of *tumah* occurs when a man dies. We are speaking of his corpse or cadaver. A lifeless body is judged with the most severity because of the consequences or potential it has for impacting others. Call it collateral damage, meaning that contact with a cadaver results in *tumah* being propagated to people, vessels, clothing, and/or food via touching or *maga* (מגע), handling or *masa* (משא), or even by sharing a common roof or *ohel* (אהל).

Now, let us turn to the man impacted. To be graphic, picture a lifeless, akimbo body. Its outstretched hand touched a man. He gets designated as a chief defiler or *av hatumah* (אב הטומא). For that man, release from this status takes seven days. All of the foregoing is so because a cadaver stands at the very top of the *tumah* pyramid. Since it is *avei avot hatumah* (אבי אבות הטומאה), when people or objects make contact with a cadaver, they become afflicted with type 2 or *av hatumah*.

Next in line is a *metzora*. One afflicted with *tzaraat* (צרעת) has also contracted type 2 *tumah* (similar to a man who has contact with a cadaver). A *metzora*'s *tumah* is called *av hatumah*, because it passes on *tumah* to those who touch, handle, or treat him. Transference also occurs when he enters a residence or *biah* (ביאה). People or objects that are recipients of contracting this second, type 2 layer of *tumah* are called *vlad hatumah* (ולד הטומאה). Incidentally, note that although they suffer the consequences of having contracted *tumah*, they are not categorized as type 3 per se. Remedy from this type of *tumah* requires the passage of time—he waits until the evening. Another ramification or outgrowth of the *metzora*'s reach (type 2) is that he transmits *tumah* to any type of furniture upon which he sits or *moshav* (מושב). Thus, if a man sits on, say, a divan on which a *metzora* had sat, he contracts *tumah*. He remains in that defiled state until sunset. On a lenient note, a fellow who pays a visit to a *metzora* does not become defiled simply by being in his presence.

Tanach students are generally more familiar with this next grouping, type 3 *tumah*. Mundane ritual impurity occurs commonly with ordinary life events ranging from menstruation to childbirth. People affected by these states include a *zavah* (a woman who has had abnormal vaginal bleeding), a *niddah* (a woman who is impure from menstruation), a *yoledet* (a woman who has given birth), a *zav* (a man who has had an abnormal seminal emission), and a *bo'el niddah* (a man who is impure from having engaged in relations with a *niddah*). Specific cases pertaining to women include certain vaginal disorders or post-childbirth issues discussed in later *parshiyot* in this volume.

Type 4 defilement refers to that transmitted by a carcass of a *treif* animal. A man contracts this contagion when he either touches or carries it. Ritual impurity remains with him until that evening.

The blighted eight creatures, when dead, follow next and are type 5. Even on a horizontal bar with them is a man who ejaculates. Both transmit ritual impurity to other people or vessels, via physical contact. However, mere carrying or handling of the object in question fails to pass on contagion. Also, if a man touches one of the blighted eight creatures' carcasses, for example, he does not have to launder his clothing. Defilement stops at the man's person.

Further down the totem pole, type 6 is *tumah* incurred from the carcass of a kosher animal. Note that the animal in our example died of natural causes. Those touching it are ritually impure until evening.

And finally we come to the last rung on our *tumah* ladder, type 7 defilement. This occurs when a kosher bird dies. Here, a man sustains impurity in a most limited and narrow manner. That is, if he swallows it. But should he touch or carry it, the man does not become *tamei*. The Torah delineates these gradations.

Upon examination of our chart outlining *tumah*, five questions come to the fore. Let us address them.

1. Assuming that man is the most complex and delicate organism of God's creations, how is it that embedded within him is the very highest level of *tumah* (type 1)? What is the logic that dictates that man's potential for *tumah* exceeds that of animal carcasses?

2. There are times in a man's life when he suffers from some malady. Physical imbalance is manifest should he become a *zav* or *metzora*. For a woman, menstruation or childbirth likely impacts her inner balance. Be that as it may, why do human beings generate *tumah* while they are alive, while even *treif* living animals or birds do not? If we advance that a man out of kilter triggers *tumah*, should not an animal's maladies also be the source of spiritual contagion? Yet this is not the case.

3. Let us consider cases of kosher animals that have been ritually slaughtered. No part of them gives off *tumah*. A Jew can freely touch or handle them without fear of defilement. Yet should that same kosher species die of, say, a heart attack, a man does become impure by touching or handling it. Why? The moment an animal dies, we can posit that man frowns upon it. The natural reaction is to recoil, and thus the deceased animal becomes foreign to him. Given that, why should a carcass not be impure irrespective of how its death came about?

4. According to the sages, carcasses of impure (nonkosher) birds cause *tumah* only if they enter a man's throat.[146] Why is that particular human anatomy the tipping scale for defilement? Why does a *treif* bird carcass leave no palpable aftereffect if it comes into contact with other parts of a man's body (such as his hands or arms)? To better put this question into perspective, what makes *treif* birds different from *treif* animals that bring defilement to man when he touches them? Also, why doesn't the Torah write explicitly about *treif* birds in the context of *tumah* at all?

5. Lastly, why is the Torah mum on the subject of nonkosher fish vis-à-vis *tumah*?

The Ralbag posits that these questions may be answered by taking man's exalted nature into account. He delves into a discussion about how man is qualitatively greater than his subcomponents, many of which share commonality with animals. Hence, when man's life force wanes and he perishes, his death is a markedly different event from that of an animal. Devoid of man's subliminal existence, a lifeless body plunges into great upheaval, vacuum, chaos. Consequently, drained man transmits *tumah* in a way lifeless animals cannot. Those interested in understanding the Ralbag should read more, but for our purposes, his theory does not seem plausible.

Let us put things into perspective and comprehensively answer all five questions. When a man passes away, the severity of his cadaver's *tumah* rates in the most intense category. Two reasons provide rationale. One is *b'bechinat hapo'el* (בבחינת הפועל) or from the perspective of the active agent—in other

---

146. *Torat Kohanim* 11:40.

words, due to the corpse itself—and two is *b'bechinat hamekabel* (בבחינת המקבל) or from the perspective of the receiver of the impurity, meaning because of what derives from a state of death, or more accurately, how that condition affects others.

To begin with, when a man dies, his body becomes acrid and putrid. Decay and decomposition offend those within close proximity. When a person passes, say, in a house, the air quality within that entire building structure reeks. Palpably, the aura surrounding a dead man's space cannot be escaped, just as it cannot be mistaken.

When we consider a case in which a person expires inside an enclosed area such as a tent, that tent gets impacted in a way that, perforce, is felt by everyone present. *Tumah* is prevalent and pervasive. Given man's physical sophistication while alive, in death his human mechanism goes into total disarray. Really, the resulting chaos is all-encompassing as a once-supple body rapidly loses oxygen and, in a manner of speaking, altitude. A nosedive results, a freefall from mighty heights. This precipitous drop happens at breakneck velocity, meaning that basic biological forces previously exerted to maintain man's intricate harmony now accelerate his breakdown and cause his physical being to hurtle toward disintegration. Human decomposition far outpaces that of animals. (A day or two after animals die, there is hardly any malodor.) In sum, man's death is incomparably more significant than an animal's.

Our discussion now analyzes the impact of the person or object subjected to *tumah*. There is one basic principle, though it contains what we may call a mirror application: (a) objects most strongly affect others with similar makeup or composition, and (b) two dissimilar objects are less apt to be affected by contact with each other.

What does this principle mean? Man is most affected by a cadaver, since man is both the source and the receiver of the *tumah*. Accordingly, his level of *tumah* runs at full capacity. Compare that to a man who comes into contact with a dead animal; he is subject to a far lesser dose of *tumah*.

This axiom's answer provides guidance. To illustrate, take the cases of a man who becomes a *metzora* and one who oozes particular bodily fluid—a *zav*. We can expand our illustration to a *bo'el niddah* or man engaged in sexual intercourse with a woman who is impure from menstruation, or to a *zavah* or female oozing particular bodily fluid, or to a *yoledet* or woman after childbirth, or even to a *tamei met* or man who comes into contact with a corpse. The Torah considers these situations fundamental aberrations that detract from a potentially balanced state of being. In other words, whether it is an extreme case of a person getting close to a cadaver or a condition whereby his or her body's natural harmony has been compromised, *tumah* results.

Sometimes *tumah* occurs when a Jew eats forbidden food such as pig, bugs, or rodents. Spiritually, he has received a decisive strike to his delicate wiring. Preventing jolting blows to a Jew's hypersensitivity is exactly what lies behind many of Heaven's directives.

- Certain places are off limits (rooms where a corpse lies).
- Certain foods may not be ingested (*treif*, etc.).
- Certain life forms may not be touched, handled, or carried.
- Certain activities are deemed abominable.

In short, the Torah demands that Jews steer far away from anything that will upset their highly impressionable, chiseled souls. And when a Hebrew flounders, it is incumbent upon him to bring an appropriate compensatory sacrifice. Seen in this light, sacrifices are the means to patch up a breach in the relationship Jews have with their Maker. Before a sacrifice is offered, an offender's *tumah* ushers him out of the Hebrew encampment. Remedy begins when he immerses in a *mikveh* and launders or changes soiled clothing.

Interestingly, at the end of a woman's menstrual period, no sacrifice is required. This is for the obvious reason that menstruation is perfectly normal and healthy. Nonetheless, she is considered *temeah* on account of uterine discharges. By contrast, men's and women's excessive and unnatural discharge renders them both *tamei*. Seemingly, those fluids are symptomatic of imbalances. Even more extreme is the case of *metzora'im*. The Torah requires them to bring a sacrifice, highlighting a radical departure from normative symmetry.

Why do women bring a sacrifice after childbirth or aborted pregnancies? This is due to placenta expulsion, etc. Note that in those latter cases only a small sacrifice is offered, consisting of two turtledoves or pigeons.

Let us consider the following forms of *tumah*. Someone who came in contact with a corpse, a man who had a seminal ejaculation, one who touched a dead reptile, or a man who entered a room where a *metzora* was present—all are cases that do not necessitate atonement. Obviously enough, these circumstances are unavoidable no matter how hard he tries.

Returning to better understand man's potential for *tumah*, note how death utterly saps him of vitality while simultaneously activating rigor mortis. The Torah assesses damages associated with the cessation of life and how it impacts a fellow man. As we have written, it is advisable to be highly vigilant when it comes to distancing oneself from any level of *tumah*. Setting boundaries for *tumah* deriving from live, domestic animals, however, is fairly impossible. Frankly, standard solicitude does not pass muster. Extra care is needed.

It is equally true that animal body fluids are not nearly as noxious as those exuding from humans. For that reason, their fluids do not cause man *tumah*. However, *tumah* will be contracted through handling of dead animals.

Slaughtered kosher animals do not give off *tumah*, as opposed to when they die of disease or natural causes. Ritual slaughter takes away an animal's life when it is fully viable or in the pink of health. No breakdown in any of its internal systems occurred. Consequently, there is no perceptible difference after its life forces abate. Hence, man's handling of it does not cause him ritual impurity. Contrast that scenario to one where an animal died of natural causes. Perforce, there had to have been prior pathology. It is that resultant aftermath of disease that ushers in contagion. Touching or transporting it triggers *tumah*. This is a contributory rationale for the Torah prohibition on eating kosher animals that have not been ritually slaughtered. It also explains why a thorough postmortem examination is carried out by experts after ritual slaughter. See the Rambam's *Mishneh Torah*.[147] The Ralbag posits that the reason kosher animals do not cause ritual impurity to man is that they were expressly created to serve man and provide him with food.

Attempts to apply our gained knowledge to discussions regarding *tumah* generated by *treif* dead birds run into difficulties. In fact, we will see that these fowl fly, if you will, under the Torah's radar. Why? One, dead nonkosher birds stir little ill effect or damage. Since they are so vastly different in makeup from man, he is impervious to their demise.

In addition, there is a practical consideration at work. *Treif* fowl hardly ever roam where man dwells. Dogs and cats are incomparably more prevalent than eagles or hawks. For that matter, kosher birds are neighborhood

---

147. Rambam, *Mishneh Torah*, Hilchot Avot Hatumah 1:2.

fixtures. Therefore, nonkosher animals, reptiles, or dead kosher animals produce *tumah*. Dog, donkey, or horse carcasses are cases in point. Proximity and mundaneness explain why their deaths generate *tumah* but not those of birds in the wild.

Statistics play a part in the mix, too. For that reason, a nonkosher animal's carcass generates a more severe form of impurity than that of a kosher animal's carcass. Why? By and large, kosher animals will be slaughtered before disease progresses to the point that they will succumb to illness. Additionally, the same (rare) likelihood exists that kosher animals will die of natural causes as that nonkosher birds will be found winging it around city boulevards. Both categories' *tumah* severity ranks low. Lowest on our totem pole is *tumah* whose source is carcasses of kosher birds. Its damage is negligible, and its rate of occurrence is most infrequent. Apropos, its *tumah* is only contracted as a man eats it, attesting to its attenuated magnitude of impurity. Only vaguely does the Torah cover this *halachah*.

Concerning the subject of fish and *tumah*, Scripture also says sparingly little. That is because when fish come out of water, death quickly ensues. Verses do not differentiate between live and dead fish, nor do they pin *tumah* on someone who touches or handles them. Bereft of hides, horns, hooves, or other parts of value that animals have, fish have minimal redeeming value. Still, they are good food.

Striving for Holiness

"On the other hand, a spring or cistern of gathered water shall be ritually pure. And someone who touches their carcass will be ritually impure."[148] Allusion is made to nonkosher fish while they are still in their natural marine habitat. Fastidious-minded Jews are advised against touching them. Similar care is taken by those individuals to avoid touching food or seeds that have come in contact with water unless they are preparing to eat them imminently. All the more so, alacritous Kohanim who eat sacred foods assumed extra caution in their eating habits, expending leonine efforts to steer away from contracting *tumah*.

Here's another observation on a Jew's behavior. He goes to great lengths when it comes to handling liquids. This is so because liquids possess properties

---

148. Vayikra 11:36.

capable of laying the groundwork for bringing on food impurities. In contrast, people are not so finicky about food. To wit, folks regularly eat food cooked in various ways. They also like food to come in a variety of colors. But would a man even think to drink water that isn't perfectly clear or wine whose appearance is off? Therefore, solid foodstuffs are not as susceptible to *tumah* as the Torah-specified liquids. The same holds true for legumes. Until they have been moistened, they haven't been readied for human consumption, and subsequently they do not become *tamei*.

In this vein, earthenware vessels needed to be watched from potential invading forces of *tumah*. Contact with *tumah* from the inside of clay utensils turned it into something quite noxious. Hence, if it did contract impurity, there was no remedy, and it had to be smashed to bits.

Metal utensils are a radical departure from those made of pottery.[149] Briefly, they were essentially clean, so purity was just a matter of rinsing them out with water. Metal vessels used for cooking on fire, though, needed to pass through fire as a means of purifying them if they required remedy.

This concludes our two final remarks on this *parashah*. Essentially, it all boiled down to one thing. The Torah intends for Jews to attain the very highest levels of holiness. All forms of baseness get robustly rooted out. Explanation and elucidation are meant to offer readers guidelines into this esoteric topic of ritual purity and impurity. The following *parshiyot* delve into finer details and will be elaborated in their appropriate sections.

Readers, take note that the Ralbag takes a totally different tack than we have put forth. Let students study both approaches and choose the one that makes the most sense to them.

---

149. Abravanel lightly touches on metal vessels here despite the fact that the Torah does not.

PARASHAT TAZRIA

ON LEPROSY

First *aliyah*

"And Hashem spoke to Moshe, saying: Speak to Bnei Yisrael, saying: When a woman conceives and gives birth to a son, then she shall be [ritually] impure for seven days, just as when she menstruates she shall be [ritually] impure."

A Note on Terminology

Because this volume delves into arcane areas of spiritual defilement or contamination, and because the Torah employs terms and concepts that modern readers may find recherché, we present here a lexicon to serve as a primer into the subject. Since English translations may have foreign and/or undesirable connotations, we will generally prefer to simply transliterate the Hebrew and refrain from attempting to translate it.

baheret Baheret (בהרת) appears to have been a distinctive spot, quite noticeable and conspicuous.

baheret levanah A subcategory of *baheret* is a white, distinctive spot called *baheret levanah* (בהרת לבנה).

beharot beharot levanot Prevalent white body spotting or *beharot beharot levanot* (בהרות בהרות לבנות) necessitates a priest's house call and diagnosis.

bohek Pale body dots or *bohek* (בוהק), though concerning,

are not problematic, as this is straight-up seborrhea.

gibe'ach Shedding beard tufts or *gibe'ach* (גבח) is a harmless condition but can turn to chagrin should discoloration arise.

kere'ach Similarly to *bohek* (בוהק), common head balding or *kere'ach* (קרח) presents no issue so long as there is no discoloration.

metzora A *metzora* (מצורע) is a Biblical "leper," that is, a person who is suffering from *tzaraat* (צרעת).

michvah   Burns from fires
or *michvah* (מכוה) present
their own headaches for the
examining priest. Strange things
may happen after a burn heals.
Namely, rawness bordering
on bright pink or *michyat
hamichvah baheret levanah
adamdemet* (מחית המכוה בהרת
לבנה אדמדמת) or a white spot
or *michyat hamichvah levanah*
(מחית המכוה לבנה) grows.

michvah perachah   If the resulting
spot from a healed burn
invades the skin, then the priest
pronounces *tzaraat* (צרעת);
however, this form of *tzaraat*
is called *michvah perachah*
(מכוה פרחה). It is a *nega tzaraat*
(נגע צרעת).

mispachat   A *mispachat* (מספחת)
falls into a subcategory of
sapachat (ספחת). It may describe
a benign pale-looking skin
discoloration. As such, it is
neither a *nega* (נגע) nor *tzaraat*
(צרעת). Alternatively, that
infected region may erupt and
signal *tzaraat*.

nega   A telltale or confirming
mark on the skin of one who
suffers from *tzaraat* (called a
metzora) is a *nega* (נגע). An
attending priest, upon seeing a
patient's *nega*, will pronounce

the onset of the malady. A *nega*
can spread, shrink, or stay the
same. Similarly, it can darken,
become lighter, or sit tight.

nega amok   Also, we read in this
section about sick skin giving off
a sunken or lower-tier look. This
is *nega amok* (נגע עמוק), resulting
in proof-positive pathology or
nega tzaraat (נגע צרעת).

nega hanetek   Hair loss on the
head or *tzaraat rosh* (צרעת ראש)
and of the beard or *tzaraat
zakan* (צרעת זקן) may be
combined to read *nega hanetek*
(נגע הנתק).

nega tahor   *Nega*, by itself, fails to
impart enough information. The
man bearing it could very well
be exhibiting a benign mark or
nega tahor (נגע טהור). Contrast
inconsequential *nega tahor*
with debilitating *nega tzaraat*
(נגע צרעת).

nega tzaraat   A positive diagnosis
or rash may be designated as a
nega tzaraat (נגע צרעת).

nega tzaraat b'beged tzemer
Apart from a man's body,
a man's woolen or linen
clothing may become defiled.
Respectively, the contamination
on clothes items is called *nega
tzaraat b'beged tzemer* (נגע צרעת
בבגד צמר) and *nega tzaraat*

b'beged pishtim (נגע צרעת בבגד
פשתים). Variations on this
tzaraat take into consideration
warp or *shti* (שתי) and weft or
erev (ערב) threading, leather, or
items made of leather.

netek Baldness may constitute yet
another leprous sign or *nega*
(נגע). Hair loss may occur on the
head or beard. Commentators
divide on whether or not
discoloration (plus baldness)
comes into the picture. In
addition to *nega*, this infirmity
has a second name: *netek* (נתק).
See also *nega hanetek.*

niddah A woman who is
spiritually impure due to
menstruation is a *niddah* (נידה).

pechetet A denigrating word for
blighted material and leather is
pechetet (פחתת). More detailed
description of accursed garment
material or garment parallels
words used when we wrote
about balding and receding
hairlines. Thus, they are *pechetet
b'karachto* (פחתת בקרחתו)
and *pechetet b'gabachto*
(פחתת בגבחתו).

sapachat Commentators find it
hard to agree on what *sapachat*
(ספחת) was. We translate it
either as a whitish blotch,
discoloration, or skin scabs.

se'ar ba'nega Verses speak of
body hair affected by diseased
epidermis as *se'ar ba'nega* (שער
בנגע).

se'eit *Se'eit* (שאת) has a white or
whitish blotchy appearance.
A subcategory of *se'eit* is a
white blotch referred to as *se'eit
levanah* (שאת לבנה).

se'eit hamichvah Sometimes,
skin healing from burns will
give off early warning signs,
only to have an aftergrowth's
progress arrested in its tracks.
The Torah labels this a harmless
discoloration or *se'eit hamichvah*
(שאת המכוה).

shechin Translating the skin
infection whose fame derives,
one may advance, from the sixth
plague in Egypt proves elusive.
Thus, *shechin* (שחין) has been
dubbed an infection, pustule,
boil, or blister. The disorder
has multiple root causes, but
injudicious exposure to heat
or sun is not one of them. To
elaborate, *shechin* may develop
from *se'eit levanah* (שאת לבנה)
or *baheret levanah adamdemet*
(בהרת לבנה אדמדמת), a further
branch-off from *baheret levanah*
proper).

shechin perachah When sufficient
evidence of *baheret levanah*

adamdemet (בהרת לבנה אדמדמת)
is present, a determination is
made that the chap has been
afflicted with *nega tzaraat*
(נגע צרעת), a manifestation
of galloping boils or *shechin
perachah* (שחין פרחה).

tamei/temeah   Ritual impurity is
designated in the masculine as
tamei (טמא) and in the feminine
as *temeah* (טמאה).

tzaraat   Biblical leprosy, which
refers to a spiritual rather than
a physical defilement, is called
tzaraat (צרעת). Signs, symptoms,
and descriptions leading to
positive diagnosis of *tzaraat*
(or ruling it out) are as follows:
Flesh maladies are referred to as
se'eit (שאת) or *sapachat* (ספחת)
or *baheret* (בהרת).

tzaraat mameret   After conclusive
tests come in proving the
presence of *tzaraat* (צרעת) in
fabric, the Torah refers to the
much-maligned wool, linen,
or leather as *tzaraat mameret*
(צרעת ממארת).

**tzaraat porachat b'karachat/
gabachat**   On the head, this
is *tzaraat porachat b'karachat*
(צרעת פורחת בקרחת), whereas

on the forehead it is called
tzaraat porachat gabachat (צרעת
פורחת גבחת). Alternatively,
this *tzaraat*'s name tacks on a
combo slew of other terms we
have introduced (שאת הנגע לבנה
אדמדמת בקרחתו או בגבחתו).

tzaraat rosh/zakan   The Torah
depicts head-hair dysfunction or
beard loss as *tzaraat rosh* (צרעת
ראש) or *tzaraat zakan* (צרעת זקן).

tzarevet hamichvah   The
innocuous condition called
tzarevet hamichvah (צרבת המכוה)
is another name for *se'eit
hamichvah* (שאת המכוה).

tzarevet hashechin   Confusingly
enough, *shechin* does not always
bespeak an infectious version
of the ailment. It may be a
false alarm mimicking the real
McCoy. The Torah calls this
pseudo-lesion *tzarevet hashechin*
(צרבת השחין).

zav   When a man's penis oozes or
drips, Tanach refers to him as a
zav (זב).

zavah   In Tanach, a woman
exhibiting certain vaginal
discharge or oozing is called a
zavah (זבה).

Ritual Impurity after Childbirth

After the Torah broached the subjects of impure animals and birds so far as a Hebrew's permitted diet and handling them was concerned, it next delved into questions dealing with ritual impurity of men and women—both when they are alive and then ultimately as it pertains to them after death. As prefaced in the previous *parashah*, the recent Torah sections adhere to neat patterns and to a structured hierarchy of spiritual defilement. Nothing about the progression is willy-nilly.[1] Beginning at the top of the pyramid (reflecting the most severe) is defilement as it pertains to man. Its tentacles, in a manner of speaking, have the greatest reach, exceeding that of animals and birds. Accordingly, the Torah's treatment of man's ritual defilement necessitates more detail than had been provided when the subject heading pertained to animal-based defilement.

Rashi, quoting the sage Rabbi Samlay, learns a juxtaposition of this *parashah*'s opening sections this way. The reason our section commences with women after childbirth is that this marks man in his very earliest developmental stage. Or possibly it informs readers that the majority of *tzaraat* (spiritual or Biblical leprosy) is on account of sexual relations at ill-chosen times. Illustrations of such include cohabitation when a woman is impure due to menstruation or when a man's wife experiences technically defined vaginal discharge or oozing. Sexual intimacy at the wrong time can bear directly upon newborns. *Tzaraat* latches on to them from birth. This explains why laws concerning a woman after childbirth precede those dealing with *tzaraat*. Finally, the Torah hints at three root causes of *tzaraat*'s curse and why that affliction occurs more often than many other ailments.

First, *tzaraat* can result after a man ingests ritually defiled food. It is axiomatic. Second, exposure to a human corpse or animal carcass makes man susceptible to *tzaraat*. Lastly, if a woman conceives while in certain times in her monthly cycle, this produces a predilection for her children to become *metzora'im*. Because of these three chief events, our section begins with a woman giving birth. Afterwards, verses will deal with *tzaraat*.

---

1.   Note that Abravanel's treatment of the subject skips around somewhat, and his essay on the first *aliyah* will actually include material from each of the first four *aliyot* of this *parashah*.

Tzaraat is, in fact, an alarum to:

- Study the dietary laws punctiliously.
- Learn the laws of ritual defilement.
- Heed the laws of family purity.

The first two warnings appear in the prior *parashah*. Our present one starts, "When a woman conceives." It delineates the applicable laws on the subject. Statutes governing *tzaraat* follow immediately afterwards. Look again at this Hebrew phrase: "*Ishah ki tazria v'yaldah zachar*" (When a woman conceives [תזריע] and gives birth [ילדה] to a son [זכר]).[2] Women create life similar to land bringing forth produce. Her seed or *zera* (זרע) is her son or daughter.

If a woman gives birth to a boy, "then she shall be *temeah* for seven days."[3] Counting seven days begins after her son is born. The simile "just as when she is impure due to menstruation, she shall be [ritually] impure" teaches about how to relate to post-birth blood. It is viewed as menses. In Hebrew, the word for a woman who is impure due to menstruation is *niddah* (נידה). As Rashi says, the word implies a time associated with a general and overall heaviness in the head and limbs, a feeling that persists for days. Monthly, nature expels unneeded fluid buildup from a woman's body in a pattern that has been compared to lunar cycles. Just as a one-month time period can be broken down to four cycles of the moon—neatly divided into four weeks—so too it is with women, whose period lasts for a week. Apart from what happens during a woman's cycle, most human illnesses also assume a seven-day course. These patterns correspond to lunar sub-cycle phases. That explains why, as we will soon see, priests place suspected *metzora'im* in quarantine for seven days before they perform a second observation to confirm and pronounce their conclusions.

Seven days is also the time frame whereby a newborn still acutely feels the trauma of childbirth. It is during that time that new mothers experience heavy bleeding normally attributed to expelling the placenta and residual stored blood accumulated during pregnancy because normal menses ceased.

"And she shall remain for thirty-three days while she experiences ritually pure blood. She shall not touch sacred things, nor should she come

---

2. Vayikra 12:2.
3. Ibid.

to the Mikdash until the days of her ritual purification process conclude."[4] Thirty-three days is the time a woman needs to rid her body of the buildup during pregnancy when she was not menstruating.

Talmudic sages differ on human embryology.[5] Rabbi Yishmael opines that development for boys occurs on day forty-one, and day eighty-one for girls; however, a majority of sages assume that a fetus (male or female) reaches its critical mass at forty-one days after conception. The Ramban follows rabbinic consensus.[6] This finding, most likely, was based on surveying pregnant women. They claimed to have felt movement on day forty-one for boys, day eighty-one for girls. Logically this theory holds water, if you will, because boy's natures and traits are more heated than those of girls. These characteristics follow their respective genders throughout their lives. In conclusion, given that these innate traits exist, it makes sense that a boy fetus will develop at a more rapid rate than a girl fetus.

Embryology, then, is a chief determinant to our verse's math. That is, Heaven devised a way to link former fetus and uterine wall lining development to postnatal days of purification. Hence, for a boy we arrive at forty days (including the first seven days) in order to return a mother's womb to its pre-pregnancy state. An operative rule of thumb is this: the number of early pregnancy days when menses abated equals the post-birth days of excess bleeding. That total (forty for boys) corresponds to the time when a male fetus reaches a critical stage of its development. Critically, should a pregnant woman experience bleeding during this first trimester, it is not considered menstrual bleeding on the same level as postnatal blood (when she counts days eight to forty). But for the first seven days after she gives birth to her baby, that blood is categorized as ritually impure.

After delivery, a woman must physically separate herself from others for seven days. Isolation ceases after the first week and marks the time she returns to her dwelling and to her husband. In fact, a *yoledet*'s social rehabilitation comes in stages, because though she sits at home after day seven, she still may not touch sacred food or visit the Mikdash. "[Still,] she shall not touch sacred things, nor should she come to the Mikdash until the days of her ritual

---

4. Vayikra 12:4.
5. BT *Niddah* 30a.
6. Abravanel relies on medieval science to explain these passages and backs Rabbi Yishmael's opinion.

purification process conclude." According to the Ramban, the Hebrew term *tehorah* (טהורה) describes a state of perfect purity, such as described in "pure and untainted gold"[7] or "and purify Bnei Levi."[8]

Let us continue explaining our verses that teach how a woman is purified after giving birth to a girl. According to Rabbi Yishmael, who subscribes to variant embryology for males and females, a girl takes eighty days to reach her critical mass. Even the sages accede that the physical makeup for boys tends to be more boisterous or bouncier than that of girls. Thus, a woman's complete recovery process is lengthened after giving birth to a girl. Essentially, a female's nature builds up at a slower and more methodical pace, so that undoing those pent-up body fluids is also stretched out. Symmetry is the centerpiece of the Ramban's approach too. All in all, women who give birth to girls are *temeah* for fourteen days and afterwards count sixty-six days for their bodies to return to pre-pregnancy ritual status quo.

"And when she finishes her purification process after giving birth to either a boy or girl, she brings a year-old male sheep for a burnt offering and a male turtledove or pigeon for a sin offering to the entrance of the Tent of Meeting to a Kohen."[9] Fairly, students read this verse in puzzlement. Why must she bring a burnt and sin offering? Had she sinned? Is that why the next verse conveys "And the priest makes atonement for her"? What does the Torah's order of these two obligations reveal?

The sages instruct that, in practice, sin offerings precede burnt offerings. Their ruling appears ironic considering that whenever the subject of sacrifices is broached in the Torah, discussion commences with burnt offerings.[10] Regarding a woman after childbirth, the sages answer this. At childbirth, a woman foreswears her husband from ever having intimate relations with her again. *Halachah* provides dispensation for oaths under duress, such as one occasioned during labor. Obligating a woman to bring a sacrifice comes out of recognition that her blurted-out oath necessitated divine forgiveness.

But here is a straightforward answer. Really, the Torah requires a new mother to bring a burnt offering because of her profound appreciation for having been delivered from a harrowing childbirth experience. She offers

---

7.   Shemot 25:39.
8.   Malachi 3:3.
9.   Vayikra 12:6.
10. BT *Zevachim* 90a.

a sacrifice to her Maker as a means of getting closer to the Almighty, her Redeemer from danger. Another classic idea is being expressed and acknowledged. Namely, a person's safety is not compromised unless he or she is culpable as a result of transgression.

This sentiment is expressed in the Talmud. "Tribulation does not befall a man had he not sinned."[11] Crouching in her birthing chair, a *yoledet* suffers aplenty. Consequently, she is obligated to bring a sin offering. This process acknowledges that in a religious sense there arises the need to make amends. Still, she first brings a burnt offering as a means to enhance piety and cleave to God. Her burnt offering is a one-year-old sheep. And if she assumes that she must be guilty of inadvertent sin, she brings a sin offering to curry catharsis.

In sum, a woman after birth brings a burnt offering because she aspires to ever greater otherworldliness. This is followed by a sin offering based on an assumption of wrongdoing, though she has no clear recollection of any malfeasance in particular.

In accordance with a new mother's moral probity, our verse conveys, "she brings a year-old male sheep for a burnt offering and a male turtledove or pigeon for a sin offering to the entrance of the Tent of Meeting to a Kohen."[12] More details ensue. "And he shall offer it before the Almighty."[13] At heart, the main thrust of her two sacrifices is the first one, the burnt offering. "And the priest makes atonement for her."[14] This refers to her second sacrifice, the sin offering.

"And her womb has been emptied from blood."[15] A Kohen pronounces her renewed state of ritual purity. Sort of. In fact, at this juncture a *yoledet* has only been cleared from having afterbirth blood categorized as menses. Recall that until she counts additional days (thirty-three for a boy and sixty-six for a girl), she is still forbidden to partake of sacred food or visit the Mikdash. Importantly, though, receiving a Kohen's pronouncement is a key initial component in her achieving full ritual purity.

---

11. BT *Shabbat* 55a.
12. Vayikra 12:6.
13. Vayikra 12:7.
14. Ibid.
15. Ibid.

Skin Disorders

"And Hashem spoke to Moshe and Aharon, saying: [If] a man's skin produces a swelling and blotch or *se'eit* (שאת), or a scab and discoloration or *sapachat* (ספחת), or a bright spot or *baheret* (בהרת), and these lead to *tzaraat*, then he shall be brought to Aharon the Kohen or to one of his descendants [who are also] priests."[16] Aharon was included in this divine communiqué, together with Moshe. This attests to his acumen as an accomplished dermatologist. More than that, he excelled at discerning between various types of outbreaks afflicting garments, causing them to develop rashes.

Though *metzora'im* experienced skin disorder symptoms, *tzaraat* was not, per se, a medical illness. Instead, it should be viewed as a spiritual imbalance that mimics common skin disorders. When marks cropped up on a man's epidermis, this conveyed to him that disequilibrium had struck. Oozing skin mirrored something sinister festering under his skin. "[If] a man's skin produces a swelling and blotch or *se'eit*, or scab and discoloration or *sapachat*, or bright spot or *baheret*." Initially, pus-filled pimply gook rested on the skin's surface. In pernicious cases, it ate away chunks of flesh.

As a general rule, any disturbance to man's naturally harmonious inner balance manifested itself on his skin. However, skin rashes of this sort could not be contained. Like pollen or airborne dust, such an affliction traveled. In turn, these irregularities affected—and infected—those in close proximity to him. *Tumah* marched. "[If] a man's skin produces a swelling and blotch or *se'eit*." Insofar as man is durably designed, disruptions to his wellness may occur and rock that pristine state. If spiritually caused rashes are left unchecked and untreated, collateral damage to others will prove hard to manage. No similar threat applies to man from diseased animals. Concern for public safety and welfare prompted the Torah to issue cautionary statements, raising awareness of leprous outbreaks. Certainly, other diseases were known to man, but none carried such dire consequences as *tzaraat*. In a snap, these skin lesions could spread like a brushfire, bringing a pandemic to the Hebrew camp's doorstep.

From the outset, readers need to know that in the Tanach, *tzaraat* is not a medical condition but rather an affliction of the soul, as the Torah says, "And you shall not cause your souls ritual impurity."[17] Spiritual blotchiness stands

---

16. Vayikra 13:1–2.
17. Vayikra 11:33.

front and center. The ailment took to the air, polluting every drop of oxygen in its path, unlike medical diseases doctors treat. It was contagion by transcendental asphyxiation. Of course, medical pathology lacks the wherewithal to defile man's soul any more than smog in the air we breathe could defile us spiritually. It goes without saying that infirmity lacks four-wheel drive to desecrate the Mikdash or the Hebrews' holy encampment.

Checkups by Kohanim had nothing to do with their acumen in natural sciences or medicine. Most perceptibly, they understood the inner workings of the soul, and their fingers felt the spirit's pulse. Examination of the heart produced an innocent or guilty verdict.

Pronouncing purity or impurity was the call and domain of trained Kohanim. In addition, Kohanim were entrusted to offer sacrifices on behalf of penitent *metzora'im*. Unquestionably, priests were the "go to" people, as it says in Sefer Devarim: "Pay great attention to the symptoms of *metzora'im*, and heed all that which the Kohanim will instruct you."[18]

Let us provide workable definitions for these skin lesions linked with *tzaraat*.

1. **Swelling and blotchy *se'eit* (שאת).** According to Ibn Ezra, the term implies a burn; however, this is not accurate. When skin is exposed to fire or the sun, it darkens. Yet *se'eit* is whitish. Another difficulty with this definition is that intense heat swells skin, often causing blistering. But our section's verses state, "And its appearance is depressed within the skin's flesh."[19] Finally, other types of *tzaraat*—take for example *shechin* (שחין) or *michveh* (מכוה)—are symptomatic of burning but not *se'eit*. Bottom line: *se'eit* implies an excess of something. In this case, it is an overproduction of flesh or a skin discharge emanating from man's epidermis. Building on etymology, a play on words emerges. Arrogance—airs of the excellency of dignity or *yeter se'eit* (יתר שאת)—brings *se'eit*.[20]

2. **Scab and discoloration or *sapachat* (ספחת).** This disorder features pus whose source came from outside the body. It is a

---

18. Devarim 24:8.
19. Vayikra 13:3.
20. The term *yeter se'eit* appears in Bereshit 49:3.

communicable disease. The Hebrew term is, of course, instructive. "Please attach me" or *sefacheni* (ספחני) "to one of the priest's shifts."[21]

3. **Bright spot or *baheret* (בהרת).** Here the skin looks white to the point of being bleached. "White" or *bahir* (בהיר) "as the skies."[22] An affected man's body has an oversupply of white humor or perhaps pigment.

Leprous outbreaks presented themselves in four distinct ways. The first one, *se'eit,* was a very noticeable blotch as white as snow. A subcategory of this first outbreak was a blotch that shared the same shade of white as the whitewash used in the Beit Hamikdash. The second one, *baheret,* had the color of white wool. Its subcategory had the whitish color of the membrane that surrounds the contents of an egg. Some writers describe *se'eit* in more of a rouge tone. Because of its particular hue, it gives off a superimposing appearance. Thus, the color seemed to rise above the others akin to what master artists utilize in their paintings: *trompe l'oeil.* The third type of outbreak is *sapachat.* Blackness blanketed infected areas. Finally, *baheret* could be either whitish or pinkish.

The challenges of matching these colors when no swatches or palette avail themselves are manifest. For that reason, it is far preferable to paint with one color that fits all. *Blanco* pretty much says it all. Whiteness was assumed to come about as a result of excess body fluid buildup. Now, when it came to other maladies such as boils or *tzaraat shechin u'michveh* (צרעת שחין ומכוה) or rashes, the dominant tone was deep red leaning toward black on a color chart. Yet other dermatological disease mostly affected the scalp or chin, though hair discoloration may have occurred anywhere on the body. That kind of *tzaraat* gave a blond tint associated with hyperactivity of a body's red forces.

Out, Damned Spot

"And if there will be on the flesh of his skin a *nega tzaraat,* he shall be brought before Aharon Hakohen or one of his sons."[23] Two additional skin maladies are being described. One is a case of *nega adamdam* (נגע אדמדם), and the second

---

21. The term *sefacheni* appears in I Shmuel 2:36.
22. The term *bahir* appears in Iyov 37:21.
23. Vayikra 13:2. Here, Abravanel's commentary does not run systematically. Our translation follows his Hebrew original.

is a *tzaraat porachat* (צרעת פורחת). Bad blood is the root cause of these two pathologies. *Nega* conveys damaged and painful skin. The operative words are hurt and misery. Both are learned from the Hebrew cognate *tzaar* (צער), denoting severe discomfort.

"He shall be brought before Aharon Hakohen." Where leprous symptoms persist, then determining a diagnosis is not at a person's whim or fancy. Our verse stresses as much, so if a likelihood of *tzaraat* exists, the suspected patient will be dragged before Aharon should he not come of his own accord.

"Before Aharon Hakohen or one of his sons." Aharon was the preferred or prime address for diseased men. If a chap, however, could not walk the longer distance to Aharon's examining room, then it was perfectly acceptable to make an appointment with his sons.

What did these examinations reveal? "And the Kohen saw the *nega* on the skin of his flesh. And the hair on the *nega* turned white, and the appearance of the *nega* was deeper than the skin of his flesh—it is *tzaraat*."[24] Body hair color is generally dark or fair. Both shades are considered normal and healthy. Our verse states that it blanched unnaturally.

A second symptom presented an appearance of unevenness surrounding the skin. It looked sunken. Because of discoloration or abnormal texture of the pathology, an observer would attest to it looking recessed or deep-set. A confluence of both of these factors leads a priest to his diagnosis. The patient is stricken with a leprous patch or *nega shel tzaraat*. Without further ado, judgment concludes. It is simply a matter of the priest's examination and resultant conclusion: the patient is pronounced *tamei*. When cases are open and shut (meaning both irrefutable symptoms are present), it is pointless to quarantine the patient.

The matter proceeds altogether differently when both signs are lacking or at least may be lacking. "And if the *baheret* appears whitish in the skin of his flesh, yet the depth dimension does not appear, and its hair has not turned color."[25] Two doubts surface. One, perhaps skin coloration is not that distinctly white, or two, his body hairs did not turn pale. When that occurs, the priest treads cautiously with his prognosis, which is a verdict. "And a Kohen isolates

---

24. Vayikra 13:3.
25. Vayikra 13:4.

the *nega* for seven days."[26] Time off and time out is deemed expedient to flush out the true nature of the patient's illness.

What does the seven-day wait accomplish? It is an adequate time frame for the disease to incubate and progress or heal by itself. Uncommonly, sometimes resolution may require a two-week wait-and-see period. Medically, priests are looking for a man's body to regain its former red and white balance or yin and yang, if you will. Besides, during this time period a man is careful not to go out and hobnob with friends and neighbors. Bustle and strenuous activity saps the body of the proper rest it needs to get the body functioning full strength. Lastly, the Torah's demand for a man to isolate himself is sensible because if it turns out that he did contract *tzaraat*, he will transmit it to others. Some commentators widely miss the point on this verse, as per below.[27]

Their misguided approach lacks logic. Why shouldn't a Kohen take proactive and heroic steps to help him? "And you shall certainly heal him"[28] is the Torah's ready dictum and modus operandi. According to the Ralbag, the seven-day quarantine played a practical role. Bed rest gave the body a fighting chance to neutralize foreign antibodies. This brings us to the last verse in this first *aliyah*.

Second *aliyah*
***"And the Kohen shall again examine him on the seventh day.
And behold if the affliction had dimmed
and not spread on his skin,
the Kohen shall pronounce him ritually pure. He is scabrous.
And he shall launder his clothing and be pure."***

"And the Kohen shall again examine him [for a second time] on the seventh day."[29] The priest is looking to determine the disease's momentum. Did telltale

---

26. Ibid.
27. One writer explains that during the seven-day trial, the patient is locked up behind bars. This prevents his family and friends from administering therapeutic food and drink, let alone medicine. The whole point of the test was to let nature run its course—without outside intervention. "And a Kohen isolates the *nega* for seven days." The verb "isolates" (והסגיר) is transitive, meaning that the officiating priest issues an order for the patient to be incarcerated.
28. Shemot 21:19.
29. Vayikra 13:6.

signs accelerate or decelerate? Of course, there is a third possibility. Maybe matters stood still. If so, the Kohen tacked on an additional week of seclusion.

Chiefly, the attending Kohen was looking to see that the disease was checked. That means that even if there was no visible improvement of dermatological symptoms, it was sufficient to get a pass, since no deterioration took place. Word got out that the patient was released from isolation. Psoriasis-like chapping, though annoying, did not signal an intrinsic mishap within his body's temperament. To be sure, scabbing is one step beneath *se'eit*. He therefore garnered a clean bill of health, since his disease was on the mend. Our verse is explicit that the patient must clean his clothes. Implicitly, however, it is understood that he needs to submerge himself in a *mikveh*. Why? It is on account of his having been quarantined. Reasonable doubt is enough to presume *tumah*. Deduce from here that all *metzora'im* placed in isolation must submerge and launder clothing—even if it turned out to be a false alarm.

Sometimes, initial close calls progressed into a full-blown problem. "And if *mispachat* certainly spread on the skin after he had been examined to determine ritual purity, he needs to be examined again."[30] To clarify, this teaches that two weeks have already elapsed. In that interval, a patient had been originally examined, placed in quarantine, and declared fit. But after two weeks of downtime, the patient noticed a worsening of his condition. Namely, his psoriasis-like scabs spread with a vengeance. That is to say, after the patient was checked by a Kohen and remanded for house arrest with his skin lesions showing signs of improvement, the man was pronounced ritually pure. But alas, dormant symptoms returned and resurfaced. It could be said that now the gravity of those diagnostic signs exceeded that of those measured after his quarantine. Essentially, his condition was not at a pre-isolation level. Since the affliction had shown signs of improvement, the fact that he returns to the condition that prompted the examiner to isolate his patient in the first place means trouble.

Another examination is scheduled. "And the Kohen performs a checkup, and behold, *mispachat* has broadened on his skin. The Kohen pronounces that he is ritually impure. It is *tzaraat*."[31] This attests to the patient's declining condition.

---

30. Vayikra 13:7.
31. Vayikra 13:8.

"When a man displays a *nega tzaraat*, then he shall be brought to a Kohen."[32] Prima facie, it seems as if this verse is redundant. In fact, it is not identical to an earlier verse but rather introduces new *halachot*. For one, there is a warning issued to priests. They need to be on the lookout for whitish *se'eit* on skin causing "the hair on that spot [to be] blanched,"[33] suggesting disease. *Tzaraat* symptoms cause normal dark hair to whiten.

In Torah parlance, "pus oozes from an afflicted region."[34] This latter phrase depicts a festering, nasty surface wound. How? Note that dead skin is generally dry and cracked, whereas the verse's term "spot is blanched" connotes aggravated or aggressive skin degeneration. Nasty lesion eruptions are highly suggestive of advanced stages of *tzaraat*. That symptom alone alerts Kohanim to a patient's condition. "It is acute *tzaraat* on the skin of his flesh. And the priest proclaims his *tumah*. Quarantine is unnecessary, for he is [definitely] ritually impure."[35] Isolation is prescribed for patients exhibiting possible signs of *tzaraat*. As stated, this gives a man a chance to hopefully combat the affliction or deal with it in the event that he cannot shake it. However, in our case, isolation is counterproductive. Nothing is gained by forestalling an obvious diagnosis. In summary, the verse is not redundant but rather reveals new information heretofore not imparted.

"It is acute *tzaraat* [leprosy] on the skin of his flesh." In the medieval era, "acute leprosy" was known as pestilence. Prognosis for those afflicted was, to understate, dim. In particular, spreading sores led to high incidents of mortality. Until now in this discussion, we have established that *tzaraat* can be attributed to an imbalance of white versus red forces within man.

At this juncture, the Torah unfurls a startling revelation, and one that by all accounts seems counterintuitive. Logic dictates that if a small region of a man's body is afflicted, and ritual defilement is pronounced, then all the more so should a priest declare *tzaraat* when an entire body is engulfed by it. Or to put it another way, a body wholly covered by skin disease is a body that is totally out of whack so far as the white and red forces are concerned. True, a *metzora's* body may be said to be battling this illness, yet all of its gargantuan efforts don't change the picture. The victim, one might reason, is beyond help.

---

32. Vayikra 13:9.
33. Vayikra 13:10.
34. Ibid.
35. Vayikra 13:11.

Here is where the Torah tosses a zinger. "And if *tzaraat* breaks out all over…from head to toe."[36] For as far as a Kohen's eye can see, only sick skin peers back out at him. The Talmud lists twenty-four anatomical parts: ten fingers, ten toes, two ears, nose, and genitalia.[37] And the administering Kohen's verdict is: *tahor* (ritually pure). "And the priest shall see and behold *tzaraat* covers all his flesh. And he proclaims the man's affliction to be *tahor*. It has all turned white—he is *tahor*."[38]

The presiding Kohen's assessment is that no inner imbalance exists because that particular man's disposition is fully functioning. In conclusion, anybody whose antibody and immune system can wage a full-court battle is deemed pure, and gets a clean bill of health to boot. The matter is akin to a body's high fever killing bacteria or diarrhea expelling harmful germs, and the like. At the end of the day, regained health will return.

"And if on the day of his examination, [a patch of] healthy flesh appears, he will be considered *tamei*."[39] After having concluded that a body filled with affliction is deemed *tahor*, this verse throws a monkey wrench into the equation. That is, if one region of his otherwise sickly body heals, then a priest is called in to reevaluate the patient. Essentially, a reversal will occur, because now the man's body is giving off mixed messages. His body is riddled patchwork, since it is no longer all decrepit (that is, it no longer displays its quirky measure of wellness). The concluding few verses provide more details about what a Kohen might actually observe and how he ought to classify the skin disorder. "If the healthy skin blanches again…"[40]

Now that the subject of *tzaraat* has been elucidated, the following *aliyah* takes up the matter of another dermatological malfunction.

---

36. Vayikra 13:12.
37. See Rashi on Vayikra 13:12.
38. Vayikra 13:13.
39. Vayikra 13:14.
40. Vayikra 13:16.

Third and fourth *aliyot*
"*And when previously infected flesh with* shechin *heals.*"

Below are laws governing two other unseemly disorders: *shechin* (boils) and *michvah* (burns). Boils are the subject of this third *aliyah*, whereas burns will be taken up in the next one. Sometimes, boils are referred to as *tzaraat hashechin* (pox).

Boils or burns results when a man's body produces a surfeit of what we have identified as either a feverish red or black humor. "And when previously infected flesh with *shechin* heals."[41] When the Torah here speaks of "flesh," it may refer to either a man or a woman, as another verse proves: "When any flesh comes to bow down before Me."[42]

Boils present themselves differently and make up distinct types. Strictly speaking, it is not *tzaraat*, but there is a common underlying thread with it. Namely, a body exhibits signs that a foreign agent invades. The natural immune system identifies, locates, and mounts a defense against the intruder. Consequently, excess red forces are pushed to the fore of the outer skin layer. Defense mechanisms produce a preternatural heat, which in turn causes skin to boil or rash as described in this *aliyah's* opening verse. To clarify, it really means that pesky physical conditions hamper normal functioning and healing.

Now the Torah gets specific. "And in the place of the *shechin*, a *se'eit levanah* [whitish bump] or a *baheret levanah* and *adamdemet* [white and red bright spot] erupts. And he must be examined by a Kohen."[43] When a man's body healed itself from what had been a boil, another issue surfaced. Thus, it was not vibrant skin that replaced the boil, but rather a disconcerting, troubling sign. Lingering pus gave way to a wide swath of either a "*se'eit levanah* or *baheret levanah* and *adamdemet.*" Wonderful this new prognosis was not. Trading worrying skin lesions (boils) for another skin condition marked by oozing and discoloration brought zero relief, let alone comfort. In fact, this latest development had nothing in common with our earlier discussion of *nega'im*. The chief difference becomes apparent when there is an analysis of boils. Febricity is fueling the evolving problem. Pinkness or redness results on a patch of skin.

---

41. Vayikra 13:18.
42. Yeshayahu 66:23.
43. Vayikra 13:19.

Enter an administering Kohen to examine the patient. "And a Kohen makes an examination. Behold, it appears low in the skin or hair turned white."[44] A priest and physician looks to see if one area of skin surface differs from the rest, meaning that discoloration is severe enough to give an appearance of elevated or sunken skin; then he pronounces *tumah*. Actually, he may even come to that conclusion if what had been normal dark body hair turns white. Either sign (skin or hair discoloration) seals a verdict. "It is a *nega tzaraat* which erupted out of the *shechin*."[45]

Here is what happened. When the man's body resisted disease by producing a fever blister, remains lingered on even after that original boil subsided. However, festering under the barely healed skin came a second eruption, comprising a different pathology. Though *tzaraat hashechin* had precious little to do with *tzaraat*, since it grew in the place where pox had appeared, the verse makes a connection. The Ralbag hypothesizes that it was a compromised immune system within the body that could not shake off *tzaraat* other than at the spot where the boil appeared.

"But if a Kohen sees it and behold…and it is lighter, a Kohen shall isolate him for seven days."[46] As stated above, a priest pronounces *tumah* when either one of the two telltale signs are presented. But if only a minor alteration can be seen, or if the trend to complete healing persists, then it is not deemed a *nega tzaraat*. What is it? "It is a *tzarevet hashechin*, and a Kohen pronounces him *tahor*."[47] Slight skin discoloration is normal after a bout with boils, and the recovering patient is expected to improve steadily with time. No further intervention is required.

Laws governing burns are similar to those promulgated concerning boils. It comes down to renewed heat appearing where blisters had erupted. Protracted fever is, to state the obvious, not a natural state of affairs and must be understood as an aberration to a healthy organism. Fairly, one wonders why the Torah needed to teach essentially identical passages twice.[48] The answer is that boils and burns are different diseases.

We continue with the fifth *aliyah*.

---

44. Vayikra 13:20.
45. Ibid.
46. Vayikra 13:22.
47. Vayikra 13:23.
48. Abravanel does not comment in detail on the fourth *aliyah*, concerning burns.

Fifth *aliyah*

"And when a man or woman has a nega on the head or beard."

It is appropriate for this section to follow in this sequence since a *netek* is, generally, a by-product of a problematic situation in which red humor dominates the white one.[49] This illness strikes in places where hair grows. For a woman, this dysfunction affects her head, while for a man it may appear either on his head or beard. The Hebrew term *netek* implies removal. A flare-up of this disease explains why there is hair loss—it is on account of body fluid buildup in that particular hairy region.

The Torah distinguishes between balding or *karachat* (קרחת) and receding hairlines or *gabachat* (גבחת), though there can be overlap as well. Namely, these two conditions share things in common and are thus interchangeable. Balding is normally associated with hair loss in the back and/or on the sides of a man's head, whereas receding hairline refers to the front. Root causes— excuse the bald pun—of both conditions occur when a man or woman's white humor goes into overdrive.[50]

But actually, there is a distinction between the two conditions. Balding results when the back part of the brain has too much white humor, whereas receding hairline results when the front brain lobe displays excessive red and black humor (or high levels of blood volume).[51] At any rate, these conditions are akin to imbalances leading to *tzaraat* and thus written about in our *parashah*.

"And behold, if it appears sunken in the skin, and it sprouts a thin yellow hair."[52] Jaundiced-looking hair that is not its typical dark color traces back to excess red humor or sick blood. To the attending Kohen, symptoms of hair loss or blanched discoloration give an illusion of two-tiered skin layers. Another diagnostic at the priest's disposal was an up-close look at the infected area. They shaved it in order to better examine affected hair follicles.

---

49. A parenthetical preface is necessary. It is not entertained that we are speaking about hirsutism or polycystic ovary syndrome, medical conditions that may result in a woman growing a beard.
50. Abravanel speaks of "humor," as was the wont of ancient thinkers. To modern readers, this terminology and conceptualizing is antiquated.
51. Ditto previous note.
52. Vayikra 13:30.

Note that our verse relays two conditions that tip the scales in favoring a man's *tumah*: "sunken in the skin" or *mareha amok min ha'or* (מראה עמק מן העור) and "short yellow hair" or *se'ar tzahov dak* (שער צהב דק). The word *dak* in this context means "short." Because of decaying, the smoky vapor necessary for growth of hair is not activated. Effectively, underlying disease curtails and thwarts normal hair production. That shortcoming plus tarnished skin lands the patient outside the Hebrew camp. He is *tamei*.

"Then a Kohen will pronounce him ritually impure."[53] Let us deduce the inverse. Namely, if neither of the two signs appears, or even if one is present but not the other, then seven days of isolation are prescribed. "And when a priest will examine the *nega* on the *netek*, and behold, it does not appear sunken from the skin…then the priest shall quarantine him."[54]

A man's seven-day lockup is only step one in determining the condition's true nature. "And the Kohen shall examine the *nega* on the seventh day, and behold the *netek* did not spread, nor did yellow hair sprout, and the appearance of the *netek* did not seem sunken in the skin. He shall be shaved [with special care paid] not to shave the *netek*."[55] This procedure allows the attending priest to mark and chart the disease's progression.

At the end of this second seven-day incubation period, a final assessment will be made. "And the Kohen shall examine the *netek* on the seventh day, and behold the *netek* had not spread in the skin, and its appearance does not seem sunken in the skin, the priest will pronounce him ritually pure."[56] After laundering his clothing, he resumes his former status of ritual cleanliness.

What happens if the patient's illness shows signs of recrudescence after it looked as if he had licked it? "And if the Kohen examines him, and behold, the *netek* broadened in his skin, then there is no further need for a priest to reexamine for the purpose of finding albinic hair, for he is defiled."[57] To make matters clear, this verse refers to a time period after a patient had been pronounced clean. That is, sometime later he notices a return of his symptoms. Remission had been short-lived. The Torah teaches that just one recurring sign

---

53. Ibid.
54. Vayikra 30:31.
55. Vayikra 13:32–33.
56. Vayikra 13:34.
57. Vayikra 13:36.

suffices, and there is no reason for a priest to have the infirmity confirmed by the second symptom of yellow hair.

This *halachah* is only valid when the patient experienced a recurring spreading *netek*. Namely, a patient was quarantined twice. He shaved after week one, ushering in a lull. He emerged unscathed and was pronounced pure. Week two witnessed a *netek* proliferation or reactivation of his sickness. We adduce that even if after a surcease of symptoms (meaning no new *netek*), if a jaundiced patch of hair began to sprout, a priest would still decree: *tamei*. How can we deduce this? See a later verse: "And if in his estimation, the *netek* did not progress, but the dark hair grew there, the *netek* is healed, and he is pure. And the Kohen will pronounce him ritually pure."[58] Ergo, if yellow hair grew, he must be impure.

After the Torah concludes these sections dealing with *nega'im*, boils, and burns, it continues to take up other matters related—at least on the surface—to *tzaraat*. Drawing clear demarcation lines, the end of this fifth *aliyah* and the beginning of the sixth convey skin conditions that mimic *tzaraat* but do not result in a patient becoming *tamei*.

"When a man's or woman's skin develops white spots, [they are] rash spots appearing whitish."[59] The Torah generalizes this case afflicting men and women in contrast to the beginning of the next (sixth) *aliyah*, which only impacts men. What does it convey? It stresses that acne marks erupting on the skin are white, but their color does not render a person ritually unclean. The Hebrew term *bohek* (בוהק) is synonymous with *beharot* (בהרות). Both describe benign skin boils. Topical eruptions are pale yellow or even white. At any rate, these shades are not indicative of an advent of *tzaraat*.

Discussion now proceeds to the next *aliyah*, in which other innocuous skin disorders are brought up, beginning with those affecting males.

---

58. Vayikra 13:37.
59. Vayikra 13:38.

Sixth *aliyah*
"And when a man's head loses hair, he is ritually pure."

This verse teaches an application of laws pertaining exclusively to men, for the simple reason that balding is rare among women. Women do not go bald because they have more and longer hair than men on account of their having more body fluids.[60] A receding hairline, even to the extent of full baldness, does not constitute concern for pronouncing *tumah*. The same can be said for loss of hair near a man's face. "And if hair falls out from his face area, it is [an extension of his] forehead or *gibe'ach* (גבח). And still he is ritually pure."[61] Similarly, if a man's hair production surceases or if he sheds due to illness, he is ritually pure.

"But if a blanched and pinkish sore grows on the bald back part of his head or forehead, it is a leprous eruption on the bald back part of his head or bald forehead."[62] Identifying the specific region of a man's bald head is the key here. Disease may break out behind his crown or in front of it. The latter is often called a receding hairline.

What pathology is presented? Sores such as *se'eit, sapachat, baheret,* or *netek* appear. After careful examination, a qualified priest proclaims his patient *tamei*. "He is ill; he is ritually defiled. The Kohen shall determine his unequivocal ritual impurity."[63] These cases, being blatant, do not call for a patient's isolation, since his condition is well advanced and beyond question. After the Torah concludes its remarks regarding how *tzaraat* may manifest itself in multifarious ways, it pronounces uniform guidelines.

"Any *metzora* who has a *nega* shall rend his garments and not cut his hair. And he shall mask his mouth."[64] Our verse speaks about a diagnosed *metzora*. The Torah obligates him to publicly assume rites and customs associated with a man who observes mourning. To be perfectly clear, he is not mourning family members. He is required to publicly bemoan his compromised conduct,

---

60. Common observation bears out that balding in women is rare—certainly rarer than balding in men. Abravanel explains the reason for this according to belief prevalent in the fifteenth century.
61. Vayikra 13:41.
62. Vayikra 13:42.
63. Vayikra 13:44.
64. Vayikra 13:45.

salacious behavior that caused him illness. "Man's folly derails him," observes King Shlomoh.[65] Medical illness follows moral lapse.

"He shall rend his garments."[66] This is a requirement to tear asunder his clothing. "And not cut his hair."[67] *Metzora'im*, in the style of mourners, sport slovenly hair. The Ralbag explains that this means the *metzora* must cover his hair. More plausibly, the Torah is teaching that his head is uncovered, in contradistinction to his mouth, which gets covered up. Mouth masks are effective against spreading disease. Needless to say, this getup draws attention, broadcasting the turpitude of the *metzora*. A social magnet he wasn't. Whoever saw this creep approaching would likely cross to the other side of the street.

"Defiled! Defiled!" he cries aloud.[68] If anything, instructions for a *metzora* are abrasively visual and vocal—right in the face. Practically, his ostracization improves the odds that others will not contract his catching disease. While stricken, he must dwell outside the Hebrew camp. Again, this serves to stem a pandemic. When priests examine patients, naturally these follow-ups are performed outside the encampment. After a former *metzora* regains spiritual footing, he returns home. More of this will be explained.

"And if his clothing catches *tzaraat*."[69] This verse describing leprous symptoms invading clothing raises more than a few eyebrows among readers. We have discussed how this dreaded malady attacks particular limbs or regions of a man's or woman's body. We put forward how it resulted from moral misalignment. Hence, an obvious question glares: How does an inanimate article of clothing develop leprous signs? Not to mention that later in this *aliyah* we read: "It is a malignant form of *tzaraat* and is ritually impure."[70] The Hebrew adjective "malignant" or *mameret* (ממארת) connotes pain and discomfort. See the following Scriptural support for this: "a prickly or *mamir* (ממאיר) bramble...nor a painful thorn."[71] Being divorced from sense perceptions, clothing and skinned animal hides are immune from experiencing physical pain. Full stop.

---

65. Mishlei 19:3.
66. Vayikra 13:45.
67. Ibid.
68. Ibid.
69. Vayikra 13:47.
70. Vayikra 13:51.
71. Yechezkel 28:24.

Classic commentators have assayed to explain this admittedly bizarre phenomenon—but with little success.[72]

---

72. In most acerbic language, Abravanel takes the Ralbag, Ramban, and an anonymous writer to task. Interested students should look to the original texts; their respective opinions are condensed here for reference.

Ralbag explains how inanimate objects can contract leprosy, and what it means in practical terms. In so many words, he writes that inanimate objects may turn colors (green or red) if their fluid makeup gets invaded by foreign bodies. The process resembles decomposition commonly observed in trash heaps. He adds that the Torah requires affected clothing and threads to be burned to ensure that Jews will not derive benefit from this scourge. Abravanel responds that the Ralbag's comments are patently delusional. Wellness and illness, he emphasizes, are limited to living man. Flora or fibers cannot contract sickness any more than stones or sitting chairs. Finally, the root cause of leprosy symptoms stems from blood abnormalities, something that those aforementioned objects do not possess.

Ramban takes a position that this passage (among others) does not belong to the world of nature as we know it. The reason *tzaraat* attacks clothing (and later we will read in Parashat Metzora about it infecting houses) is solely because the Jewish nation is inherently and indissolubly connected to their Maker. Since this bond exists with Hashem, He finds ways to engage and engender the relationship. One way is to provide a Jew's body with "reminders." Other spiritual wake-up calls include Heaven-sent pestilence to their clothing and houses. This keeps Jews, in a manner of speaking, constantly on their toes, not to mention on their best behavior. Should sin crop up in their conduct, oozing skin lesions on their body erupt. Ditto for disease infecting their clothing and homes. In a word, *tzaraat* is an expression of God's profound displeasure. "When you come into the land of Canaan that I give to you for an inheritance and I will send *nega tzaraat* in a house in the land that you own" (Vayikra 14:34). This refers to a divine sign striking houses of which Jews take possession. This can only transpire in the Holy Land, insofar as it is God's inheritance and the place where He resides. The Ramban concludes that this phenomenon is akin to *tzaraat* afflicting clothing and thus only occurs in the Land of Israel. Abravanel notes that no such local-to-Israel limitation phrase is found in our passage dealing with contaminated clothing, fibers, and animal skin hides. Finally, in utterly rejecting the Ramban's approach, he points out that these verses are very specific and limited to wool, linen, hides, and warp and weft threads. If the matter is supernatural, then why doesn't *tzaraat* attack other Jewish possessions, such as for instance wine goblets, mattresses, sandals, or paperweights?

Abravanel quotes from a writer whom he fails to name or identify. This coxcomb advanced the following theory. Torah sections discussing *tzaraat* need to be considered from a prism of moral preaching or homiletics. Namely, piety must be carefully nurtured, and any breach to proper conduct upsets a man's inner calm, resulting in the creation of something spiritually untoward and even grotesque. Moreover, this thinker depicts an unwanted appendage attaching to and growing on a pristine soul. The operative image is as if a man dons soiled and foul clothing. Is it not despicably offensive? This message presupposes that there is a mind and body relationship, so that if a man mires in manure, not only will his clothes reek of the stench, but his soul will reel from the effects too. *Tzaraat* is that quagmire. Concluding, this commentator asserts that the Torah is hyperbolic when it comes to clothing contracting *tzaraat*. Don't other verses in Tanach employ such literary devices? Don't we have the verse "And you cause pain through stones to any good portion of land" (II Melachim 3:19)? Afflicted walls and houses need to be viewed as no more than literary license. Abravanel refutes this third writer.

Let us provide a better way of approaching these seemingly logic-defying subjects. Some objects that people wear or otherwise use closely are affected by a proprietor's deeds, or rather, misdeeds. Consider an article he wears close or snug to his body. Examples of such objects are those made out of silk, linen, wool, or animal hides. Contrast those with other harder materials, such as armor or coat of mail. These are not impacted by a wearer's behavior. Part of the explanation of this phenomenon is not just the molecular composition of metal versus linen, but also the fact that linens and wools conform more closely to a person's contours. For example, leather shoes mold to one's feet. Even when upcoming verses talk of warp or *shti* and weft or *erev*, this same principle applies. "They who work in combed flax...and its foundations shall be smashed."[73] Picture a loom used to weave cloth. The basic premise is that a loom holds the warp threads taut in order to facilitate crisscrossing weft threads. Briefly, weaving is a manufacturing process consisting of intersecting longitudinal threads (warp) with traversing threads (weft). These stitches are essential for producing woolen and linen garments. Let us examine how animal hides are manufactured and become clothing. Whether they are unworked hides or shaped to make leather shoes, they are influenced by the person wearing these items.

Having prefaced these ideas, let us proceed. The Torah has concerns that perhaps a *metzora*, while exhibiting symptoms of the illness, will be quarantined. During isolation, what would happen if he were to wear those pliable articles of clothing and shoes? And further imagine what would occur if the contaminated warp and weft formed his bedding? Very possibly those garments and hides would pick up a *metzora*'s germs and bacteria. His body fluids would be all over undergarments and bedding. Staining would leave its notorious and noxious mark. Most commonly, these markings assume a greenish or reddish hue. Be clear. These are not bright greens or reds, but rather they are like the color of dried blood, mucus, or pus. Other variations of colors appeared on what should have been a plain white garment.

The sages teach that these *halachot* only apply to white, but not to other colored garments, even if those colors are natural and not artificial.[74] This is a result of practical considerations. Stains and marks can only be discerned on white garments. One need not look far to see real-life cases. When a

---

73. Yeshayahu 19:9–10.
74. Mishnah *Nega'im* 11:3. See also *Torat Kohanim*.

man with a fever perspires, his undergarments or pajamas get discolored to varying degrees. The determining factor is locating the infected body part and the garment closest to it. This approach holds the key to better understand verses discussing how *tzaraat* affects certain clothing items, while others are impervious. After a *metzora* becomes healthy, the Torah issues a stern warning. He should not put on those articles of clothing, shoes, and so on that he lounged around in when disease peaked. Had the Torah not required a man to burn them, he might have suffered a relapse due to contact with contaminated clothing.

"It is a *nega tzaraat*, and he must show it to a Kohen."[75] Quarantine measures for clothing are designed to protect a person's money. It would be profligate to destroy garments before ascertaining contamination. "And he examines the *nega* on the seventh day. If the *nega* has spread on the clothing or in the warp or weft..."[76] This refers to a man's stain on a given undergarment, warp, weft, or animal hide. A positive result is issued. "It is a malignant form of *tzaraat* and is ritually impure."[77] The verse conveys how the *metzora*'s clothing tested positive and carries lethal germ samples. In summary, the Torah is not talking about a blighted undergarment or hide per se, but rather describes the *metzora*'s condition: he is ill. Consequently, his undergarments have been afflicted due to their having been worn by a highly contagious *metzora*. Incinerating them is deemed judicious.

"Or any leather article onto which the pestilence has spread."[78] A thorough inspection must be made, and whatever leather goods had come into contact with the *metzora* must be burned. Why? Presumably, lethal germs penetrated those articles, since the verse is speaking about those items he handles regularly.

"But if a Kohen examines and behold, the *nega* had not spread to the clothing or in the warp or weft or any other leather article..."[79] Inconclusive results do not mean that the patient's ordeal is behind him. He launders his clothes and is whisked away for a second seven-day interval. This time frame suffices to reassess matters.

---

75. Vayikra 13:49.
76. Vayikra 13:51.
77. Ibid.
78. Ibid.
79. Vayikra 13:53.

Seventh *aliyah*

"And a Kohen shall examine [it] after the nega has been laundered, and behold, [even] if the nega has not intensified and the nega has not spread—it is ritually impure. Burn it in a pyre. Decrepit is the front or back [of these intimate clothing articles]."

A critical point is made here. The patient's clothing has been washed. After an attending priest examines these garments, he notices that the disease has not spread. Note, even though there has not been a worsening of the *nega* (the stain has not widened), a positive verdict will nevertheless be handed down. Without any doubt, the priest proclaims that the patient is *tamei*. In order to have been declared ritually pure, there would have to have been a modicum of improvement. Mere stabilization or maintaining status quo does not do the trick. Contaminated samples are shown to the fire, for they are a bane.

What do the two Hebrew terms *b'karachto* (בקרחתו) and *b'gabachto* (בגבחתו) mean? Both cognates are familiar to us, because we came across them in the previous *aliyah*. There we said that they specified terms outlining a man's balding patterns. A *kareach* has no hair in the back of his head, whereas a *gabeach* describes a receding hairline. Those same definitions apply here. But instead of sketching a bald head, the terms here take into account the inside (קרח) or outside (גבח) parts of clothing. Decisively, the Torah rules that if either the inside or outside of the garment has had close contact with a *metzora*, one law pertains. Woolen or linen articles and animal hides have been defiled. This reflects the facts on the ground. Sometimes pesky stains will perspire through both sides of a garment, and other times only one side streaks.

"And if a Kohen examines, and behold, the *nega* has dimmed after being laundered, then he shall cut that strip away from the garment or from the animal hide or from the warp or weft."[80] This means that stains from the *nega* either cleared entirely or somewhat abated as a result of being laundered. Amelioration does not bring total relief in the sense of being deemed *tahor*. "He shall cut that strip away from the garment." That swatch is snipped away and burned.

---

80. Vayikra 13:56.

Remedial steps just mentioned do not spell closure of this *metzora*'s ordeal. He must pay close attention to his condition, because even though he seems to have turned the corner and to have beaten his illness, vigilance is still required. "And if it reappears on the clothing, or on the warp or weft, or on any leather object, it has spread. Burn anything defiled with *nega* in a fire."[81] The fact that *tzaraat* resurfaces shows that these articles had not truly been cured. Only a brief respite had been granted. Germs or bacteria had lain dormant but now reared their ugly heads. At this juncture, the final resort meant charring all contaminated items, since earlier stopgap measures (snipping away swatches) proved futile.

"And should either the garment or warp or weft or any object that you shall launder result in the *nega* healing, then you shall launder it once more and it will be deemed ritually pure."[82] According to our verse, one washing is not sufficient, and priests will not proclaim purity unless and until a second wash cycle is complete. As stated above, this repeat washing refers to immersion in a *mikveh*.

"These are the governing laws pertaining to *nega tzaraat* found in woolen or linen clothing, or on a warp or weft, or any leather object—either in cases resulting in their purification or defilement."[83] Dénouement and summary bring an end to this *parashah*. The importance of closure cannot be overstated, for it compartmentalizes statutes dealing with *metzora'im* versus those discussing clothing and household items. Having established a demarcation between the two, it should nevertheless not be entertained that one is wholly independent of the other. In fact, man is front and center concerning these loathsome stains on clothing and the like. We will take up a new subject in Parashat Metzora—the topic of pestilence-stricken dwellings and houses.

Before moving on to the following *parashah*, let us turn our attention to the Torah's sequence. Why did it place the section of *tzaraat* afflicting clothing before that of disease-infested houses? Simply, garments are more likely than houses to be affected by a *metzora*'s germs, sputum, and other body fluids. Instructively, this sequence also emphasizes that one who wishes to get rid of *tzaraat* must sanitize clothing worn during his illness.

---

81. Vayikra 13:57.
82. Vayikra 13:58.
83. Vayikra 13:59.

In review, consider how the Torah here in the seventh *aliyah* never brought up a perfectly reasonable scenario. What would be the statute in cases where an infection cleared up after the first week of isolation? Another fair question is this: What does the *halachah* say about inconclusive *tzaraat* signs and symptoms? Consider that after one week of quarantine, leprous spots darkened. What says the Torah?

From what is explicit in this section, we can do simple math. Namely, should discoloration worsen during the first week, then a suspected *metzora's* clothing would not have to be snipped, trimmed, and torched. Contrast that treatment to situations where week two had passed and discoloration had been pronounced. There the Torah is explicit. Sullied garment swatches were to be cut away and burned. Now let us back up and deduce. If after week one, there was a noticeable darkening, then the prescribed advice would be to launder the garments and continue isolation for a second week.

On what grounds is this logic compelling? We must assume that the Torah does not distinguish between cases where discoloration becomes visibly more pronounced. Now let us make another reasonable assumption. Which deciding factor must be given prominence? It is the second sign. Thus, if the *nega* had not spread, this consideration takes precedence and ultimately drives *halachah*. The result: the man's garments must be laundered before he is sent back to quarantine.

We now answer our earlier query. Though it is not written, what would the Torah demand if after week two either the spot darkened or spread? Although that situation was not raised, another verse is explicit regarding leprous stains keeping the same color intensity despite it not having spread. The upshot was that despite two factors leaning toward leniency having been observed (no discernible coloration and no spreading), still a verdict came down hard. This seems, on the surface, counterintuitive. Why? Compare instances where marks did not darken or spread to those in which it had both darkened and spread. When a spot lingers, it triggers a judgment of *tumah*. The same holds true for infected skin areas that linger. Essentially, darkening does not budge or remove the *tumah* stigma. Another thing. Darkening and spreading does not indicate low-level *tumah*, so that it is possible to deduce the obverse in cases where coloration had neither deteriorated nor spread.

This much should be plain. Increased incidence of *nega* does not derogate instances where *tumah* signs are stable. Hence, if a compromised appearance deteriorates but does not spread, then the law is as if the color both dimmed and spread. All the more so will a *tamei* verdict be delivered should the affected coloration worsen *and* spread out. See the Ralbag's comments on this *parashah,* and especially his concluding remarks.

PARASHAT METZORA

MORAL MELTDOWN

First *aliyah*

> *"And Hashem spoke to Moshe, saying:*
> *These will be the governing laws for one smitten with* **tzaraat**
> *on the day he recovers spiritual purity.*
> *And he will be brought to the Kohen."*

Following the Torah laying out laws for those stricken with *tzaraat*—whether on the skin or on the undergarments—this *aliyah* delves into the "day after." That is, upon concluding his stint in isolation, when the day of his purification arrives, "he will be brought to the Kohen."[1] Exactly when does this appointment take place? It does not refer to the final stages of his malady, when skin lesions are still present. This is derived from the following verse, "And the Kohen leaves the camp."[2]

Visiting hours, per se, were scheduled beyond the encampment confines. And examinations took place a safe distance from population centers. Under no circumstances did patients enter the camp for their checkups. Thus, we can deduce from the appointment's venue (a Kohen's office inside the camp) that *tzaraat* signs had fully subsided. This *aliyah*'s section goes into greater detail, as we learn about purification steps to which a recovered *metzora* adhered.

Rehabilitation began with a Kohen's initiative. "And the Kohen leaves the camp." Call it a well-leper checkup. It is on this occasion that, providing that all symptoms have passed, the road back home commences. "And the Kohen examines, and behold, the *nega hatzaraat* has healed from the afflicted man. And for a man who will be rehabilitated, a Kohen requests [he take] two living kosher birds, some cedar wood, and crimson wool, and hyssop."[3] The tab for these items is picked up by the guy undergoing rehab.

---

1. Vayikra 14:2.
2. Vayikra 14:3.
3. Vayikra 14:4.

As far as the birds are concerned, any kosher kind will do, so long as they are alive. Some commentators explain that the term "living" or *chayot* (חיות) connotes wild versus domestic types. How? They translate the word as "flyers." Birds in the wild are generally more adept at taking to their wings than their rotund, domesticated cousins, who barely manage to clumsily glide or thump down from barn rafters.

Cedar wood was used due to its merit of having been considered the finest of all trees. "Standing tall like a cedar of Lebanon,"[4] praises psalmist King David. Next on the list was crimson wool or *shani tolaat* (שני תולעת). This red string received an outer coat of blood. And finally, there was hyssop or *ezov* (אזב). The contrast between the tallest trees in the forest (cedars of Lebanon) and the lowliest ones (hyssop) could not have been more marked. King Shlomoh noted the disparity: "And he spoke of trees, from the cedar of Lebanon to the hyssop growing from walls."[5]

"And the Kohen ordered that one of the birds be slaughtered over an earthenware vessel containing fresh water."[6] This instruction called for pristine spring water previously unused by man. What was the fate of the second bird? "And he shall take the living bird along with the piece of cedar wood and crimson wool and the hyssop, immersing the live bird in the blood of the slaughtered bird [that had dripped] in pure spring water."[7]

What happened next? "And he shall sprinkle that upon the man rehabilitating from *tzaraat*, and he pronounces him ritually pure or *tahor* (טהור). Then the live bird gets released to the open fields."[8] To the blue skies, that is where the freed remaining bird flew.

"And he who is purifying himself must launder his garments and shave off all of his hair and wash in water. And he is *tahor*. And afterwards he may reenter the encampment but dwells outside his tent for seven days."[9] Quarantine for this healed *metzora* is a thing of the past. Still, he is not allowed to move back home. This signals that he may not yet engage in intimate

---

4. Tehillim 92:13.
5. I Melachim 5:13.
6. Vayikra 14:5.
7. Vayikra 14:6.
8. Vayikra 14:7.
9. Vayikra 14:8.

relations with his wife. Sexual intercourse is strongly inadvisable to patients newly recovering from serious illness.

We have provided a straightforward explanation for these verses. The sages, however, reveal a deeper side.[10] They hold that *tzaraat* is a consequence of disrelished traits. Specifically, it results from a man's arrogance. Divrei Hayamim records that underlying reason leading to Uzziyahu, the king of Yehudah, suffering a bout of *tzaraat*. "And as a result of his contempt, *tzaraat* emblazoned his forehead."[11] In accordance with this homily, the rabbis issued stern warnings. Purportedly, conceit lifts a man tall like towering cedar trees, but his downfall cuts him down to the size of the lowly hyssop. Fortunately, a remedy avails itself. Far better when a man gains level-headed perspective that allows him to not take himself so seriously. Effective object lessons can be found in the remaining two items used by reformed *metzora'im*: silk worms and hyssop.

All told, there are four observations worthy of analysis when discussing the debilitating and harrowing experience suffered by one who contracts *tzaraat*. One, he loses feeling in his flesh, a feeling akin to pins and needles. Two, his inner harmony gets whacked out of kilter, causing foul moods. Three, his natural facial countenance dulls or yellows. An ashen complexion indicates liver disorders and produces a slew of undesirable side effects. And finally, fourth, offensive body odor lingers stubbornly.

Note too that there are two ways in which a *metzora* gets put out—literally. First, he is forced into quarantine, where he dwells as a social outcast bereft of his co-religionists' comfort or company. Second, he is prevented from ascending to God's Mishkan and is thus deprived of divine communion. Since his state of *tumah* resulted in two cut-offs, it follows that his rehabilitation seeks to make two amends. Reentry into the Hebrew camp heralds his return to health and social standing. Bringing a sacrifice aids in helping him attain atonement while reestablishing close relations with his Maker.

With these aspects of a *metzora's* purification process in mind, let us ponder particular points associated with his first day of renewed purity. Recall how his performance and execution utilizes four props, for lack of a better

---

10. *Torat Kohanim* 14:35.
11. II Divrei Hayamim 26:19.

word. These avouch for his regained vigor and clean bill of emotional health. What are these four match-ups?

Symptoms of *tzaraat*	Rehabilitating props
loss of feeling and sensation	live birds, meaning he has regained life
inner turmoil	cedar wood is durable and sturdy
ashen complexion	crimson wool's healthy rosy coloring
foul odor	hyssop has delightfully enticing fragrance

In sum, these four objects provide excellent countermeasures to his former plight. Indeed, all point to the emergence of a new, vital man.

"And the Kohen ordered that one of the birds be slaughtered over an earthenware vessel containing fresh water. And he shall take the living bird along with the piece of cedar wood and crimson wool and the hyssop, immersing the live bird in the blood of the slaughtered bird [that had dripped] in the pure, spring water."[12] This rite is, of course, very suggestive. At the outset, both birds were alive. On Hashem's command, one was killed. Consider the fate of two men. One falls ill and dies. The other recovers and lives. Both are subject to the Almighty's decree.

What symbolism should we grant to the earthenware vessel? Man resembles a clay dish created at the Potter's hand. Unquestionably, all creatures are putty in His palm. "One of the birds be slaughtered over an earthenware vessel containing fresh water." Spring water represents timeless Torah, Holy Writ close to man's heart. This first bird's slaughter and death resulted, metaphorically, from desultory lip service to Torah observance.

The following point also carries rich meaning and is inter alia levelled at a common misunderstanding held by some people regarding *tzaraat*. A live bird is dipped into a potion consisting of fresh water, bird blood, cedar wood, and hyssop. This conveys how *tzaraat*'s contagion is not spread in the manner of other germs and bacteria. Doctors and scientists do not properly understand this scourge we commonly translate as *tzaraat* or pestilence. It is a function of God's will—nothing more and nothing less. Transgression causes

---

12. Vayikra 14:5–6.

a Jew to experience a lowered resistance. Susceptible, he may ultimately grow deathly ill.

Now let us turn to better grasp the import of the wood and plant pieces placed in the spring water, in addition to the crimson wool strand. Taken as a whole, these represent a healthy man both in body and spirit. Man's wonderfully diverse systems are keenly designed to allow for his self-sustenance. Though his balance or harmony may encounter misalignment if exposed to unseemly influences (say, bird blood), it doesn't. Man is resilient. The slaughtered bird stands in for a *metzora*. When *tzaraat* strikes, one may mistakenly think that the victim hangs on tenuously, since the aggressive illness attacks with a vengeance. But man does not succumb. As ominous as this plague could be, not all is irreparably lost. God watches over the Hebrews, protecting them from catching it—despite exposure to the killer disease represented by blood.

Symbolism of the slaughtered bird's blood conveys a second message, too. "And he shall sprinkle that upon the man rehabilitating from *tzaraat*, and he pronounces him ritually pure."[13] At root, a *metzora*'s ordeal and recovery is a bigger story. It is a universal story about human triumph, as King Shlomoh observed, "seven times will a righteous man fall but [each time] he picks himself up."[14] Buoyancy, the wise king reveals, means that the upright not only stand after tripping, but they also do not retain traces of former evil influences that caused downfall. The sages put it pithily: It is not the viper that kills, but rather sin.[15]

"Then he shall release the live bird to the open fields."[16] To a pastoral place of peace, that is where a reformed *metzora* goes. Newly cleansed, he is readmitted to the Hebrew encampment. No further restraints harness him. He is as free as a bird. Quarantine and ostracism are a thing of the past. Note that since these are not sacrificial birds, the slaughtered one is not burned.[17]

"And the one undergoing cleansing must launder his clothes and shave off all of his hair. And he washes in water and is deemed ritually pure."[18] This is straightforward. Laundering his clothes is expedient, because this clothing

---

13. Vayikra 14:7.
14. Mishlei 24:16.
15. BT *Berachot* 33a.
16. Vayikra 14:7.
17. Abravanel points out but negates Ralbag's assertion that the priest offered the slaughtered bird as a sin offering.
18. Vayikra 14:8.

belonged to a *metzora*, once tainted by *tzaraat*. A clean start is predicated upon a clean break from anything tinged and connected to his sordid, leprous past. Shaving his hair contributed an additional break with his erstwhile nettlesome complaint. Part of the malady manifested itself in hair loss. Had a *metzora* not been required to systematically crop his hair, then his geographic scalp—a tuft missing here and a tuft missing there—would be a dead giveaway. Now that his head has been shaved, new hair will grow back evenly and healthy-looking.

Without a doubt, Jewish wisdom's layers of sagacity abound as the tradition encourages *metzora'im* to glean life lessons. Formerly, he had sunk to levels of depravity. On account of them, calamitous punishment rocked him. Later, he got hold of himself. Annealed by the ordeal, he welcomes a clear-headed return to authentic values. Torah grants catharsis, instructing ways to reclaim spiritual balance and purity. Undesirable personality traits—like soiled garments—agitate as in a vigorous wash cycle. Add to that a haircut and shave. Coiffed and sporting a pressed suit, a man is set to tackle his demons.

If the cleansing process sounds simple, that is because it is. "And he washes in water and is deemed ritually pure." No meds. No treatment. No therapy. Just a slap of cold water does it. This is exactly as the prophet Elisha prescribed to Naaman, the king of Aram's chief of staff. "Go and wash in the Jordan River seven times."[19] Perhaps the prophet took a leaf out of our passage dealing with *tzaraat*.

"He may reenter the encampment but dwells outside his tent for seven days."[20] As previously stated, this sole limitation on his movement within the Hebrew encampment reflected how sick he had been and how his full recovery comes in stages. At this sensitive juncture, returning home and resuming sexual relations with his wife would likely have slowed a full rebound. Thus, refraining from intimacy for an additional week makes good sense. There is another angle. Namely, all remedial steps until now were designed to help him regain entrée to the Hebrew encampment. Basically, this measure only amounted to a ticket out of quarantine. Still, sticky remnants of wrongdoing had not completely been shaken. Waiting another week in the wings, as it were, was one more proactive course of action.

---

19. II Melachim 5:10.
20. Vayikra 14:8.

Sacrifice filled in that last missing piece. But before sacrifice was permitted, preparation was needed. Dwelling outside his home for seven days helped in that direction. It provided spiritual readiness.

Recapping, then, these two birds should not be viewed as sacrifices, but instead convey that a *metzora* had shed his spots and was healthy. Our discussion has also elucidated the rationale behind the need to use cedar wood, crimson wool, and hyssop. Finally, we better understand why there were two purification steps. One allowed a healed *metzora* entrance to the encampment; the other brought him to the banquet hall of the King's palace.

The Torah provides protocol for his seventh day of purification. "And it will be on the seventh day, he shall shave off all of his hair—hair on his head and on his beard and eyebrows—and all of his hair he shall shave off. And he shall launder his clothing and bathe himself in water. And he is ritually pure."[21] The Torah demands a repetition of purification acts on the seventh day. Shaving and bathing are crucial steps in his personal growth. They usher in a new inner self and mark the end of a spoiled former stage. Staying a course toward his rendezvous at the Mikdash required as much. And more.

"And on the eighth day he took two unblemished sheep and a one-year-old unblemished female sheep and three *esronim* of fine flour mingled with oil, and one *log* of oil."[22] The first sheep was a guilt offering, the second one a sin offering, and the third sheep served as a burnt offering. Note these sacrifices dovetail with an overall schema that reveals perfect divine providence, a modus operandi tailor-made for the Chosen Nation.

Judaism posits that man always receives his just deserts, meaning that reward and punishment are measured and precise. Turning to a *metzora*, it is assumed that his guilt and sin landed him this mighty blow. Continuing, let us consider whether he had knowledge of his wrongdoing. Assuming that, he would be required to bring a sin offering. However, if his transgression was perpetrated without awareness, then he would be obligated to bring an *asham talui*, as has been stated earlier. Those two possibilities explain why he brings two of the three sheep mentioned in our verse.

Let us understand the sequence of these first two sacrifices. It is a working assumption (and King Shlomoh has memorialized this in Scripture) that no

---

21. Vayikra 14:9.
22. Vayikra 14:10.

man is inured to or sheltered from life's challenges and vicissitudes. Simply (under)stated, nobody is perfect. Wittingly or not, there are bound to be accidents. Sacrificing a guilt offering at the outset acknowledges man's reality head-on by atoning for inadvertent sins. Sheep number one accomplishes this. After it follows a female sheep used for a sin offering. In ascending order as far as severity is concerned, this sequence is logical because lighter issues are best tackled before more complex (grievous) ones. Finally, when a man makes amends for errors (either with knowledge or without it), he is positioned to bring a burnt offering, since it attests to altruistic man's yearning to gain intimacy with his Maker.

Nothing has been spelled out regarding what the altar receives or to what an attending priest is entitled. Earlier in Sefer Vayikra this has been stated.[23]

Second *aliyah*
"And the Kohen took blood from the guilt offering and the Kohen placed it on the right earlobe of the man being purified and on his right hand and on his right big toe."

The Torah stipulates more remedial action for a healing *metzora*—this time in the form of three sprinkles of blood. Another similar dash is ordered to be taken from the *log* of oil that comprises part of his gift to the Mikdash. Remaining oil is cupped in the hand of the officiating priest.[24]

Our verse is explicit that an officiating Kohen takes a dab of blood from the first sacrifice (guilt offering), placing it on the patient's right earlobe, right thumb, and right big toe. Next, this procedure is repeated with oil.

Here is a twist. "And leftover oil that is in the priest's palm he daubs on the patient's head. And the Kohen brings him atonement before Hashem."[25] Here are the reasons that this is performed. One, those are the particular anatomical parts that *tzaraat* attacks first. This is because those limbs have little flesh, hastening the affliction. Two, this daubing conveys how true healing comes from Above when the victim repents of misdeeds and redoubles performance of mitzvot. Truism: When Heaven's regime for healing is administered, it

---

23. Parshiyot Vayikra and Tzav.
24. Note that Abravanel does not comment on this *aliyah*'s opening verses.
25. Vayikra 14:18.

supersedes the need for patients to seek conventional medical advice. This counsel applies to healing *tzaraat*, and allusion is made to bloodletting. That procedure sought to offer relief from blood vessels in the ears en route to the brain.[26] Sometimes, bloodletting centered on a man's chest cavity, where cardiovascular arteries connect to his arm. Another area where bloodletting commonly occurred was in the leg, since it links up with the liver.

Fluid for daubing	Where it is daubed
blood from the guilt offering brought by the *metzora*	right earlobe of the man being purified and on his right hand and on his right big toe
leftover oil that remains in the priest's palm from the *metzora*'s offering	The head of the man needing purification

Greater emphasis regarding Heaven's wonderfully effective way of healing cannot be more pronounced. Not only are doctors told to refrain from standard methods of medicine (bloodletting), but also those standard anatomical regions (ears, arms, and legs) don't have blood taken from them, but rather an attending priest actually adds blood to those regions. A loud broadcast publicizes: God does not call for typical healing that usually includes brain, heart, and kidney bloodletting. On the contrary, blood is taken from the guilt offering and daubed on a patient's ears, hands, and legs. Most important, the treatment worked wonders.

Let us analyze why priests spilled drops of oil on patients. Clearly, this procedure did not look to reduce a man's body fluids, again a common practice to combat pestilence. Repentance, not medicine, nurses a patient back to health. Taking charge of his destiny trumps everything else. When queer notions entered his head, heart, or kidney, he invited affliction. Dashes of blood on those places signal patching-up impulses that had led him astray in the first place.

Why does the Torah stress the right limbs time and again? The right side is considered predominant and stronger than the left. "And leftover oil that is in the priest's palm he daubs on the patient's head. And the Kohen brings him

---

26. Abravanel alludes to common medieval practice and medical convention.

atonement before Hashem." As stated, *metzora'im* are given ample opportunity to address wrongdoing and set things straight. Here, an overall counsel is shared. Namely, oil, which symbolizes wisdom, conveys that he should remember at all times to keep his smarts and intelligence well lubricated, for this is the basis of right living.

To be sure, dashes of blood and daubs of oil bespeak rich imagery. This is especially true when we consider that the blood had been pooled from the guilt offering but not from the sin or burnt offering. Why? Exclusively, it is over the guilt offering that a *metzora* admits his transgression before God. On the merit of his repentance, forgiveness is granted. We have mentioned above that rams most befit guilt offerings on account of their considerable worth and value. Here, however, the verse settles for an unblemished sheep, presumably due to it being of relatively similar cost to rams. Turtledoves or pigeons, on the other hand, may not be used as ram or sheep fill-ins, for their value is too disparate in comparison. For one thing, fowl are oviparous (and thus lower on a biological scale), whereas sheep are viviparous. Another reason sheep fit the bill as worthy substitutes is that they provide ample quantities of blood needed for sprinkling.

Third *aliyah*
"And if he is poor and cannot afford it,
then he can suffice with one sheep for a guilt offering
to be waved to attain atonement and an isaron *of flour*
for a gift offering plus one log *of oil."*

As we explained at the conclusion of the last *aliyah*, the Torah did not allow for any fudging when it came to guilt sacrifices. Leniency was, however, permitted when it came to sin or burnt offerings if a patient was indigent. "And two turtledoves or two pigeons for which he could afford to pay…one served as a sin offering, the other a burnt offering."[27] Two turtledoves or pigeons sufficed. For that reason, blood for sprinkling always had been taken from guilt offerings. Sheep, then, remained the constant.

---

27. Vayikra 14:22.

"And with his right finger, the Kohen sprinkled from the oil in his left palm seven times before God."[28] No mention is made of dashing blood here. Why? The Kohen's body language tells a story. That is, when he sprinkles oil "before God," it suggests his heartfelt prayer on behalf of his patient. The holy of holies—the Almighty's haunt—hears the Kohen's fervent prayer on behalf of the man that he should be blessed with a life of good health. Symbolically, oil reflects sound health; seven dashes of it intimate lasting blessing.

Before continuing to the fourth *aliyah*, let us rethink this. What can be learned from the somewhat atypical order and sequence of a *metzora's* sacrifices? Previously, we suggested that the order was significant. Adequate blood needed to be collected initially in order to have enough for the sprinklings. Since the guilt offering was brought first—and had it been a turtledove or pigeon, there would certainly have been a blood shortfall—there needed to be a sheep used for a guilt offering. See our discussion in Parashat Vayikra, where it stated that guilt offerings were always rams.

Sin and burnt offerings were established on a sliding-scale basis. This reflected their main essence, namely that they had to be brought with full religious intent or *kavanah*. Consequently, the Torah granted leeway. "And he shall offer…that which he can afford for either the sin or burnt offering with its meal offering, and the priest shall bring atonement to the one who comes to purify himself before the Almighty."[29] These are the *aliyah's* concluding remarks. This aptly summarizes how the first step of attaining ritual purity seeks to allow a healed *metzora* reentry to the Hebrew encampment. Second, the process aimed to accord him a place in the Mikdash, as it says, "one who comes to purify himself before the Almighty."

---

28. Vayikra 14:27.
29. Vayikra 14:30–31.

Fourth *aliyah*

"And Hashem spoke to Moshe and to Aharon, saying: When you come to the land of Canaan that I bequeath to you as an inheritance, I will place the leprous curse or **nega tzaraat** *in the houses—in the land of your inheritance."*

Not even remotely is this phenomenon of diseased houses a natural occurrence. Not a smidgeon.[30] How is it that blood and other fluid imbalances that cause *tzaraat* can be determinants for bringing pestilence to houses? It is hardly reasonable let alone defensible to ascribe vitality to structures of stone.

Here is the thing. So far in this *parashah* we have been discussing how a *metzora* regains spiritual purity. These steps, as noted, stressed heavy dosages of pure and unadulterated divine providence. Remedial acts were not only preternatural but ran counter to conventional methods of medical knowledge and practice. Thus, bloodletting and so forth was waived. All "normative" pathology theory was abandoned, and in its stead a series of measures was adopted, including sprinkling blood and oil, bathing, and laundering, not to mention offering an array of sacrifices.

While supernatural momentum had been gaining steam throughout the previous *aliyot*, this section should be seen as an extension thereof. Houses contracting illness is, well, perfectly otherworldly. Juxtaposition of these sections mentally prepares readers that something beyond the pale of "normalcy" is about to roll out. Indeed, it provides a heads-up for rationally minded readers to temporarily suspend their human reason. Yes, rehabilitation for a *metzora* defies logic, just as certainly as does this upcoming subject dealing with kaleidoscope walls in houses.

When Jews enter the land, they are hereby informed that it is a land on which God's eyes are constantly trained. "When you come to the land of Canaan that I bequeath to you."[31] Outlandish, maybe, but Jews heard from Moshe that divine providence—when it comes to Israel—just may on occasion toss in some brow-knitting house partition patterns. "That I bequeath" reveals just how far the Creator went in pulling natural stops, tugging divine strings.

---

30. Abravanel's position differs from that of the Ralbag.
31. Vayikra 14:34.

But why would Hashem buck the natural order that He established? What was the point? One possibility is to serve as a cautionary. God warns man to turn to reflective repentance and extirpate misdoing. It is as if building stones yelp or house rafters wag fingers at property owners: *Jews—come back home to Hashem your Almighty. Discern well what is pullulating on your walls. If meaningful change does not transpire, there will be these dreadful symptoms climbing on your abdomen, on the trunks of your children…*

Clearly, the sages had this connection in mind when they wrote homiletically about the juxtaposition of these two Torah sections featuring toxic house *tzaraat* after a section dealing with that affliction upon man.[32] Alternatively, there is another reason that explains the Torah's sequence. That is, after Jews enter the Land of Israel, they will apprehend *nega tzaraat* in Canaanites' former dwellings. Ringworm and rashy wall marks apprise them of pagan practices that had been performed there. By revealing locations where idolatrous outrages had been perpetrated, Jews learned which Canaanite houses needed to be destroyed. Thus, *nega tzaraat* is no less than Heaven sent, with clearly illustrated X-marks-the-spot targets, no less. According to this approach, verses concerning leprous houses of idolatrous ill repute bring to the fore an important observation. Namely, Heaven validates and confirms that just as divine marks must be viewed as…well, divine, so too were those symptoms of *tzaraat* that had infected man. Both ailment and its cure had divine providence's furious scribbling all over them. This approach finds support in Moshe's words in Sefer Devarim. "Pay attention to *nega hatzaraat* to observe it intently and to do all that which the Kohanim instruct you—as I have commanded, you shall keep and do them."[33]

Had Moshe's co-religionists still harbored doubts as to divine providence's proactive posturing, he removed any guesswork. "Remember what Hashem your Almighty did to Miriam along the way when you left Egypt."[34] As a punishment to Miriam for speaking disparagingly against her brother Moshe, she had been stricken with *tzaraat*. Not medicine but rather Moshe's fervent prayer healed her.

---

32. *Vayikra Rabbah* 17:4.
33. Devarim 24:8.
34. Devarim 24:9.

"And the homeowner comes and informs the Kohen, saying: Apparently I have seen something like a *nega* growing in my house."[35] The Torah is teaching proper reticence and apprehension to homeowners. Instead of presuming to be expert in matters of pestilence, they should defer to priest specialists. Kohanim, and not afflicted homeowners, pronounce either impure or pure verdicts. Torah in general but *tzaraat* in particular is the purview of the people's priestly educators. "Apparently I have seen something like a *nega*." Note the homesteader's tone, expressing doubt. A house call with a qualified priest is arranged.

Before a Kohen arrives, and out of acknowledgment that his word on these matters is final, he issues a directive to the homeowner. "And the priest demands: And they shall remove all contents from the house before the priest arrives to inspect the *nega*. [This he does] so as not to proclaim all contents impure. And afterwards the Kohen comes to inspect the house."[36] Manifestly, removing house contents is an expedient and spares a homeowner the additional trouble should the priest deliver a guilty verdict rendering those movables ritually impure.

What are the symptoms a Kohen looked for when he inspected house walls? "And he looks at the *nega* and behold, the *nega* is on the walls of the house. [They are either] greenish or reddish colors, appearing indented within the house walls."[37] The Torah records two telltale signs: appearances of discoloration and indentation. Though they could either be green or red stains, their color's hue or pitch was nonetheless intense. As far as the second symptom was concerned, it looked as if it was deeply inset within the walls of the house.

"And the Kohen walked out of the house to its entrance. And he placed the house in quarantine for seven days."[38] While the priest stood in the main doorway before anyone had an opportunity to enter, he proclaimed his opinion that more time was needed before making a final determination. Not mincing words, he called for a seven-day time out, just as was the case involving a suspected *metzora* or a suspected garment worn by a *metzora*.

---

35. Vayikra 14:35.
36. Vayikra 14:36.
37. Vayikra 14:37.
38. Vayikra 14:38.

"And the priest returned on the seventh day and made an inspection. Behold, the *nega* had spread on the walls of the house."[39] Symptoms had certainly become exacerbated, and wall blotches bled beyond their original borders. "And the priest ordered that they remove the contaminated stones. And they shall heave them beyond the city limits to a soiled area."[40] This means that those affected stones were pried loose from the wall and shunted beyond city borders, where they permanently lay—alfresco—in a predesignated hazardous waste dump. This measure protected others from contracting pestilence.

More curative steps had to be taken. "And the house needed to be sanded down around the infected area. And the debris that they scraped was dumped outside the city to a soiled area."[41] Here students notice a difference between contaminated houses and clothing. When it came to a *metzora*'s clothing that had tested positive, the entire garment was placed in a fire; however, that was not the case with contagious house stones. Only those impacted stones were taken away, but the others were not touched.

"And they took other stones and brought them as replacements. And he took other plaster and plastered the house."[42] Stopgap measures allowed time to elapse before reevaluation was assessed. "And if after the stones had been removed and the plaster sanded and new plaster applied, [yet] the *nega* returned and spread inside the house, then the Kohen shall come and make an inspection..."[43]

To no avail, three vigorous steps had been adopted to stem the house's downslide. "And behold, pestilence spread in the house. Malignant *tzaraat* has possessed the house. It is ritually impure."[44]

Draconian measures are adopted. "And he completely wrecks the house—its stones and its wood and all the plaster comprising the house, and he transports these beyond the city limits to a soiled area."[45] Levelled and carted off, the cancerous house is no longer.

---

39. Vayikra 14:39.
40. Vayikra 14:40.
41. Vayikra 14:41.
42. Vayikra 14:42.
43. Vayikra 14:43.
44. Vayikra 14:44.
45. Vayikra 14:45.

Before continuing, consider these two points. Had the pestilence not spread but merely remained the same, then the Kohen would not have issued his fateful verdict, meaning that the house—even with its queer markings— would have been deemed ritually clean. The Hebrew verb for sanding and scraping or *yaktzia* (יקצִיע) is in the singular. That work was performed by a priest.

Before the house had been destroyed, recall, a Kohen had pronounced it ritually impure. Several governing laws now call aloud for practical ramifications of that damning verdict. "And anyone who comes to the house while it is under quarantine shall be ritually impure until the evening."[46] It doesn't matter if a man entered the no-entry zone on day one or day seven, the result is identical. He contracts *tumah*. If that house had already been condemned and a man enters that area, a fortiori he remains *tamei* until evening. That is the case for his person, but not for the clothes on his back, though the next verse will make this explicit.

"And one who sleeps in the house shall launder his clothing. And one who eats in the house shall launder his clothing."[47] According to Jewish tradition, *tumah* occurs even if the person doesn't actually eat, as long as he was in the affected house for the time it takes to eat a satisfying quantity of bread, or if he went to sleep there.[48]

"And if the Kohen enters and inspects, and behold, the *nega* had not progressed in the house after replastering the house, then the Kohen shall deem the house ritually pure, for the *nega* healed."[49] The return of the Kohen spoken of here takes place after the third set of seven days, after the *nega* had been scraped and plastered over. Since the disease had been arrested, the house is proclaimed pure—reminiscent of the clean bill of health given to a *metzora* whose affliction does not worsen. "For the *nega* healed."[50]

Priests are looking for a steady decline in the wall's blotchiness. Since no decline had been noticed, the disease is stabilized and the house set on a healing course. This is not a matter of guesswork. A stabilized condition in

46. Vayikra 14:46.
47. Vayikra 14:47.
48. See *Torat Kohanim*, chapter 14.
49. Vayikra 14:48.
50. Ibid.

a disease as violently aggressive as *tzaraat* is a sure-fire sign of its abatement and reversal.

Let us clarify a difference between this affliction affecting clothing versus a house. Pathology infecting clothing attacks a man's property of limited or modest value. Indicative of this is the fact that the Torah is not particularly concerned about finding ways to preserve it. In contrast, a house is landed property. Its loss represents a major financial setback for families. For that reason, it behooves Heaven, as it were, to find mitigating circumstances. However, in other ways the two cases overlap and share governing laws. In effect, this economizes, because some verses in the clothing section apply to the house section and vice versa. To illustrate, there is no doubt that when a garment has a leprous spot, it will cause *tumah* for a man sitting or sleeping on it, just as is the case for a man entering, sleeping, or eating in a contaminated house.

However, when clothing is proclaimed leprous, they burn it either entirely or partly. No tincture composed of birds, cedar tree wood, crimson wool, and hyssop cleansed it. Not so with house dots. "And to disinfect the house, he takes two birds and cedar wood and crimson wool and hyssop."[51]

After verses elaborate more details, this fourth *aliyah* concludes: "And [it] makes atonement for the house. And it is ritually clean."[52] Are students to believe that the house sinned and was in need of forgiveness? Of course the notion of a house having capacity to transgress is senseless drivel. Really, the Torah alludes to the house owner's lapse. When he processes that his ordeal is designed to be a warning, he internalizes an important message sent from Above. God is nudging him to repent in order to merit divine compassion. It is the homeowner's own well-being at stake, his healing on the line. An agonizing agent—an arduous pestilence—knocks at his door. Literally. That is why a house gets healed exactly as does a *metzora*. Advice for man crouches at his front deck, personally delivered to his home address. A discerning man gathers as much. Not to a lifeless peppered house, not to polka-dotted cold stones, and not to indifferent pocked wooden planks does the Almighty speak. This is a communiqué for man's ears only.

---

51. Vayikra 14:49.
52. Vayikra 14:53.

Fifth *aliyah*
"And Hashem spoke to Moshe and to Aharon, saying:
Speak to Bnei Yisrael and say to them:
Should any man develop oozing from his flesh,
he shall be deemed ritually impure."

Digestion and Proper Sexual Conduct

Prefatory remarks are in order.[53] To begin with, see Sefer Bereshit.[54] Doctors and anatomists identify three stages in man's digestive tract. The first one (let us call it stage 1) is his stomach, where food processing initiates the breakdown of food. Concentrated nutrition next travels to the liver, veins, and arteries, where it is absorbed and assimilated. Waste material and excess food intake get eliminated through the intestines and colon after having passed through the liver. Some waste is passed through the urinary tract. Clearly, at those latter points of exit, no nutritional value remains from the food originally ingested. Because it is of no value, it does not and cannot remain in a man's body.

Technically speaking and as a testament to nature's ways, *halachah* does not deem man's waste product an object that causes or triggers defilement or *tumah*. Obviously enough, man cannot live without ridding himself of these unwanted products regularly. After a man relieves himself, he need only wash his hands and make a blessing. Not surprisingly, normative and everyday *halachah* of bathroom habits applies to officiating priests in the Mikdash. Despite their holy workplace, there was no overriding and overbearing *halachah* for the priestly habitués. Hence, when a Kohen relieved himself on duty, he did not contract *tumah*. Nor would passing urine or moving his bowels require him to take a recess from his post until sundown.

We now progress to how doctors understood the second aspect of man's digestive system (stage 2). The liver performs this role after nutrients get passed to it from the stomach. This organ takes the choicest component of food, transforming it into blood. Of the rest, it produces other bodily fluids which may neatly be compartmentalized by color code: white, red, or black.

---

53. Abravanel builds on medieval medical theory and philosophy.
54. See *Abravanel's World: Bereshit*, Parashat Toldot, first *aliyah*.

As food is redistributed throughout man's body, it continues to nourish it. This process contributes to a healthy organism. At the same time, remaining waste products are secreted either through body perspiration or coughing. At this intermediate stage (stage 2 of three stages) of separating usable from unusable food, a man may rid himself of undesirable product via diarrhea or bleeding.

While still in this stage 2 category of digestion, note that these above-mentioned methods of expelling excess waste do not usher in *tumah*. Thus, nosebleeds, bloodletting, or blood in the stool (say, from hemorrhoids) are not status-altering *tumah* events. Expelling waste and excess fluids is a crucial bodily function, critical to preserving good health.

The third category of digestion (stage 3) occurs within a body's organs.[55] Note that stage 3 differs from the first two. How? It is marked by absorption or metabolism within man's body, whereas stages 1 and 2 emit outside of the body. After stage 3 is complete, there is, in effect, barely a trace of nutritional value remaining. Consequently, a healthy fellow excretes worthless excess. When? Commonly, a body expels redundant fluids—perspiration—during physically demanding tasks. Other evacuative fluids exit during sexual intercourse. So, for a man, we are referring to sperm he ejaculates into a woman. Activated by intercourse or ovulation, a woman's fluid is associated with her internal reproductive organs (eggs, uterine lining, etc.). In essence, a man and a woman mirror each other, except that a man's release is, shall we say, external, versus internal for a woman.

Another thing. After sex, a male's sperm and corresponding woman's reproductive body fluids may wash out during a woman's period. Alternatively, they will become the stuff of human conception. More about this soon.

These biological prefatory remarks pave the way to get a better handle on our verses. How does man's anatomical mechanism serve to shed light on moral dissonance? This brings us to a discussion of *tumah* in terms of an oozing man or *zav* (זב) and oozing woman or *zavah* (זבה). We will explain some dynamics of a woman who is impure due to menstruation, a *niddah* (נידה), and a woman after childbirth, a *yoledet* (יולדת).

---

55. Abravanel records the opposing opinions of the twelfth-century Islamic scholar Ibn Rushd (known in Latin as Averroes) and the eleventh-century scholar Ibn Sina (known in Latin as Avicenna).

In the case of a *zavah*, *niddah*, or *yoledet*, it is paramount to establish that their *tumah* is not a function of vaginal oozing or bleeding. To illustrate and by contrast, consider a woman who experiences violent bouts of diarrhea stemming from pernicious kidney malfunction. Prodigious amounts of bleeding do not render her *temeah*. Nor do physicians attending to or treating kidney patients contract *tumah*. Take it as elementary that the amount of blood a menstruating woman loses is less than that of one whose bleed comes about as a result of kidney impairment. Determining *tumah*, then, is not a function of quantifying hemorrhaging. Rather, it is a matter of tracking the source of blood (or oozing) loss. Only when it originates in her uterus is she *temeah*.

Why does the source or location tilt the scales of *tumah*? To better understand, we consider what happens after a husband and wife share physical intimacy. A man's seed and a woman's egg burrow inside her womb. Uterine blood mixes with them. When a man ejaculates and a woman's ovary drops an egg, then *tumah* results. Raw material of semen and eggs consists of potential refined nutrition for a healthy body. Indeed, a body is the less for not having tapped it or capitalized on it. Stage 3 has been deprived of valuable nutrients; had a man not wasted some of the potential of his body, that material could have been used more constructively in aiding his bodily and digestive needs.

Now, we apply our knowledge to men and women who malign themselves and betray their higher calling. Wastrels and roués squander rich bodybuilding substances. In a man's case, he fritters away invaluable material, robbing body tissue of vitality. To clarify, we are not speaking about normal spousal relations. Instead, we are talking about fornication outside of matrimony. Essentially a dissocial act, illicit sex is distasteful debauchery. Hence, it creates *tumah*. Moreover, others in contact with rogue rakes are impacted and contract their defiled fate.

Things look very different for responsible marrieds. Their sexual intimacy stresses propagation of family. Since their mindset measures most reputably, the Torah provides dispensation. They are not *tamei* for seven days. Also they do not have to bring sacrifices. But they are required to immerse their bodies in water. In the evening they are *tahor*.

Unmistakably, the Torah broadcasts divine agenda. Immersion in cleansing waters and a forced "time-out" until sunset is instructive. It serves to chill excessive interest in and performance of sexual intercourse. Heaven counsels married couples: moderation.

Couples flouting moderation exhibit conduct often seen among rapscallions and lechers. Far more preferable is when spouses contain themselves, meaning that they take a break after intercourse. Yet some act as if their sex drive is irrepressible. They indulge repeatedly. Bouts follow in succession, another and another all day long. Spiraling, things simply spin out of control. Reiterating, it is all the more reprehensible when a man wastes semen as he squanders sound judgment, good sense, and well-being. Surrendering to the moment equates with a surrendering of self-discipline. Moral meltdown.

In efforts to shame ill judgment, the Torah slaps a degenerate with a verdict of *tamei* until the evening. In this unflattering column of impetuous rogues are rascals who sought their kicks by giving in to sexually suggestive fantasies. From that point, connect the dots to nocturnal emissions. And the result? Misconduct lands a scamp in *tamei* status until nightfall. Of course, he will need to shower and clean himself up.

Abundantly clear is this: the Torah does not profess that the *tumah* of a *zav* or *zavah* came about insofar as they had fallen ill—in a medical sense. Similarly, there is no insinuation that some cruel trick of nature alone activated *tumah*. In sum, neither illness nor nature explains *tumah*. What does? Consistent with current medical opinions,[56] the matter of *tumah* rests with the comingling of a woman's uterine blood and a man's seed, as advanced above.[57]

Intrinsically, a man's and woman's body fluids are of highest quality when located within optimal anatomical parts (or functions). Sexual intimacy results in a mixing of some of these fluids, weakening them and hence beckoning *tumah*. Caveat: this is not the case when husband and wife approach their love life responsibly.

Circling back, we summarize what we have learned before answering upcoming questions about certain women's and men's issues. Regarding women, we are speaking about one (a *zavah* or *yoledet*) who experienced particular gynecological phenomena. For her, why does the process stretch

---

56. Prevalent circa 1500 CE.

57. Abravanel cites contemporary physicians who discerned between blood circulating in a woman's veins or arteries (deemed high quality) versus uterine blood (deemed low quality). By the same token, these doctors maintained that a man's plasma circulating in the blood system ranked far superior to those seminal fluids he ejaculated.

out over seven days, and why does it culminate with her bringing a sacrifice after she has become *tehorah*? For men, discussion centers upon those who ejaculated. What does that event convey?

First, we contrast the cases of *zavah* and *yoledet* with other bodily functions we identify as nature running its natural course.[58] Generally speaking, a person expels waste product (excrement or urine) because it no longer stores value for the person. Since both are by-products of stage 1 digestion (discussed above), they must be discarded so as not to undermine a person's health. In that category we add, say, blood from bloody noses or rectal bleeding. Blood in stool, too, does not trigger *tumah*. Why? These are waste materials from stage 2 digestion. Again, had a person not expelled these from his body, he would take ill.

Now to answer our questions. In the case of a man who releases semen, he becomes *tamei*, since this is a by-product of stage 3 digestion. Had a man not ejaculated, that fluid potential could have been used for his benefit. That is, semen's chemical and biological makeup offers a man more while it circulates inside his body. Now he is, in fact, all the worse or weakened for having parted with this useful bodily fluid biochemistry. Sperm, exposed to an outside and foreign environment, is putrid. Whoever or whatever it touches contracts *tumah*. Caveat: when a man engages in level-headed lovemaking with his wife, the Torah extends him a dispensation, lessening the ill effects of having ejaculated.

We move on to the subject of a man who becomes a *zav*. Recall, this is a libertine who experiences uncontrolled oozing from his genitals. His case is quite severe, because it involuntarily reoccurs. With each episode of oozing, his health declines. Doubtless, the direction is a deleterious one.

The next topic takes into account a woman who becomes a *niddah*, *zavah*, or *yoledet*. Normatively speaking, all three cases render a woman *temeah*. Furthermore, our premise takes into consideration that this woman suffers, to adopt a medical term, from sexual polyphagia. Semen has mixed with vaginal secretions. Both entered her womb. The combo decomposes in a noxious manner. By way of highlighting just how bad the situation grows, her case stands on par with *tzaraat*.

---

58. A *niddah*'s case is slightly different and is discussed shortly, together with that of a *zavah* and *yoledet*.

Presently, we have grouped together the categories of a *niddah*, *zavah*, and *yoledet*. For accuracy's sake, however, a *niddah* must be decoupled from that grouping. Why? Menstruation is nature's way of expelling unused uterine blood. The thing is critical. Since this fact cannot be disputed, the Torah drops its obligation for her to remain *temeah* for a week just the same way it releases her from bringing a sacrifice after her period concludes. A *yoledet* does not get such treatment, as she bleeds prodigiously after delivery. Another factor that gravitates in favor of a *yoledet* waiting seven days and offering a sacrifice is the danger inherent in delivering a baby.

What must be said about a *zavah*? This is a woman who continually—and involuntarily—oozes from her genitals. The Torah renders her *temeah* owing to a clear-cut assumption that she behaves as a bawd. Unguarded with men, she conducts herself loosely and trots unhinged.

Heaven castigates her unchastity. She counts seven clean days, after which she brings a sacrifice. A *zavah's* vaginal bleeding is of the vilest type. Consequently, her contagion spreads to those who touch her. Should she enter the Mikdash, she sullies the holy place as well.

We have concluded our disquisition. Note, however, that conspicuously missing from it is the Torah's treatment of a Jew who comes into contact with a cadaver and is therefore afflicted by *tumat met* (טומאת מת). This is all the more striking when we consider that this particular form of *tumah*—so egregious—tops its class category of *tumah*. How extreme is it? Exclusively, only the ashes of a red heifer or *parah adumah* (פרה אדומה) provide recourse, and his return to normalcy. "And you shall take for the *tamei* ashes from a burnt purification offering."[59] Featured in Parashat Chukat, the mystifying topic of the red heifer will be discussed at length. Also there, we will learn laws governing a Hebrew who has contact with the dead.

Male Oozing as a Result of Malfeasance

"And Hashem spoke to Moshe and to Aharon, saying: Speak to Bnei Yisrael and say to them: Should any man develop oozing from his flesh, he shall be deemed ritually impure."[60] After concluding our lengthy prefatory discourse

---

59. Bamidbar 19:17.
60. Vayikra 15:1–2.

on various afflictions and conditions affecting men and women, we return to provide running commentary on this *parashah*'s final three *aliyot*.

In fact, the opening verse is not describing a general body oozing disorder. Instead and narrowly, pus oozes from a man's "flesh" or sexual organ. Also, our verse speaks of a man who is powerless to stop seminal emission. He is incontinent. This condition contrasts with other types of ejaculation. In the Torah, free-volition or voluntary ejection of sperm is referred to as *keri* (קרי).

"He shall be deemed ritually impure." That is, the man is *tamei*. Though his fluid is not intrinsically impaired (because it is stage 3 of digestion), still it affects his whole person. Seminal oozing or evacuation carries ritual impurity when it drips out. Medical practitioners attribute his disease to, in so many words, an unchecked libido. In short, this sex fiend fritters away an inordinate amount of time in bed.

In terms of laying out a hierarchy of ritual impurity, a *zav* is graded as an *av hatumah* (אב הטומאה).[61] By way of comparison, his level is likened to those of a dead rodent or *sheretz* and a *neveilah*. In practical terms, the ramifications are extensive. Suffice to say that it means that his severe condition impacts clothing and objects. Additionally, his fellow man will contract *tumah* if certain conditions are met (namely, if someone carries [משא], touches [מגע], or causes him to move [הסט]).

"And this shall be his ritual impurity when he oozes, regardless of whether his flesh runs because of his oozing or is blocked because of his oozing."[62] What are the parameters of his disease? Two possibilities are presented. Either seminal pus drips uncontrollably or it oozes from his flesh and becomes thin and flimsy in appearance, like saliva. Likely, his disorder is akin to a man attempting to pass kidney stones. Besides an intense burning sensation, there is a thick, coarse pus buildup too thick to be ejected. At any rate, this verse conveys that regardless of its particular symptoms, both presentations render him *tamei*. Indeed, a man's soul holds great contempt for loose morals which triggered loathsome signs of *tumah*. Interestingly, it may very well be that in every other regard the patient enjoys excellent health.

"Any bedding upon which an oozing man will lie contracts ritual impurity."[63] Sheets, mattresses, towels, and the like are all included in this verse.

---

61. See the chart of rankings of the various types of *tumah* above in Shemini, seventh *aliyah*.
62. Vayikra 15:3.
63. Vayikra 15:4.

Put a bit differently, they are organic outgrowths of a *zav*. As such, they catch and spread his disease. "And a [second] man who touches his bedding shall launder his clothing and wash in water. And he remains ritually impure until the evening."[64] Seemingly, the rationale for these particular objects spreading disease is straightforward. Since he regularly sits or lies down on chairs or bedding, and given that his evacuations are involuntary, it follows that he oozed while sitting or lying on his personal effects.

"And any seat upon which an oozing man rides is ritually impure."[65] This applies to anything from saddles to bike seats. Since these are things upon which he rides, it is presumed that motion or jerking causes pus to leak out. Verses teach that uncleanliness lasts until sunset. Note that some more extreme situations demand laundering and the passage of time, but that is not always the case.

Circling back to the *zav*, the sages propound minutiae regarding this *halachah*. Thus, even if a *zav*'s bed consisted of ten stacked mattresses and he is on the top tier, all of the bottom mattresses contract *tumah*.[66]

Now our discussion returns to the case of a second man who has contact with a *zav*. *Halachah* takes into account different kinds of contact, each with potentially varying ramifications. A man who carries a *zav*-contaminated article is treated more onerously than had he merely brushed up against or casually touched defiled items.[67]

Switching subjects, we turn to *zavim* and observe nuances between them. In other words, some *zavim* require stricter treatment reflecting their grossly defiled state. By extrapolation, we determine that had a *zav* begun his cleansing process but not completed it, and yet he still contacted other people or articles, then leniencies will apply. "And anyone whom a *zav* touches."[68] The verse speaks in common terminology. The *zav* touches a person or object with his hands. Note two things. First, the Torah instructs us that the *zav* spreads defilement if the contact had been via his hands or through any other of his limbs (e.g., he kicked someone or something). Second, "And he had not [yet]

---

64. Vayikra 15:5.
65. Vayikra 15:6.
66. *Torat Kohanim*, Vayikra 15:6.
67. See Vayikra 15:7.
68. Vayikra 15:11.

washed his hands."[69] The *zav*, we now learn, had not immersed himself in a *mikveh* as a means of removing his *tumah*. To explain, even though the verse says that the *zav* had not washed his hands, it means that he had not immersed his entire body.

Here is the scenario. We are speaking about a man who had displayed all of the signs of a *zav* (read: he oozed). Later, his symptoms abated. In order to complete his purification process, he needed to comply with the Torah's instruction. Part of his compliance meant immersing in a *mikveh*. Before that happened, the *zav* was careless and defiled others (or other objects).

"And if a man who oozes shall touch an earthenware vessel, it shall be shattered. But any wooden vessel he shall rinse in water."[70] The sages add that contamination occurs even if he touched the outside wall of the clay vessel.[71] This important detail avoids a possible misunderstanding that may crop up by contrasting this passage to an earlier one. See Vayikra above.[72] There it was advanced that clay vessels contracted ritual impurity only when contact had been made with its interior. But our verse, which seems to unnecessarily repeat something about earthenware, really conveys a new *halachah*. That is, if a *zav* touches any part of the clay object—even its exterior part—it shall be shattered on account of its *tumah*. The earlier reference limits *tumah* to the interior when the tainted implement is found inside the vessel but does not touch it. This passage elucidates another angle.

How does a man who had contracted gonorrhea heal after Heaven causes his unseemly symptoms to subside? "And when a man who oozes recovers from his pus emissions, then he shall count seven days of purification and launder his clothing. And he shall wash in spring water and then he is ritually clean."[73] It has been suggested above in the section dealing with cleansing a *metzora* why counting seven clean days is prescribed. Here we propose an additional rationale. Throughout the Torah, seven days is the uniform time period when speaking about all forms of healing. This is a borrowed allusion or throwback to the seven days of creation. This establishes a goodly and inspirational model leading directly to the Creator.

---

69. Ibid.
70. Vayikra 15:12.
71. *Torat Kohanim*, Vayikra 15:12.
72. Vayikra 11:33.
73. Vayikra 15:13.

Laundering an oozing man's clothing is considered expedient, especially because he likely spilled his issue onto his garments. There it penetrated the fabric's fibers and lodged. "And on the eighth day he shall take two turtledoves or pigeons and come before God, to the entrance of the Tent of Meeting. And he shall present them to the priest. And the priest shall designate one for a sin offering, the other for a burnt offering."[74]

When a *zav* marshals the requisite courage, he admits that weakness landed him in his present predicament. Womanizing wrought grief. Acknowledging as much, a sin offering is in order. But it is self-reflective resolve that enables him to bring a burnt offering. This sequencing of events has merit, to be sure, but there might be another direction afoot. Perhaps seminal oozing had not been caused by sin, but rather as a result of other pathologies. In deference to this distinct possibility, the Torah calls for leniency. His modest sacrifice consists of only two turtledoves or pigeons.

Sixth *aliyah*
"And when a man emits semen, then he shall wash his entire body in water and he is deemed tamei until the evening."

After the previous section explained laws concerning cases of chronic seminal discharges, it takes up a comparable but not identical subject. It pertains to a man who emits semen of his free volition. This may occur as a result of masturbation, where he spills or wastes his seed, or during sexual intercourse. "And when a man emits semen."[75] The latter case does not, of course, have tinges of transgression. Naturally, there are appropriate times for spousal physical intimacy. Consequently, he is not required to wait seven days to regain ritual purity, nor must he bring a sacrifice. The sages corroborate.[76] They write that when a man or woman oozing fluid from their genitalia experience a cessation for three straight days, then they are exempt from bringing a sacrifice. Additionally, they are only deemed *tamei* until the evening.

---

74. Vayikra 15:14.
75. Vayikra 15:16.
76. Though Abravanel alludes to [Talmudic] sages, in fact he brings this law in the name of the Rambam, *Mishneh Torah*, Hilchot Mechussarei Kapparah, chapters 2–5.

"And when a woman has sexual relations and the man ejaculates inside of her, they shall wash in water and remain ritually unclean until the evening."[77] The subject of our verse is a sensible married man. Because of our working assumption, we better comprehend the Torah's moderate and convenient requirement.

To be clear, steamy scenarios do not warrant laissez-faire consequences. To illustrate, consider sex addicts or other philandering types. Protracted sex is anathematic to Torah values. These bottomless fits of grossly exaggerated fornication—common among paramours with adulteresses—bring harsh and unpleasant reprisal.

Our verse, though, does not speak of scoundrels. The main subject is a sexually balanced fellow. After ejaculation, he is advised to refrain from repeated intimacy for the remainder of the day. Given that sound counsel applies to a married man, it is all the more appropriate for a guy who aimlessly ejaculates. He should sense shame. In our context this means washing up and remaining *tamei* until the evening.

In bygone eras, righteous individuals garnered praise for outstanding self-mastery for never having spilled their seed in vain. *Tzaddikim*, they were able to accomplish this by suppressing sexual fantasy. For them, nocturnal emissions were a thing never experienced. As written above, we can trace semen's biochemistry. When we do, we would know that while still in its internal organs where produced, it is robust.

That changes when sperm is emitted from the body. Oxidization quickly putrefies it. Out of its original element, it morphs into malodorous material. For this reason, semen is a source of *tumah*. Just as it is a superlative substance when united with a woman's egg to create a zygote, there is a flip side. Namely, when that opportunity to create life fails, the substance takes on a whiff of putrefaction or death, similar to the *tumah* associated with a cadaver.

After the Torah concludes its treatment regarding a *zav*—regardless of whether the emission is prodigious or little—it moves to discuss laws governing a case where a woman has oozing vaginal discharge. But first the verses open with regular menstruation and its halachic ramifications. "When a

---

77. Vayikra 15:18.

woman will ooze, her oozing being blood from her flesh, for seven days she will be in a state of *niddah*, and whoever touches her will be *tamei* until evening."[78]

The verses refer to a woman's monthly period. Roughly seven days out of every month, she evacuates excess blood from her uterus together with other discharges. In the case of sexually active women, semen and other bodily fluids in the uterus (including unfertilized eggs) get discharged. "When a woman will ooze, her oozing being blood from her flesh" means that her discharge is different from oozing that comes from an oozing man. For one, her discharge is bloody. As stated, since this is a natural monthly period, the Torah does not demand a sacrifice from her.

Women who menstruate count seven days in anticipation of additional days of cleansing. During this time, a woman may not cohabit with her husband. Flouting this prohibition carries stiff repercussion. To wit, a child born of such an ill-timed tryst is prone to flaws in character and temperament.

"And whoever touches her will be *tamei* until the evening."[79] This same law applies to anything upon which she lies or sits. They are ritually impure. Thus, if a man touches her bedding or chair, for example, he is *tamei* until evening. Ritual cleanliness is restored after he launders his clothing and washes himself, and time elapses (meaning sunset).

Our sages list five types of discharge that trigger *tumah*.[80] Countering those, they instruct regarding other types of discharge, which are considered *tahor*. To overly simplify, distinction centers upon tracing the cause or source of the bleeding. If it comes from her womb, she is a *niddah*. However, if she experienced a traumatic impact or injury to her pelvic region, she remains *tahor*.

The rabbis explain more details regarding a *niddah*.[81] They teach that even if a woman saw only a drop of blood during her seven days of menstruation, she is still considered *temeah* for seven days. That count begins from the time she last saw blood. Since this is the governable law when a woman menstruates, the verse specifies: "Then she shall be considered a *niddah*—for seven days she is a *niddah*."[82] Monthly menses is being referred to. Etymologically

---

78. Vayikra 15:19.
79. Ibid.
80. BT *Niddah* 19a.
81. *Torat Kohanim* 15:19.
82. Ibid.

speaking, the Hebrew term *niddah* (נידה) alludes to separation and isolation, as in Psalms: "I would wander afar [ארחיק נדד]."[83]

Another rabbinic observation is derived from our verse. "And if a man will have sexual intercourse with her, he contracts her *niddah* impurity, and he is ritually impure for seven days. Any bed upon which she lies is ritually impure."[84] The subject at hand is *tumah* and not sexual impropriety. Elsewhere the Torah promulgated punishment for a man who has intercourse with a *niddah*.[85] Stressing the specific facet of ritual impurity, the verse highlights laws featuring a man having relations with his wife while she is ritually impure due to menstruation. Possibly, this occurs while they are making love. For all intents and purposes, the law is uniform. Namely, her husband contracts *tumah* and remains in that state for a week.

Next, these final verses of the sixth *aliyah* discuss more details of a woman who oozes blood at unexpected times. "And a woman who oozes blood not at the regular time of her state of *niddah* or if she oozes blood beyond her state of *niddah*, all the days of the flow of her impurity shall be like the days of her state of *niddah*. She shall be impure."[86]

What does "not at the regular time of her state of *niddah*" mean? Using the time frame from when a woman ceases (or more accurately, should cease) menstruation, she sees more—and atypically timed—bleeding. Again and to her surprise, "or if she oozes blood beyond her state of *niddah*." The verse describes a case where a woman's flow begins at the normal time of her period but then inexplicably continues day after day.[87] "All the days of her flow."[88] She will be *temeah* as a *niddah*. More verses in this sixth *aliyah* detail treatment of beds or chairs upon which she lies or sits.

A central question is this: What difference does it make whether a woman bleeds at the usual time of her anticipated period or at an unexpected time? If menstruation occurs at an expected time, then even if she experiences a single drop of bleeding—minute as a seed—she becomes *temeah* for seven

---

83. Tehillim 55:8.
84. Vayikra 15:20.
85. Vayikra 20:18.
86. Vayikra 15:24.
87. Abravanel's words here are enigmatic and it is not possible to chart out her bleeding. He writes that "she does not stop bleeding for another eleven days. All told there are fourteen days after the seven days of her menses."
88. Vayikra 15:26.

days. This is also true if she saw blood during her regular seven days. She must immerse herself in the evening, and by so doing, she reestablishes her ritual cleanliness. There is no need for her to count seven clean days.[89]

However, if she experiences bleeding for one or two days, but it is not her expected menstruation time (the first seven days had already elapsed), then *halachah* recognizes her as a moderate oozer or *zavah ketanah* (זבה קטנה). But, if she sees blood for three consecutive days, then she is designated differently. She is a chronic oozer or *zavah gedolah* (זבה גדולה). Should there be a one-day break from bleeding, *halachah* demands that she count seven clean days before immersion in order to retake spiritual purity.

According to our example, then, it emerges that when we add up all of her days of oozing we arrive at eleven. To those eleven days tack on seven more days of menstruation. But here's an important thing. Since not every woman is capable of discerning between her days of oozing and days of menstruation—for the matter can be misleading—virtuous Jewish women from time immemorial have taken stringencies upon themselves. How does the matter resolve itself? If a woman experiences modest spotting, say the size of mustard seed, then she accepts upon herself an obligation to count seven clean days as is customary for a *zavah*. Above we differentiated between moderate and chronic oozing. A practical difference between the two will be this: a moderate oozer is exempt from bringing a sacrifice, while a chronic one must do so.

---

89. See *Shulchan Aruch*, Yoreh Deah 184.

Seventh *aliyah*
"And you shall caution Bnei Yisrael about [matters of] spiritual impurity."

This dire warning serves to protect Jewish life and limb. More forcefully and fatefully, it sets out to preserve Jewish spiritual life. "That they should not die as a result of their *tumah*—in their defiling My Mishkan that is in their midst."[90] This verse asserts that the mystical Shechinah has a seat in every Jew's carefully crafted soul. This is explicitly derived from the phrase "My Mishkan that is in their midst."

Another Scriptural verse unhesitatingly reiterates, "For Hashem your Almighty walks inside your camp, so it must be kept holy. And neither shall there be seen in your midst anything untoward, [otherwise] Hashem will turn away."[91] Spic-and-span without an ounce of ethical laxity—that is the standard by which Hebrews are ordered to keep their encampment's decorum.

Messages creating high bars of religious probity conclude our *parashah*. How appropriate, then, that this same thread connects it to the upcoming *parashah*—Acharei Mot. Verses pertaining to Yom Kippur service and ritual state unequivocally, "And you shall atone for all things sacred from spiritual impurities of Bnei Yisrael…on behalf of the Kohanim and the congregation, there shall be forgiveness."[92]

---

90. Vayikra 15:31.
91. Devarim 23:15.
92. Vayikra 16:33.

תפילה קצרה

יהי רצון מלפניך, ה׳ אלקי,
שתזכני להפיץ את דברי הרב דון יצחק אברבנאל באופן ראוי ונכון.
ולוואי וזכות זו תעמוד לאשתי, לבניי, לנכדיי ולכל בית ישראל, לחיים ולשלום.
ויהי רצון שנזכה ונחיה ונראה בביאת הגואל ובבניין המקדש במהרה בימינו, אמן.

תם ונשלם שבח לאל בורא עולם